MW01062177

A Scandalous Providence

The Jesus Story of the Compassion of God

A Scandalous Providence
The Jesus Story of the Compassion of God

E. Frank Tupper

Mercer University Press
Macon, Georgia

ISBN 0-86554-469-7

A Scandalous Providence: The Jesus Story of the Compassion of God
by E. Frank Tupper

Copyright © 1995
Mercer University Press
6316 Peake Road
Macon, Georgia 31210-3960

Library of Congress Cataloging-in-Publication Data

Tupper, E. Frank (Elgin Frank), 1941–
    A scandalous providence : the Jesus story of the compassion of God
    / E. Frank Tupper.
    xii + 468 pp.   6 x 9" (15 x 23 cm.)
    Includes bibliographical references and indexes.
    ISBN 0-86554-469-7 (alk. paper)
    1. Providence and government of God. 2. Jesus Christ—Person
    and offices. I. Tilte.
    BT135.T86   1995
    231'.5—dc20   95-5765
                                                                      CIP

Contents

Part Two: The Politics of Compassion
Marian Wright Edelman: A Prophetic Voice for Our Children
Archbishop Oscar Romero: The Politics of Liberation
Langdon Gilkey: Premier American Theologian

Conclusion

Chapter Six

The Healing of the Epileptic Boy
The Experience of Providence: *Grace*
Suffering and Prayer
The Elimination of Suffering through Healing Grace
The Confrontation of Suffering through Sustaining Grace
The Risk in Suffering of Promissory Grace

Chapter Seven

The Experience of Providence: *The Silence of God*
The Agony of Gethsemane
Prayer and Providence
The Problem of Limitations
God's relationship to the World
Suffering in Christian Experience
Concluding Questions

Chapter Eight

The Experience of Providence: *Solidarity with the Crucified Christ*
The Case against God: The Suffering of God's World
The Death Cry of Jesus—Godforsakenness
The Weakness of God
The Uniqueness of the Death of Jesus
The Mystery of the Death of God
The Tragic History of Suffering Humanity
"God Lay Dead on the Sabbath"

Preface

THIS BOOK IS NOT THE BOOK that I intended to write. When I first contemplated doing a book on providence more than fifteen years ago, I anticipated an exercise in systematic theology—an identification and analysis of the patterns of providence in the crucial events of the story of Jesus. The narrative rendering of "The Providence of God in Christological Perspective"[1] constitutes the enduring link between my original expectation and this publication. While my conversation with theologians who have written the most significant proposals on providence remains, notably, Karl Barth, H. H. Farmer, and Langdon Gilkey, sometime after my first lectures on providence in 1986 this project shifted from systematic theology toward pastoral theology.

The methodology and content of this pastoral theology integrates biblical narrative, theological analysis, and contemporary stories into a unitary essay by sustained theological reflection on issues central to a reformulation of the doctrine of the providence of God. Whether innovative or not, the format indicates my intention to move through a constructive proposal on providence into the practice of church ministry. I hope the categories, insights, and perspective in this essay will be helpful to those who struggle to understand and interpret the meaning of Christian faith in contemporary life. Seminarians preparing for ministry and various practitioners doing ministry are probably the ones who will find this book most valuable. Former students and sensitive readers will recognize nonetheless the theological structures that unite the different parts of this proposal into a distinct perspective on the providence of God.

Whoever endeavors to write on the theme of providence does not work so much on one doctrine as the point where almost all doctrines converge. This intersection illuminates different theological viewpoints, occasions sometime sharp disagreement, and invites conversation of all

---

[1]E. Frank Tupper, "The Providence of God in Christological Perspective," *Review & Expositor* 82 (1985): 579-95.

sorts, critical and constructive. Since I have benefited from discussion
with students on the essentials of this proposal on providence, I welcome
the continuation of the conversation through publication, and I intend to
learn from it. Thought provoking questions from classroom and seminar
required multiple revisions of this manuscript, the clearest evidence to me
of the ongoing necessity to rethink and refine various aspects of any
interpretation of the provision of providence. Of course, whether or not
my narrative rendering of the providence of God through the epochal
moments in the story of Jesus actually works is an entirely different
question.

   Limitations of different kinds are identifiable in this essay. First, the
theological method that shapes this book has taken different turns in the
courses of its writing, but methodological continuity endures. "A Brief
Methodological Interlude" lies between the "Introduction" and Chapter
One, and it sketches my operating assumptions. However, I have not
attempted to justify a narrative approach to theology apart from the cogency of this project.[2] Those for whom theological method is not a
priority may choose to move immediately from the Introduction to
Chapter One. Second, except for quotations and poetry, I have used
inclusive language wherever possible to be sensitive to feminist concerns.
The issue is much larger than language, because hierarchical structures
that subordinate women to men deny the full humanity of women in the
blessing of creation (Gen 1:26-27) and the grace of reconciliation (Gal

---

[2]A sampling of the literature on narrative and theology would include: Stanley
Hauerwas and L. Gregory Jones, eds., *Why Narrative? Readings in Narrative Theology*
(Grand Rapids: Wm. B. Eerdmans Publishing Co., 1989), perhaps the best introductory
materials; Ronald F. Thiemann, *Revelation and Theology: The Gospel as Narrated
Promise* (Notre Dame IN: University of Notre Dame Press, 1985), an exercise in
theological method and a brief rendering of the Gospel of Matthew—with extensive
bibliographical references in his "Notes"; Garrett Green, ed., *Scriptural Authority and
Narrative Interpretation* (Philadelphia: Fortress Press, 1987); David Ford, *Barth and
God's Story: Biblical Narrative and the Theological Method of Karl Barth in "The
Church Dogmatics"* (Frankfurt: Verlag Peter Lang, 1981; 1985); and the works of Hans
Frei, *The Identity of Jesus Christ: The Hermeneutical Base of Dogmatic Theology*
(Philadelphia: Fortress Press, 1975); *The Eclipse of Biblical Narrative: A Study of
Eighteenth and Nineteenth Century Hermeneutics* (New Haven: Yale University Press,
1974); *Theology and Narrative: Selected Essays*, ed. George Hunsinger and William C.
Placher (New York: Oxford University Press, 1993).

3:28). My sympathetic reading of feminist theology ranges much wider than footnotes document, an omission that I regret. Third, the ecological crisis requires more attention within the theme of providence than I have given it. The brief references to the crisis indicate the fact of my awareness but not the measure of my concern. All three of these areas are addressed in other literature, but these are limits that I recognize in my own work.

Numerous persons have contributed to my work in various ways: Phyllis Pleasants gave manuscript form to my first class lectures on providence in July 1986. Several colleagues have read different parts of the manuscript in process: Alan Culpepper, Andrew Lester, Tom Graves, Wolfhart Pannenberg, James Hyde, Paul Duke, Karen Smith, Temp Sparkman, Kay Shurden, Bill Leonard, Ragan Courtney, and Marvin Tate. Richard F. Wilson of Mercer University responded to the entire project with critical insight and comment. William L. Hendricks and William B. Rogers of Southern Seminary generously read the entire manuscript and made helpful suggestions. Tish Gardner and her staff in Offices Services have diligently and efficiently turned my hand-written drafts into typed-copy. Dale Melton and Michael Groves graciously compiled the indexes. Scott Nash of Mercer University Press has given me freedom, guidance, and considerable patience in the completion of this book. I am especially indebted to Wayne Oates and Roy Honeycutt. When I almost shelved this project in 1990, Wayne Oates read my work and nurtured its progress forward. As provost and president of Southern Seminary, Roy Honeycutt supported and encouraged me at every stage of this endeavor.

What I have written would not have been possible without the strength and encouragement of friends: Bill Leonard, Larry McSwain, and Walter Shurden, who stood by me when most needed; Stephen Shoemaker, Bill Johnson, and Louie Bailey, ministers of Crescent Hill Baptist Church and thus to my entire family; Ginger Miller and Nina Pollard, who made a place for me at the table. To all these and others I am grateful.

For reasons known to them better than anyone else, I dedicate this book to my children, Elgin and Michelle, with the prayer that they will experience life as a sacred journey in the providence of God.

E. Frank Tupper
Holy Week 1995

For Elgin and Michelle

Introduction

JESUS WAS BORN under a cloud of sexual impropriety and hounded as a refugee to exile in Egypt. He grew up in Galilee of the Gentiles, and he lived his life a ridiculed Nazarene.

Standing in line at the Jordan River, Jesus submitted to John's baptism of repentance. Shortly afterwards he went everywhere preaching the good news of the Kingdom of God, forgiving sins and offering salvation to anyone who would receive it. With great compassion Jesus healed the sick, some outside in and others inside out. He trafficked with the people of the land, ritually unclean but his acceptance unqualified. Crowds constantly followed him: a captivating teacher, a fascinating storyteller, a master of incisive oneliners. He was branded a glutton and a drunkard, a friend of tax-collectors and sinners, because they all saw dignity in the reflection of his eyes and the Welcome of God in the warmth of his smile. He celebrated the arriving Kingdom of God at every shared meal, the anticipation of the messianic banquet in the eschatological future of God.

Without any credentials Jesus redefined the Law, setting himself above it and promising salvation without it. He made himself Lord of the Temple, his Father's house, whose Presence he dared to convey beyond Temple grounds to every dusty little town. He broke the Law of the Sabbath and spoke of the destruction of the Temple. He was an arrogant blasphemer against God and a charismatic threat to the rule of Rome. He died a criminal's death on a Roman cross, rejected and alone, and worse, a Godforsaken "King of the Jews."

Some of the scrubby lot who followed him, unlearned men and suspect women, rumored a few days later that God had raised Jesus from the dead, a rumor turned fact after six weeks of telling. Ridiculous! Incredulous! Absurd! The resurrection of a crucified Nazarene? Scandal, all of it, from beginning to end. Scandal, scandal indeed.

An interpretation of the providence of God in the light of the story of Jesus Christ is inevitably "a scandalous providence." The message and ministry of Jesus did not fulfill the messianic hopes of his people under Roman military rule, though we seldom note it. Similarly, the providence of God does not conform to the expectations of the faithful among the family of God in the church, though we are reluctant to admit it. The essential characterization of providence, however, is a comprehensive affirmation of God's loving care and purposeful guidance of the history of humanity in the movement of creation, an affirmation of faith that encompasses the innumerable sociopolitical arenas of corporate humanity on the one side and the particularity of the life story of each of us on the other.

The providence of God is one of the most difficult themes in the enterprise of Christian theology, and only the formative importance of providence surpasses its perplexing intricacies. The very core of the definition of providence is the provision of God for us in the joys and sorrows of life. Indeed, the scope and depth of the providence of God is staggering: Providence addresses everything that happens in the world throughout world history, events great and small, which includes the brief existence of every one. Precisely because providence shapes the short story of each of us, providence may well be the most intimately personal of all the doctrinal themes of Christian theology. In the increasing complexity of life and relationships, the fundamental question is: What does the provision of God mean for us in situations of critical human need? This question acknowledges the necessity of the help and guidance of God in the whole of life, a question quite urgent in times of crisis. If the formative importance of providence is not to be lost in its perplexing intricacies, therefore, the connection of serious reflection on providence to the multiple stories of our lives must be a continuing concern in every stage of theological formulation.

A Story to Be Told

Since providence declares God's positive purpose in the process of creation and special concern for humanity in the dynamics of history, a Christian understanding of providence is nothing less than an interpretation of the loving care of God in relationship to creation, history, and each of our lives. This affirmation of the providence of God presupposes the activity of God in the history of Israel and its culmination in the story of Jesus the Christ: the gracious proclaimer of the arriving Kingdom of God, a derelict Galilean on an oppressive Roman cross, and the surprising whispers of a startling Easter dawn—a story remembered and retold in the ongoing life of the church. Ultimately the providence of God is less a doctrine to be explored than a story to be told, the story of the compassion of God disclosed in the story of Jesus. Contextualized in the history of Israel on the one side and in the ongoing history of the church on the other, *the Story of Jesus constitutes the definitive Story of God*, the story that says, "God is love," the story that tells the tale of what "God is love" actually means.

The fundamental paradigm for understanding God's relationship to the world is the Incarnation of God in Jesus Christ, a metaphor that presupposes and depends upon "the Story of Jesus." Thus Jesus Christ, whose personhood is constituted in the particularity of his history, is the definition and the expression of the providence of God, the disclosure of its meaning and content. God has revealed in the various experiences of Jesus what God actually intends for all of us; and, accordingly, Jesus has shown us how a person should respond to the ever present concern of God. While the providence of God is quite vivid in Jesus' life and ministry, the death and resurrection of the Nazarene are most significant in the demonstration of Jesus' resolute trust in God and of God's ultimate identification with Jesus.

Providence derives from the Latin *providere*, which means "to provide," a combination of *pro*, "before," with *videre*, "sees." Thus providence already has a double meaning, fore-seeing and seeing-for, making provision for what is foreseen. However, any serious attempt to conceptualize the theme of providence today will accentuate the provision of God,[1] emphasizing thereby the centrality of the compassion of God and

---

[1]See Karl Barth *CD* III/3: 3-4. Barth locates the material derivation of the word "providence" in Genesis 22:14, 8. In that passage Abraham named the place where God had prevented him from offering up Isaac as a sacrifice, Jehovah-Jireh ("The Lord will provide"), remembering Isaac's earlier question about the lack of a burnt offering and his response, "God will provide" (22:8), accroding to the Vulgate: *Deus providebit*. Barth argues that the modern German translation of *Vorsehung* is not so dynamic and accurate a translation of *providentia* as the earlier German *Fürschung*. Barth does not deny that God "sees before," but he accentuates that God "sees about." Thus providence refers primarily to the provision of God. Cf. Wolf Krotke, "Gottes Fürsorge für die Welt:

the openness of the movement of history. Since the conceptualization of providence aims to describe how God relates to and works in the world, the possibilities of providence at any given moment occur in the matrix of converging natural events, the variable configurations of historical contingency, and the participation of ever widening circles of human agents. Yet the interpretation of providence through the dynamics of the Incarnation of God in Jesus Christ is not a self-evident enterprise that only requires conceptual explication. Rather, the providence of God elaborated through the story of Jesus eludes the symmetry of the smooth answers of faith and thwarts the precision of interlocking conceptual analysis. The work of providence in the journey of Jesus does not provide a teleological design for every circumstance on the basis of the plentiful provision of God, but a story wherein the compassion of God intersects and sometimes collides with the burnt ground of human tragedy.

The commonplace word to characterize the limits in methodology, conceptualization, and application in theology is "ambiguity." While all interpretations of providence in conjunction with reality are fraught with difficulty, ambiguity does not give adequate expression to our fumbling answers to providential questions. Sometimes we are overwhelmed with baffling confusion in the midst of the incomprehensible, all efforts to discern the providential activity of God simply an exercise in futility. What God is doing or not doing in a given situation remains beyond our view. Accordingly, the endeavor to formulate a constructive proposal of the providence of God through the story of Jesus does not eliminate ambiguity but entails more knotty complexities and unfathomable depths than the category of ambiguity can comprehend. The use of ambiguity does require us to acknowledge the limitation of information available and the frustration of elements unexplainable. Beyond the obscurity and the inexactitude of ambiguity, however, the story of Jesus confronts us with the immensity of the density of the mystery of God. Karl Barth titled his exposition of the Incarnation, "The Way of the Son of God into 'the Far Country,' "[2] a graphic statement of the indefatigable compassion

---

Überlegungen zur Bedeutung der Vorsehungslehre," *Theologische Literaturzeitung* 108 (April 1983): 241-52. The fundamental reality of the overflowing compassion of God, not the traditional category of foreknowledge, is the essential concept for the affirmation of the provision of providence.

[2]The phrase is from Karl Barth, *Church Dogmatics*, IV/1:157.

of God and the desperate plight of fallen humanity. The way into the far country is always east of Eden but inside the land of Nod, a place where all humanity dwells in estrangement from God.[3] When he embarks on this path, therefore, whether knowingly or not, this Journeyman is marked for death. Alas, the cry of dereliction of the crucified Nazarene is a death cry into Darkness that scandalizes the hallowed Name of God, the Holy One of Israel.

A Neglected Theme Impossible to Neglect

The difficulties in formulating an authentic and helpful understanding of the providence of God dare not be minimized. The problems in framing a contemporary interpretation of the providence of God baffled many,[4] if

---

[3]Note Genesis 4:15b-16.

[4]Cf. Roger Hazelton, *God's Way with Man: Variations on the Theme of Providence* (New York: Abingdon Press, 1956) 6: He comes at the doctrine of providence "not systematically but strategically": "I have conceived this book as a group of variations on the providential theme, modeled frankly on a musical and not the usual architectural pattern." Also, W. G. Pollard, *Chance and Providence: God's Action in a World Governed by Scientific Law* (New York: Charles Scribner's Sons, 1958), whose thesis is the subtitle of the book and focuses on the convergence of "biblical Providence and scientific causality"—a very restricted perspective. Cf. Albert C. Outler, *Who Trusts in God: Musings on the Meaning of Providence* (New York: Oxford University Press, 1968) x. Though the outline of his essay came easy, he says, its subtitle describes the character of his work, i.e., "musings," much less than a constructive reformulation of the meaning of providence.

In 1960 Langdon Gilkey attempted to write a "doctrine" of providence as a companion piece to his volume on creation, but he found his "thinking devoid of any available method" and his "mind empty of relevant and credible concepts" as well as the disintegration of his life "into meaningless pieces" (Langdon Gilkey, *Reaping the Whirlwind: A Christian Interpretation of History* [New York: The Seabury Press, 1976] vii).

Georgia Harkness, *The Providence of God* (Nashville: Abingdon Press, 1960), provides one of the most thoughtful and helpful perspectives during the late 1950s and early 1960s. Note the multiple concerns in the "Introduction": petitionary and intercessory prayer, miracle, the reality of God's providential care, and the possibility of life after death (9-16). These concerns inform her entire essay. She interprets providence to refer to the goodness and power of God in the ordering, sustaining, and guiding of all creation, i.e., nature, biological life, and human persons. "However, it is in the destinies of human individuals that belief in providence centers. Both a positive Christian faith in providence

not all,[5] post-World War II academic theologians. Ironically the historic importance of the doctrine of providence is overshadowed only by its general neglect, "the forgotten stepchild" of contemporary theology.[6] Among the classical doctrines of Christian theology, providence remains the only doctrine that modern theology has not reformulated with new vitality, relevance, and realism. Several historical factors combined to undermine confidence in the approach to and construction of theological proposals on the providence of God: (1) the dissolution of the concept of historical progress in the aftermath of World War I; (2) the shock of radical evil and the consciousness of its demonic depths throughout most of this century; (3) the acceptance of scientific naturalism as the explana-

---

and the perplexities connected with it find their focus in God's care of the individual person" (17). In her interpretation of providence Harkness excludes an interventionist model of God's activity in the world, she rejects predestination and the identification of providence with it, She locates "special providence" in "general providence," and she carefully reformulates the traditional view of divine foreknowledge in terms of the dynamic wisdom of God. Harkness, fails, however to clarify the mode of God's provident activity in the world in relation to the enormity of the problem of evil. She says: "God is not the helpless victim of evil forces beyond His control, nor is He an arbitrary and despotic celestial dictator. He is the Maker of heaven and earth, within which He has delegated to men enormous powers to work with Him or to thwart His oncoming creativity" (91). Harkness' response to the problem of evil reflects minimum attention to providence in nature and history. Can a theological understanding of providence concentrate on "the destinies of human individuals" and not address the issues of nature and history? No, because providence always occurs in the context of creation and history. Nevertheless, Harkness offers one of the most meaningful interpretations of providence prior to the 1970s.

[5]Note especially Karl Barth, *CD*, III/3:1-423; also, G. C. Berkouwer, *The Providence of God*, trans. Lewis B. Smedes (Grand Rapids MI: Wm. B. Eerdmans Publishing Co., 1952). Cf. Austin Farrar, *Love Almighty and Ills Unlimited* (London: Collins Press, 1962).

[6]Langdon Gilkey, "The Concept of Providence in Contemporary Theology," *The Journal of Religion* 43 (1963): 174. Gilkey asks: "Why has Providence in our generation been left a rootless, disembodied ghost, flitting from footnote to footnote, but rarely finding secure lodgment in sustained theological discourse?" (171). Gilkey presents a sharp critique of Barth's volume on providence: When finished reading Barth's formulation of providence, Gilkey says, "one feels one has read a comprehensive, strong, and credible doctrine of God's rule in the world, with an amazing successful balance between divine sovereignty and human freedom in which neither seems to have been sacrificed." Upon reading the next section of *CD*, III/3, on "*das Nichtige*," Gilkey admits to utter confusion, because Barth's discussion of evil reduces his doctrine of providence "to a shambles" (188).

tion for occurrences in nature; (4) the emphasis on human autonomy in the making of history; (5) the rediscovery of Jesus' eschatological vision of the Kingdom of God.[7] These multiple factors offered a frame of reference for interpreting life in the world without reference to the provident action of God and shattered the historic sense of continuity between the Biblical Story and our ongoing contemporary story. The consequences for the question of a workable theological method focused on the availability of useful categories of interpretation, the identification of a comprehensive pattern of conceptualization, and the structure of a coherent and convincing line of argument. These disquieting historical realities and attendant methodological problems account for the neglect of providence in most contemporary theology.

Such neglect is theologically untenable because the doctrine of providence comprehends directly the most crucial issues for Christian faith: divine sovereignty and human freedom, radical evil and the goodness of creation, petitionary prayer and the availability of God, the meaning of life and the mystery of death. The complexity and scope of these problems undergird the conclusion that providence is not so much a discrete locus of doctrine as a comprehensive symbol for the question of the relationship of God, the world, and human history.

The concept of providence has historically included God's preservation of creation, the concurrence of God's activity with human action, and God's governance of creation and history.[8] While preservation is some-

---

[7]Gilkey, *Reaping the Whirlwind*, 223-36.

[8]The renewal of the discussion of providence includes Peter R. Baelz, *Prayer and Providence: A Background Study* (New York: The Seabury Press, 1968), admittedly a modest contribution; Langdon Gilkey, *Reaping the Whirlwind: A Christian Interpretation of History* (New York: The Seabury Press, 1976), a major constructive proposal; Michael Langford, *Providence* (London: SCM Press, 1981), a contribution to the conversation.

See Peter T. Geach, *Providence and Evil* (Cambridge: Cambridge University Press, 1977), "The Stanton Lectures 1971–1972." Geach rejects the traditional understanding of "foreknowledge" necessary for any contemporary interpretation of providence, but he defines providence to mean that God knows the future by controlling it. The problem of the compatibility of the good Creator's control over the world amid the multiple forms and magnitude of evil in the world is a contradiction that finally invalidates his proposal. Conversely, precisely because of continual irresolvable problems, Maurice Wiles, *God's Action in the World* (London: SCM Press, 1986), considers the entire enterprise of formulating a constructive understanding of God's activity in the world a dubious one.

times reframed as the continuation of creation, the question of the concurrence of God's activity in conjunction with human action and the conceptualization of how God governs creation and history are significant points of disagreement and debate. The difficulty of formulating a comprehensive understanding of providence notwithstanding, the question of the providence of God continues to assert itself and must finally be faced: How does the loving care and guiding presence of God actually function in the history of humanity and in each person's life?[9] The question of a meaningful understanding of God's compassionate activity in corporate

---

See David J. Bartholomew, *God of Chance* (London: SCM Press, 1984), who accentuates the element of chance in reflecting on God's activity in the world and addresses both Geach and Pollard (125-35); more recently, John Polkinghorne, *Science and Providence: God's Interaction with the World* (Boston: New Science Library, 1989), a major contribution, creative and credible; also, Keith Ward, *Divine Action* (London: Collins Religious Publishing, 1990), who endeavors to interpret biblical faith in a personal God active in a scientifically-understood, open universe.

Cf. Peter Hodgson, "Providence," *A New Handbook of Christian Theology*, ed. Donald W. Musser and Joseph L. Price (Nashville: Abingdon Press, 1992) 394-97. Unlike premodern theology, e.g., Augustine and John Calvin, with its monarchical model of God's unilateral action in the world and linear view of history moving toward a fixed goal, modern theology finds the question of providence in the areas of individual life, history, and nature most complex. Though individuals experience providence in suffering and disappointment as the strength to go on, history is a significantly more difficult problem. Through influence and persuasion God "shapes" definite patterns of transformation and liberation in history with specific structures toward justice that involves individuals, communities, and institutions. "History itself remains deeply ambiguous, a tragicomic process by which synthesis of values and praxis are achieved through confrontation and compromise, prevail for a while, then break down" (396). The pattern of history is spiral and not linear, open and incomplete: "The goal of history, never attained but only approximated, might be described as 'communicative freedom' or 'boundless communication.' " Such communication involves "a dialogical rationality" that questions everything, eliminates all privileges, transcends every provincialism, overcomes all distortions, and establishes new forms of community. Behind this article see Peter Hodgson, *God in History: Shapes of Freedom* (Nashville: Abingdon Press, 1989). The work of Hodgson cannot be discounted or dismissed, because he demonstrates an awareness of the formidable theological problems that threaten to scuttle any constructive reformulation of providence in contemporary theology.

[9]Barth, *CD*, III/3:58. Karl Barth aptly summarized: "God fulfills His fatherly lordship over His creation by preserving, accompanying, and ruling the whole course of its earthly existence." From time to time throughout this essay, I will engage Barth's proposal on providence, one of the most substantive treatments of providence in this century.

human history and the journey of an individual's life presses relentlessly for some answer.

The interpretation of the providence of God in the light of the story of Jesus does not alleviate the abstruseness of the task, because Jesus himself contributes to the contemporary crisis of the providence of God. Jesus said:

> Ask, and it will be given you; search, and you will find; knock, and the door will be opened for you. For everyone who asks receives, and everyone who searches, finds, and for everyone who knocks, the door will be opened. Is there anyone among you, if your child asks for bread, will give a stone. Or if the child asks for a fish, will give him a snake? If you then, who are evil, know how to give good gifts to your children, how much more will your Father in heaven give good things to those who ask him! (Matt 7:8-11)

The prayers for daily bread in modern times have sometimes been answered with an abundance of warm bread. Yet at other times the prayers for bread have been silenced amid the shrieks and screams of those buried under an avalanche of stones. And in the torrential downpour of the rubble of stone, the cry is not for bread but a crying out for one another, the smell unmistakably the smell of fear, indeed, of death.

With the coming of Jesus Christ, however, God does something radically new, which requires the rethinking of everything about providence. God's historic work of providence in caring for creation and God's work of reconciliation in overcoming alienation are intrinsically interwoven together. Indeed, God's work of reconciliation illuminates and clarifies God's providential work in the whole of creation and thereby uniquely in the arena of contingent human history. In Jesus Christ, the mystery of the providence of God converges with the vision of the Kingdom of God. Therefore, the understanding of the providence of God on the basis of the story of Jesus requires the integration of providence, Christology, and eschatology.

Precisely because the providence of God is more a story to be told than a doctrine to be explained, I propose a narrative rendering of the providence of God in the light of the Synoptic telling of the epochal moments in the story of Jesus. *Chapter 1*: The experience of Jesus in baptism indicates the intention of God to bless every person as the son and daughter of God. *Chapter 2*: The Matthean infancy narrative accentuates

the decisive action of God to accomplish specific goals through providential guidance as well as the compassion of God for families who
suffer the death of children. *Chapter 3*: Jesus' response to the temptations
in the wilderness declares the continuing goodness of creation as the
arena of God's activity to overcome all forms of evil. *Chapter 4*: Three
themes highlight the good news of the Galilean ministry of Jesus: the immeasurable compassion of God, responsibility and authenticity in prayer,
and divine activity in the form of miracles. *Chapter 5*: The contextual
dynamics in the transfiguration of Jesus underscores the political thrust
of the providence of God. *Chapter 6*: The healing ministry of Jesus
focuses initially on the epileptic boy but moves quickly to the expressions
of grace in conjunction with illness in other stories of the New Testament. *Chapter 7*: The agony of Jesus in Gethsemane occasions reflection
on the silence of God in situations of inescapable human tragedy. *Chapter
8*: The execution of Jesus with the death cry of Godforsakenness requires
careful analysis with regard to the suffering of God. *Chapter 9*: The
affirmation of the resurrection of Christ crucified moves the enterprise of
providence beyond history into eschatology. Each decisive event in the
Synoptic recounting of the good news of Jesus reveals a specific and
different experience of providence, each form with contemporary significance for interpreting God's involvement in the contingency of human
history as well as the journey of every individual's life.[10]

Since the Story of Jesus is the paradigmatic Story of God, we must
interpret our innumerable stories in the light of the story of Jesus, that is,
the recollection of the story of Jesus within the canonical Gospels. Of
course, a reciprocity of interpretation will occur in the endeavor to understand some of our contemporary narratives through the disclosure of God
in the narration of Jesus' history and destiny, but the priority of the
Gospel story endures. Reflection on contemporary lived experience will

---

[10]My analysis of the story of Jesus is framed on the structure of the Gospel of Mark,
but the life and teaching of Jesus require continual reference to the Gospels of Matthew
and Luke. Indeed, chapter 2, "The Bethlehem Massacre," originates entirely from the
Gospel of Matthew, and chapter 3, "Who Trusts in God," mostly so. Chapter 6 "Grace
and Healing," moves beyond the Gospels to the Letters of the Apostle Paul, and chapter
9, "The Vision of the Providence of God," concentrates inevitably on the Synoptic
Gospels as well as Paul in 1 Corinthians 15. For the purposes of this essay I have
concentrated on the Synoptic Gospels with only occasional references to the Gospel of
John.

undoubtedly illuminate some dimensions of a Gospel story heretofore unrecognized, wrongly understood, or perhaps overemphasized; nevertheless, the story of Jesus finally encircles and reframes our stories into the ongoing story of God. That the Story of Jesus is the paradigmatic Story of God that encompasses the stories of each of us is the essential thesis of this narrative rendering of the providence of God.

Inasmuch as reflection and research is the basis of constructive theological proposals, the personal investment of the theologian in formulating a particular perspective on a given theme is seldom included in its conceptualization—for good reason: A theological essay must be evaluated on the basis of the cogency of its argument rather than an appeal to the author's experience. Of course, personal experience impacts and shapes a theologian's constructive work in a variety of ways. Life experiences can turn a person toward the question of God that eventuates in an affirmation of faith and a vocation in theology.[11] Again, the experience of God in the crucial circumstances of life can decisively shape the perspective and substance of one's theological work.[12] Moreover, the

---

[11]See Wolfhart Pannenberg, "How My Mind Has Changed: God's Presence in History," *The Christian Century* 98 (11 March 1981) 260-63. Pannenberg has said that a series of experiences led to his affirmation of the Christian faith. The single-most important experience happened on 6 Janaury 1945, when he was sixteen years old. Pannenberg has written: "On a lonely two-hour walk home from my piano lesson, seeing an otherwise ordinary sunset, I was suddenly flooded by light and absorbed in a sea of light that, although it did not extinguish the humble awareness of my finite existence, overflowed the barriers that normally separate us from the surrounding world" (261). Several months earlier, he had narrowly escaped an Allied bombardment of Berlin, and a few weeks later his family had to flee their eastern German home because of the Russian offensive. He did not know that January 6 was the day of Epiphany or realize that "Jesus Christ had claimed [his] life as a witness to the transfiguration of the world in the illuminatory power and judgment of his glory." But he began to search for the meaning of life and wanted to understand his extraordinary experience of January 6. Subsequently, he had a teacher of German literature who did not fit his image of a Christian, whose impact influenced him to turn to the study of theology at Humbolt University in East Berlin in 1947. Before long, he knew that he would be a theologian for the rest of his life. Cf. Wolfhart Pannenberg, "An Autobiographical Sketch," *The Theology of Wolfhart Pannenberg*, ed. Carl E. Braaten and Phillip Clayton (Minneapolis: Augsburg Publishing House, 1988).

[12]Gilkey, *Reaping the Whirlwind*, 131, refers to two experiences in life which he initially experienced as fate but were transformed into creative destiny: "a war interment camp and a divorce." Cf. his several references to his interment as a prisoner of war: 333,

working theologian's experiences and encounters in life may occasion a dramatic change from an earlier theological perspective to a new orientation with a revised agenda.[13] Finally, some theologians identify the social location within which they work in order to clarify the context and content of their theological proposals.[14] Although I do so with some hesitation, I have decided to include some aspects of my life experience in this essay. My purpose is not to authorize or justify my theological conclusions but to contextualize the final formulation of the perspective on the providence of God that unfolds in this essay. The matrix in which this understanding of providence has been finally hammered out proved to be the most difficult years of my life. Though my narrative rendering of the providence of God in the story of Jesus is in some ways inextricably bound up with a particular story in my life, the truthfulness of the perspective on providence that I propose does not depend on my personal experience. Yet the concerns in this essay are more than theological

---

n. 62; 343, n. 40; 345, n. 51; 349, n. 66; 427, n. 37. Gilkey published a detailed account of this formative experience, *Shantung Compound* (New York: Harper & Row, Publishers, 1966). More importantly, see Langdon Gilkey, "A Retroperspective Glance at My Work," *The Whirlwind of Culture*, ed. Donald W. Musser and Joseph L. Price (Bloomington IN: Meyer-Stone Books, 1988) 1-35. Gilkey provides a remarkable account of his life, which includes the decisive impact of internment as a prisoner of war and the story of the failure of his marriage in divorce. He could have left any reference to these two events in his life out of *Reaping the Whirlwind*, but he decided for the sake of clarity to identify these pivotal experiences in his book on providence and to detail them in his retrospective examination of his life's work. Cf. Jürgen Moltmann, "My Theological Career," *History and the Triune God* (New York: Crossroad, 1992) 165-82.

[13]See Thomas Oden, "A Personal Interlude: A Path toward Postcritical Consciousness," *The Word of Life*, vol. 2 of *Systematic Theology* (San Francisco: Harper & Row, 1989) 217-20; for his account of the reversal in his theology, see Thomas Oden, *Agenda for Theology* (San Francisco: Harper & Row, 1979).

[14]The importance of self-involving discourse that identifies the social location of the theologian charaterizes the work of proponents of African-American theology, the various voices in feminist theology, and Latin/South American advocates of liberation theology. A sampling of these perspectives would include: James H. Evans, Jr., *We Have Been Believers* (Minneapolis: Fortress Press, 1992); Elisabeth Schüssler Fiorenza, *In Memory of Her: A Feminist Theological Reconstruction of Christian Origins* (New York: Crossroad, 1983); Gustavo Gutiérrez, *A Theology of Liberation: History, Politics, and Salvation*, trans. Sister Caridad Inda and John Eagleson (Maryknoll NY: Orbis Books, 1988; 1973). But note Peter C. Hodgson, "A Personal Epilogue," *Winds of the Spirit: A Constructive Christian Theology* (Louisville: Westminster/John Knox Press, 1994) 332-37.

issues to me, because the questions embedded in the theme of the providence of God are significant dimensions of my experience and affirmation of Christian faith.

A Personal Context

The story begins on 4 September 1981, but it has a specific and unique context. After sabbatical research on the theme of providence at Oxford University during the 1979–1980 academic year, I returned with my family to Louisville and regular seminary teaching responsibilities in July, 1980. I continued my work on the theme of providence, and in the Spring of 1981 I convened my first graduate seminar on "The Providence of God." When the 1981–1982 school year began in late August, I had a Faculty Address on "The Providence of God in Christological Perspective" ready for presentation on October 7. Unexpectedly everything providential suddenly plummeted into a dark and ambiguous abyss. On Friday, September 4, Betty, my wife for eighteen years, had her annual check-up, which unexpectedly included consultation for surgery with the almost certain diagnosis of breast cancer, and a few days later she had a modified radical mastectomy. Since the malignancy had metastisized, we turned from surgery to chemotherapy for treatment, a process so debilitating, sometimes excruciating, that it intensified the sense of the disease. Nevertheless, chemotherapy promised a fifty percent chance for recovery from the illness that now threatened her life.

At the time our son, Elgin, had just turned eleven, and our daughter, Michelle, only seven. Betty went through chemotherapy for almost a year, with the disease apparently arrested. She began to put her life back together, and the family began to function again. In January of 1983, we suspected recurrence, a suspicion confirmed through surgery in early February.

The recurrence of cancer in my wife and the mother of our children constituted nothing less than a personal crisis of faith for me. She had endured surgery that initially decimated her sense of feminine identity. She had gone through the ordeal of chemotherapy—a terrible experience. She had regained the use of her right arm. She entered psychotherapy after chemotherapy, and she had begun to find life again. The regimentation of regular hospitalization and continued recuperation at home had drained the entire family and bruised, indeed, frightened, Elgin and Michelle.

Then everything fell apart. You lean into the promise of hope. You pray in the stammering of hope. You live through the courage of hope. But one word, "recurrence," smashed hope into millions of cellular pieces, each one with the sentence of death.

Shortly after confirmation of recurrence early in February of 1983, I had the most memorable dream of my life. The dream addressed the turmoil in my life concerning the threat to our family. I was living on the edge of faith, lecturing daily to my students about the grace of God and staring nightly into the empty Darkness of death. The dream expressed the crisis of my faith—a personal crisis in the providence of God.

> During the near darkness
> Of the hour before dawn
> I watched my teachers and mentors
> Following one by one behind each other
> But beyond me,
> Unaware of me
> Standing off in the shadows.
> Conscious of each other
> And their purposed destination,
> They wore dark robes with hooded cowls
> Which almost hid their faces
> As they hastened, one after the other,
> On some sacred pilgrimage.
>
> Sure the last one had gone by,
> I fell in line and followed—
> Not knowing where or why—
> Dressed in ordinary clothes,
> No robe, no fold of piety
> To cover me.
>
> The path we followed single file
> With shredding darkness on all sides
> Suddenly opened into a vast field of grass
> Awash in the brilliance of morning sunshine.

I saw my monkish mentors gathered in silence
On the other side of the field of green
Ringed in a semi-circle around an immense
Painting of the Sea:
A magnificent scene—
The distant sky a churning grey and blue,
White-capped waves breaking,
Waters crashing against a rocky shore,
A collage of blue and green,
White, black and grey—
A swirling, dizzying portrait
Of the Sea.

I moved around the half-circled masterpiece
From one corner to the other
Finding no place to stand.
I could not see their painting of the Sea.
I could not join in the stillness
And silence of their captivity.
I felt deep disappointment sweep over me,
Why did I not have a place to be?
Disappointment sank into despair:
Did they not know the difference
Between a painting—even a masterpiece—
And reality, the indescribable wonder of the Sea?

Without knowing how or why
I suddenly found myself beyond the edge
Of the painting,
Behind it,
Dropping gently yet rapidly
Through a comfortable smoky haze.
When I stopped descending,
An unnoticed silence discontinued.

I stood alone on the wet, sandy shore
In the presence of the Sea.
Its waters extended endlessly,
Beyond the horizon
Touching infinity.

The sounds of waves rolling
And crashing against the shore
Roared like the majestic dawning of creation,
Deafening in its might.
Colors blurred into every shade
Of blue and black and green and white.

I tasted salt in my mouth,
And breathed it into my life.
The light of the eastern sky broke through
Billowing clouds of cotton and blue,
Dark clouds receding, retreating before the light.
Towering black cliffs loomed massive behind me,
Laid alongside one another
Like giant steeples of stone
Reaching up until lost in the mist
Of blanketing clouds above.

I stood in the awesome, infinite Presence of the Sea,
Of ineffable Mystery.
And simultaneously I saw myself from above,
One speck on a vast, shining shore,
A shoreline stretching farther than the eye could see,
Lost in the distance to the embrace of the Sea.
And I felt significant.
I felt significant only because of my insignificance.
Yet I stood in the Presence of Ultimate Reality,
Of Another, of the Holy Other.
I felt acceptance and affirmation,
Security and peace.

I belonged to the Sea.
It had let me be
To become a valued entity.
It had named me,
To forget me now an impossibility.

God knew me.
God knew my name,
The journey of my life.
And God loved me.

Two profound impressions lingered: ecstasy and peace. And when ecstasy became memory, peace wanted to stay. Later I realized that I had nothing more but nothing less than my mentors and friends: a vision of the Sea, a masterpiece emblazoned on the memory of my mind, nothing more but nothing less.

A short time later, I dreamed another dream, a dream that would recur again and again in my sleeping, a nightmare ever more real when awake. It was a nightmare of sheer torment.

> Night on a dark stormy sea—
> Winds howled
> As wave after wave crashed against
> The craggy shore.
> Running, running out of breath
> But I was always running,
> Running alone in the darkness,
> Driven by an overwhelming sense of fear,
> No, terror.
>
> Icy waters lapped at my heavy feet.
> The cold chilled me to the bone.
> The wet sand pulled at every footstep.
>
> Whenever I looked over my shoulder
> At the sea,
> I saw him staring at me—laughing.
> His dark face etched on the white surf
> Of rushing waves
> Was a face of terror.
>
> Large, lidless eyes—
> They stared, glared, ensnared my mind.
> A wide mouth with massive, shining teeth
> Formed a vicious grin
> That spewed mocking laughter.
> His sinister cackling filled the night,
> Rising and falling with the wind.

As the waves would ebb and flow,
I could read the cold, white, night light
That blinked out his name:
CHAOS . . . CHAOS . . . CHAOS. . . .

Whether asleep or awake, I knew that I lived in the grip of chaos, the
terror of a Storm. What did this recurring nightmare mean? Had I encountered the dark side of God? No, I knew from the outset the name of
this tormenting face: "Chaos." Only later did I realize that its "mocking
laughter" and "sinister cackling" identified this face in the night with evil.
Chaos threatened to claim the place of God, and lurking in and behind
the face of chaos, disguised and hidden within it, I glimpsed the demonic.
Why was I surprised?

I do not know how I survived those months, now a lifetime ago, but
Albert McClellan recorded a conversation, an intimate conversation,
between the two of us alone one afternoon in the Faculty Lounge. He
penned the conversation into his daily journal, calling the entry. . . .

Frank's Soliloquy

*In the faculty lounge today Frank Tupper said that many contem-
porary theologians had abandoned the hope of resurrection, noting:
"That disturbs me greatly." He said that he personally accepted the
affirmation of his teachers but without their concern for detail. Then
he spoke of his wife's condition. He said, "The first time in chemotherapy we had so much hope, but now there is so little hope, now
we are suspended." We were alone in the lounge, and Frank was
sitting slightly turned away from me. He talked of his students and
resurrection reality. He said that the students understand so little of
pain, and nothing of death. His words were softly spoken, as if he
were talking to himself. "I would not believe in God if I did not
believe in Jesus." The way he said it was startling, almost as if
without Christ no one believes in God. Then I said, "Yet most people
would say that if it were not for God they would not believe in
Jesus." Frank's answer, "Yes, and that is because they have not lived*

long enough in Mark's Gospel—the desperation of Gethsemane and the desolation of the cross."[15]

Of course, I cannot speak for anyone else, *only for me.* This I know: Without the story of Jesus I would not believe in God. Or more probably, God simply would not matter. The story of Jesus enables me to envision God as One who genuinely cares for each and all of us. In Jesus, God confronts the Darkness face to face, Incarnate, for our sake. Jesus is Light to the gentle face of God. The story of Jesus says that God laughs with us in our joys and weeps with us in our sorrows. God strengthens us in the helplessness of our hoping, God stands with us in the uncertainty of our believing, and God waits for us in our yearning to be loved. Ultimately the lonely companionship of Jesus in the suffering of his passion made my painful journey a sometime story of faith.

---

[15]Adapted. Personal correspondence from Albert McClellan.

A Brief Methodological Interlude

THE PROBLEM OF THEOLOGICAL METHOD is a major issue in contemporary theology, nowhere more difficult than theologizing about the providence of God. Although I prefer a more inductive rather than deductive approach to theological method—which characterizes what I have done in this volume—a brief sketch of theological method may assist the reader in understanding and engaging the chapters that follow. Three methodological concerns shape this theological essay: First, a study of providence requires the integration of providence, Christology, and eschatology through the Gospel narratives, a point already made in the Introduction.[1] Second, the use of the Gospel narratives to fashion an interpretation of the providence of God on the basis of the story of Jesus requires the identification of the genre of the canonical Gospels and the role of critical consciousness in the theological exegesis of the Jesus traditions. Third, the significance of theological models for illuminating the relationship of God to the world warrants a brief analysis of the model of providence that has taken shape in writing this book and that subsequently informs each chapter of it. In this brief Interlude, therefore, I will sketch the theological rationale in my appropriation of the Gospel traditions and the model of God's action in the world that undergirds this project. An evaluation of the adequacy of my treatment of these methodological issues finally turns on the cogency of the proposal on providence in the entirety of this project.

Interpreting the Gospels

The endeavor to interpret the providence of God in the light of the epochal moments in the Synoptic telling of the story of Jesus requires an

---

[1]See the Introduction, 1-5, 9-11.

explanation of my understanding and use of the Gospel traditions. Although every effort to identify the Gospels with a particular literary genre has its limitations, Roland M. Frye, professor of English Literature at the University of Pennsylvania, has argued persuasively for the characterization of the Gospels as "dramatic history."[2]

The Genre of Dramatic History

The Gospels preserve historical traditions about Jesus of Nazareth but not in the sense of biographies or histories, chronicles or annals. Hence the question: To what kind of accounts of history do the Gospels belong? The genre of dramatic history. This genre includes the historical plays of William Shakespeare (*Henry V*), George Bernard Shaw (*Saint Joan of Arc*), and Robert Sherwood (*Abe Lincoln in Illinois*),[3] and these works of dramatic history exhibit characteristics that one finds in the canonical Gospels. Frye offers a helpful definition of the genre:

> A dramatic history is a literary work that presents a basically historical story with economy and narrative effectiveness, which remains essentially faithful to the historical tradition but which may alter elements of that tradition as appears necessary in order to represent *multum in parvo*, and which is designed to convey important insights and understandings (both factual and interpretative) to a wide audience.[4]

---

[2]Roland M. Frye, "A Literary Perspective for the Criticism of the Gospels," *Jesus and Man's Hope*, Vol. 2, ed. Donald G. Miller and Dikran Y. Hadidian (Pittsburgh: Pittsburgh Theological Seminary, 1971) 193-221. For a response, see Paul J. Achtemeier, "On the Historical-Critical Method in New Testament Studies: Apologia pro Vita sua," *Perspective* 11 (1970): 289-304. For Frye's reply, see "On the Historical-Critical Method in New Testament Studies: A Reply to Professor Achtemeier, *Perspective* 14 (1973): 28-33. Dan O. Via, Jr., *Kerygma and Comedy in the New Testament* (Philadelphia: Fortress Press, 1975) 97, says: "Frye's suggestions ring true to me . . . but I would like more precision." Conversely, Charles H. Talbert, *What Is a Gospel: The Genre of the Canonical Gospels* (Philadelphia: Fortress Press, 1977) 22, n. 48, says: "From my perspective, grouping Shakespeare, Shaw, and Plutarch together creates more problems than it solves," but Talbert ignores Frye's disclaimer about Plutarch and one of Frye's primary examples, namely, Robert Sherwood, *Abe Lincoln in Illinois*. Talbert favors the genre of an ancient form of biography (133-35).

[3]Frye, "A Literary Perspective," 206-10.

[4]Ibid., 219, n. 28.

Shakespeare, Shaw, and Sherwood obviously intended to be interesting to their audiences, but they aimed to do more: Their dramatic vehicles had a vision to proclaim, a message to impart. The role of imagination is critical in a dramatic history, for the audience must engage the imaginative vision of the playwright with its own imagination, if the dramatic history is to come alive for them. Unlike historical fiction, which uses the past as a colorful point of departure, an historical drama has a commitment to the original historical situation of the chief character of the play, a commitment to the events and circumstances that convey the significance of the central figure. Moreover, these playwrights designed their presentations to attract as broad a general audience as possible, which made condensation all the more important, because brevity is more effective than prolixity for such an audience. What the dramatist chose to present about characters and events had to be representative of the entire story. Accordingly, different literary devices are employed to tell the story fairly and convincingly: Thus chronology may be altered or telescoped, and later insight may be shifted to an earlier period for the sake of narrative effectiveness. The use of representative persons, incidents, and actions, says Frye, constitutes an essential key: "What is shown represents a vastly larger canvas of life that cannot be shown."[5] Therefore, the narrative depiction must portray with great brevity the life and significance of the central character in a compelling dramatic presentation.

Robert Sherwood gives a good working definition of the author of a dramatic history: "He is, at best, an interpreter, with a certain facility for translating all that he has heard in a manner sufficiently dramatic to attract a crowd," but he is neither a news reporter nor a scholarly critic.[6] The dramatic historian must not only omit considerable material, but he may structure representative events that communicate concisely and summarily the pattern of many different things that did occur. Throughout there is "a steadfast effort" to represent the historical protagonist as truthfully as possible, because "a strict regard for the plain truth" remains a fundamental concern.[7] Whatever the range of his poetic license, Sherwood

---

[5]Ibid., 209.

[6]Robert Sherwood, *Abe Lincoln in Illinois*, "The Substance of 'Abe Lincoln in Illinois' " (New York: Charles Scribner's Sons, 1939) 189.

[7]Ibid., 190. Sherwood says: "However, in the case of a play about the development of the extraordinary character of Abraham Lincoln, a strict regard for the plain truth is

knew that he could not afford to falsify a tradition that would be familiar to many in his audience. Similarly, G. B. Shaw demonstrated a basic concern for the essential truth in history, but he acknowledged the necessity on occasion to present an "inexact picture of some accidental facts" for the sake of the truth itself. Through the inevitable sacrifice of verisimilitude, Shaw declares, he "has secured in the only possible way sufficient veracity" to convey a persuasive and truthful understanding of his story to the people whose interest he intends to capture and retain.[8]

The Gospels as Dramatic History

As surely as differences exist between the writings of Shakespeare and Sherwood within this literary genre, so do differences endure between the Gospels of antiquity and modern examples of dramatic history. Certain formal characteristics of this genre do apply nonetheless to the Gospels: (1) While neither chronicles nor biographies, the Gospels aim to provide an authentic presentation of the historical events and persons that they narrate. (2) All the evangelists intend to attract the attention of a broad audience and to present their message as convincingly as possible. (3) The Gospels remain relatively short but quite compelling, and each can be read within two hours. (4) Finally, the location of the Gospels in the genre of dramatic history helps to explain the differences between the Gospels without "disintegrating" criticism. Frye says: "Chronology may be rearranged, incidents diversely selected, emphases shifted, and episodes presented in distinctive light." Such differences are not problematic

---

more than obligatory; it is obviously desirable." He continues: "[Lincoln's] life as he lived it was *a work of art*, forming a veritable allegory of the growth of the democratic spirit. . . . Furthermore, just as Lincoln's life needs no adornment of symbolism to make it pertinent, his character needs no romanticizing, no sentimentalizing, no dramatizing" (190, italics added). Subsequently he writes: "While I have made a steadfast effort to reflect the character of Lincoln as truthfully as I can, I have been less faithful in the portraits of the other historical characters who appear in this play," without grave injustice to any of them except possibly Stephen A. Douglas. "These other characters had to be used, for dramatic purposes, not as people important in themselves but as sources of light, each one being present only for the purpose of casting a beam to illuminate some one of the innumerable facets of Lincoln's spirit" (197).

[8]So Frye, "A Literary Perspective," 210. Cf. G. B. Shaw, Preface to *Saint Joan* in *Selected Plays* (New York: Dodd, Mead and Co., 1949) 2:313-14.

but intrinsic to the genre. "Though they may represent conflicting and contradictory traditions, they do not necessarily do so, for such variations at the author's discretion are inherent in the methodology of dramatic history."[9]

The characterization of the Gospels as dramatic history is helpful for understanding the similarities and dissimilarities between the canonical Gospels--the fundamental difference between the Synoptic Gospels and the Fourth Gospel on the one side, and the variations and parallels between the three Synoptic Gospels on the other. The evangelists framed four different narratives that integrate diverse materials so distinctively and effectively that each Gospel constitutes a unique literary work in its own right. Frye observes, "Remarkable skill is evident in the selection, arrangement, and presentation of material by each of the four evangelists, and each Gospel deserves to be treated as a literary unit."[10] As the writers appropriated their various sources in the distinct shaping of each of the Gospels, their work included not only an elemental continuity but also a pervasive discontinuity. The discontinuity refers to "a basic transmutation rather than mere incorporation" of the different sources into the striking literary quality characteristic of the Gospels.

Does the identification of the Gospels as dramatic history lead us beyond a precritical stage of interpretation into a critical stage? Several reasons sustain an affirmative answer. First, we do not have a lengthy biography of Jesus that would enable us to evaluate the adequacy of a dramatic history about Jesus, e.g., the Gospel of Mark. Conversely, we can read Carl Sandburg's extensive biography of Abraham Lincoln and evaluate the reliability of Robert Sherwood's dramatization of *Abe Lincoln in Illinois*. For the story of Jesus such analysis rests almost entirely on a comparative examination of the canonical Gospels. Moreover, while Robert Sherwood provides a commentary to explain his use of sources and his employment of various literary devices,[11] the authors of the Gospels do not provide such an explanation. The endeavor to determine what sources a given evangelist utilized and what literary

---

[9]Frye, "A Literary Perspective," 211-12.

[10]Ibid., 220, n. 41.

[11]Note Sherwood's lengthy analysis of what he has done in *Abe Lincoln in Illinois*: He provides supplementary notes to identify the resources that he has used (189-201) and a scene by scene explanation of how he has adapted the material (201-50).

devices informed the shape of a Gospel tradition remains the task of biblical scholars who work with multiple methodologies but whose results are only more or less probable. Therefore, precisely because the genre of dramatic history with its characteristic traits exists independently of the Gospel traditions, the identification of the Gospels with their distinctive literary features as instances of dramatic history stimulates and energizes a critical consciousness in the interpretation of the stories of Jesus.[12]

Second, the canonical Gospels are written from the vantage point of the conclusion of the story of Jesus—the Roman execution of the Nazarene as "King of the Jews" and the confident witness of his disciples to Jesus' resurrection from the dead. All the Gospels are written retrospectively, and the numerous stories of Jesus are remembered and retold in the light of his destiny--the resurrection of the Christ crucified. Thus the Gospels in their similarities and differences are creative depictions of the story of Jesus Christ through the intertwining of historically referenced and historically represented traditions, all of which constitute the narrative world within which the Christian community lives and church theologians work.

Third, the narration of the passion of Christ in the Gospel traditions is disproportionate in measure to the stories of the life and teaching of Jesus. Yet the answers to the questions of why he died and whether or not God raised him from the dead do not answer in and of themselves the questions of what he said and what he did. The questions of the words and deeds of Jesus have their own integrity, which in turn affect the questions of his death and resurrection. All the questions are asked

---

[12]For a stimulating discussion of the kind of problem that Frye's approach generates, see Roland M. Frye, "The Synoptic Problems and Analogies in Other Literature," *The Relationships Among the Gospels: An Interdisciplinary Dialogue*, ed. William O. Walker, Jr. (San Antonio: Trinity University Press, 1978) 261-302. Frye offers a provocative conclusion to his essay: "My proposal is that *first* we use the readily available techniques of secular literary-historical criticism for bringing the character of Jesus to life literarily, *then* we compare the figure (or figures) of Jesus emerging from the four Gospels (each with its distinctive presentations and emphases, and *finally* we may be able better to assess the historical figure who lies behind the four characterizations and his relevance to us: *we can only get back to the Jesus of history through the Jesus of literature*" (302). In the same volume of essays see William H. Farmer, "Basic Affirmation with Some Demurrals: A Response to Roland M. Frye" (303-22), and the comments of Joseph B. Tyson, "Literary Criticism and Gospels: The Seminar" (323-41).

together, because all the questions converge in the question of who Jesus was—and *who Jesus is*. This question, the question that gathers all other questions together, draws us into the narrative world of the Gospels and invites to read with a second naiveté.

Reading with a Second Naiveté

What does it mean to enter the narrative world of the Gospels and to read with a second naiveté?[13] The movement is from the first naiveté of a precritical interpretation into innocence lost in historical-critical interpretation. The first naiveté accepts without question the literal sense of the text and lives naturally in the world of symbols that are indigenous to the text. The achievement of critical consciousness negates the innocence of the first naiveté, and it renders precritical interpretation helpless and perhaps embarrassed in the dissonance between a literal reading and modern historical consciousness. Whether one accepts his larger hermeneutical proposals or not, Paul Ricoeur offers helpful guidance.

> For the second immediacy that we seek and the second naiveté that we await are no longer accessible to us anywhere else than in hermeneutics; we can believe only by interpreting.[14]

Believing on the other side of modernity occurs through a hermeneutic of postcritical interpretation. The hermeneutician suspends critical judgment and accepts provisionally the orientation and affirmations of the believer. The hermeneutician does not "feel" the awareness and commitments of the believer in a first naiveté but "re-feels" them in an a-critical posture, that is, "as if" he or she were a precritical interpreter who did read with a first naiveté. This experience of a second naiveté requires a reenactment through a creative and sympathetic imagination.

Subsequently the hermeneutician attempts to account conceptually for the possibility of living in the believer's world. The task is to demonstrate

---

[13]See Lewis S. Mudge, "Paul Ricoeur on Biblical Interpretation," in Paul Ricoeur, *Essays on Biblical Interpretation* (Philadelphia: Fortress Press, 1980) 4-9.

[14]Paul Ricoeur, *The Symbolism of Evil*, trans. Emerson Buchanan (Boston: Beacon Press, 1969) 352, probably the most widely quoted reference of Ricoeur to "the second naiveté."

that the symbols that belong to the world of the narrative are actually reality-detectors that cannot be abstracted from the narrative itself. Living in the Gospel narratives through a second naiveté results in the illumination of the depths of reality that could otherwise not occur apart from the symbols of the narrative world in the Gospels of Jesus Christ. The movement is from the hegemony of an historical-critical interpretation that negates the *sensus literalis* of the text to the positive reception of the literal meaning of the narrative in postcritical interpretation.

The priority of the Biblical Story in its irreducibility and unrepeatability is crucial. James McClendon has stated it eloquently: [We are called] "to see past and present and future linked by a 'this is that' and 'then is now' vision, a trope of mystical identity binding the story now to the story then and now to God's future yet to come."[15] Reading with a second naiveté does not mean that we find our stories in the Biblical Story; on the contrary, postcritical interpretation requires us to accept the priority of the Biblical Story and to make it self-consciously our story. The heart of the Biblical Story is the Story of Jesus, but the epochal moments in the Story of Jesus are not instantiations of universal religious truth that serve essentially to illuminate our stories. Rather, the Story of Jesus, the Story of Jesus as the definitive Story of God--this Story incorporates and transforms all our stories. The Biblical Story defines for us the nature of reality and the vision of the world within which we do reflective theology. Whatever the limitations of his theological program, George Lindbeck has seen this issue correctly:

> Intratextual theology redescribes reality within the scriptural framework rather than translating Scripture into extrascriptural categories. It is the text, so to speak, which absorbs the world, rather than the world the text.[16]

When the hermeneutician enters the world of the Biblical Story, reading with a second naiveté and suspended critical judgment, the task is to discern the depiction of reality disclosed therein. As the Biblical

---

[15]James Wm. McClendon, Jr., *Doctrine: Systematic Theology, Volume 2* (Nashville: Abingdon Press, 1994) 45.

[16]George Lindbeck, *That Nature of Doctrine: Religion and Theology in a Postliberal Age* (Philadelphia: The Westminster Press, 1984) 118.

Story encircles and reframes the modern world, the interpreter will move to reclaim critical judgment, but always careful not to elevate extra-biblical norms into the basic framework of theological explanation. Of course, a second naiveté is *a second naiveté*—on the other side of historical-critical explanation. A critical consciousness will necessarily inform reading with a second naiveté, but the reciprocity of interpretation between the biblical traditions and contemporary lived-experience will maintain the priority of the understanding of reality disclosed in the Biblical Story through its hermeneutical key, the Story of Jesus. The recognition of the Gospels as dramatic history will enhance reading with a second naiveté, because the genre of dramatic history enables the interpreter to live in a biblically-defined world view without sacrificing the critical consciousness that the second naiveté requires.[17]

A Model of Personal Agency

The interpretation of how God relates to and works in the world is essential to the conception of a biblically-defined worldview, which poses the question of an appropriate model of God's providential activity in nature and history. The models of providence in contemporary theology tend to be variations of the monarchical model on the one side and differing forms of a process or existential model on the other. Is there a viable model of providence that moves between the monarchical model with its emphasis on divine sovereignty and a process or existential

---

[17]See especially Garrett Green, " 'The Bible As . . .': Fictional Narrative and Scriptural Truth," *Scriptural Authority and Narrative Interpretation*, ed. Garrett Green (Philadelphia: Fortress Press, 1987) 79-96. In this closely argued essay Green accepts the characterization of biblical narratives as "fictive" or "fictionlike," but he argues nonetheless for the truth of the Gospel story. However, he does not specify what essential narratives constitute the Gospel story, a critical theological issue. The affirmation of "fictive" elements (82, 83-84, 90-91, 93-94) is not contrary to the genre of dramatic history, especially in conjunction with "imagination" (85-86, 88-90, 92-93), but the use of these terms requires much more precision.

Cf. Kevin J. Vanhoozer, *Biblical Narrative in the Philosophy of Paul Ricoeur: A Study in Hermeneutics and Theology* (Cambridge: Cambridge University Press, 1990) 148-89, an especially illuminating discussion of Karl Barth, Hans Frei, and Paul Ricoeur—plus Green's essay.

model with its stress on human decision-making within the dynamics of nature and history? The alternative that I propose is a personal model with an accent on creative transformation through the power of the future. Whereas the monarchical model sacrifices historical realism to the control of God, which dramatically mitigates and sometimes negates human freedom, historical contingency, and natural causation, the process model sacrifices the sovereignty of God to historical realism for the sake of the responsibility of humanity in the ambiguities of nature and history.

The tension between these perspectives on providence roots partly in different patterns of the interpretation of the Scriptures. Although any model for providence must be defined through a critical appropriation of the biblical traditions, a sketch of my understanding of the personal model of God's activity in the world in terms of engaging transformation will help to clarify the conceptualization of providence that takes concrete form in this book. My critical evaluation of the monarchical model of God's relationship to the world informs directly or indirectly every chapter of this project, and my critique of the process model with its existential dimensions in historical passage comprises the Appendix, "Gilkey on Providence."[18]

The Mode of God's Activity in the World

"Engaging transformation" best describes my understanding of God's activity in the world in terms of a model of personal agency. As the power of the future who participates in every present, God actively engages all aspects of creation and every human situation. God not only establishes the possibilities available in any given moment, but God also acts as one agent among others in shaping the specific configuration of a sequence of events. That God participates in the movement of nature and history does not mean that God determines the conclusion of every developmental process or historical progression. On the contrary, God acts alongside other agents amid the variables in a particular situation. The givens in the development of a process condition what human agents can do, and these same givens inviting and limiting human possibilities condition in similar fashion what God can do—a similarity within a still

---

[18]See the Appendix, "Gilkey on Providence," 441-54.

greater dissimilarity. God's engaging participation transcends the various forms of human participation, a transcending participation that occurs partly through the interconnected activity of God with all events simultaneously on the one side and ultimately as the integrating horizon of every moment of actualization on the other. God is an active agent in every present as one agent among others who contributes to the specific configuration that occurs, and, concurrently, God is the horizon of the future who integrates each sequential movement together and unites all historical progression retrospectively.

"Transformation" describes what God can and does do in a specific situation, but the measure of transformation ranges from very slight to the surprisingly new. Such transformation presupposes that God has possibilities with regard to every situation that transcend the possibilities that are intrinsic in the situation itself. The givens in a concrete situation, however, do fundamentally condition the possibilities available to God that transcend it. That is, the options that God alone brings to bear on a particular situation will be coherent with the givens that structure the possibilities in the situation itself. Thus the possibilities that are available to God exclusively are not of a fundamentally different kind, or at least not contrary to, those immanent possibilities in a developing configuration on the way to actualization.

How can one recognize even tentatively the actualization of possibilities accessible to God alone that transcend yet cohere with those in the concrete situation? Although the discernment of God's action cannot be sharply distinguished from what would otherwise occur without reference to God—because what *coheres* will be consistent with what *inheres* in the arrangement of variables on the way to the future—the element of "surprise" in varying degrees will stamp those positive developments that God contributes to a situation from the transcendent possibilities available only to God. Since whatever coheres from the transcending side of God cannot be abstracted from whatever inheres within the nexus of the event itself, God's providential activity as one agent among other agents with regard to each and every situation remains hidden from those who interpret events without reference to God. The action of God converges with natural causation in historical contingency and apparently coincides with the development that actually transpires. Yet the retrospective integration of a specific historical configuration from the horizon of the future determines its final shape, which allows the interpreter the opportunity to discern the form of providence and its measure by looking backwards: The affirmation of providence occurs through the construal of this particular story in the light of its conclusion. Of course, even the conclusion of a specific process belongs to the continuing movement of the larger history of which it is a part, which means every conclusion is always penultimate and superseded.

The Historic Aspects of Providence: Preservation

The understanding of providence in terms of a personal model of engaging transformation addresses the historic aspects of providence on the basis of preservation, concurrence, and governing.[19] First, God is the source and ground of all possibility in the history of creation, and God maintains all that God has created. A sharp distinction between creation and preservation is not possible, however, because God preserves the structures that constitute creation and accepts the limitations that the continuity of creation implies. That God creates in the freedom of love means the gracious preservation of the integrity of creation through divine freedom. The self-limitation of God in relation to creation originates in the decision to create and continues in fidelity to the ongoing existence of the world. Yet the self-limitation of God is not a self-contradiction, for God chooses this limitation in the plenitude of divine freedom in order to produce a relatively free and contingent creation. Thus the possibilities that exist in any given moment cannot be abstracted from the past, not for the creature and not for God.

Does God preserve chaos and Nothingness in the continuing blessing of creation? The existence of humanity in the world is a critical reference point: That God actively sustains humanity in the movement of creation through history does not mean that God preserves sin, because sin is a distortion of humanness, an alien and an intruder. Rather, God sustains *humanity* in its sinfulness. While the preservation of human creaturely existence inevitably means humanity fallen into sin, God does not preserve sin itself. In similar fashion God maintains the movement of creation in history that invariably includes the chaos of an unfinished and

---

[19]For a careful and interesting analysis of providence in church tradition, see Thomas C. Oden, *The Living God,* vol. 2 of *Systematic Theology* (San Francisco: Harper & Row, 1987) 270-315, esp. 279-94, 300-302.

discordant creation as well as the demonizing of historical passage through the cumulative sin of corporate humanity and the ever present threat of the specter of Nothingness. God preserves what God has made but not what God has rejected and not made—yet which nonetheless exists. Beyond the negative powers of sin, chaos, and Nothingness, God sustains the goodness in the purpose of creation and the opportunities that contribute to the fulfillment of the intention of creation.

The Historic Aspects of Providence: Concurrence

Second, God is an active agent in the contingency of history, and God has chosen to act in concurrence with the temporal givens, historical and natural, alongside human agents and other creaturely factors.[20] When human agents cooperate with God, they assist in the achievement of God's purpose. Conversely, when persons fail or refuse to cooperate with God, they frustrate God's immediate intention and may exercise some negative impact on the accomplishment of a long-term goal. The realities of nature prove even more complicated than the response of human agents in the interpretation of concurrence, because natural causation that informs any situation relative to humanity in history is not as available to God as human agency. Natural causation, nevertheless, does not lie beyond the persuasive activity of God.

Wolfhart Pannenberg has suggested that all reality exists as a single field of force,[21] and that God impacts in different ways and at different levels those natural processes that shape a specific development or occurrence within the field of force in terms of the possibilities available to God. Nancey Murphy poses another model:[22] Within the hierarchy of being a superior agent can change the otherwise natural direction of a particular process without destroying the causal interconnections that occur in a complex system comprehending natural processes. For exam-

---

[20]Ibid., 281-86. Oden interprets primary and secondary causation with a sensitivity that magnifies the cooperation of divine power with subordinate powers. He judiciously avoids divine omnicausal determinism.

[21]See Wolfhart Pannenberg, *Systematic Theology*, 2 vols., trans. Geoffrey W. Bromiley (Grand Rapids MI: Eerdmans Publishing Co., 1994) 2:76-115.

[22]See Nancey C. Murphy, "Does Prayer Make a Difference," *Cosmos as Creation*, ed. Ted Peters (Nashville: Abingdon Press, 1989) 235-45, esp. 242-45.

ple, a small boy can decide to pull a wagon uphill against the force of gravity, a force that would otherwise push it downhill: While it would be a violation of the law of gravity apart from the action of a higher agent, the boy, such action is not a violation of any physical law in the context of the entire system, that comprehends a human agent, a wagon, and natural law. Constraints do exist, for a fifty-pound boy cannot pull a two-hundred pound wagon uphill.

If such systems are to be useful in the interpretation of God's action in relation to natural causation, the fundamental question of when, how, and to what extent a specific system proves viable to describe the action of God with reference to the complexity of an event requires considerable more data before the question is answerable. The level of God's impact on natural causation in any given setting hinges in principle on the range of possibilities available, but the measure of human collaboration in conjunction with the active investment of God in relation to the process may turn out to be the critical factor. Indeed, the nexus of historical and natural causation at a crucial juncture in the development of a situation often proves to be decisive. While the measure of human concurrence varies from situation to situation, God always acts and interacts with the multiple factors in the give and take of a contingent historical process, working with the givens therein to move an identifiable sequence to its attainable goal. Like preservation, therefore, concurrence includes a divine self-limitation: On the basis of the possibilities that inhere in and/or cohere with a particular configuration, God shapes its progression in concurrence with creaturely agents who participate in its actualization.

Concurrence describes God's active participation in the movement of nature through history with special reference to human agents, individual and corporate, despite the persistence of evil in the whole of creaturely existence in the world, but God does not act in concurrence with evil. Rather, God acts in opposition to all instances of evil, working in each to fashion some good, whether significant or slight. God does not cooperate with that which God does not will. Thus concurrence remains an eminently positive category that describes God's action in conjunction with responsive human agents, though the measure of such response will vary considerably. Yet engaging transformation through the concurrence of God's action with cooperative human action can be quite decisive and produce something dramatically new—without resorting to the monarchical model of the unilateral intervention of God.[23]

The Historic Aspects of Providence: Governance

Third, God governs creation and all creaturely events in history. If God rules as the power of the future, the integration of a particular historical progression will happen retrospectively, attaining and receiving definitive form only through its conclusion. Its meaning is not only recognizable from the endpoint, but it is also determined from it. The integration of a temporal movement is certainly informed by the possibilities of the present on the basis of the past; nevertheless, the distinctive character of a contingent process happens through the power of the future that ultimately defines what it is. God guides the movement of history through the continuing integration of contingent occurrence from the horizon of the future. God is the power of the future: God is the future of every present become past and every future becoming present. Thus history, which must include the history of nature, has a teleological or eschatological structure. The living God does not rule and overrule historical development with the scepter of monarchical control nor does the Creator God essentially sustain a process that lacks an ultimate goal. Rather, God establishes all the possibilities of each moment of history, God acts alongside other agents in the contingency of events to effect a particular historical progression, and God integrates retroactively everything that occurs from the horizon of the future: Ultimately God guides each contingent configuration in the dynamics of historical progression within the process, and God superintends the entire multifaceted movement in all its interconnected complexity from the frontside.[24]

---

[23]Although the terms "intervene" and "intervention" can be used as synonyms for "act" and "action," I use these terms only with reference to an interventionist model of God's relationship to the world, i.e., unilateral intervention.

[24]One of the most controversial issues in the conceptualization of the providence of God is the appropriate definition of omniscience. As early as 1935 H. H. Farmer expressed his rejection of the traditional understanding of predestination, omniscience, and foreknowledge, which claims that God knows everything from the beginning of creation to its end. See H. H. Farmer, *The World and God: A Study of Prayer, Providence and Miracle* (London: Nisbet & Co., 1935) 253, where he argues that such a view denies human freedom and divine sovereignty. It "depersonalizes man and his relation to his

The hidden work of God in the structures of nature and contingency

world in a way that no juggling with the concept of freedom can overcome," and it protects the sovereignty of God by giving God "nothing to be sovereign over." It attributes to God "an achieving purpose in regard to man, but in a way that gives that purpose nothing to achieve, and no 'man' in respect of whom to achieve it." Farmer concludes: "All that is left is the unspeakably sterile and depressing spectacle of omniscience playing an everlasting game of patience with itself, all possible combination of the cards being already known by heart" (253).

Paul Helm, *The Providence of God* (Downers Grove, IL: InterVarsity Press, 1994) espouses the view of providence generally and omniscience particularly that Farmer decries. Helm's "risk-free view" of the providence of God contains many questionable statements, especially with regard to evil and suffering (18, 204, 208, 211, 213-16), but he caricatures any alternative to his own perspective: "If we believe in a 'risk' view of providence, based upon an incompatibilist view of free will, or for some other reason, then *there will be many occurrences in our lives which are as surprising to God as they are to us*. In these circumstances, it will be impossible for us to see our lives as *a response to what God has ordained*, since on this view God has ordained only a portion of those events that befall us, that proportion which does not involve the free choices of human creatures, and which those free choices in no way effect" (215-16, italics added). The supposition of "many occurrences in our lives which are as surprising to God as they are to us" is as faulty as the impossibility "for us to see our lives as the response to what God has ordained." What happens to us does not surprise God, and we respond not so much to what God has ordained [predetermined?] but to God personally. Indeed, Helm argues from the no-risk view of providence "that Christians can be *confident* that everything that happens to them does so by the divine will," whereas the risk view of providence "would make for *chronic uncertainty*, in that the believers are never in a position to know by what agency what occurs in their lives has been produced, whether by the agency of God, or by some other agency . . ." (230, italics added). The charge is unreflective and without substance. We have the Biblical Story as well as the Story of Jesus as its hermeneutical key, and the Holy Spirit continues to provide the gift of discernment to the Christian commnuity and for the Christian pilgrim within it. Has Helm carefully read T. J. Gorringe, *God's Theatre: A Theology of Providence* (London: SCM Press, 1991) as he implies? (Helm, *The Providence of God*, 228, 241). Or do the two references to Gorringe's work, both quotations from Gustavo Gutiérrez, suggest otherwise? Like other comtemporary theologians, Gorringe recognizes the necessity for a redefinition of the "Knowledge, Power and Providence" of God (47-68).

For an earlier discussion among conservative evangelicals, see David Basinger and Randall Basinger, editors, *Predestination and Free Will: Four Views of Divine Sovereignty and Human Freedom* (Downers Grove, IL: InterVarsity Press, 1986) especially the essays: Bruce Reichenbach, "God Limits His Power," 99-124, with responses, 125-40; and Clark Pinnock, "God Limits His Knowledge," 141-62, with responses, 163-77.

of history includes divine judgment against human sin and demonic evil. In a pattern something like cause and effect, the judgment of God is immanent within historical progression, because the consequences of sin are built into perverse actions and attitudes, individual and corporate. Sooner or later the presumption of pride and prejudice as well as corrupt systems of monstrous evil falter under the judgment of God working in history, and they bring down retribution upon themselves. Oftentimes evil miscalculates its strength and overreaches itself, occasioning judgment. This immanental principle of divine judgment, of sowing and reaping, is the negative side of the rule of God in history. Beyond judgment God endeavors to coordinate the multifaceted movement of history in all its complexity and for all its participants toward whatever measure of fulfillment that exists on the horizon of creaturely possibility.

Yet the self-limitation of God also belongs to God's providential ruling, because God cannot integrate into a historical sequence what does not cohere with it, regardless of God's work of retroactive integration from the horizon of the future. Whether radical distortion through the collusion of sin, chaos, and Nothingness or the consequences of the immanental judgment of God in history, a specific course of events can be so negative and so destructive that the aggregation that occurs seems to be solely the unwanted given of fate that accumulates and extends from the past. Only when a specific and ongoing stretch of negative inevitability shifts contingently toward positive possibility, only when the surprisingly new transforms fate into destiny, only then is it possible to discern the providential guidance of God in the turn toward a constructive goal. Oftentimes, however, such a turn happens in the wake of great cost and loss, and providence appears too little and too late. The critical aspect of providence that addresses such historical developments is the governance of God, but the divine governing occurs in conjunction with preservation and concurrence. God's ruling and overruling in the guiding and governing of history happens in the temporality and contingency of God's action, reaction and interaction with the dynamic movement of the history of creation.

A Christian interpretation of the historic aspects of preservation, concurrence, and governance in God's providence requires the Christian theologian to concentrate on the action of God in Jesus Christ. Neither the story of Joseph (Genesis 37-50) nor the Book of Job discloses for us the definition of the providence of God in the midst of human joy and grievous suffering. Jesus of Nazareth is the paradigm of the provision of God for us in the multiple contexts of life in the world. The historic aspects of the providence of God are gathered decisively together in the rule of God, but the essential disclosure of the divine ruling has occurred in the enactment of the Kingdom of God in Jesus' mission and ministry as well as its culmination in his death and resurrection. The prolepsis of the Kingdom of God has already happened in human history in the life and destiny of the Nazarene. And through our participation in the story of Jesus we experience the providence of God available to us individually and corporately in the sacred journey of life.

Chapter One

Blessing—The Intention of Providence

THE WILDERNESS. A place of desolation. Deserted. Almost non-inhabitable. The Jordan River its marshy boundary. A place for the beginning of "good news"? Yet the movement had begun, the first prophet in Israel for generations: at least a would-be prophet with a sweet and sour diet of locusts and wild honey; an ascetic with the unkempt smell of mud and river; a bizarre coat of camel hair wired round his waist with a wide leather girdle. He had suddenly and unexpectedly appeared: Wind burned, sun dried, and weathered brown. Hair raggedly shorn, beard matted together. A fierce countenance with craggy, compelling features. Penetrating eyes narrowed with the far-sight of glaring sunlight. An unforgettable voice that split the sound of the air heavy with years of silence. A voice crying in the wilderness, John preached repentance: "Repent, for the Kingdom of [God] has come near." And more: "Prepare the way of the Lord, make his paths straight" (Matt 3:2-3b).

A *coming*, a Kingdom coming—that's what he prophesied. A *revolution*, a Messiah—that's what he promised. A *scandal*, an outrage, baptizing Jews—that's what he did. The initiation rite for Gentiles who converted to Judaism, John required of Jews. The Baptizer placed the children of Abraham on the same level as Gentiles, calling them to the washing of repentance for inclusion among the true people of God.

He preached to different groups the same message of repentance, of readiness, but with specific and distinct application (Luke 3:10-14):

To the multitudes:
"Whosoever has two coats must share with anyone who has none; and whoever has food, must do likewise."
To tax-collectors:
"Collect no more than the amount prescribed for you."

To soldiers:

"Do not extort money from anyone by threats or false accusation, and be satisfied with your wages."

The proclamation of John the Baptist signaled the beginning of a new age in Israel. Preaching at the Jordan River for the necessity of preparation for the coming day of the Lord, the Baptist aroused all kinds of excitement and expectation. He especially stirred hope for the coming of the Messiah and the fulfillment of dreams long overdue for the Kingdom of God. Jesus heard the call of the Baptizer, and he traveled from Galilee to Judea to be baptized by John. Among many others who had already responded to John's message, confessing their sins through baptism, Jesus submitted to John's baptism of repentance in their company. What does John's summons to baptismal repentance and Jesus' identification with baptismal responsibility say about the providence of God? In his baptism Jesus experienced the refreshing Presence of God anew in his life. The energizing Spirit of God enveloped Jesus and a Voice came from heaven: "You are my Son, the Beloved; with you I am well pleased" (Mark 1:11).

The purpose of this chapter is to explore the providence of God in Jesus' experience of baptism. Beyond the identification of the form of providence in this epochal moment in his life, the chapter concentrates on the identity of God and its implications for understanding God's relationship to the world, searching for a model of divine activity in the world that coheres with the Gospel narratives and contemporary Christian experience. A brief survey of the realities of evil and suffering in the Gospel traditions contrary to the providence of God poses problems that will occupy themes throughout this essay.

The Experience of Providence: *Blessing*

The characterization of Jesus' experience with God in his baptism comprises a singular moment with two simultaneous aspects: the experience of God's Presence as unconditional love and as absolute claim, that is, as gift and as demand.

Jesus' Abba Experience: Gift. On the one side, Jesus' consciousness of sonship presupposed an awareness of God as *Abba* Father—the gift of the invigorating Presence of God in terms of the love of mother and father for son and daughter. His *Abba* experience[1] is essential to the understanding of the providence of God in the life story of Jesus. In fact, the knowledge of God as the *Abba*-come-near is indispensable for Jesus' message of the dawning Kingdom of God.

Jesus' Vision of the Kingdom of God: Demand. On the other side, Jesus' vision of his messianic mission in behalf of the Kingdom of God constituted the fulfillment of the message of John the Baptist—the absolute demand of the inbreaking Kingdom of God. Jesus experienced the demand of the Kingdom as the summons to freedom, as fulfillment instead of obligation or duty.

What form of providence of God did Jesus experience in his baptism? Not the beginning point but a heightened awareness of himself as "the blessed child of God." *Blessing*: He received the gift of acceptance and affirmation, the promise of nurture and guidance. *Blessing*: He heard the summons to vocation and responsibility, the commissioning of work and ministry. Since the gift and the summons happened at his baptism within the community of John and his disciples, Jesus knew his own providential experience required participation in a graced community.

Receiving the blessing of God, Jesus modeled divine providence for every human being. All infants and toddlers, all youngsters, male and female, all maturing men and women, all those creased with age—God intends for everyone to hear the affirmation of blessing within an accepting and responsible community. God wants each and everyone to experience life as the good gift of love. We are God's sons and

---

[1]The phrase *"Abba* experience" is from Edward Schillebeeckx, *Jesus—An Experiment in Christology* (London: Collins, 1979) 256-71, 652-61. Schillebeeckx sums up his perspective: "[I]n Jesus' time what the *abba* signified for his son was authority and instruction: the father is the authority and the teacher. Being a son meant 'belonging to'; and one demonstrated this sonship by carrying out father's instructions. Thus the son receives everything from the father. . . . The son also receives from the father 'missions,' tasks that in the name of his father he has to make his own" (362-363). Yet Schillebeeckx emphasizes: "Jesus' familial expression for God, *Abba,* without any further qualifications suggestive of transcendence . . . quite certainly points to a religious experience of deep intimacy with God" unlike anyone else (263). Schillcbccckx does not explore the significance of Jesus' *Abba* name for God with reference to patriarchy.

daughters, and God nurtures a gifted response in us to life's opportunities. In this gifted identity as God's children, God purposes meaning and significance for individual fulfillment within community relationships. Every person should find life as a blessed child of God and know that he or she belongs to ever enlarging circles of brothers and sisters.

The twin poles of gift and demand characterize God's providential Presence of compassion in the world, but the structure of the polarity is significant. We experience God as sustaining Presence and as absolute demand. That is, we experience God's unqualified demand in the context of grace wherein the resources necessary to begin to fulfill that demand are already available. This is preeminently true in the life of Jesus. His *Abba* experience defined his vision of the Kingdom. So the *Abba* experience of unconditional love defines the Kingdom way of absolute demand: The ultimacy of the call of the way of God evokes the response of surrender to the persuasion of love. Thus the priority of the Presence of God as grace precedes the summons of God as command, an ontological priority rather than a temporal sequence. Whether recognized or not, the environment of grace undergirds the conviction of demand, because grace is the context in which demand occurs. So it is gift and demand, not demand and gift, always therefore with the priority of grace. Jesus experienced life as the blessed child of God, and God intends for every person to experience the grace and value of life with the deep sense of blessing within a community of graced people.

The Identity of God

John's proclamation in messianic expectation preceded the public ministry of Jesus, and John's ministry and message remain the presupposition for Jesus' proclamation and activity. The Gospel narratives locate Jesus' call at his baptism: The Spirit of God descended on him, which identified Jesus with the beginning of the messianic age. The heavens opened with the proclamation: "You are my Son, the Beloved." Beyond the echo of royal coronation from Psalm 2:7, the Gospel traditions add a significant word to the pronouncement: "the *Beloved*." The Old Testament knows that the only son is the beloved son, and Isaac is the classic example. Therefore, Jesus had a filial relationship to God similar to the relationship of Isaac with Abraham.

God, the *Abba* of Jesus

The union of Jesus with God wherein he heard himself addressed as "the beloved Son" presupposed his prior awareness of God as *Abba*. The characterization of God as *Abba* roots in the Nazarene's intimate relationship to God, a relationship essentially unprecedented in the history of Israel. Although some of Jesus' contemporaries occasionally addressed God as "*Abba*," Jesus customarily did so.[2] What proved unique to Jesus? He did not suddenly and singularly address God as *Abba* in first century Judaism. This word of address for God did not originate with him nor did it belong exclusively to him. Jesus did nonetheless uniquely use "*Abba*" as his normative characterization of God, something fundamentally new. Yet the issue involved much more than the naming of God *Abba* in prayer. Jesus had the unique mission of proclaiming the inbreaking Kingdom of God and granting eschatological salvation to those who accepted his message. The *Abba* experience points to the depth of Jesus' personal relationship to God throughout the entirety of his life, a relational intimacy that nurtured and sustained him in the fulfillment of his mission. So the *Abba* experience summarizes the uniqueness of Jesus' communion with God, an experience confirmed and heightened in his baptism that experientially anchored his proclamation of the Kingdom of God and its dawning in his ministry. Through his distinctive sense of the Presence of God and commissioning by God, Jesus was conscious of a difference in his relationship to God and that of all others. Accordingly, Jesus spoke of God as "my Father" and "your Father" but never as "our Father." The disciples spoke to God as "our Father," but they did so in community with Jesus and with the authorization of Jesus. The beginning of the Model Prayer in Matthew 6:9 with "Our Father" does not relativize Jesus' unique use of *Abba* to address God; on the contrary, the "Our Father" of the disciples' prayer presupposes the audacity of the customary invocation

---

[2]Wolfhart Pannenberg, *Systematic Theology*, 2 vols., trans. Geoffrey Bromiley (Grand Rapids MI: Eerdmans Publishing Co., 1991) 1:260. Since God is addressed as Father in Judaism at the time of Jesus, especially in Pharisaism, Pannenberg says: "The intimacy implied by invoking God as *Abba* typifies the relation of Jesus to God, but we should not set it in antithesis to the Pharisaic piety of the time" (260). He notes that *Abba* occasionally occurs in the Talmud with roots in the first century, which requires a revision of Jeremias' portrait of the uniqueness of Jesus' address to God as *Abba*.

of Jesus. The *Abba* experience of Jesus shaped his prayers, it stamped his message, and it founded his ministry: It is the source and secret of Jesus' life. Thus Jesus' *Abba* experience constitutes the key to his relationship to God, it denotes the uniqueness of his person, and it occasioned the radical breakthrough of the Kingdom of God that he embodied and proclaimed.

Where did the assurance of the salvation of God through the arriving of God's Kingdom originate? It was certainly not a given in Jesus' historical context nor anticipated specifically in Israel's messianic hope. Jesus lived in a history drenched with misery and suffering, a history that did not provide any grounds for his unqualified confidence in the salvation of God that distinguished his message and ministry. Rather, the hope of salvation signaled in Jesus' proclamation of the inbreaking Kingdom of God expressed his lifelong trust in his *Abba* God, the unfathomable and intimate sense of God that defined his life. The vision of the salvation of God that grasped Jesus with unprecedented boldness and stunning clarity rooted in his sense of the Presence of God in the midst of the tragic suffering of his people: On the one side, he encountered the incredible, immeasurable history of the suffering of humanity through illness and natural disaster, violence and injustice, military occupation and brutal subjugation, dehumanizing exploitation and excruciating oppression. On the other side, Jesus had from early on a unique relationship to God, the *Abba* God, *whose Presence he had lived and breathed all his life*, the Holy One of Israel who stands against and promises to overcome the murderous forces of evil.

Jesus' deep *Abba* experience nurtured his messianic response to this historic contradiction: He proclaimed the liberating rule of God to be present, already confronting and changing the suffering history of his people. Jesus knew God to be the compassionate *Abba* who vigorously offers hope for a new future to God's children. Such a promise in the provident activity of God could not be read off the pages of human history, but it required an awareness of God's deliverance in a past remembered and the hope of God's salvific action in a future now coming.

God—Person and Mystery

The fundamental presupposition of Jesus' experience with God concentrated in his baptism is the relational awareness of God as personal. The biblical traditions magnify God as personal: From the call of Abraham (Gen 12) through the unique experience of Moses (Exod 3-4) to the passionate proclamation of the prophets (e.g., Isaiah, Jeremiah, Hosea), the people of God encountered God in terms of personal relationship. Through divine initiative, God confronted the chosen people as eminently personal. Moreover, the experience of God in human life confirms this perspective. The mystery of personhood includes openness to an engaging encounter with another and the gift of friendship from the other. Through the dynamics of personal relationship one experiences the personhood of the other and the affirmation of one's own personal identity. To ignore another person denies the human dignity of the other, and to manipulate another person uses the other as an impersonal object. The presence of another person demands respect and resists manipulation, the claim in the personhood of another and the promise in relationship to the other.

If one knows the living God as personal, God must be apprehended in one and the same moment as unconditional love and absolute claim. The multifaceted structure of personal relationship stamps the Christian sense of the Presence of God, but it does not exhaust it. The radical otherness of God transcends the most intimate personal experience of God, a point all the more important because the emphasis on personhood accentuates God's availability to us in Christian life. God is immanent and transcendent, a transcendening immanence, an evasive and hidden Presence, a revealing that discloses a concealing. Therefore, the revelation of God in Jesus Christ does not eliminate but accentuates the incomprehensible depths of the mystery of God.

The British theologian H. H. Farmer speaks surprisingly and eloquently of the mystery of God that endures precisely in the experience of God as personal: "a vast penumbra of awareness of the infinite, mysterious, divine reality, from the depths of whose transcendent and *unimaginable being*[!] there comes forth this revealing resistancy and succoring promise, of personal purpose."[3] It is *God*, not another creature

---

[3]H. H. Farmer, *The World and God: A Study of Prayer, Providence, and Miracle in*

like ourselves, *Who* is apprehended as personal. God is personal, but God remains impenetrable and ineffable Mystery. Thus the encounter with God takes the form of the elusive Presence of Another who is always Thou.

The Significance of God's *Abba* Identity

What is the significance of Jesus' identification of God as *Abba* for a contemporary understanding of the providence of God? This question cannot be answered apart from an investigation of Jesus' use of *Abba* in the hierarchical and patriarchical context of his own time and place. Thus far I have not addressed the contemporary debate about the character-ization of God as Father in Christian tradition, but I have used the Aramaic address of *Abba* in an effort to be sensitive to the concerns of others and to anticipate my own proposal. Now some of the difficulties must at least be acknowledged, because the reservations and criticisms concerning the image of God as "Father" are significant and require a response. Furthermore, because the image of the Kingdom of God apparently authorizes a monarchical model of the providence of God, the significance of the name *Abba* for interpreting the Kingdom of God and the model of providence that it implies requires analysis and evaluation.

The Problem of Patriarchy

What is the theological status of the name of God as "Father"? Some contemporary theologians argue that Father is the proper name of God that inheres in the story of Jesus, the revelatory name of God that is theologically non-negotiable.[4] However, many feminist theologians have

---

Christian Experience (London: Nisbet & Co., Ltd., 1935) 26 (italics added).

[4]See Carl E. Braaten and Robert W. Jensen (ed.), *Christian Dogmatics* (Philadelphia: Fortress Press, 1984) 97, who argue that the Trinitarian formula of "Father, Son, and Holy Spirit" is God's proper name, the proper name for God in liturgy, devotion, and theology. The argument is that "Father" is preferred over "Mother" because "it is decisive for Israel's God that we are not of God's own substance, that God's role as our parent is not sexual, that God is not even metaphorically a fertility God." Why is "fathering" allowed? "The choice between 'Mother' and 'Father,' as terms of filial address to God, was and

argued that the characterization of God as Father is hopelessly patriarchal and intrinsically sexist,[5] a name which is not essential for the gospel of Jesus Christ.[6] Can the characterization of God as *Abba* transcend the hier-

---

Kimel, Jr., "The God Who Likes His Name," *Interpretation* 45 (1991): 117-32 and 147-58 respectively.

[5]The literature in feminist theology against the essential name of "Father" for God is voluminous. See Sallie McFague, *Models of God* (Philadelphia: Fortress Press, 1987) 203-207, footnotes for her chapter, "God as Mother"; also Johannes-Baptist Metz and Edward Schillebeeckx (ed.), *God as Father?*, "Concilium," 143 (New York: The Seabury Press, 1981); Anne Carr and Elizabeth Schüssler Fiorenza (ed.), *Motherhood: Experience, Institution, Theology*, "Concilium," 206 (Edinburgh: T. & T. Clark, 1989).

[6]Elizabeth A. Johnson, *She Who Is: The Mystery of God in Feminist Theological Discourse* (New York: Crossroad Publishing Company, 1992) 80-82, argues against the metaphor of *Abba* as Jesus' essential characterization of God. Word count reveals that God is called Father 4 times in Mark, 15 in Luke, 49 in Matthew, and 109 in John. To make her point, she quotes James Dunn who says it is difficult to dispute that here is "straightforward evidence of a burgeoning tradition, of a manner of speaking about Jesus and his relation with God that became very popular in the last decades of the first century" [James D. G. Dunn, *Christology in the Making* (Philadelphia: The Westminster Press, 1980) 30]. However, she fails to mention Dunn's dependency on Jeremias, who had already concluded that the Gospels reflect *"a growing tendency to introduce the title 'Father' for God into the sayings of Jesus"* [Joachim Jeremias, *The Prayers of Jesus*, "Studies in Biblical Theology," Second Series, 6 (London: SCM Press, 1967) 30]. Actually Dunn concludes: "*Abba* (Father) was a characteristic feature of Jesus' prayers" (26). Though Elizabeth Johnson uses Dunn's analysis to substantiate her point, he draws the opposite conclusion: It is extremely difficult to avoid the conclusion, Dunn says, "that *it was a characteristic of Jesus' approach to God in prayer that he addressed God as 'abba' and that the earliest Christians retained an awareness of this fact in their own use of 'abba' "* (26).

Indeed, Dunn considers Jeremias to have overstated Jesus' singular usage of *Abba* for God in Judaism, but he concludes: "In short, *the evidence points consistently and clearly to the conclusion that Jesus' regular use of 'abba' in addressing God distinguished Jesus in a significant way from his contemporaries"* (27). The claim for the distinctiveness of Jesus' *Abba*-prayer has deep roots in contemporary documentation more than any alternative view (27-28). Johnson will only say: "While it is historically most probable that Jesus sometimes addressed God with the Aramaic *abba*, the paternal metaphor is not necessarily as frequent or as central as a literal reading of the text might suggest" (80). Conversely, Dunn recognizes the increase of the word count of "Father" in the Gospels, but he still considers *Abba* the distinctive characteristic of Jesus' address to God.

The jump in word count from Mark to Luke and Matthew does not surprise me, because Mark contains very little of the teaching of Jesus, most significantly the absence

archy of patriarchy and the subordination of women to men?[7] Does the
Abba-come-near in the proclamation of Jesus critique and relativize the
patriarchical structures of social and family life? Patriarchical structures
elevated the father in the family to ultimate control and intrinsically
subjugated the wife, children, and others in the household to the man of
the house. What did Jesus do? He called for a reconstruction of family on
the basis of the summons of the *Abba* God, a call that takes precedence
over the authority of any earthly father and actually justifies the rejection
of natural family ties. When the family of Jesus came to the house where
he was teaching in order to take him home, did they do so because they
thought him insane or because of his patriarchical responsibility as the
eldest son to care for his mother and younger siblings? Jesus responded
to their inquiry:

---

of the Model Prayer that occurs in Luke and Matthew (but not in John). If *the parables*
were to stand or fall as the distinctive and unique mode of Jesus' teaching on the basis
of the difference in the number of parables in Mark over against the number in Luke and
Matthew, we would have to conclude that the increase in the number of parables indicates
a contagious use of "parables" from Jesus to his disciples in the "burgeoning" oral
tradition of the first century. *Therefore, while Jesus most probably used parables
occasionally as a teaching method, the use and number of parables in Matthew and Luke
does not necessarily mean that 'parable' was as frequent or as characteristic a teaching
devise of Jesus as a literal reading of the text might suggest.* Of course, such a conclusion
would be erroneous. If Mark is to play a significant role in clarifying the way Jesus
addressed God, only Mark among the Gospels reports Jesus' Gethsemane prayer, "*Abba,
Father.*"

Johnson does acknowledge that whenever Jesus used *Abba* in speaking of God, such
usage "connotes an intimacy of relation between Jesus and God, along with a sense of
God's compassion over suffering, willing good in the midst of evil" (81).

Jesus' *Abba* is not a patriarchal figure who dominates but a subversive metaphor of
any form of domination in favor of mutuality and equality. To me, the *Abba* of Jesus is
always working to create a community of mutuality in opposition to the structures of
patriarchy. Johnson's concern that the Father symbol in Christianity "grew hardened and
fixed in alliance with patriarchal rule, thus imprisoning rather than releasing the good
news it was originally intended to convey" (82), is regrettably true. But the re-
patriarchicalization of the church through the use of the metaphor "Father" does not
justify the rejection of the importance of Jesus' *Abba* symbol for God.

[7]See Sharyn Dowd, "Reflections on the Inclusive Language Debate," *Lexington
Theological Quarterly* 27 (1992): 16-25, for a clear delineation of options among feminist
theologians and her own surprising conclusion.

"Who are my mother and my brothers?" And looking at those who sat around him, he said, "Here are my mother and my brothers. Whoever does the will of God is my brother and sister and mother!" (Mark 3:31–35)

Jesus understood the call of the *Abba* God to have priority over all family obligations and patriarchical responsibilities, which required the restructuring of the family in the light of the identity of God. Indeed, Jesus gave God the *normative* name of *Abba*, an intimate address of affection and respect, a revisioning of the reality of God. Beyond Jewish familial usage, only the activity and teaching of Jesus defined the meaning and significance of his name for God. Jesus taught in word and deed that YHWH, the covenant God of Israel, had come so remarkably near that YHWH had taken the name of *Abba*. If the activity of Jesus interpreted the meaning of *Abba* to his followers, however, one of the initial acts of Jesus poses a formidable problem: the calling of the Twelve, all circumcised Jewish males like Jesus himself. The constitution of Israel into twelve tribes through the twelve sons of Jacob con-textualized the action of Jesus in his selection of the Twelve, because he reconstituted thereby the new Israel of God, indeed, a new family of God. The problem of patriarchy was certainly not eliminated through the position of the Twelve but apparently reinforced. Yet the issue is not so one-sided as it seems.

If the Gospel portraits of Jesus' relationship to women are valid, if Jesus was as intentional in his relationship to women as the Gospels portray, he adopted a revolutionary posture against the structures of patri-archy in favor of the equal blessing and full humanity of women alongside men. In fact, an intriguing question emerges: *Did Jesus know that patriarchy could be dismantled only from the inside?* As a rabbi with his disciples, all Jewish and all male, Jesus had access to places of privilege and power that would otherwise be denied him but from within which he could voice the judgment and purpose of God. As a man with other men Jesus exposed the oppressive structures of a male-dominated and father-regimented hierarchical society. Yet Jesus' rejection of patri-archy was all the more difficult, because these hierarchical forms rooted in and had the authorization of the sacred traditions of his people. For the sake of clarity, I must anticipate the conclusion of my argument: The Jewishness of Jesus and the Twelve did not mean the priority of Jews over Gentiles, despite the ministry of Jesus almost exclusively to his own people. Likewise, the gender of Jesus and the Twelve did not justify the authority of the male over the female, the subordination of women to men, despite the absence of women from the circle of the Twelve but present nonetheless among his most faithful disciples.

The dissent from patriarchy and the affirmation of the equal humanity of women with men runs through the *whole story of Jesus*. Unlike the Twelve who thought mothers and children an intrusion, a patriarchical posture, Jesus welcomed these women and their children with warmth and blessing, sharply criticizing his disciples (Mark 10:13-16; Luke 18:15-16). He rejected divorce on the basis of the covenant of marriage in "one flesh," marital oneness that meant the repudiation of the treatment of women under men's property rights (Mark 10:2-6). As a dinner guest at the house of Simon the Pharisee, Jesus allowed a prostitute to wash his feet, affirming her bold extravagence while criticizing Simon's inaction and attitude (Luke 7:36-50).[8] A diverse group of women whom Jesus had healed followed him alongside the Twelve during his Galilean ministry, regularly caring for Jesus and the Twelve out of their own resources (Luke 8:1-3). Against the complaint of Martha, he affirmed the place of Mary with the Twelve, teaching them together: He believed women could be taught the Torah as well as men (Luke 10:38-42). Jesus engaged a scandalous Samaritan woman in public conversation, shocking his disciples (John 4:7-30). In the Temple overlooking the treasury he called the disciples to him and singled out a poor widow who gave two copper coins as the model of devotion in giving (Mark 12:41-44).

Jesus had women among his disciples in Galilee, and they accompanied him to Jerusalem (Mark 15:40-41). Only these women among the disciples followed Jesus all the way to his cross and saw his burial in a borrowed tomb (Mark 15:47). With the confident affirmation of women equal with men, Jesus commissioned these women as the first witnesses

---

[8]See Robert Hammerton-Kelly, *God the Father: Theology and Patriarchy in the Teaching of Jesus* (Philadelphia: Fortress Press, 1979). Hammerton-Kelly is graphic: "And in a breathtaking scene, whose full significance has yet to be understood, he let a whore wash his feet, let her perform a service for him that was the characteristic sign of a wife's duty to her husband" (Luke 7:36-38). Who is the more scandalous of the two—the woman in her daring assertiveness or Jesus in his affirming acceptance?

of his resurrection (Mark 16:1-8), despite their subsequent lack of credibility with the apostles (Luke 24:1-11).

The significance of the normative address of God as *Abba* is pivotal for understanding the attitude of Jesus toward the marginalized generally and women particularly. Jesus reconstituted the people of God in calling the Twelve, but he demonstrated a stunning openness and respect for women alongside them, because women no less than men are created in the image of God (Gen 1:27), recipients of the same blessing and summons of new creation in the Kingdom of God. From the acceptance of the prostitute who washed his feet to the call of women who declared his resurrection, Jesus dramatically undermined the societal structures that subordinated women to men and affirmed the equality, the solidarity, of women with men in the new family of God. In the context of patriarchy Jesus' use of the *Abba* image functioned subversively, and Jesus' lifelong *Abba* experience nurtured his radical insight and his scandalous action. The experience of God as *Abba* revealed the heart of Jesus' relationship to God and the key to his proclamation of the grace of God for the blessing of all his disciples—women and men, the broken-down and the upright, insiders and outsiders alike.

Questions surface immediately. Just how unique was Jesus' invocation of *Abba* to God in the social and religious context of his life and ministry? Can the *Abba* image sustain the weight and significance attributed to it? What does the *Abba* image mean in the life of the church today? Although the contemporaries of Jesus used *Abba* occasionally to address God, they would not make it normative for their relationship to God in prayer, because it would have been too familiar and therefore quite inappropriate. Conversely, when he prayed, Jesus characteristically addressed God as *Abba*.

The word *"Abba"* probably originated as a babble word of small children, but it should not be construed to mean something like "Daddy,"[9] an unfortunate mistake occasionally encountered.[10] Rather, adult children

---

[9]So James Barr, " 'Abba, Father' and the Familiarity of Jesus' Speech," *Theology* 91 (1988): 173-79.

[10]See Joachim Jeremias, *The Central Message of the New Testament* (New York: Charles Scribner's Sons, 1965) 72: "It was something new, something unique and unheard of, that Jesus dared to take this step and to speak with God as a child speaks with his father, simply, intimately, securely." Jeremias clearly overstates the case. The uniqueness

used it in addressing their fathers and as a courtesy in speaking to older men. Yet *Abba* belonged primarily in the everyday conversation of the family, a word of affection and respect for the father in the home. Unlike patriarchical language of authority and control, *Abba* resonates with the warmth and freedom of family togetherness.

The breakthrough in the familial characterization of God as *Abba* clarifies Jesus' little noticed prohibition against calling anyone on earth *Abba*, "for you have one Father (*ho patēr* [*Abba*])—the one in heaven" (Matt 23:9). With this mandate did Jesus shift the regimentation of patriarchy from human social structures to the disciples' relationship to God? On the contrary, the normative characterization of God as *Abba* and the exclusive utilization of *Abba* for God would establish a familial vision of God whose attitude and posture toward us is lovingly parental —the intimacy and joy of the best in familial relationships. The address of *Abba* to God articulates the parental character of God's relationship to all the Nazarene's disciples. Jesus did not abolish patriarchy in the name of his *Abba* God on earth in order to establish the patriarchal rule of God over men and women alike from heaven! Rather, Jesus rejected the hierarchy of patriarchy in favor of the parental God of love, a familial God who mothers and fathers all of God's children. Jesus revised language for God through the familiar *Abba* to address God, and he modeled a messianic servant rather than a Messiah King that corresponded to his revisioning of God in relationship to humanity. This radical transformation in Jesus' vision of God was not an isolated revelatory moment without continuity with the past, because the heritage of Jesus included not only the use of paternal images but also various maternal images for God.[11] Thus the numerous maternal images for God in the Old Testament, e.g., Hosea 11:1-4, provided a context not only for a nonpatriarchical vision of God but also for a maternal/paternal experience of God for Jesus. Contrary to the structures of patriarchy, Jesus realized that his *Abba* experience subverted all authoritarian forms of domination and control in favor of mutuality and equality. Through the invocation of

---

of Jesus lay in his normative address to God as *Abba*, not in his original and exclusive use of it. Cf. Schillebeeckx, *Jesus*, 259-61.

[11]See Jeremias, *The Prayers of Jesus*, 11: In Oriental antiquity, long before Moses and the prophets, ". . . the word 'Father,' as applied to God, thus encompasses, from earliest times, something of what the word 'Mother' signifies for us."

Abba to God, therefore, Jesus abrogated all hierarchical structures for the sake of egalitarian family relationships of brothers and sisters with one another.[12]

Other layers of New Testament tradition contain some affirmations of patriarchical power, but countervailing passages in the Gospels continue to accentuate the protest of Jesus against patriarchy on the basis of his characterization of God as *Abba*. Luke 9:59-62 is of special importance, because Jesus rejected inviolate family ties in favor of the Kingdom of God. Jesus said to one man, "Follow me." He responded, "Lord, first let me go and bury my father," the final duty of a son for his father; but Jesus charged: "Let the dead bury their own dead." Another said, "I will follow you, Lord; but let me first say farewell to those at my home." Jesus told him not to look back to his family but forward to the Kingdom of God. The call of God, the *Abba* come near, relativized all the established obligations and sacred responsibilities of patriarchy that surfaced in other New Testament traditions. The reassertion of patriarchical authority occasioned the entrenchment of patriarchical and hierarchical structures in the history of the church, which has endured until now. The re-patriarchicalization of the church on the basis of an authoritarian and oppressive use of the image "Father" does not warrant the rejection of the centrality of the *Abba* image for Jesus himself. Rather, the *Abba* God of Jesus summons us to the de-patriarchicalization of the Christian community in the name of and in faithfulness to Jesus Christ.

The significance of Jesus' *Abba* image of God can be summarized as follows: (1) Although he did not invent the *Abba* name for God, Jesus'

---

[12]Rosemary Radford Ruether, *Sexism and God-Talk: Toward a Feminist Theology* (Boston: Beacon Press, 1983) 136, says: "Relation to God no longer becomes a model for dominant-subordinate relations between social groups, leaders, and the led. Rather, relation to God means we are to call no man Father, Teacher or Master (Matt 23:1-12). Relation to God liberates us from hierarchical relations and makes us all brothers-sisters of each other." Elsewhere she writes: "When discussing fuller divinity to which this theology points, I use the term God/ess, a *written* symbol intended to combine both the masculine and feminine forms of the word for the divine. . . . This term is *unpronounceable* and inadequate." She does not intend to use this language in worship, where terms such as "Holy One" or "Holy Wisdom" may be preferable" (46, italics added). However, neither "Holy One" nor "Holy Wisdom" contains the warmth and intimacy of the *Abba* of Jesus, a flaw in her transition from theological reflection to the worshipping life of the church.

customary use of the *Abba* address made it normative and therefore unique; moreover, it conveyed a vision of God whose relationship to humanity is not patriarchical but lovingly familial. This normative status of the name *Abba* lies behind the use of "Father" (*ho patēr*) in the Model Prayer of Matthew 6:9 and Luke 11:2. (2) While the address *Abba* retained elements of the spontaneity and intimacy of children, adults used *Abba* as an expression of their affection and respect for the father in the home—not exclusively but primarily a word of familial address. This parental posture of God toward Jesus' disciples is fundamental to the New Testament traditions and accounts at least partly for the increasing use of the image Father in the Gospel narratives. (3) The elements of warmth and gratitude in the translation from Jesus' Aramaic to the Gospel's Greek is not lost with *ho patēr*, but a shift does occur. The move away from variations of *Abba* to *ho patēr* is less intimate and more reverential but still familial. The shift is especially clear in Matthew with the invocation of the Model Prayer, "Our Father *in heaven*" (6:9). (4) Beyond all specific instances of the use of *Abba*, the image itself functioned subversively in the teaching of Jesus, undermining the authoritarian structures of patriarchy and nurturing egalitarian relationships in the Kingdom's gathering of the family of God. (5) The Aramaic *Abba* on the lips of Jesus in Mark's memory of his agony in Gethsemane is surprising and extraordinary, but the measure of his intimacy in prayer corresponds to the level of intensity in his petition as he faced the cross. (6) Paul used the Aramaic *Abba* in Romans 8:15 and Galatians 4:6, a word otherwise unintelligible to his Gentile audience, because he knew it to be Jesus' normative address to God and important for the relational life of the worshiping church as Jews and Gentiles, brothers and sisters together.

Is the address *Abba* essentially sexist and hopelessly patriarchical? On the contrary, in the name of God as *Abba* Jesus affirmed the equality of women with men and decisively breached the wall between men and women that founded patriarchical rule. The divisive wall did not fall apart immediately, but the rift in its center fissured in every direction, from top to bottom and inside out. Permanently and irreparably fractured, the wall has slowly but surely crumbled. The characterization of God as *Abba* has broken down the hierarchical wall of patriarchy from the inside, because, Jesus said, God is not the patriarchical lord of the house but the gracious *Abba* who fathers and mothers the entire family.

The familial name of God as *Abba* is of immeasurable significance for understanding God's relationship to humanity—male and female, Jew and Gentile, [slave and free]. Through the story of Jesus we know ourselves to be the children of God, a dramatic new moment in the disclosure of God's providential care for all of us. God intends for every human being to experience life as "the blessed child of God." The parental naming of God as *Abba*, therefore, means the individuated naming of each one of us as the special concern of God—children known, children loved, and children blessed.

If a great variety of New Testament scholars and systematic theologians are correct, that the *Abba* of Jesus is "a wholly nonpatriarchal Father," the translation of *Abba* with "Father" is overburdened with misunderstanding that requires more than an accurate translation. *Abba* is a metaphor that requires conceptual transposition, the metaphor of "a Motherly Father" or "a Fatherly Mother."[13] Is this conceptual transposition viable? On the one side, the biblical traditions use maternal imagery to characterize God, all the more noteworthy and significant because it occurs in essentially patriarchical traditions. On the other side, the form of contemporary family life includes not only the pattern of the nuclear family but also the two-career marriage with children, the blended family, and the single-parent family. These diverse expressions of family life require a style of parenting that negotiates and integrates traditional male and female roles, so that mothers do fathering and mothering and fathers do mothering and fathering. Therefore, when I employ the *Abba* image, I intend an *Imma-Abba* metaphor, that is, "a Motherly Father" characterization of God. *Abba* means to speak, think, and feel God as nonpatriarchical, the maternal/paternal *Abba*.

Some theologians argue for the exclusiveness of the Father image and reject the metaphor of a Motherly Father as a wrong-headed accom-

---

[13]To get beyond patriarchal structures I began to use two images in the mid-to-late 1970s: "God fathers and mothers. . . ." "God is 'the Motherly Father.' " Women in my theology classes heightened my sensitivity to the issue. Cf. Jürgen Moltmann, *The Trinity and the Kingdom: The Doctrine of God* (San Francisco: Harper and Row Publishers, 1981) 164. Moltmann writes: "[A] father who both begets and bears a son is not merely a father in the male sense. He is a motherly Father too. . . . He has to be understood as the motherly Father of the only Son he has brought forth, and at the same time as the fatherly Mother of his only begotten Son."

modation to modern secularism, here, feminism. The argument is: The term "Father" is more separable than "Mother" from the sexual role in reproduction; therefore, it preserves quite explicitly the transcendence of God overagainst all creaturely existence. The argument is misplaced. The issue is not the role of male versus female in the process of birthing nor the preservation of transcendence from collapse into immanence. The issue is the quality and character of the relationship of God to us disclosed through the self-revelation of God in the story of Jesus. This relationship is not masculine in contrast to feminine but comprehensively parental. The gracious mercy and love of God has come to us through the gift of Jesus the Christ, enabling us to become who we are intended to be, "the blessed children of God." Through Jesus we experience God as *Abba*, the Motherly Father, the God of an ever transcending immanence. This blessing is the gracious gift of God who mothers and fathers everyone in the circle of the family of God and who affirms each of us as children, as brothers and sisters with one another. So the usage of biblical language and corresponding personal pronouns is always qualified, because God is never simply a non-maternal Father but always "the Motherly Father," "the Fatherly Mother."

Lest the point be missed, Jesus was rejected and crucified because he relativized the Law in the name of God who gave the Law. In the name of his merciful *Abba* Jesus stood with those whom the Law excluded: the prostitutes and tax collectors, collaborators with the Roman occupying powers for money; women and children, significantly less than and subject to the disposal of men; the lepers and the demon-possessed, untouchables, disfigured outside and within; the people of the land, ordinary people rendered ritually unclean through their everyday work; unconverted Gentiles, Roman soldiers who trusted the word of grace and healing. Jesus taught that the God of love liberates from oppressive and depressive societal structures through the creation of a new family that offers a place of love and equality for each family member. Jesus envisioned a family of God constituted through the *Abba* experience of all family members— without hierarchy or patriarchy, chauvinism or sexism, racism or class. In the name of God, the God whom he named *Abba*, Jesus rejected the walls of privilege that divided the children of the God from one another. The blessing of God embraces all of those who belong to the new family of the God through the midwifery of Brother Jesus.

The Problem of Monarchy

Since the word "kingdom" inevitably connotes "monarchy," does the image of the Kingdom of God within the discussion of providence require "a monarchical model" to conceptualize God's relationship to the world? Monarchy was the normative pattern of social and political life in the ancient world, wherein the king ruled through unilateral power to dominate those under his control, whether through benevolence or tyranny. Monarchy meant the sovereign rule of the king through royal decree: The choice to act or not to act in order to enforce his will in any situation, the option to use all power at his discretion without the necessity of explanation, the right to hold the life of each of his subjects in his hand to do whatever he might command—all these privileges belonged within the king's sovereign right. Thus the king could rule arbitrarily without concern for consistency in the treatment of his subjects.

The monarchical model of God's relationship to the world accentuates this pattern of sovereignty generally and providence specifically.[14] That God rules and overrules through the unilateral exercise of supernatural power is the essence of the monarchical model of God's providential action in the world. God preserves the givens of natural causation and historical contingency as long as these serve God's purpose. From time to time, however, God radically alters natural causation to change fundamentally or eliminate completely what would otherwise occur in the arena of creation; correspondingly, God overrules the contingent configuration of historical events shaped by human activity, a divine overruling that directly changes the progression of events contrary to what would otherwise occur. Plainly said: God controls nature and history for God's purposes, ruling and overruling the regularities of natural causation or the decisions of human agents that would distort or frustrate the specific purpose of God. Although the cooperation of persons in a particular

---

[14]See Julian N. Hart, "Creation and Providence," *Christian Theology: An Introduction to Its Traditions and Tasks*, Rev. Ed., ed. Peter C. Hodgson and Robert King (Philadelphia: Fortress Press, 1985; 1982) 141-66, for a history of the monarchical model and the continuing challenges to it. For a description and critique of the traditional monarchical model in Augustine and Calvin, see Langdon Gilkey, *Reaping the Whirlwind: A Christian Interpretation of History* (New York: Seabury Press, 1976) 159-87. Cf. McFague, *Models of God*, 63-69.

historical situation may be the means whereby God chooses to accomplish a certain goal, such bilateral concurrence is not a condition for the achievement of God's purpose. Rather, the sovereign God always has the power to intervene directly and unilaterally in the actualization of a specific goal, whether large or small.

The monarchical model of God's supernatural contravention in the processes of nature and the dynamics of history excludes the concept of the self-limitation of God, for it is a conceptual and linguistic contradiction that denies the sovereignty of God. Such a self-limitation would subject the Creator to the rule of natural law and reduce God's prerogatives to the concurrence of sinful human agents. Rather, God rules the whole of creation for divine ends, which includes the preservation of regularity *or* its contravention, and God determines the specific direction of historical passage, which sustains, qualifies, *or* negates human decisions moving history forward. That God acts sometimes in one way and at other times in another lies in the wisdom and purpose of God that is beyond human understanding. Nothing is impossible for God, and everything in nature and history is under God's immediate control.

Since the story of Jesus authorizes or confirms the mode of God's power in the world, a critique of the monarchial model of God's relationship to the world begins with the activity and proclamation of the Nazarene. What does Jesus' *Abba* experience mean in relationship to his message of the Kingdom of God and its implications for the providence of God? The traditional interpretation has been: "Only where God rules as Lord is God the Father." This explanation, however, construes the relationship backwards. Rather, "Only where God is Father does God reign." Jesus did not proclaim the Kingdom of the Lord God but the rule of the gracious and forgiving *Abba*, the reign of fatherly and motherly love, not lordly rule. So Jürgen Moltmann concludes: "In this kingdom there are no servants; there are only God's free children. In this kingdom what is required is not obedience and submission; it is love and participation."[15] The monarchical model of providence with its emphasis on lordship and sovereignty does not exhibit the familial qualities of God nurturing love and participation, freedom and responsibility. Rather, the interpretation of the rule of God in terms of the power to control is a

[15]Moltmann, *The Trinity*, 70.

fundamental distortion of the teaching and activity of Jesus. The endeavor to control through contravening force is visibly contrary to the authentic cry for human freedom, and the arbitrary use of force to establish and maintain control contradicts the essence of genuine human community. Yet authentic human freedom and genuine human community are essential to the vision of the Kingdom of God. Against the ancient rule of monarchy through dominating power and hierarchical control, therefore, Jesus' vision of God as *Abba* served to preserve both the distinctive sovereignty of God and the reality of human freedom within the New Testament hope for the Kingdom of God, and Jesus embodied the Kingdom that he proclaimed as a liberating experience with God that nurtures an accepting community of brothers and sisters together.

Precisely here a deeper and more fundamental problem lies embedded within the monarchical model of the providence of God. This model conceives of God preeminently as the Lord God, and the lordship of God occurs through the exercise of omnipotent power.[16] God is the Lord God almighty who must have all power and who may then be merciful, but then again, may not. The mercy and love of God are subordinated to God's power and lordship. The Lord God says, "I will be gracious to whom I will be gracious, and will show mercy on whom I will show mercy" (Exod 33:19), one proof-text to be isolated and cited among other proof-texts. The monarchical vision of God differentiates the lordship of God from the love of God, giving priority to a worldly conception of sovereignty as the power to control rather than to Jesus' vision of God's rule as the liberating reign of love. The *Abba* God of Jesus is the God who is love. Thus the affirmation, "God is the Lord," must be in agreement with the disclosure, "God is love." Only the love of God is almighty. The lordship of God must be accomplished through the love of God, because the love of God cannot be differentiated from or subordinated to the power of God. Thus the power of God-ruling is one and the same as the rule of God-loving. Since the hierarchical conception of power as the power to control is central to the monarchical model of God's providence, it inevitably distorts Jesus' proclamation of the King-

---

[16]See Eberhard Jüngel, *God as the Mystery of the World*, trans. Darrell Guder (Grand Rapids MI: Eerdmans Publishing Company, 1983) 21-22. Although Jüngel's critique focuses on the worldly necessity of God, it applies equally to the monarchical model of the providence of God.

dom of God as the rule of *Abba*-love blessing all participants as beloved children.

Finally, the monarchial model of God's relationship to the world intensifies the problem of human suffering rather than relieves it. The insurmountable problem consists of the innumerable circumstances wherein vast segments of humanity are left in the lurch, suffering and dying unattended: God neither delivers them from their plight nor provides for them in their need. When a great tragedy occurs, whether to a region in the clutch of a natural disaster or a community wracked with the explosion of violence or a family with a youngster terminally ill, the monarchical model of God who rules and overrules with the power of a king offers little solace and comfort. If God really has the power to intervene in nature and history whenever, wherever and however God chooses, why does God not do so? The monarchial model of a do Anything, Anytime, Anywhere kind of God cannot account for the failure of God to act to prevent a colossal catastrophe or to deliver a segment of vulnerable humanity from some monstrous evil. The alternative explanations for the absence of the provision of providence would include the judgment of God against human sin, the purpose of God in shaping human character, or the inscrutability of the will of God beyond human understanding. Yet none of these alternatives is self-evident, and the dramatic measure of human suffering qualifies them all. The inaction of God in situations of critical human need raises the questions of the love of God, of the identity of God who is love, most poignantly. "Nothing is impossible for God" before a crisis, during a crisis, or after a crisis proves to be the affirmation of a promise gone unfulfilled or an abstraction unrelated to the concrete circumstances of a crisis becomes a calamity.

The *Abba* God of Jesus, however, responds to the multiple crises of human existence with some measure of mercy and grace. God has established the processes of creation and preserves the contingency of human history, and God works with the flexibility in natural causation and the variables of historical contingency to accomplish providential goals. Yet God does not negate natural and historical causation for the benefit of persons in especially painful straits. Rather, God works with the possibilities and limitation that faithfulness to creaturely existence in the dynamics of creation entails. Through the decision to work in conjunction with environmental givens, temporal development, and human agency, God acts with the creativity and restraints of love to anticipate and respond to humanity's need with provision and care. Ultimately the problems in the monarchial model of God's relationship to the world require another model of providence that affirms the self-expenditure and the self-limitation of God in the Jesus story of the compassion of God.[17]

[17]Karl Barth, *CD*, III/3, has proposed a monarchical model of God's relationship to the world that he thinks will transcend the problems evident in previous formulations of this model. Two problems undermine his proposal. First, Barth elaborates his understanding of providence under the rubric of "God the Father as Lord of His Creature" (58). That is, God rules all creaturely occurrence as Father and King. Barth develops his perspective under four headings: "The Divine Preserving" (58-90), "The Divine Accompanying" (90-154), "the Divine Ruling" (154-238), and "The Christian under the Universal Lordship of God the Father" (239-88). Barth intends to integrate the identity of God as the Father of Jesus Christ with the historic identity of God as the King of Israel. As Barth expounds the lordship of God in preserving, accompanying, and ruling, however, he accentuates the rule of God in such a vigorous monarchical fashion that the familial characterization of God in the story of Jesus does not substantially inform or shape his exposition. The subsection on "The Christian under the Lordship of God the Father" becomes supplementary, because the historic themes of preserving, accompanying, and ruling have already been defined with minimal reference to Jesus' vision of God. The conceptualization and elaboration of Barth's proposal does not rely enough on the New Testament traditions generally and the Gospel traditions particularly. The integration of the identity of God as the Father of Jesus Christ with the identity of God as the King of Israel occurs through the inappropriate subordination of God's *Abba*-ruling to God's monarchical control.

Second, Barth separates his exposition of divine providence in Paragraph 49, "God the Father as Lord of His Creatures" (58-288), from his discussion of the problem of evil in Paragraph 50, "God and Nothingness" (289-68). God denies the benefit of the divine preservation, concurrence, and rule, of God's fatherly lordship, to Nothingness. Yet providence still comprehends Nothingness. Indeed, it requires the rethinking of providence. The new investigation, however, does not relate the problem and reality of Nothingness to the fundamental aspects of providence explored in Paragraph 49, that is, preserving, accompanying, ruling, and fatherly lordship. Theological and conceptual disclaimers notwithstanding, the narration of the Biblical Story and the experience of the church in history invalidate Barth's exposition of the doctrine of providence apart from the historic threat and power of Nothingness. These two methodological moves appear to strengthen Barth's presentation, a monarchical model of God's relationship to the world that claims to be distinctively Christian, but Barth's doctrine of providence proves fatally flawed. The monarchical model, when only qualified, cannot comprehend the centrality of Jesus' vision of the *Abba* God or address effectively the human experience of evil and suffering.

The providence of God in the numerous stories of Jesus affirm the provision of God in the face of the ordinary and extraordinary human need. The God of love improvises with a surprising activity that encompasses the resources in nature and the concurrence of human agents. The strategy of love in the activity of providence reflects flexibility and adaptability, a weaving of purpose in and through the contingency of history. So God rules and overrules in the accomplishment of providential purpose with a creativity that does not coerce or overwhelm but nurtures and guides. Obstacles are met not only with deliberation and strength but also with sensitivity and persuasion. Neither the investment of time nor the maintenance of processes run counter to providence, because patience and faithfulness characterize the activity of God. Within the difficulties of providential action, God demonstrates a love that sustains the good and confronts the evil, a confrontation through a transforming Presence that turns evil insofar as possible toward the good. When the tragic consequences that inhere in evil become effective and therefore destructive, God labors to limit unnecessary and innocent suffering with an ever present consolation. Yet the providence of God through the power of love displays a level of weakness that chaos and Nothingness threaten to overwhelm and perhaps absolutely destroy. Although God does not cease to act for the benefit of all creatures in the entirety of creation generally and for human persons created in the image of God particularly, the activity of the God of love in the complexity of history is not simple or self-evident. Rather, the discernment of providence at work in the world presupposes an ongoing trust in the transforming Presence of God in the life of the Christian. Does trust in the providential activity of the God of love prove to be consistent with the Christian's actual experience of life?

The worshiping church recites the Apostles' Creed: "I believe in God the Father Almighty, Maker of heaven and earth. . . ." How do persons within a Christian community translate their confession of faith into meaningful but realistic existence? God loves us like a Father, the church assures us. Then thirteen-year-old Janet is diagnosed with leukemia. Her father, a respected attorney in the community and active in the church, secures the best specialists to be found anywhere. They draft a profile of Janet's illness and match it with the most effective treatment available. The parents pray for Janet, their only child. The church prays, which includes the prayers of adults and youth alike. As treatment begins, Janet's life is regulated with a medical program designed to save her life.

Janet's mother devotes her time almost exclusively to her daughter. Treatment continues, but the condition of the young teenager deteriorates. In less than three months she hovers near death. Medication to relieve her pain leaves her feeling drugged, so she refuses anymore than enough to make it bearable. Late one evening, unaware of her father and mother beside her, Janet dies.

Some of the faithful say, "Yes, God loves us like a Father, but. . . ." God's love is "a different kind of love," or it is "an inscrutable love." Others ask, "What is the purpose of Janet's death? God always has a purpose for what God does or does not do. God is God! God is in control. Perhaps we simply cannot understand. . . ."

The physician who led the team of specialists and therapists works under the weight of fatigue. He has watched too many children die, now one of his daughter's closest friends, her father one of his friends. He knows the senselessness of it all. "My God," he says alone, "if we suffer, how much more must God suffer." This Christian physician has revised the traditional vision of God as an all-powerful monarch who rules the world unilaterally like a king, but who somehow remains "the Father Almighty, Maker of heaven and earth." He has intuitively connected "all-powerful" with God's work of "creation," and the context of creation wherein God works with parental compassion implies an inevitable self-limitation. He believes the God of limitless love has worked alongside and with them all in the effort to save Janet's life. Why does the church not say so?

The physician's plight is the theologian's task. The ever recurring problem of the death of children with the best of medical care and spiritual nurture dethrones the traditional understanding of God as a heavenly monarch who has unlimited power with specific reference to the time and place of the dying of a child. God is not a do Anything, Anytime, Anywhere kind of God. Such an idea is an untenable assumption and a misleading abstraction. Actually the *Abba* God knows the reality of limits immeasurably more than any father and mother attempting to care for a sick and dying child. The self-limitation that God has chosen in the act of creation, the limitations[18] that are God's within

---

[18]The concept of the self-limitation of God that shapes my understanding of the providence of God includes the following elements: (1) God did not create the universe and humanity within it on the basis of any insufficiency in God but out of the over-

the structures of creation, refer the grief and pain of parents who watch their children die to the experience of the shared life of the community of faith. When healing does not occur, say pain-scarred witnesses in the fellowship of faith, God suffers with deep empathy alongside fathers and mothers in their pain and grief. God shares their sorrow and stands beside them in their mourning with some measure of sustaining grace and with at least fragile hope for love yet to be.

In the givens of a specific historical context of desperate human need—with the particular limits and transforming possibilities intrinsic within it as well as the transcendent possibilities available only to God beyond it—God always does the most God can do. Whatever God does, it will be coherent with the givens in the situation, because these givens inevitably condition the action of human agents as well as the response of God. Put simply: *God always does the most God can do.* On what grounds do I make this statement? Is it anything other than an assertion that "the providence of God" is compatible with any and every state of affairs? First, Jesus characterizes God's parental care as always more than the care of the best mothers and fathers (Matt 7:9-10). The analogy says that God is more engaged and at least equally active, that God is more

---

flowing joy of life within God. (2) The eternal God created *ex nihilio*, out of nothing, which underscores the power of God, the creative power of the transcendent God who is love. (3) The self-limitation of God for the sake of a relatively-independent creation and a significantly-free humanity is God's own choice, a self-chosen limitation that does not denote any inherent limitation in God. (4) The act of self-limitation coincides with God's act of creation and continues through God's ongoing activity and providential guidance of the history of creation (5) The self-limitation of God in relationship to creation does not restrict God's action to the source and ground of all possibility, because God creatively engages every aspect of the movement of creation in history: God acts and interacts within the dynamic configuration of natural processes, historical contingency, and human agency—actively engaging through the Holy Spirit all the factors that compromise historical passage. (6) The *self-limitation* of God coheres with the *self-investment* of God to bring creation and all human history to the fulfillment of the positive purpose of God: The Incarnation of God in Jesus Christ constitutes the definitive disclosure of God and the passionate assurance of the goal of creation in the coming Kingdom of God. Thus, this understanding of the self-limitation of God distinguishes a genuine personal model of God's relationship to the world from an unqualified monarchical model with its implicit historical determinism as well as from various existentialist and process models that minimize God's purposeful participation in and direction of the history of creation en route to eschatological fulfillment.

saddened and grieved than the most concerned father and mother for a suffering and dying child. Second, that God always does the most that God can do in a specific context of human need does not mean that God is trapped in a closed system without any alternatives in response to a particular situation of human crisis or adversity. Within the interconnectedness and complexity of ever enlarging circles of human relationships, engaging the possibilities intrinsic in the situation and uniting them with the possibilities transcendent within God alone, God responds to the particular circumstances of our lives in the world, and the alternative that God engages will be as lovingly parental as the best father and mother.

Third, what God can do in a given context is only visible and describable "after the fact," that is, in the light of what God has done. Yet patterns in God's response to recurring situations of need can be provisionally discerned, an extremely difficult but necessary theological task. *Theology is not a risk-free intellectual exercise.* Fourth, the analogy of the activity of an earthly father for the sake of his child facing death is eminently appropriate. Like the good mother of a dying child, always attentive and sometimes surprisingly resourceful, God works within the limits and possibilities available to God to relieve the situation of critical human need. God does not withhold relief from God's children who suffer. While these brief comments do not resolve the debate with those who question the providence of the God of love, the form of the debate must be reframed. The realities of life require the rejection of the monarchical model of a God with unlimited power who allegedly loves us like a good Father, a God housed in the lofty palace of splendored monarchy who rules and overrules through the unilateral exercise of sovereign power. The God of Jesus does not rule the world with the absolute and unilateral sovereignty of a king.

The primacy of the biblical image of the Kingdom of God must be distinguished from all theological models of God's relationship to the world. The various attempts to describe the providence of God in terms of the monarchical model assume too quickly that the image of the Kingdom of God authorizes this model of divine activity in the world. In fact, the monarchical model is a theological proposal that appropriates the Scriptures, but it is not identical with the vision of the Kingdom of God contained in Scriptures. Unfortunately the church's preference for hierarchical patterns of authority throughout most of its history has perpetrated a studied commitment to the monarchical model of the

contained in Scriptures. Unfortunately the church's preference for hierarchical patterns of authority throughout most of its history has
perpetrated a studied commitment to the monarchical model of the
providence of God. Yet the critical factor that prevents the simple identification of the image of the Kingdom with the model of monarchy is the
story of Jesus who reveals God as *Abba*. Although the monarchical model
of God's relationship to the world does recognize and accentuate the
sovereignty of God, which is its continuing contribution, it distorts the
kind of power and the mode of authority in Jesus' teaching about the
Kingdom of God, which is its fatal flaw.

Is the hope for the Kingdom of God a yearning for the singular
lordship of almighty God over all other powers that threaten humanity
and oppose God? OR: Is the hope for the Kingdom of God a longing for
the celebration of a graced humanity in the safe embrace of the family of
the good *Abba* of Jesus? The choice is too sharp, because each contains
dimensions of the other; nevertheless, the difference in orientation
remains. The issue finally turns on the kind of power that stamps the
contextual rule of God on the basis of the story of Jesus. My conclusion
is: The centrality of the image of the Kingdom of God is irreplaceable,
because it stamps the story of Jesus Christ; correspondingly, the stories
of Jesus Christ must always be remembered and retold, because these
stories interpret and define what the Kingdom of God means. The story
of Jesus does accentuate the sovereignty of God, the reign of fatherly and
motherly love, but the stories of Jesus do not validate the unilateral
activity of God in terms of the monarchical model with its accent on the
power to control. The power of God in the story of Jesus is not domina-
tive power but donative power. In the Gospels the power of God is the
power of self-giving, the scandal of the strength of weakness: The God
of Jesus is the God of a vulnerable compassion.

Another Metaphor and a Different Model

Since the monarchical model of God's relationship to the world stumbles
on the story of Jesus, or better, the Jesus story of God, another metaphor
is needed to illuminate the image of the Kingdom of God that would
imply a different and more appropriate model. A good metaphor to translate "the coming Kingdom of God" is "the coming Home-Coming of

God," the *Abba* God of Jesus Christ: In *the coming Home-Coming of God* the servants of God through covenants with Noah and with Abraham become *children of God* through the new covenant in Jesus the Christ. In the coming Home-Coming of God all the children of God become *brothers and sisters* with one another through the love of God in their *crucified brother*, Jesus of Nazareth. In the coming Home-Coming of God all the brothers and sisters of Christ become *friends* who genuinely learn to like each other through the warming wind of the creative Spirit of God.

The coming Home-Coming of God contains elements that are central to Jesus' vision of the Kingdom of God. First, the metaphor is essentially eschatological, a vision of the future of humanity with God. Though the sovereignty of God is not explicit, it is nonetheless implicit in this metaphor. Second, the present and the future are intertwined, because the *Abba* of Jesus intends for the celebration of the future banquet of the coming Home-Coming of God to begin in the historical present. The coming Home-Coming of God reflects the "already" and "not yet" in the vision of the oncoming Kingdom of God. Third, the metaphor contains intrinsic and profound ethical significance. Beyond individual standards of personal integrity, those who follow Jesus are summoned to exercise an ongoing evaluation of the structures and patterns of sociopolitical life, working to change those forms that prove to be inadequate expressions of life in the human family under the guidance of God. Fourth, the metaphor of the coming Home-Coming of God contains a depth of pastoral concerns for life inside and outside the church. The brothers and sisters of the Christ bear the bruises and brokenness of life as well as the distortion and disorientation of sin. We all need the goodness of nurture, the mending of life, and the belonging of friends.

The metaphor of the coming Home-Coming of God gives expression to elements intrinsic to the image of the Kingdom of God. The reconceptualization of the image of the Kingdom on the basis of the identity of God as *Abba* moves the image forward into this new metaphor, a metaphor that stimulates and encourages the vision of human life within family-defined relationships. The qualification of the Kingdom of God with the image of *Abba* understands relationships in terms of a healthy family under the leadership of One who is always the Motherly Father. Nevertheless, the coming Home-Coming of God is vulnerable to sentimentality that can minimize the continuing need for change, perhaps more so than other metaphors that interpret the primary image of the Kingdom of God. In its explication of the image of the Kingdom of God, the metaphor of the coming Home-Coming of God must be constantly redefined on the basis of God's activity in the history of Israel through Jesus Christ for the Church, and the story of Jesus must remain the continuing reference point for defining the purpose and activity of God. Therefore, the coming Home-Coming of God is an important interpretive metaphor, but it is always subordinate to the primary metaphor of the Kingdom of God, which Jesus personified through his mission and destiny.

The metaphor of the coming Home-Coming of God suggests an eschatological model for conceptualizing God's relationship to the world and our responsibility to God in the world. God is the loving *Abba*-come-near in Jesus Christ with an intimate creativity for the benefit of all humanity. A helpful analogy for envisioning the relationship of God to the world is the work of a Master Weaver with an ever lengthening tapestry. God is the future of every present become past and every future become present. That is, God always stands on the frontside of the "now" of the human story and constantly strives to weave together with purpose and creativity a tapestry of ongoing human history. Each moment in the particulars of nature within the contingencies of history shaped through human decisions provides the materials and the direction for the Master Weaver to continue to work. The engaging possibilities open to the Master Weaver depend on the available resources in the tapestry at any given moment: the kinds of thread and fibers; the variety of colors; the thickness or thinness of the fabric; lengths, short or long; texture, the looseness and density of the weave; and from wherever they originate, the patterns, or apparent lack of patterns already visible. The Master Weaver works with all these elements in the continuing task of fashioning a tapestry with some strength of character and with splashes of beauty through the multiple possibilities available within the design that the Weaver constantly re-imagines in pursuing his immediate purposes for the accomplishment of his ultimate goal.

A translation: God works in each and every moment with the variable factors available to God, integrating some measure of purpose in the movement of human history wherever possible and however minuscule —with long and short stretches, or sometimes only streaks, without hint of pattern or meaning. The "materials" that God utilizes are not just the "stuff" of history, but especially human agents in the historical situation whom God engages. Thus, doing the work of providence, God especially interacts with individuals and groups in the freedom of their decision-making, constantly engaging each individual and every kind of group for a positive response that contributes to God's immediate and ultimate purpose. God works with the givens available, a creative moment but a constant limitation. Yet possibilities are not simply determined from the givenness of historical progression.

As God steps back into the futurity that is God, providing a new finite future of historical contingency, God simultaneously releases new possibilities from within the creativity of the intention of God. Sometimes an improbability becomes a probability, with a trajectory of future possibility heretofore unlikely and perhaps unforeseen. At other times God rigorously engages the participants in a specific situation, and through the interaction of the present and future transforms it into a new configuration that could not have occurred without the creative participation of God. These new possibilities out of the future cohere with the possibilities in the givens of human history, but, however slightly or extensively, they stretch and shape, push and pull, enlarge and rearrange the possibilities within the givens of historical passage into new possibilities perhaps unanticipated and unforeseen.

Since God always engages history from its frontside, surprises happen that contain essential elements of continuity and, from the vantage point of the previously unanticipated, elements of discontinuity as well. God gathers the disjunctures of the unanticipated into a surprisingly unexpected but integrated historical progression. Conversely, tragedy occurs with the bent of an enduring negative continuity. Both the surprises and the tragedies of history are visible only retrospectively. Is this an interventionist portrayal of God's activity in the world? Is this another form of the monarchical model of God's relationship to the world, different only in its portrayal of unilateral intervention through the location of God on the frontside of history? No, because the new configurations of possibilities introduced through the constant interaction and personal participation of God cohere with the possibilities in the givens of historical passage. Thus providence still happens in conjunction with the specificity and concreteness of its historically-defined context.

God occupies a unique position in each moment of human history, engaging the transition from the past into the present toward the future. Simultaneously, God engages the movement of history with the creativity of personal interaction from the future with interpenetrating possibilities in the present. To return to the analogy, the Master Weaver re-envisions possibilities toward the immediate and long-term design of the tapestry from the frontside that coalesces with the givens at this present point in the tapestry, working with purposeful imagination in the continuing movement of the tapestry weaving its way forward. The analogy is limited, of course, but it suggests the form of an eschatological model of God's relationship to the world. Though beyond the limits of this essay, the eschatological model of God's continuing activity in the world entails a specific understanding of historical actuality and future possibility. Without minimizing the givens, the restraints, the limits in actuality, *possibility* has priority over *actuality*.

The creativity of God not only embraces the limitations that the past imposes on the present, but the imaginative activity of God includes the newness that the future offers to the present. Such newness always comes with an appropriate measure of coherence that intersects but does not break the elements of continuity and contrast in history's advance forward. The possibilities in the movement of time herein described presupposes the futurity of God. The eschatological model of the providence of God does not connote the unilateral intervention of God but the ongoing transformation of history through God's continuing, engaging interaction with it. Actuality does in fact condition possibility, which includes the possibilities impinging on the present through the future of God. The priority of possibility does not mean that God does not continue to work within limits. Actuality resists possibility. Significant, even severe limitations remain. Yet an indeterminate measure of mystery at the intersection of the future with the present broadens and enlarges in varying degrees the open possibilities available in the present from the past. The eschatological model of God's relationship to the world affirms an element of newness that impinges on every present, whether actualized or not, but it does not minimize the tragic in historical passage. On the contrary, the eschatological model of the providence of God bears the tragic in history with a stark realism that sometimes threatens to overwhelm hope, the continuing viability of the promise of the blessing of God.

The Contrasts in the Gospel Traditions: A Startling Ambiguity

The Gospel narratives indicate an awareness of the providence of God with both compassion and realism. Providence roots in the goodness of creation and God's continuing concern for humanity in the contingency of history. Yet the penetrating observations and the probing questions of Jesus reflect a profound realism, sometimes obscured.

Indiscriminate Creation

Matthew 5:45 accentuates the stability of creation and the non-discriminatory activity of God. Jesus said:

> [God] makes his sun rise on the evil and on the good, and sends rain on the righteous and on the unrighteous.

God's good providence happens in the orderly cycles of nature, and the rhythm of nature benefits everyone alike, regardless of how they stand before God. The reverse is also true, because discord in nature batters everyone alike: droughts and floods, tornadoes and hurricanes, volcanoes and earthquakes. The providence of God accentuates the relative stability in nature for humanity's benefit, but a biblically-informed providence recognizes the destructive elements that are present in nature and endanger human life. Indeed, Jesus concluded the Sermon on the Mount with a parable about hard rain, rising floods, and strong winds, all battering houses built on rock or sand (Matt 7:24-27). The Gospels know the negative side of the natural world whether we listen to them or not. Nature both nurtures and threatens our fragile human existence. Those who mourn the devastation and the dead in a violent natural disaster invariably ask, "Why?"

Useless Anxiety, Ever Present Suffering, Fearful Danger

In Matthew 6:25-34 Jesus urged his listeners not to be anxious "about your life, what you will eat or what you will drink, or about your body, what you will wear." These concerns are not unimportant, but God already knows our basic human needs. Over against the security of things Jesus charged his listeners to put their trust in God. Look at the birds and flowers: Though "the birds of the air" do not sow, reap, or store food, the good *Abba* feeds them. If we humans are really of "more value" than they, we should trust God to provide food for us. Again, "the lilies of the field" neither toil nor spin, but these wild flowers are clad with beauty surpassing the grandeur of King Solomon. The God who lavishly adorns the flowers will be even more purposeful in providing clothing for us. The *Abba* God of Jesus values humans created in the image of God more than all else in creation, and the providential activity of God focuses upon us. Since God intends to bless our lives whatever the measure of our faith, always working together with us, God will provide for us insofar as possible, but without guarantee. Beyond appropriate concern for daily needs, nevertheless, constant worry about food and clothing in the face of an uncertain tomorrow not subject to our control is unhealthy and self-destructive. Preoccupation with tomorrow distracts from the legitimate concerns of today and threatens trust in God today and tomorrow.

Jesus said: "But strive first for the kingdom of God and his righteousness, and all these things will be given to you as well" (6:33). Is this statement an unqualified promise of the provision of God for all our needs? The force of the affirmation cannot be denied, but Jesus offered an important qualification. Instead of overanxiety about tomorrow, "Today's trouble is enough for today" (6:34b). The persistence of trouble of all kinds day after day means that the provision of God is not an unqualified promise but an affirmation of God's providential intention.

The interpretation of the providence of God in Matthew 6:25-34 demands immediate attention to the parable of "the judgment of the nations" in Matthew 25:31-46. Within the parable Jesus identified the deprived and marginalized who are neglected and ignored in the daily traffic of life: the hungry, so many, some starving, jobless and begging for bread; the thirsty, dried inside and out, thirsty for water from the cup of another's hand; the stranger, alien and alone, yearning for someone's word of welcome; the naked, cringing in daylight embarrassment and shuddering in nighttime cold, ordinary clothing their worn-out call; the sick, needy but shunned, the repulsive smell of body waste amid the acrid air of death, longing for the comfort of a visitor's touch; the imprisoned —condemned, repudiated, and isolated, non-persons who grind down their hope for anyone to reach through the bars of their rejected humanity. The providence of God for the marginalized and the dispossessed depends on the gift of human compassion and the agency of human provision, an implication of the parable that we already know. Without the energy of compassion extended to them, those who suffer remain in their need, sometimes desperately so.

In Matthew 10:26-33 Jesus sent his disciples on mission into an oftentime hostile world with his word of the Kingdom of God. Under threat of persecution and death he urged them not to fear their enemies. Precisely in these situations of danger Jesus affirmed the passionate concern of the *Abba* God for each of them, indeed, all of us. He said:

Are not two sparrows sold for a penny? Yet not one of them will fall to the ground apart from your Father. And even the hairs of your head are counted. So do not be afraid; you are of more value than many sparrows. (10:29-31)

If God sees the life and death of creatures like sparrows, hardly worth a half-cent to humans, how much more does God care for us. We are so intimately known and eminently valued that God constantly catalogues the number of hairs on every head, a striking metaphor of the extent of God's concern.

What an astounding claim! Dare we believe that the One who created all that is knows the name and sees the face of every human creature on this obscure speck of dust called Earth—a speck almost invisible in the vastness of the universe? It sounds arrogant, even worse, utterly naive. Yet the message of Jesus originates in this startling and incredible affirmation of the passionate concern of the *Abba* God for all of us. On the basis of God's personal concern for each one of us, the disciple can endure adversities and even face death from mortal enemies without the hopelessness of overwhelming fear. Earthly foes can kill you, but that is all. Not so with the God of the coming Kingdom. This God will not allow death the last word over children blessed and bound in *Abba* love, because the providence of God embraces eschatology: the promise of new life on the other side of death in the coming Home-Coming of God. Yet this promise poses a mystery that evokes a lingering ambivalence.

Sickness, Disability, and Birth Defects

Jesus regularly encountered people who suffered from illness and disability, and he offered healing. Numerous stories of sickness and healing in the Gospel traditions remind us of the common human problem of physical and psychic illness that afflicts all of life, sometimes with unexpected and premature death. The Gospels know multiple problems of illness and disability: the lame, the maimed, the blind, the mute (Matt 15:30b); the complete disintegration of personality (Mark 5:1-20); an epileptic son (Matt 17:14-21); a dying daughter (Matt 9:18, 23-25). Why do illnesses occur? Why are these sick among most others who are well? Why are there such variations among illnesses? Why do those with the same illness sometimes face radically different prognoses? The questions are unanswerable, but the ambiguity that they reflect remains.

John 5:2-9 describes a pool called Bethzatha with water famous for its curative powers. It attracted "many invalids—blind, lame, and paralyzed," which included a man "who had been ill for thirty-eight years." Although someone would apparently bring him to the pool, he did not have anyone to assist him getting into the pool when the curative waters stirred, which required an immediate response for only one beneficiary. Jesus confronted the man, and then healed him. What did Jesus do about "the many" others who waited at the pool? Did he heal them? If so, why does John fail to say so? If not, why did Jesus not do so? At this point the Gospel of John reflects the ever present problem of the healing of some but not others, certainly not all. The ambiguity is startling: A multitude lay ill in the hope of healing, hope that brought them to the pool almost daily, but of these apparently only one is restored.

Today families and friends invest time and energy to take the sick and disabled to medical centers with hope for relief, perhaps for cure. Some hobble with kindred help because of the increased intensity of rheumatoid arthritis. Year in and year out a family shuffles from doctors and hospitals caring for the sufferer of Parkinson's disease—more rarely, even more severely, the tragic deterioration of amyotrophic lateral sclerosis. More often, family and friends experience frustration and fatigue in the face of developing stages of Alzheimer's disease, from memory loss and confusion to unpredictable and uncontrollable behavior. Beyond the typical problems of aging, multitudes lie atypically ill and disabled around us, sometimes an entire family focused on the need to provide continual care for just one of these.

The suffering of an innocent child stirs our compassion, but such suffering seems all the more senseless in instances of brokenness at birth. The issue surfaces in John 9:1-3:

> As [Jesus] walked along, he saw a man blind from birth. His disciples asked him, "Rabbi, who sinned, this man or his parents, that he was born blind?" Jesus answered, "Neither this man nor his parents sinned. . . ."

Here the story of Jesus touches the tragedy of birth defects. The disciples voiced the options of popular theology about congenital defects: Who sinned, the fetus in the womb or his parents? Jesus rejected both options: Neither the infant nor his parents are accountable. Jesus acted to heal the man, which displayed the creative work of God in him. Beyond the specific instance of John 9:3, however, the awareness of the brokenness of life from birth, whatever its form may be, confronts us with innumerable instances of "flawed creation." Whenever we encounter children who suffer from defects at birth, we too ask: Why did this happen? Who is responsible? What can be done? The flaws are many: blind, deaf, mute; heart defects, respiratory malfunction, muscular dystrophy; physical malformation, mental retardation, Downs syndrome, cerebral palsy—and countless other afflictions, some so severe that the infant dies, perhaps mercifully. The providence of God does not protect the unborn from defective formation nor his parents from a grief of devastation. What does the providence of God mean for a severely handicapped child and her family? Even the most dispassionate and logical theology senses the quicksand of ambiguity in the birth of a broken child, because it defies responsible theological explanation.

Military Oppression, Murderous Violence, Deadly Accidents

In Matthew 5:41, early in the Sermon on the Mount, Jesus refered to the heavy weight of the Roman military occupation of Palestine:

> If anyone forces you to go one mile, go also the second mile.

The idealizing and moralizing of "the second mile" in the church and society have ripped this text from its political and military context. At any moment a Jew could feel the touch of the flatside of a Roman sword or spear on his shoulder and be compelled to serve his conqueror in some menial task, e.g., bearing the luggage or equipment of a soldier from one place to another for "one mile," at least. This was the stuff of which war was made, which the Jewish war of 66–70 CE made plain. What does the military occupation and control of a small country by a conquering imperial power say about the providence of God? Is the foreign oppression in some form of military rule the judgment of God? Do the words of Jesus constitute an affirmation of Roman rule or perhaps the necessity of accommodation in the face of insurmountable odds? The suffering of a nation under the oppression of a foreign power through military might is almost incalculable, but the injustice of oppression is hardly debatable. The endeavor to glimpse any purpose of God in the godless purpose-lessness of injustice and oppression, whether foreign or not; the effort to discern the activity of God over against the military might of a cruel foreign power; the struggle to see some creative destiny beyond the fate of massacred villages by a repressive regime of cruelty and greed—all such visionary goals shatter under the weight of the savagery of military oppression. The providence of God seems shackled in chains of suffering and death, ambiguity that evokes the question: "Where is God?"

Death through violence is the companion of oppression. In Luke 13: 1-3 Jesus recognizes the contingency of life in the murderous violence that afflicts persons in God's world:

> At that very time there were some present who told him about the Galileans whose blood Pilate had mingled with their sacrifices. [Jesus] asked them, "Do you think that because these Galileans suffered in this way they were worse sinners than all other Galileans? No, I tell you."

Apparently the Roman governor Pilate ordered the execution of a group of Galileans, killing them in the Temple as they slaughtered the animals they intended for sacrifices. Since revolutionaries thrived in Galilee, these men may have been rebels, or perhaps they were only mistaken for rebels. Whoever they were, Jesus said plainly that they did not die because they were "worst sinners" than others. The victims of violent oppression are not the object of divine judgment more deserving of death than life, because the bloody violence of human brutality cannot be explained through the simple pattern of the cause and effect of human sin. The legal violence with "official casualties" in a police action of a totalitarian regime; the brutality and death of warring gangs up and down city streets, inside schools and out; an angry household confrontation when rage explodes unexpectedly in a smoking gun—an incalculable number of murders and killings, legal and illegal, happen throughout the world everyday. The affirmation of providence is riddled with gunfire in places large and small.

Yet Jesus reinforced his point with an account of an accident, a contingency categorically removed from intentional violence and murder. He added:

> Or those eighteen who were killed when the tower of Siloam fell on them—do you think that they were worse offenders than all the others living in Jerusalem? No, I tell you.

The eighteen killed may have been visitors admiring the tower of Siloam or perhaps construction workers building the tower. Whoever they were, Jesus repudiated the idea that those killed were "worst offenders" than other inhabitants of Jerusalem. The contingency and the accidental that maim and destroy happen within the watchful care of God. Some human failure often contributes to an accident, but not all. A driver accelerating to make the yellow light at an everyday intersection, a collision with one car bent round the front of another, one dead, two seriously injured; a break in a pipe in a chemical plant, the malfunction of a safety valve inspected a few days earlier, eleven workers dead from poisonous fumes, another sixteen with lungs seared into disability; a smoke-charred house framed in early dawn, a faulty electrical connection the origin of the fire earlier in the icy night, three escaping, four small children unable— accidents happen. Though usually less dramatic than murderous violence, accidents in various configurations sometimes kill, the consequences just as deadly as murder.

Reflection on the providence of God in situations of military oppression, murderous violence, and deadly accidents underscores the fundamental realism of Jesus about the providence of the *Abba* God, a realism that is sometimes difficult to accept and understand. *Providence does not mean protection.* Is God sometimes powerless, mostly enduring evil that thwarts and perhaps negates God's providential care? This question poses a startling ambiguity.

Summary

The affirmation of the providence of God permeates the Gospel traditions in the stories of Jesus, but the reality of the difficulties and dangers of life remain visible, even if subdued. Nature is essentially good and beneficial to human life, but from time to time it produces serious threats to creaturely existence in the world. Crucial resources necessary to meet basic human needs are often but not always available, especially for the marginalized who are dependent on others for aid. Though serious illness can sometimes be cured, masses of people suffer from sickness and disability with pain and hardship. The tragedy of suffering children, especially the handicapped, underscores the limits of the handiwork of God. The violence of military oppression dominates some places, and vicious killings and deadly accidents happen everywhere else. These problems locate ambiguity in the affirmation of the providence of God: "God knows your need, but. . . ." "God genuinely cares for you, but. . . ." "God will provide for you, but. . . ." The ambiguity runs deep, because creaturely existence means daily vulnerability, sometimes mortal vulnerability. Therefore the provision of providence is not absolute but conditional, always with reference to a specific context of human need and the resources available therein.

Conclusion

The intention of the providence of God is for everyone to experience himself or herself as "the blessed child of God" within a graced community. Acceptance and affirmation, vocation and responsibility — these are the twin sides of blessing in the love of God, the good *Abba* who knows everyone of us by name. For the sake of this providence of blessing, Jesus attacked the patriarchical structures of Jewish society, the devaluation and subordination of women to men—in principle, breaking down the walls of sexism and chauvinism, racism and class that obstruct the intention of human fulfillment in the purpose of God. Jesus reframed the understanding of God as the *Abba*-come-near, proclaiming the Kingdom of God in terms of redefined family relations instead of lordly monarchical rule. He articulated and enacted a vision of the Presence of the coming of God, acting for the benefit of humanity in each moment of human life and with a promise to humanity of the coming Home-Coming of God.

Yet contrasts to the vision of the Kingdom of God permeate the Gospel traditions *with a subdued realism*. The critical difficulty is the sharp qualification of the providence of God because of the tragedy of human suffering and the victims of untimely death. These dark stains on the affirmation of providence range from the lack of everyday human necessities for life through the dreary drain of life's vitality in sickness to the murderous injustice of an oppressive military regime. Beyond all the declarations of the goodness of life within the purpose and provision of God, the providence of God often seems garbled with ambiguity and stained with scandal. If God intends for everyone to experience life as "the blessed child of God," the activity of God nurturing this destiny must be a primary concern of any constructive proposal on the providence of God, because a scandalous ambiguity permeates all affirmations of divine providence in the specificity of human existence.

A cold, grey Saturday afternoon. January cold. Wintry silence. Empty house. The telephone rang, and I answered.

"Dr. Tupper," the conversation began. "Yes," I replied. The voice identified himself, a former student in a large theology class with me almost a decade earlier, now a pastor in Texas.

As I tried to put a face with his name, he continued the conversation and inquiries: "Dr. Tupper, do you remember David? We sat together in your theology class?"

David's picture came clear immediately in my mind. I said, "Yes." I had met David in college before he came to seminary. A big, hearty, vigorous man. Now a pastor in Kentucky.

"Did you know that David is ill?"

"No."

"David is dying. He would like to hear from you. Would you call him?"

I answered with little hesitation and considerable resistance: "No, I don't think I can call him. I would not know anything that I could say to him." I had not gone through the first winter, much less the second.

"Dr. Tupper, didn't you lose your wife about two years ago?" *Lose your wife.* Odd words, I thought. A scream began to wind upward from the hollow roundedness of my mind. Abrasive words from the carelessness of a name unremembered. *Lose your wife. Lose. Wife.* He had confused the date of her surgery with the date of her death.

"No, she died in September." Yesterday. Last week. Last month. Last year.

"I'm sorry. If I had known, I probably would not have called."

With an effort toward kindness I ended the conversation.

A few days later, on Monday in fact, I changed my mind and decided to call David. I telephoned to his home, and asked to speak to David. Ordinary conversation, mundane to recount.

"Hello, David, this is Frank Tupper in Louisville."

"Hello, Dr. Tupper."

Greetings exchanged, we small talked for a few minutes. Awkward talk, bridging the years and the miles between us, between the death now at work in him and the death long worked over me.

I asked him how he felt. He did not say much about his illness. Instead, he told me about his medication, how it made him feel. Cancer. Therapy. Medication. All intruders. Now one hardly different from the other.

A long pause. Softly, deliberately, almost whispered to make sure no one else could hear, David asked me: "Dr. Tupper, is God arbitrary?" A slight pause. "Is God arbitrary?"

"We sat together in your theology class," the Saturday caller had said. *"He would like to hear from you."*

The question split open and began to unravel immediately. Is God arbitrary? Is God consistent? Am I dying because God simply refuses through medicine or miracle to heal me? Am I leaving my wife and baby son because God thinks they really do not need me? Am I sick to death because God has some judgment against me for some wrong long forgotten in the forgiveness of grace? Bottom line: Am I dying because God does not love me enough to make me well?

"No, David, God is not arbitrary. God always does the most God can do."

Again softly, almost whispered, he said: "No." ". . . That's what I thought."

A few days later I called David once more. The conversation proved less intense, less urgent. We talked about life and its many gifts—wife and son and friends. We talked about death and the hope for eternal life in God. I wandered around with metaphors for eternal life, all necessary, all inadequate: brilliant Light, an open Door, warming Presence. David listened, interested, occasionally questioning. But he had already asked and answered the crucial question, the God question. Now the pain of saying "Good-bye" occupied him much more than the contemplation of saying "Hello." He died a short time later, but he faced death believing: Life is arbitrary. God is not. Grace.

Chapter 2

The Bethlehem Massacre— The Negation of Providence?

THE DEATH OF INNOCENT CHILDREN negates the promise of providence to them, because none are able to experience life as "the blessed child of God." Tragedy shrouds the death of all infants and children. Whether the unexpected pain of death in childbirth, childhood accidents or illness; whether the helpless victims of negligence, from parental abandonment to calloused public policy; whether the murderous violence of evil tyranny against "certain" children—these and all other reasons why children die bathe them in tears of grief.

The most dramatic instance of the murder of children in this century is undoubtedly the Holocaust, a pogrom that took the lives of a half million Jewish children. Elie Wiesel, one of the survivors, described what happened to the Jews of Sighet. They were herded into cattle cars and shipped to the death camps. When the doors opened, the victims emerged on the railway platform at Birkenau—the reception center at Auschwitz. A soldier taunted them: "Didn't you know what was in store for you at Auschwitz? Haven't you heard about it? In 1944?" None of them had heard anything. They were told that their fate would be the burning flames, the smoking chimney, the oven's ashes. Wiesel thought it must be a nightmare, an unimaginable nightmare. Someone said that they were going to the crematory. Wiesel saw gigantic flames leaping up from a ditch nearby. The fourteen year old boy reports: "They were burning something. A lorry drew up at the pit and delivered its load—little children. Babies! Yes, I saw it—saw it with my own eyes . . . those children in the flames."[1] This was young Wiesel's first glimpse of the Holocaust.

---

[1]Elie Wiesel, *Night*, trans. Stella Rodway (New York: Bantam, 1960) 30.

And in one of the most widely-quoted passages in Holocaust literature, Wiesel describes the searing of Auschwitz on his deep faith:

> Never shall I forget that night, the first night in camp, which has turned my life into one long night, seven times cursed and seven times sealed. Never shall I forget that smoke. Never shall I forget the faces of the children, whose bodies I saw turned into wreaths of smoke beneath a silent blue sky.
>
> Never shall I forget those flames that consumed my faith forever.
>
> Never shall I forget that nocturnal silence which deprived me, for all eternity, of the desire to live. Never shall I forget those moments which murdered my God and my soul and turned my dreams to dust. Never shall I forget these things, even if I am condemned to live as long as God Himself. Never.[2]

The suffering and death of children is always tragic, and sometimes unspeakably evil. Any endeavor to understand the providence of God, therefore, must face the fact of the death and the murder of children. Alone among the traditions of the New Testament, the Gospel of Matthew gives muffled voice to the fate of slaughtered babies.

The Paradigm of Innocent Suffering

The tragedy of the suffering and death of children turns the inquiry of providence to the slaughter of the innocents of Bethlehem in the infancy narrative of the Gospel of Matthew. The problem for providence is staggering. Put simply: The story of the journey of the Magi in search of the Christ child suggests that the baby Jesus experienced a divine rescue from Herod's murderous rage because of the special intervention of God and that all the other male babies in Bethlehem were slaughtered because God did nothing in their behalf. The Magi, who alerted Herod to the birth of the new king, set in motion a series of events that culminated in the Bethlehem massacre. The Magi followed God's leading with a star to Jerusalem and subsequently to Bethlehem, which implicates them and

---

[2]Ibid., 32.

raises the whole question of the involvement of God in the tragedies of human history.

The story bristles with questions: Is God really the good *Abba* of the whole human family, or is God inconsistently fatherly,[3] demonstrating parental provision for some and benign neglect toward others? The same question can be asked in a different form: Does God love the baby Jesus more than the other male babies in Bethlehem, orchestrating a divine rescue for "My Son" and leaving the others for slaughter? The same question can be put still another way: Does God value the baby Jesus and the necessity of his "messianic" escape, but considers the other male children of minimum significance and therefore expendable?

These questions surface critical theological issues. *Providence*: Does God consistently exercise providence within the historically defined context of time and place, the participation of human agents, the extent of the development in the situations, and the limits and possibilities available therein or coherent therewith? If providence is always contextually defined, lines of continuity and discontinuity will precede and follow God's specific providential activity. Furthermore, the provident action of God will happen with some measure of human cooperation and within the arena of historical contingency. Conversely, if God's providential activity happens outside or independent of a historically defined context—God simply chooses when and where and how God will work, when and where and how God will not work—the interweaving of lines of continuity with lines of discontinuity will not characterize God's action, human cooperation and historical contingency will not genuinely apply. The surprises of God turn into naked actions of divine power. To the victims, God appears inconsistent and unreliable. The goodness of God

---

[3]The phrase that I began to use in 1985 to express the non-arbitrary character of God's activity is "the self-consistency of God." Surprisingly, E. Y. Mullins, *The Christian Religion in Its Doctrinal Expression* (Valley Forge PA: Judson Press, 1917) 223-24, used the same phrase in his discussion of the variation of God's activity in conjunction with the immutability of God: "By immutability we define God as unchangeable in his nature and purposes. . . . God is infinitely free in his choices of both ends and means. . . . that *self-consistency* . . . runs through all his activities. . . . he is infinitely flexible and adaptable in the execution of his purposes. . . . All these forms of the divine activity are. . . . the expression of the infinite fullness and resourcefulness of God who will not be defeated in his purposes. . . . *There is nothing arbitrary in God's action*" (italics added).

is skewed. *Election*: Does divine election mean divine protection? Does the *Abba* God favor some children at the expense of others, acting protectively only in their behalf? The meaning of the love of God for children slaughtered on the bloody bench of human history becomes a question impossible even to begin to answer. If one retreats into the inscrutability of God's will and the mystery of God's purpose, the election of God magnifies not only the importance of some but also the utter expendability of others. The children of purpose are rescued, and the rest are murdered or relegated to insignificance. *Identity*: The underlying issue upon which everything else hinges is the identity and character of God. Is God trustworthy? Is God the covenant partner with Israel for the benefit of all humanity? Is God the *Abba*-come-near in Jesus of Nazareth? Is the characterization of God as the Motherly Father only one facet and not always the central facet of God's multifaceted and transcending identity, an identity utterly incomprehensible to us? Is the essence of God *agape*? The slaughter of Bethlehem boys two years and under reverberates with all these questions and unleashes more, questions at the center of biblical faith and the ongoing life of the Church.

What does the providence of God really mean in the startling ambiguity of life in the world, the world of Jesus and our world today? The characterization of the mode of God's providential activity surfaces in this most unlikely of places—the journey of the Magi, the flight of the holy family to Egypt, and Herod's murder of the male babies in Bethlehem. Why is the Bethlehem massacre so important? Unlike the other stories in the Gospels that contain significant ambiguity, the Matthean infancy narrative describes the special rescue of the Christ child and the slaughter of the children left, a sharp contrast, indeed, an apparent contradiction in the providential activity of God in the same historical setting. Obviously questions about God's providence cannot be restricted to Matthew's story of the Christ child, but the Bethlehem massacre remains *a classic case* of *the negation of providence* for the many and the provision of providence for only one. The question is more than a question of Matthew's story line, because embedded in the story is the question of the identity and purpose of God. The persistent inquiry relentlessly pushing for a response is: Does Matthew's infancy narrative undermine and ultimately destroy the most intentional form of the providence of God disclosed in Jesus' baptism, the experience of life as "the blessed child of God"? Does God will and work for every person to celebrate the blessing of the great gift of love: "My Son" and "My Daughter"?

Preliminary Reflections on Matthew's Infancy Narrative

How should one read and interpret the infancy narrative in the Gospel of Matthew? The story contains five dreams and five prophecies, but without a strict dream-prophecy sequence. The dreams occur at critical junctures in the narrative and serve as catalyses for action, and the prophecies are Matthew's interpretation of what has already transpired. The specific function of each dream and prophecy requires a careful examination of the different scenes in the infancy narrative of the Gospel of Matthew, literally the beginning of the "good news" in the opening pages of the Scriptures of the Church.

The Purpose of Matthew's Infancy Narrative

Matthew 1 and 2 divide conveniently into four units, each with a specific purpose: the genealogy, *who* (1:1-17); the birth of Jesus, *how* (1:18-15); the journey of the Magi, *where* (2:1-12); Bethlehem, Egypt, Nazareth, *whence* (2:13-23).[4] These different scenes in the infancy narrative are carefully crafted, they reflect discernible patterns, and they answer specific questions.

Genealogy: Who? The names of the genealogy divide into three groups of fourteen each: from Abraham to King David, from David to the deportation to Babylon, and from the Babylonian deportation to Jesus. The promise of God to Abraham, seemingly fulfilled in King David but failed in the Exile, will be fulfilled in Jesus, born of Mary and called the Christ.

---

[4]Raymond E. Brown, *The Birth of the Messiah: A Commentary on the Infancy Narratives in Matthew and Luke* (Garden City NY: Doubleday & Company, 1977) 52-54. Brown utilizes and expands the brilliant essay of Krister Stendahl, *"Quis et Unde? An Analysis of Matthew 1-2,"* in *The Interpretation of Matthew*, ed. Graham Stanton (Philadelphia: Fortress Press, 1983) 56-66.

The Birth of Jesus: How? Though Joseph did not father the child, Jesus was conceived through the Holy Spirit, which further clarifies his identity as Emmanuel, "God is with us." Joseph, of the house of David, faithfully accepted Mary already expecting a child into his house. Joseph named her new-born son "Jesus" which legally located the infant Jesus in the genealogy of David.

The Journey of the Magi: Where? The birth of Jesus in Bethlehem underscored his identity as the son of David and "King of the Jews," and the Magi arrived from the east to honor him with gifts worthy of a king. The homage and faith of the Gentile Magi established Jesus' salvific significance as the son of Abraham, the Messiah through whom all the nations of the earth will be blessed.

Bethlehem, Egypt, Nazareth: Whence? The travels of the holy family began with the murderous reaction of Herod to the news of the Christ child. As the family found sanctuary from Herod in Egypt, Jesus providentially relived the experiences of Moses in Egypt as well as Israel in the Exodus. Subsequently enroute home to Judah, the family decided unexpectedly against returning to Bethlehem and turned to Galilee of the Gentiles. Their decision to settle in the city of Nazareth added the final touch to Jesus' identity: "He will be called a Nazorean" (2:23b).

The Intention of This Narrative Analysis

Although the mode of the providence of God is not a central concern in Matthew's infancy narrative, the question of how God's providential activity occurred is not contrary to the purpose of the narrative nor external to the movement of the story. Rather, what God does to accomplish God's purpose is a most appropriate question to address to the narrative. Other approaches remain quite valuable, but I offer my own proposal as a distinctive narrative rendering[5] of Matthew 1-2 with specific concern for understanding the mode of the providence of God in the events of the infancy narrative. Do the multiple exegetical and theological debates swirling around the stories of Jesus' birth invalidate the endeavor

---

[5]Narrative exegesis concentrates on the meaning of the text, posing questions and formulating answers on the basis of the narrative itself—without essential correspondence to authorial intention or determination through the lens of the reader's response. See Mark Allan Powell, *What is Narrative Criticism?* (Minneapolis: Fortress Press, 1990).

to interpret Matthew's infancy narrative with specific concern for understanding the means and the pattern of God's activity in the doing of providence?[6] While the question cannot be answered adequately apart

---

[6]The number of New Testament scholars and theologians who reject the historicity of the infancy narrative in Matthew 1-2 and its affirmation of the virginal conception of Jesus as legendary is innumerable, a judgment that apparently renders these narratives relatively useless for understanding God's activity in history. Cf. Frances Wright Beare, *The Gospel According to Matthew* (Oxford: Basil Blackwell, 1981) 84, who says: "We are obviously dealing with legendary materials that lack any trustworthy historical base."

Of special interest are those theologians and New Testament scholars who reject the historicality of the infancy narrative and the virginal conception but affirm the actuality of the resurrection of Jesus Christ himself from the dead. See Wolfhart Pannenberg, *Jesus—God and Man*, trans. Lewis L. Wilkins and Duane A. Priebe (Philadelphia: The Westminster Press, 1968) 141-50 and 88-114 respectively; Jürgen Moltmann, *The Way of Jesus Christ: Christology in Messianic Dimensions*, trans. Margaret Kohl (New York: HarperCollins Publishing, 1990) 78-87, esp. 84: "If we wished to bring out this intention of [the true humanity of Jesus in] the nativity story today, we should have to stress the *non*-virginal character of Christ's birth, so as to 'draw Christ as deep as possible into the flesh,' as Luther said" (84-85); but on Christ's resurrection Moltmann is eminently positive (212-73, esp. 215-45): "The verdict of the disciples about Jesus' resurrection is not a reflective verdict of their faith. It is a reality judgment about Jesus' fate: He has in very truth been raised" (235).

Cf. Eduard Schweizer, *The Good News According to Matthew*, trans. David E. Green (Atlanta: John Knox Press, 1975) 26-30, 32-35: "Whether a virgin birth is possible is a question only a modern would ask; virgin birth was an accepted notion to men of the New Testament period. By no means, therefore, should a man's faith be judged by whether or not he thinks a miracle like this is possible, the less so because the virgin birth plays such an infinitesimal role in the New Testament" (34). The issue is not biological but theological (35).

The singular importance of Karl Barth at this point should not be overlooked. See *CD*, I/2, "The Miracle of Christmas," 172-202. Barth believes the sign of the Virgin birth signifies the Incarnation: "Sign and the thing signified, the outward and the inward, are [distinguishable]. . . . But they are never separated in such a . . . way that according to preference the one may be easily retained without the other" (179). "The Holy Spirit by whom the Virgin became pregnant is really . . . not in any sense an apotheosised husband, but He is God Himself and therefore His miraculous act is to be understood as a spiritual and not a psycho-physical act" (201). However, Barth argues: "The man Jesus of Nazareth is not the true Son of God because He was conceived by the Holy Spirit and born of the Virgin Mary" (202). On the relationship of the resurrection and the virginal conception of Jesus, Barth asserts: "Now it is no accident that for us the Virgin birth is paralleled by the miracle of which the Easter witness speaks, the miracle of the empty tomb. These two miracles belong together. . . . a single sign. . . . The Virgin birth at the opening and the

from an examination of the text, I must underscore the reasons why I consider Matthew's infancy narrative of inescapable significance for exploring the question of the providence of God.

First, the Gospel of Matthew is a literary whole,[7] and the infancy narrative belongs to the very fabric of this Gospel. All historical-critical questions aside, God does act providentially for the sake of the Christ child in Matthew's infancy narrative, and the form of God's provident action is of such theological interest that it cannot be ignored. Whether or not the mode of God's providence in the Matthean birth narrative coheres with or counts against a particular understanding of how God acts providentially in the world cannot be decided in advance.

Second, the journey of the Magi, the rescue of the Christ child, and the implication of the Magi in the Bethlehem slaughter mandates serious deliberation on the limits of the activity of God and eventually on the

---

empty tomb at the close of Jesus' life bear witness that this life is a fact marked off from all the rest of human life . . ."—in its origin and its goal the mystery of the revelation of God (182). Barth may be right exegetically that the sign cannot be easily separated from what it signifies, here the virginal conception and the Incarnation in Matthew and Luke, but Barth explicitly refuses to make the Incarnation depend upon the virginal conception itself. The incredible flaw in Barth's exposition is the supposed parallel significance of the Virgin birth and the Easter witness of the empty tomb, which is exegetically, historically, and theologically untenable.

[7]John P. Meier, *The Vision of Matthew: Christ, Church, and Morality in the First Gospel* (New York: Panlist Press, 1979) 53, claims that "the infancy narrative becomes a proleptic passion narrative." Certain parallels are plausible: the adversaries of Jesus, the king and "the chief priests and scribes of the people" in 2:4, and the secular ruler and "all the chief priests and elders of the people" in 27:1; the rejection of Herod and all Jerusalem in 2:1-8, 16, but the acceptance of the Gentile Magi in 2:1-2, 10-11, and, correspondingly, the rejection Caiaphas and all Jerusalem in 26:65, 27:25-26 and the commission to the Gentiles in 28:16-20; the title "King of the Jews" in 2:2 and 27:37b; the Christological highpoint in the infancy narrative with the title "my Son" in 2:15b and the confession of the centurion at Jesus' death on the cross, "the Son of God," in 27:54b; nevertheless, these parallels are far from exact. Cf. Brown, *The Birth of the Messiah*, 214, n. 2: Brown sees "a parallel between burial in the tomb and a reappearance of the risen Jesus after three days in the one instance, and the flight to Egypt and return to the land of Israel in the other. The child who returns from Egypt is Emmanuel, 'God with us' (1:23); the Jesus who returns from the tomb says: 'I am with you always' (28:20)." I find this parallelism or prolepsis strained and speculative without foundation in a literary analysis of the text. Almost all the parallels of the infancy narrative to the passion narrative are imprecise.

question of the complicity of God in the tragedies of human history. The particular problem of evil and suffering in Matthew's infancy narrative confronts us with "the Job problem of history"[8] where providence and theodicy converge.[9]

Third, the entire infancy narrative calls into question the fundamental affirmation of God's providence identified at Jesus' baptism: Jesus experienced himself as the blessed child of God, a model of divine providence God intends for each and every person—infants and toddlers, boys and girls, men and women. *The slaughter of the innocents in the Bethlehem massacre constitutes one of the most important challenges to the affirmation of the providence of God in the New Testament, precisely because of the circumstances of the singular providential escape of Jesus from Herod's bloody assault on the infant sons of Bethlehem.*

Unless it should be written off as theologically irrelevant for a contemporary understanding of the providence of God, a negative judgment that itself requires substantiation, an examination of Matthew's infancy narrative to determine whether or not it contributes to a meaningful theological interpretation of the providence of God for today is in my judgment unavoidable. The essential purpose of this chapter is to analyze the story of the Christ child in Matthew 1-2 in order to discern whether it discloses a consistent and relevant understanding of God's providential activity for theological appropriation today. Beyond the infancy narrative, moreover, another question must be asked: Does the Gospel of Matthew in its entirety provide any additional insight into the providence of God that relates to the story of Jesus' birth?

---

[8]See Jürgen Moltmann, *The Trinity and the Kingdom*, trans. Margaret Kohl (New York: Harper & Row, Publishers, 1981) 48. Since God refutes the theology of Job's friends, Moltmann asks: "Does Job have any real theological friend except the crucified Jesus on Golgotha?"

[9]Yet providence and theodicy must be distinguished, because providence endeavors to understand God's working in the world without attempting to justify the goodness of God amid the suffering of the world. See Stanley Hauerwas, *Naming the Silences: God, Medicine, and the Problem of Suffering* (Grand Rapids MI: Wm. B. Eerdmans Publishing Co., 1990), especially 65-95, 126-51.

The Experience of Providence: *Family*

What is the form of the providence of God in Matthew 1-2? The initial and unobtrusive form of the providence of God in the infancy narrative is "the experience of family." The providence of God happens positively and negatively, almost always the one wrapped in the other, in the family life of the child. Indeed, the subplot in Matthew's infancy narrative, shaping the story of Jesus' birth and early childhood parallel to the birth and childhood of Moses, accentuates this point. The courage and creativity of Moses' mother and sister, Jochabed and Miriam, saved him from the death sentence of Pharoah. They nestled Moses in a floating basket among the reeds near the bank of the Nile where Pharoah's daughter would bathe, and the princess found the crying Hebrew baby boy. Miriam had been watching, and she approached Pharoah's daughter to suggest a Hebrew nurse for the child. She agreed, and Miriam brought Jochabed to her, and the Egyptian princess made his mother his nurse! Miriam's action and Jochabed's immediate availability seem part of a deliberate plan to place Moses in the care of the princess. Indeed, Pharoah's daughter named the child "Moses" and made him her son. What does the story of Moses and his rescue from Pharoah's death sentence say about the story of Jesus and his escape from Herod's orders "to search and destroy"? The linkage is intrinsic in the narrative, because the narrative world of Matthew 1-2 encircles and reframes the narrative world of Exodus 1-2: a royal death decree, creative parental action, the slaughter of male babies, fearful political intrigue, refugees on the run, obscurity and maturity in exile. Though certainly different, the story of Moses and the story of Jesus locate the initial form of the providence of God in the life of the family.

The Scenes in Matthew's Nativity—An Interpretation

The infancy narrative in the Gospel of Matthew answers two critical questions for the readers of this Gospel: "Who is Jesus?" and "Why is he from Nazareth?" The circumstances of his birth and his characterization as a Nazarene constitute the beginning and end within which the nativity is told. Close attention to the text is essential to a narrative interpretation.

The Birth of Jesus (1:18-25)

In the story of the birth of Jesus sexual impropriety looms large over the circumstances of Mary. She was an engaged maiden pregnant with a child not fathered by Joseph, her betrothed husband. Two plain facts inform the movement of the drama: First, Mary was pregnant. Second, Joseph knew Mary to be pregnant. Both Mary and Joseph, therefore, were trapped in an injurious situation with lifelong consequences. Though not recounted, some *conversation* is intrinsic and necessary in this scene of the story. How did Joseph learn of Mary's pregnancy? This question alone signals conversation, but with whom and how much? Conversation with Joseph about Mary? Conversation between Mary and Joseph? Conversation with or without the knowledge of Mary's family? Of Joseph's family? The Gospel of Matthew does not say. Joseph knew of Mary's pregnancy, and he assumed that she had been unfaithful to him. Unwilling to subject her to public disgrace, Joseph "planned to dismiss her quietly." Unexpectedly, however,

> an angel of the Lord appeared to him in a dream and said, "Joseph, son of David, do not be afraid to take Mary your wife, for the child conceived in her is from the Holy Spirit. She will bear a son, and you are to name him Jesus, for he will save his people from their sins." (1:20-21)

When Joseph awoke from sleep, he did exactly what the angel had told him. He took Mary into his house and he conferred Davidic paternity on the child, naming him Jesus. The dream did not inform Joseph of Mary's pregnancy, but it did explain the source and identity of the child she carried. The dream transformed Joseph's understanding of Mary's already-known pregnancy, because the revelatory dream provided an explanation that excluded Mary's unfaithfulness and declared it to be the work of God. Through the reciprocity of information known and revelation provided, Matthew advanced the story forward. The scandalous element in Mary's plight was obvious but not contrary to God's purpose or provident history.

Matthew guides the reader to understand the birth of Jesus "to fulfill what the Lord had spoken by the prophet":

"Look, the virgin shall conceive
    and bear a son,
    and they shall name him
        "Emmanuel,"
which means, "God is with us." (1:23)

The Christological import of Isaiah 7:14 is plain: The Christ child is not only the son of David but the Son of God. Through the creative action of the Holy Spirit the messianic child would be Emmanuel, "God is with us." Why did Matthew insert the formula of the fulfillment of prophecy from Isaiah in the middle of this scene and in a dream [!] instead of its conclusion, as he did in each of the subsequent episodes? Although the name of "Emmanuel" unquestionably affirmed the divine element in the identity of Jesus, Matthew clearly intended to conclude the scene with the accent on Davidic sonship, which Joseph conferred on the child born in his house: "he named him Jesus" (1:25b).

An important point must be registered here: The contrast between Herod and the Magi has prompted the theme, "rejected at home, accepted from afar." This theme, if left unqualified, is an unfortunate distortion and nurtures a subtle anti-Semitism. In fact, Joseph modeled the theme of "acceptance at home." He personified the description of "a righteous man," he was sensitive and sympathetic toward Mary, and he accepted the angelic announcement that explained Mary's pregnancy and his responsibility to her son. Joseph embraced the scandal of the birth of the Christ child.[10]

---

[10]Meier, *The Vision of Matthew*, 54-55, falls into this trap, which is most unfortunate. Ignoring the wholesome attitude of Joseph distorts Jewish acceptance of Jesus and inappropriately nurtures an anti-Semitism that thrives on the contrast between the Magi (2:1-12) and the Jerusalem mob who demanded the release of Barabbas and the crucifixion of Jesus under the persuasion of "the chief priests and the elders" (27:20). The crowd cried, "His blood be on us, and on our children" (27:25), which has "justified" the abuse and pogroms against all subsequent generations of Jews as "Christ-killers."

The Genealogy of Jesus (1:1-17)

The critical significance of the genealogy of Jesus unfolds only in the light of the birth of Jesus. The Matthean genealogy divides into three stages of fourteen generations each: from Abraham to David, from David to the deportation to Babylon, from the Babylonian Exile to Jesus. The title of the genealogy introduces the themes of the infancy narrative: "An account of the genealogy of Jesus the Messiah, the son of David, the son of Abraham." The obvious intent at the beginning of the genealogy is to anchor the identity of Jesus in the Davidic line of the lineage of Abraham, but the careful location of Mary at the conclusion of the genealogy deliberately breaks the usual genealogical pattern:

> And Jacob the father of Joseph the husband of Mary, of whom Jesus was born, who is called the Messiah. (1:16)

The alternation in the genealogy provides a precise description of Jesus as the child of Mary whose husband was Joseph, but it does not repeat the established pattern elsewhere in the genealogy that would otherwise read, "Joseph the father of Jesus." The genealogy is through "Joseph the husband of Mary" but not through "Joseph the father of Jesus." Behind Mary, moreover, Matthew has already included four women in his genealogy: Tamar, Rahab, Ruth, and the wife of Uriah (Bathsheba). Since the variations in the genealogy indicate the providential selectivity of God in the ancestral list of the Messiah, the role of these four women evokes questions, even consternation: What is their relationship to Mary?

These four women have two biographical features in common with Mary: First, each of these women had a well-known story of marriage that contained varying elements of sexual scandal—unions, however "irregular," which continued the lineage of the Messiah. Second, each woman actively participated in events that became part of God's purpose in the fulfillment of the messianic heritage, identifying them as the instruments of the providence of God.[11]

The widowed and humiliated Tamar played the harlot and seduced her father-in-law Judah into fathering her twin sons, at the same time

---

[11]Brown, *The Birth of the Messiah*, 73.

cleverly protecting herself and her children. The prostitute Rahab provided shelter for two Hebrew spies sent to Jericho, making it possible for Israel to enter the promised land; nevertheless, the marriage of Salmon with Rahab, whatever her "acquired virtue," contained some element of scandal. The origins of the Moabites in incest and impurity bred contempt in Israel, but the Moabite Ruth, a widow and an emigrate, took the initiative toward marriage with Boaz (at least brazen, if not scandalous) without which the Davidic line might not have originated. The adulterous affair of David with Bathsheba prompted the king to send her husband Uriah the Hittite to sure death in battle, which eventuated in marriage, judgment, and grief; but through Bathsheba's courageous intervention their son Solomon succeeded David to the throne. Matthew does not mention other surprising births in his genealogy, e.g., overcoming sterility in Sarah, because there was nothing scandalous about her marriage or pregnancy. Schemers, harlots, adulterers—these women foreshadowed the role of Mary whose pregnancy constituted a scandal: She had not lived with her husband, a scandal of no little significance. The child nevertheless was begotten through the Holy Spirit, which meant God had acted to fulfill the messianic heritage through Mary in the most dramatic irregularity possible, without a father's begetting.

At this point traditional exegesis falters. The four women in Matthew's genealogical narrative participated actively in events that subsequently advanced the purpose of God. Tamar, Rahab, Ruth, Bathsheba —each had a story already told and similarly well-known, and the genealogy puts Mary in their history of decision-making and intentional involvement. The active participation of Mary in the birth of Jesus remains "a story untold," "a narrative unavailable." That Matthew tells the story of the birth of Jesus (1:18-25) from the perspective of Joseph has contributed to the false impression of the passivity of Mary within Matthew's infancy narrative, an erroneous assumption that has lingered throughout the entire history of the Church. Matthew, on the contrary, underscores the active role of Mary in his carefully crafted genealogy prior to the narrative of Jesus' birth. The interpreter's failure to recognize this fundamental element of the deliberate involvement of Mary in continuity with Tamar, Rahab, Ruth, and Bathsheba reinforces the unexamined assumption of the *unilateral* activity of God in the birth of Jesus apart from Mary's cooperation and receptivity.

What is the issue? What is the problem? What critical concern for understanding the providence of God is inherent in the genealogy of the Gospel of Matthew? The webbed impression centuries old in the memory of the Church has assumed the unilateral intervention of God in the birth of Jesus. This entrenched perception of the unilateral action of God in the conception of Jesus has reinforced the interpretation of the divine rescue of Jesus from Herod as simply another instance of the singular intrusion of God. Though Mary's creativity and receptivity remain in Matthew's infancy narrative a story untold, the *continuity* of the *stories told* and *untold in the genealogy* must not be ignored but affirmed from the outset: God did not superimpose the divine will and purpose upon Mary any more than God did upon Tamar, Rahab, Ruth, or Bathsheba. The birth of Jesus did not happen through the unilateral intervention of God but, conversely, through God's purposeful initiative and Mary's intentional participation. Since concurrence denotes God's action in conjunction with the collaboration of human agents, the *concurrence* of God's initiative and Mary's cooperation, skillfully but firmly established in the genealogy, reframes the question of the mode of God's activity in all the scenes of Matthew's infancy narrative, which includes the providential rescue of Jesus from Herod. Likewise, the concurrence of God's initiative and Mary's receptivity nurtures a profoundly human element in the birth of Jesus the Christ at the beginning of Matthew's story of the Incarnation.

The Visit of the Magi (2:1-12)

The journey of the Magi in search of the Christ child led them to Jerusalem, the capital city of Judah, asking: "Where is the child who has been born King of the Jews? For we have observed his star at its rising, and have come to pay him homage" (2:2). The question took the form of an announcement, one that startled and troubled King Herod and with him the entire city of Jerusalem—with good reason. Herod lived in constant fear of intrigue or assassination, suspicious of every potential rival to his throne. His murderous insecurity bred rage, cruelty and unpredictability toward family, friend and foe alike.

Alerted by the inquiry of the Magi, Herod assembled the chief priest and scribes of the people who used the Scriptures to locate the birthplace of the Messiah in Bethlehem of Judah. Before the Magi left Jerusalem, however, Herod met with them secretly to ascertain the time of the star's

appearing (which would coincide with the new king's birth) and to secure
their promise to return to Jerusalem to tell him precisely where the child
could be found in order that he too might honor the new Messiah. The
Magi agreed; subsequently, they followed the star to Bethlehem and to
the house where the child was. Therein they found the Christ child with
Mary his mother, and they offered gifts, treasures appropriate for a king.
"And having been warned in a dream not to return to Herod, they left for
their own country by another road" (2:12). These words concluded the
journey of the Magi and marked the beginning of the travels of the holy
family under the leadership of Joseph.

Here a crucial question emerges for understanding the providence of
God in the care of the Christ child. What occasioned the dream of the
Magi not to return to Herod? The affirmation of revelation answers the
question generally, but what revelation means requires a more precise
definition. Did revelation through a dream happen inexplicably and compel them arbitrarily to break their commitment to Herod and return home
another way? Or did the dream warning presuppose a new context that
occasioned the compelling insight "not to return to Herod"? The mainstay
of the answer hinges on the question of significant conversation of the
Magi with Mary and Joseph. The story thus far requires and contains
conversation: The scandalous story of Mary's pregnancy and Joseph's
response already presupposed conversation, essential conversation not
recounted in the text. Again, the inquiry of the Magi about the newborn
King of the Jews contained significant conversation between the Magi
and Herod that is recounted in the text. Herod sought help from "the
chief priests and scribes of the people," he learned the prophecy heralding
the Messiah's place of birth, and he had a clandestine meeting with the
Magi before they left for Bethlehem in order to gain their promise to
return with news of the location of the Christ child. The development of
each scene contains conversation implicit and explicit in the unfolding of
the drama. Would Matthew have the readers think that the Magi stopped
in Jerusalem without telling Joseph and Mary? Hardly, because the Magi
learned only in Jerusalem and with the help of Herod that Bethlehem
would be the birthplace of the Messiah. Such a conversation demands to
be recognized in the story of the Magi. As they recounted the last part of
their journey, the reader can hear the obvious and fearful questions of
Joseph and Mary:

"You stopped WHERE?"
"You asked WHO?"
"You promised WHAT?"

Everyone in Judah knew Herod's murderous reputation to eliminate all suggested rivals to his throne. Before they arrived in Bethlehem, the Magi did not suspect Herod's evil intent. On the contrary, they trusted Herod! After the briefest conversation, however, they had to be concerned for the child whom Herod had asked them to locate under the pretense that he too might honor the newborn King. Why were they now more than receptive to a different response to Herod? A new context occasioned an ordinary conversation with extraordinary consequences. Knowledge of Herod's atrocities from Joseph would evoke grave concern, and a revelatory dream could easily transform concern into action: Avoid Herod entirely. That the providential leadership of God would likely happen in conjunction with the concrete circumstances and conversations of the Magi in Bethlehem does not detract from the revelatory activity of God. On the contrary, the alternative is abominable: If a dream with information otherwise completely unavailable could effectively warn the Magi not to return to Jerusalem to keep their promise to Herod, why did they not receive an earlier dream that would have instructed them not to stop in Jerusalem for consultation at all? The problem is larger than Matthew's story line, because the Magi are implicated in the subsequent massacre in Bethlehem—and beyond the star-led, dream-warned Magi, in some sense even God.

The Flight to Egypt (2:13-15)

This scene in Matthew's nativity begins with a dream and ends with a prophecy. Nevertheless, the context of the dream must be emphasized: "Now after [the Magi] had left." The arrival of the Magi in Bethlehem from Jerusalem, the presentation of their gifts to the Christ child, and their departure with a warning not to return to Herod—all these events occurred with Joseph's knowledge but prior to Joseph's dream. The threat of Herod had accompanied the Magi to Bethlehem, but it did not leave with them. In this context an angel of the Lord appeared to Joseph in a dream with specific instructions:

Get up, take the child and his mother, and flee to Egypt, and remain there until I tell you; for Herod is about to search for the child, to destroy him. (2:13b)

Joseph followed the instructions of the divine messenger and left Bethlehem immediately for the safety of Egypt. The understanding of the providence of God at this point in the care of the Christ child cannot avoid but inevitably requires a crucial judgment about whether or not what-turned-out-to-be a highly significant conversation about King Herod transpired between Joseph and the Magi. Did the dream introduce King Herod with his knowledge of the newborn king and his birthplace in Bethlehem into the orbit of Joseph's concern? Or did the dream warn an already concerned Joseph of the encircling murderous threat of Herod and the necessity to leave immediately for the safety of Egypt? The Magi had learned from Herod in Jerusalem the birthplace of the newborn king in Bethlehem, alerting him to a potential rival to his throne. The Magi had learned from Joseph in Bethlehem the character of Herod, alerting them to the potential threat to the child. The God-given insight that warned the Magi not to return through Jerusalem paralleled the God-given dream that warned Joseph to seek the safety of his family in Egypt. Therefore, the same people who put Jesus at risk with Herod, however unintentional, became a catalyst for Joseph in the escape of the child to Egypt.

The flight of the holy family to Egypt would not be unintelligible at all. Herod's power could not reach to Egypt, a province under Roman control. Since Egypt had long been a place of refuge for Jews fleeing tyranny in Palestine, another Jewish family's escape to Egypt would certainly not be unusual. A relatively short journey, a colony of Jews already resided in major metropolitan centers where Joseph could easily find others in similar circumstances. That providence in the escape and safety of the Christ child happened in light of the conversation between Joseph and the Magi does not minimize the working of God. Without the instruction of God in a dream would Joseph have reacted so quickly and so decisively for the sake of his young charge? The narrator concludes the scene with the text from Hosea: "Out of Egypt I have called my son." Therefore, he interprets the exile in Egypt with the grandest title for Jesus in the entire infancy narrative, "My Son."

A final word about this scene is essential for interpreting the next scene, "The Slaughter in Bethlehem." As the infancy narrative moves forward in conjunction with the journey of the Magi on the one side and the escape of the Christ child on the other, the specific focus of the narrative must be remembered: The Magi had asked, "Where is *the child who has been born king of the Jews?*" Herod had said, "Go and search diligently for *the child*; and when you have found *him*, bring me word. . . ." The Magi "saw *the child* with Mary his mother. . . ." Unsurprisingly the specific content of Joseph's dream warned: ". . . take *the child* . . . for Herod is about to search for *the child*, to destroy *him*."

The only child in Bethlehem whom the Magi and Joseph knew to be at risk was the child in Joseph's charge. Accordingly, he devoted himself to the safety of this child without reason to be concerned for any other. The critical issue for understanding God's providence is the interrelatedness of the content and context of Joseph's dream. The Magi searched for one child. Herod demonstrated interest in one child. Joseph had responsibility for one child. When the Magi brought gifts to the Christ child, Joseph knew that they had traveled a great distance, logically stopped in Jerusalem, but turned through Scripture to Bethlehem. The Magi knew of Herod's intense interest in the child, and Joseph knew of Herod's murderous insecurity about rivals to his throne. The knowledge of the Magi on the one side and of Joseph on the other constituted the context and stamped the content of Joseph's dream. The issue is not the foreknowledge of God, however defined, which would encompass all families with male babies in Bethlehem. On the contrary, *the revelation of God* at this crucial point in Matthew's Gospel happened *within the limits of Joseph's own experience*. ". . . Herod is about to search for *the child* to destroy *him*" (2:13b).

The Slaughter in Bethlehem (2:16-18)

When he realized that the Magi would not return to Jerusalem, Herod became furious. He ordered the death of all the male children "in and around Bethlehem who were two years old or under, according to the time that he had learned from the Magi." Such brutality was entirely consistent with Herod's character: He had three of his sons killed in 7 BCE, because he thought them to be a threat to his rule. When Emperor Augustus heard the news, he reportedly offered a pun on Herod's murderous insecurity and his kosher diet: "It is better to be Herod's pig (*hus*) than his son (*huios*)."[12] That Herod would slaughter all the male babies in Bethlehem from the threat of the birth of a rival king remains entirely plausible.

The wording of the text has sometimes left the impression of large numbers—hundreds, even thousands killed. If the population of Bethlehem and its surrounding area totaled 1,000 (a high estimate) with an annual birthrate of thirty (at most), because of the high infant mortality rate male children under two years of age would have numbered no more than twenty, perhaps as few as twelve or fifteen. So the lack of any other record of the Bethlehem "slaughter" is unsurprising in light of the other atrocities during Herod's rule. Yet the very calculation of *an infant mortality rate* blends the tragedy of flawed creation with the violence of *calculated murder.*

The introductory formula for the fulfillment of the prophecy of Jeremiah varies from Matthew's pattern elsewhere in the infancy narrative. Here Matthew uses the neutral term *tote* (meaning "then") instead of his usual *hina* or *hopōs* (meaning "[in order] to fulfill").[13] Matthew says to the reader: God would not have purposed the death of the children for the sake of the fulfillment of prophecy. The Bethlehem massacre was not the prophetic, pre-determined will of God. So the text reads:

> Then was fulfilled what had been spoken through the prophet Jeremiah:
> "A voice was heard in Ramah,
> > wailing and loud lamentation,
> Rachel weeping for her children;
> > she refused to be consoled,
> > because they are no more." (2:17-18)

The slaughter of the male children in Bethlehem with Rachel weeping for her children functioned as a vivid reminder of the two great tragedies that God's people had suffered: infanticide in Egypt and deportation to Assyria and Babylon. The massacre of the children in Bethlehem echoed Pharoah's slaughter of the male babies of the Hebrews in Egypt; and Rachel, weeping for her children forced into Exile, mourned again from

---

[12]Frank Stagg, "Matthew," *The Broadman Bible Commentary*, vol. 8 (Nashville: Broadman Press, 1969) 89.

[13]Brown, *The Birth of the Messiah*, 205.

her burial place near Bethlehem for her children "who are no more." Yet Matthew does not intend a sense of historical determinism that mocks the providence of God. On the contrary, he employed Jeremiah's description of Rachel crying for her children to accentuate the utter pathos of the moment. With shrieks of pain, the shock of death, and the helplessness of a massacre done, Rachel represented the mothers of Bethlehem who could find no comfort amid the lifeless bodies of slaughtered sons: "She *refused* to be consoled, because they are no more." These nameless, faceless mothers of nameless, faceless sons refused consolation for their children, "because they are no more."

Disturbing questions about the providence of God clamor for attention. While the relatively small number of male babies killed in Herod's Bethlehem massacre might account for the lack of corroboration in other literature, the role of the Magi constitutes nonetheless a major problem. They informed Herod of the birth of the newborn king and the time of the star's appearing to mark his birth. They are implicated therefore in the murder of the Bethlehem male children. Is God also implicated through the Magi for the slaughter in Bethlehem? Could God have prevented the killings but chose not to do so? If God is less than God to twelve or fifteen or twenty in an obscure, minuscule footnote within the sweep of the whole human story, a footnote written again and again, *the godlessness of God* is a story already told twelve or fifteen or twenty times over, cumulative footnotes that number hundreds, even thousands, a million times more. Can one reason against this charge that the blessing of the providence of God cannot undo a high infant mortality rate or the violence of wicked tyrants? Yes. This story still remains a problem because the Magi represent a positive response to the disclosure and promise of God, a positive response that loosed Herod in the land with a bloody sword in his hand. Can one argue that the inquiry of the Magi in Jerusalem about the birth of "the King of the Jews" was so natural as to be unavoidable? Yes. Can one conclude that the response of Herod, predictable as it may have been, was completely contrary to the will of God? Yes. Can one affirm that the providential activity of God happened within the limits and possibilities of a historically defined context, here with utterly tragic consequence? Again, yes.

The Return to the Land of Israel (2:19-23)

The final scene in Matthew's infancy narrative begins with the death
of Herod. An angel of the Lord appeared in a dream to Joseph in Egypt
with the message:

> Get up, take the child and his mother, and go to the land of Israel, for
> those who were seeking the child's life are dead. (2:20)

Matthew's use of the plural, "those," sounds wrong, but the phrase is
almost identical to the words of God to Moses in Exodus 4:19.[14] The
death of those who wanted to kill Moses allowed him to return to Egypt
to begin his liberating work; correspondingly, the death of Herod
apparently allowed Jesus to return from Egypt to the starting place of his
messianic mission. When Joseph confidently took the family back to
Israel, as the dream had instructed him, he heard that Archelaus, the
worst of Herod's sons, reigned in Judah, and "he was afraid to go there,"
appropriately so. Archelaus had been granted rule of Judah, Samaria, and
Idumea. He began his reign with the massacre of three thousand, and he
persisted in his dictatorial ways until his brutality became so intolerable
that Rome deposed him in 6 CE. Another dream warned an already
frightened Joseph to withdraw to the district of Galilee, there to dwell in
the city of Nazareth under the rule of Herod Antipas with the likelihood
of greater political tranquility.

The revelatory dream to Joseph in Egypt announced the death of
Herod and assured him of the safe return of the family to Israel. Yet the
Egypt dream was only half right and potentially dead wrong, because it
did not alert Joseph to the danger of Archelaus' reign in Judah until after
he had returned to Israel. "He was afraid," because, contrary to the
dream, Jesus remained under the threat of death. The dream in Egypt
lacked the information Joseph would need to avoid a dangerous return to
Judah, and the dream warning to withdraw to Galilee happened only after
Joseph already knew not to go home to Judah. The dream in Egypt had
proven to be inadequate, and worse, dangerous to refugees already on the
way home.

---

[14]Ibid., 217.

This story with its "awkwardness" underscores the issue that I have raised throughout: Do the Matthean dreams, revelatory to be sure, presuppose a specific context that limited their revelatory content? Had the news, the rumors, of Herod's death already swept through the Jewish immigrants and refugees like a strong east wind, which the dream confirmed but without essential information for Joseph to know how best to proceed? The question is not so speculative. The problem with a crowd of refugees is not the absence of news but the bewildering difficulty of distinguishing real news from unfounded rumor, and perhaps more difficult, determining the news in the news, the truth wrapped in the layers of its telling.

> When [Joseph] *heard* that Archelaus was ruling over Judah in place of his father Herod, he was afraid to go there. (2:22a)

The text is plain: Joseph heard through *public conversation* about Archelaus in Judah, and only then did a dream warning send him to Galilee. The text says, "when he heard," conversation more implicit than explicit, without reference to time and place, apart from the identity of the participants involved. Yet conversation occasioned the necessary context for Joseph's unwillingness to continue toward Judah and receptive to another dream warning him to withdraw to Galilee.

The incompleteness and dangerous instruction of Joseph's dream in Egypt to return home to Israel indicates again that the knowledge of God is not the problem. Rather, the contextual limitation of the dream that actually shaped its content is the issue. When and where would the announcement of Archelaus' reign in Judah have originated? How rapidly would the news have spread, and how reliable would it have been considered? It is not insignificant that Joseph's Egypt dream almost duplicated the words of the Lord to Moses for his safe return home in Exodus 4:19—no arresting new information for Joseph out of Exodus! The Egypt dream lacked dangerous specificity, but positively it gave him the confidence to leave the sanctuary of Egypt for home in Israel. Could a revelatory dream in Egypt with more specific information have sent Joseph safely to Nazareth of Galilee without changing the pattern in the narrative and the movement in this scene of the story? Perhaps. Another question must be asked: Did the imprecise dream in Egypt with the subsequent danger in Judah provide a new historical context that could occasion a dream warning to Joseph to shift direction and relocate in Nazareth of Galilee? The infancy narrative concludes with the fulfillment of "prophecy": "He will be called a Nazorean" (2:23b). Where did this prophecy originate? Why was it applicable to Jesus? When did it become so? This final scene raises most sharply the mode of God's providential activity in Matthew's infancy narrative: Does God exercise providence in conjunction with and conditioned by the historically defined context of time and place, the participation of human agents, the extent of the development in the situation, and the limits and possibilities available? What is the relationship of the content and timing of these revelatory dreams to the context within which the dreams occurred? The inter-relation of the context of the situation with the content of the dreams, the context delimiting the content, characterizes the providential guidance of God. Though most obvious here but intrinsic to the entire infancy narrative, the providence of God moves with the give and take of the historical dynamics in the story.

Critical Reflections

Revelatory dreams are essential to the Matthean story of the Christ child, and an assessment of these dreams is mandatory for a distinctive narrative rendering of the providence of God. Other difficult issues must be faced with observations that address key questions within the scope of inquiry into the providence of God.

An Assessment of the Dreams

The interpretation and understanding of the five dreams in Matthew's infancy narrative proves crucial for discerning the lines of divine providence in the unfolding of the narrative. The recurring question is: Are the revelatory dreams so contextualized in the life situation of the narrative that context essentially shaped their content? The author of Matthew may not have recognized the fundamental significance of the changing context for the new revelatory content moving through the nar-rative. This does not mean that the question of the contextualization of the providence of God cannot be asked. On the contrary, the endeavor to determine the mode of the providence of God in the infancy narrative requires us to ask how God acts in a historically defined context, an inquiry that does not distort the text but enlightens the meaning within the parameters of the text. Indeed, a sharp line cannot be drawn that delimits content to context, at most a discernible pattern, but the appropriateness of this pattern of interpretation throughout the infancy narrative can attain substantive credibility.

The first dream to Joseph was the most explicitly contextualized with the most extensive content: That Mary was not carrying an illegitimate child but one conceived through the Holy Spirit (therefore he should not be afraid to take her as his wife), and that he should name the child "Jesus." Yet even here the dream occurred in a context. The marriage of Mary to Joseph had been arranged, with about a year between betrothal and residency, during which time Mary became pregnant with a child. The deliberation of Joseph required the certainty of his knowledge of Mary's pregnancy and his own violation of the Law through acceptance of her into his house. How many already knew and how much had already been said lingers in the background, because Jesus would necessarily be born too early after Mary and Joseph came to live together to escape scandal and gossip. These factors contextualized Joseph's God-given dream that instructed him how to proceed within these specific circumstances.

The fifth dream to Joseph minimally distinguished content from context (if at all). Already and appropriately afraid, the dream warned him not to continue to Judah, which eventuated in the family's settlement in Nazareth of Galilee. The awkwardness of Joseph's need for this dream enroute to "the land of Israel" points to the "heard" news along the way of Archelaus' rule over Judah and the complete lack of such important information in his earlier dream in Egypt, i.e., the fourth dream. The Egypt dream assured Joseph of the safety of his family in Israel, "for those who were seeking the child's life are dead." Danger surfaced enroute, and a frightened Joseph "being warned in a dream" withdrew to Galilee. The Egypt dream referred only to the news of Herod's death, which created the false impression of promised safety but without warning of the danger in returning to Judah. The issue, of course, is not the knowledge of God, because God already knew who ruled in Judah. Rather, the limits in the context restricted the adequacy of the content of the Egypt dream, which could be corrected nonetheless enroute to Israel. So the journey itself constituted a new historical context and occasioned a final dream that turned Joseph in a different and safe direction to Nazareth of Galilee.

The second and third dreams revolved around Herod, and are crucial, even central, to a narrative interpretation of the providential activity of God in the story of the Christ child. Did these dreams occur in a historically-defined, conversation-informed context? The second dream roused the Magi "not to return to Herod" on their journey home. Almost simultaneously, the third dream of unmistakable divine origin awoke Joseph to the necessity of the immediate and urgent flight of the family to Egypt to escape Herod's search to destroy the Christ child. Herod was the common reference point of both dreams: Each dream presupposed the knowledge of the journey of the Magi through Jerusalem. Each dream presupposed Herod's knowledge of birth of the Christ. Each dream presupposed the keen interest of Herod in the location of the Christ child. Each dream presupposed Herod's murderous history of rivals to his throne. In Bethlehem context and content converged.

All five dreams in Matthew's infancy narrative, therefore, have a contextual reference in the life situation of the text before the revelatory dream occurred: engaging conversation. Furthermore, the subject matter of the dream had already become a concern for the dreamer prior to the experience of divine disclosure in the dream through enlightening conversation. The conversations that preceded each dream can be summarized as follows:

Dream 1:   Conversation with Joseph about Mary's pregnancy, which required his sure knowledge and his personal response;

Dream 2:   Conversation with the Magi about Herod's murderous insecurity, which Joseph and all Judah already knew;

Dream 3:   Conversation with Joseph about Herod's intense interest in the child, which was certainly not to locate and honor him like the Magi;

Dream 4:   Conversation with Joseph about Herod's death, which promised safety in Judah without qualification;

Dream 5:   Conversation with Joseph about Archelaus' reign in Judah, which occasioned his turn to Galilee for the safekeeping of his family.

All five dreams shaped decisions and informed the action in each scene of the drama, each movement in the narrative. Every dream nonetheless presupposed specific references in the life situation of the text in conjunction with the revelation and leadership of God: engaging conversation. Therefore, the infancy narrative in the Gospel of Matthew counts against the understanding of divine providence in terms of the unilateral intervention of God. The revelatory dreams that moved Matthew's infancy narrative forward were special acts of God, but these providential actions of God did not occur arbitrarily, but in a historically defined framework informed through the common element of human conversation.

Observations—Not Generalizations

A narrative understanding of the providence of God does not permit comprehensive generalizations about human existence. On the contrary, a genuine narrative interpretation of God's providence cannot be abstracted into universal truths that leave the narrative behind, because the truths in the narrative are inseparable from the narrative. Questions can still be put to the story that evoke observations from the story, observations relevant to the lives of those in conversation with the story for understanding their own storied existence.

(1) The readers of Matthew would not have a problem with the "miracle" of Jesus' birth, but they would have a problem with a sexual scandal at the beginning of the Gospel. *Question*: Why would God choose for Mary to become pregnant so long before her marriage that she became subject to gossip, humiliation, divorce? Why would God not communicate the divine purpose to Mary and Joseph earlier, with the birth of Jesus inside the parameters of public morality and apart from the whispers of sexual scandal? Why put Mary with Tamar, Rahab, Ruth, and Bathsheba? *Observation*: God does not always work God's purpose within the boundaries of public respectability and community expectations. The work of God can take the form of *scandal, a risk that heightens the need for trust* but does not contradict *the self-consistency of God*. Furthermore, the entire infancy narrative, from the genealogy to the residence of Joseph's family in Nazareth, reflects the reality of various kinds of scandal in a family's experience. The genealogy knows more scandal than the irregular unions of Tamar, Rahab, Ruth, and Bath-

sheba. Perhaps the pain of scandal belongs with any serious reflection on the "family" as the initial form of the providence of God, whether public scandal happens in every family or not. Sometimes a family is scandalized only from within, scandal known to various family members but kept from the public: drunkenness, adultery, spouse abuse, incest, child abuse, theft, deceit, slander, and the list goes on in the privacy of family life. Families are ragged things. Yet within the realism of ongoing family life, Matthew's infancy narrative says that scandal, public or private, does not in itself destroy the providential work of God.

(2) The readers of Matthew would have little difficulty with the pilgrimage of the Magi to Judah in search of the Christ child, Gentile astrologers though they be. *Question*: But why should they alert Herod to the birth of "a newborn king"? Was the stop in Jerusalem inevitable? *Observation*: The entanglement of the purpose of God with the givens of human decision-making that thwart that purpose remains unavoidable. The path of providence always includes human agency and historical contingency. Distorted insight, limited understanding, irreversible decisions, unfortunate intersections, hostile opposition, luring oppression, human weakness, flawed character—God works with these kind of negative variables in shaping the purpose that God intends for a particular time and place. Patterns of providence are exceedingly difficult to discern because even the patterns are broken with deep cracks and smeared with dark stains. The journey of the Magi underscores the entanglement of the leadership of God with forces hostile to God's purposes and the risks in every venture of providence.

(3) The readers of Matthew would have no problems with the rescue of the Christ child to Egypt. *Question*: But why did God ignore or abandon the other families of Bethlehem with young sons who needed rescue, too? Why did God not provide instruction to the other fathers of toddling sons in Bethlehem? Could God have done so but chose not to do so? *Observation*: God has chosen to work within certain limits: God acts, but God alone does not determine the shape of events in human history. God does not control everything, and God does not control anything completely. Could God have prevented the murder of the infants in Bethlehem? If the providence of God happens within the limits of an historically conditioned context, if context is critical for content, the answer would have to be "Probably not," indeed, a cautious but necessary "No." Why did God not provide instruction to the other fathers of

toddling sons in Bethlehem? They did not have a specific context that would identify their sons to be at risk. A warning would have been context-less, conversation-less, and meaning-less. Does such a conclusion detract from the Godness of God? On the contrary, the difficult but painful "No" preserves the very Godness of God, the identity of God as the *Abba* of Jesus. Conversely, the temptation to affirm what might have been—the comfortable sound of "Yes"—is the temptation to construe all the children slaughtered with the sword of evil tyrants in some sense as the handiwork of God (if not the elect, the benign neglect of God). A narrative understanding of the providence of God must wrestle with the awareness of *the radical self-limitation of God*, regardless of the conceptual and linguistic difficulties involved. God is the all-comprehending reality moving history toward its goal but not without human activity that resists God's control.

(4) The readers of Matthew would have responded positively to the fulfillment of prophecy in the different scenes of the infancy narrative. *Question*: But why must Rachel weep again in prophetic memory for the loss of her children in this senseless massacre in Bethlehem? *Observation*: The history of promise and fulfillment does not imply a deterministic understanding of the human story. God does not simply control history in the rhythm of promise and fulfillment. Matthew uses the text from Jeremiah already once fulfilled to accentuate the tragedy of the Bethlehem slaughter. These murdered children were the victims of fate, the unwanted given that negated their intended destiny. "Rachel weeping for her children" was a graphic description of what had happened instead of the prophetic fulfillment of what God intended to occur. Matthew knows "the Job problem of history." Yet the action of God in the story of the Magi and the rescue of Jesus happened in the midst of violence and ambiguity in the little town of Bethlehem. And sometimes God seems only one step, even a half step removed from complicity for the most tragic and evil events. The tragedy remained nonetheless a human tragedy: "Rachel weeping for her children," "wailing and loud lamentation," "she refused to be consoled, because they are no more." Since "the experience of family" is the initial form of the providence of God, the life of a healthy family ought to be enlarged to include some place for a great sorrow.

(5) The readers of Matthew would not have a problem with the sojourn of the holy family in Egypt. *Question*: But why take permanent residence in Nazareth of Galilee, a despised, scorned, insignificant town?

Observation: The purpose of God happens in the context of human need and historical possibilities on the one side and in conjunction with the ravages of evil and the promise of the good on the other. In fact, the providence of God has a history and a geography. Providence always has a history: specific persons who are agents and recipients, sometimes more active than passive and other times more passive than active, always within a particular series of events that are contingent even when purposed, God always working to accomplish God's will through the engaging human response of a Mary and Joseph, of Magi, and of ordinary people in the most ordinary places. Likewise, providence always has a geography: specific places where people come and go, stopping in between, some places distant and far and other places familiar and near, God always stretching God's will in and around and through places of human activity, Jerusalem and Bethlehem, Egypt and Judah, and all the ordinary Nazareths in the most ordinary Galilee worlds. The providence of God always has a history and a geography, a geography and a history, forged together in narrative. Providence is not a precept to be explained but a story to be told. The place of safety at one point in time can become the source of confusion at another, and worse, worse indeed, *a scandal.*

The Compassion of God

The Gospel of Matthew begins with the importance of children, the generations of the sons of Abraham and David. The focus of the entire infancy narrative centers on the birth, the identity, and the providential concern of God for the child born in Bethlehem, exiled to Egypt, and home-towned in Nazareth. Yet the narrative does not minimize the importance of the slaughter of the innocents in Bethlehem nor the deeply warranted grief of their parents. The interest in children in the Gospel of Matthew does not end in Nazareth but continues through the ministry of Jesus.

The Importance of Children

Jesus used the paradigm of a child to identify the appropriate attitude of the disciples for entering the Kingdom of God: He literally called a child and put him in the midst of the disciples, urging them: "Truly I tell to you, unless you change and become like children, you will never enter the Kingdom of [God] (Matt 18:3). Discipleship requires a "turning," becoming like a child, ready and willing to embrace new attitudes, new values, new commitments, that is, the experience of conversion. Greatness in God's Kingdom requires the disciple to become as humble as the child is dependent, for humility is the posture of service.

That Jesus loved little children is an observation so commonplace in the life of the church that any reference to it seems redundant and unnecessary. In a patriarchical society, however, children were not valued as children in themselves. Yet Jesus put himself in strikingly solidarity with children:

> Whoever welcomes one such child in my name welcomes me. If any of you put a stumbling block before one of these little ones who believe in me. . . . (Matt 18:5-6a)

Jesus identified so closely with the little ones, that to welcome them in his name meant to welcome him. The interface of "child" and "little ones" in this text locates children among the little ones, all little children and the little people who are commonly neglected or exploited. Comparison of verses 5, 6, 10 and 14 supports this double reference. Matthew 18:10-14 invites providential interpretation. Jesus said:

> *Take care that you do not despise one of these little ones; for I tell you, in heaven their angels continually see the face of my Father in heaven.* What do you think? If a shepherd has a hundred sheep, and one of them has gone astray, does he not leave the ninety-nine on the mountains and go in search of the one that went astray? And if he finds it, truly, I tell you, he rejoices over it more than over the ninety-nine that never went astray. *So it is not the will of your Father in heaven that one of these little ones should be lost.*

Both Matthew and Luke recount the parable of the lost sheep, but Matthew brackets the parable with striking words without parallel elsewhere. Moreover, Matthew 18:10 and 18:14 precede and conclude the parable of the lost sheep. To whom do the "little ones" refer in these verses? What motivated the novel announcement that angels in heaven represent these little ones on earth? Why are these verses found only in the Gospel of Matthew? The words of Jesus are puzzling: "in heaven their angels continually see the face of my Father in heaven"? Since the idea of guardian angels was certainly not universal, it is very significant that Matthew alone assigned such angels who already see the face of God to the little ones who are often minimized and sometimes despised. These angels are cosmic powers who actualize God's rule of the universe and communicate to God all the troubles of humanity. The universal sovereignty of God is for the benefit of the little ones who are of such great importance to God: "their plight is seen, their prayer is heard." God is personally concerned for each of the little ones and "stands alongside them with his beneficent will."[15]

Why do these words of Jesus appear exclusively in Matthew? What do they mean? To whom do they refer? Only Matthew narrates Herod's slaughter of the innocents in Bethlehem. That is at least part of the answer. The same Gospel that recounts the massacre of the male babies in Bethlehem tells the reader that God does not neglect or forget the little ones, neither little children nor little people. Rather, God always sees and knows, values and loves, the faces of the little ones. "My Father," Jesus insisted, "My Father" does not will the death of any little one, which includes any little child. The *Abba* God did not intend that babies die in Bethlehem—not for the sake of the fulfillment of prophecy, not for the exposure of a totalitarian state, not for the disclosure of God's rescuing grace, not for the realism of a high infant mortality rate. God did not intend for any little children to die in Bethlehem. So when Jesus spoke of the compassion of God, the God of fatherly and motherly love, he spoke in behalf of children, all children. The death of any little baby remains contrary to the will of the *Abba* God. These two sayings of Jesus, unique to the Gospel of Matthew, address at least indirectly the tragic slaughter of the children of Bethlehem. Does Matthew say more?

The Blessing of Children

Jesus demonstrated a captivating openness to children, but the disciples did not share his attitude. Matthew 19:13-14 says:

---

[15]Schweizer, *Matthew*, 365-68. Though Schweizer says the identification of the little ones "undoubtedly refers to the disciples" (365), Stagg recognizes the context is more inclusive ("Matthew," 182).

Then little children were being brought to him in order that he might lay his hands on them and pray. The disciples spoke sternly to those who brought them; but Jesus said, "Let the little children come to me, and do not stop them; for it is to such as these that the kingdom of heaven belongs." And he laid his hands on them. . . .

The disciples thought children an intrusion, a classic example of the patriarchal attitude toward children, but Jesus invited them with a warm welcome. Jesus "took them up in his arms, laid his hand on them, and blessed them" (Mark 10:16), including some infants (Luke 18:15a). The story of Jesus blessing the children says what God does intend for children—the experience of the blessing of God in their lives. Though brushed with different strokes, the three Synoptic Gospels paint a portrait of little children hanging all over Jesus, surrounding him, with Jesus touching them, blessing them in the name of his *Abba* God. Matthew's presentation of Jesus is two-pronged. God does not will for any of these little ones to perish. And beyond the statement of what God does not want, Jesus invites the children to him and blesses them in the name of God whose Kingdom yet comes.[16] The same Jesus who experienced the intensity of God's blessing in his baptism extended God's blessing to children, the special concern of God. The blessing of God with the grace of affirmation and the assurance of familial belonging is the good gift that God intends for each and every child.

Conclusion

The infancy narrative in the Gospel of Matthew proves to be one of the most difficult and most important Gospel narratives for the interpretation of the providence of God. The issue hinges on the mode of God's providential activity in the world: Does God work providentially in the different scenes of Matthew's drama through unilateral intervention or

---

[16]Schweizer, *Matthew*, 384. He says: "Jesus is not simply to 'touch' the children but to lay his hands on them and pray for them." I would add: The expression "such as these" connects children with the Kingdom of God and implies an inclusive definition of the "little ones." Contrary to the valuation of children in patriarchal society, which the disciples reflect, children were important to Jesus precisely as children.

within a historically defined context with its intrinsic limits and transcending possibilities? A narrative analysis establishes the mode of the providence of God through historical contextualization, which coheres with the approach to the providence of God characteristic of this essay.

Several lines of inquiry converge into an interpretive network that shapes my perspective and establishes my conclusion. First, the different persons in the scenes of the drama were active participants and purposeful agents in the story of the Christ child. Everything that occurred required "engaging conversation" among the persons in the story. Second, though the revelatory dreams are essential to the movement of the drama, each dream happened in a specific context that shaped the dream's content and therefore the appropriate response of the dream's recipient. Third, the specification of the fulfillment of prophecy always applied after the fact, which illuminated the purpose of God, but the prophecies did not predetermine the events therein described. The configuration of the story of Jesus in the light of Old Testament prophecies was Matthew's own creative discernment, because he selected the texts and located their interpretation. Fourth, the historically-defined context that the journey of the Magi shaped in Jerusalem and moved to Bethlehem did not contain any reference points to indicate the other male babies to be at risk. What God "could" have done to rescue them would have been context-less, conversation-less, and meaning-less. The providential activity of God delimited to a historically-defined context constitutes a radical self-limitation of God that allows tragedies in Bethlehems the world over. Finally, the infancy narrative belongs to the fabric of the Gospel of Matthew, and the interpretation of the nativity must "fit" the understanding of the Gospel as a whole, a "fit" that moves the reader beyond the infancy narrative to Matthew 18 and 19. God did not intend for any little children to die in Bethlehem but to experience life as the blessing of God, the intention of providence for each and every one.

When Susan entered the hospital for delivery of her child, the word passed throughout their circle of friends. We had celebrated the birth of the Christ child during the season of Advent, the lighting of the Christ candle on Christmas Eve. Now we waited for news of the baby's birth, a new gift to a family whose warm friendship had touched almost all. Then the tragic message stunned friend after friend: The baby had died. The baby had been healthy when her mother entered the hospital, delivery scheduled for the next day. Yet in between times, after arrival in the hospital but before the morning of her birth, the infant died in her mother's womb.

On Saturday morning, a terrible Saturday morning, friends gathered in church: the Sanctuary of Advent had become the Ramah of Tears. The pastor and the couple entered the sanctuary, and the memorial service, already at graveside begun, could begin for us all. The baby had been named, death certified, and buried in Christmas ground. The baby's name was Rachel, and she was no more.

January 2

Rachel

> A voice was heard in Ramah
> Echoing through dark corridors of sterile tinsel.
> Seeking consolation for a desolate manger.
> Herod is loose in the land.
> Is this love's end?
>
> Oh, Mary, weep with us;
> Weave us a shroud, Hannah.
> Play us a dirge, Sarah;
> Elizabeth, come near.
>
> Simeon saw:
> a sword that pierced the heart
> of one called to be mother.
>
> Weep with us, Mary.

MJ

A young woman who had lost her own baby son at five months wrote a poem for the service. She intended to give expression to her anger—the anger of her own woundedness brought again from the dark, the anger in the senselessness of another child lost. Despite her intentions and to her great surprise, Annie wrote instead a litany of praise.

Gloria Patri
(For the Children)

Glory be to the Father
        who cradles children in his arms,
        who rocks them gently as they sleep.
And to the Son,
        who called the children to him,
        who knew that they contained the kingdom.
And to the Holy Ghost
        who hears the cries of all the children,
        who speaks for them to the Father.
As it was in the beginning,
        Creation in its fullness
        before death claimed the children.
Is now and ever shall be:
        abiding love surround the children
        from life through death and back again.
World without end,
        always children of the Father
        who cradles children in his arms.
Amen, Amen.

                                        AH

When posted on the sign of the city limits of the Bethlehems the world over, the litany sings of the compassion of God.

When I heard on Friday the tragic word that called us together on Saturday morning, I stopped at the home of my friends to express my sympathy in their grief. Unexpectedly a conversation began, a conversation that the church tolerates from time to time for people in crisis or for those in grief. After a while, without intending to do so, some one of us broke the silence with the inevitable question, "Why?" The question shattered the silence within us, and addressed the silence of God. "Why?"

"There are some things," I said, "that even God cannot do." With the innocence of love in a cradle of grief, Dan responded with upturned face, widened eyes and sharp voice: "Why not?"

My answer: "Limits, limits." ". . . God always works with limits."

The thought behind the words remains plain to me even now. God always does the most God can do in the specificity of any given situation with its particular limits and possibilities.

After a year or so, they took the risk—better, they found the courage —to try again. And though Samuel arrived almost three months too soon, he grew to match their courage. He became a great blessing and lives greatly blessed.

Chapter 3

Who Trusts in God?

EVERYTHING WAS LIFELESS in the barrenness of the wilderness, and he struggled against the emptiness of the silence. He could hear the sound of himself panting for breath. Forty days and forty nights without food—the sun had almost bleached him dry, and the hunger inside twisted uselessly in search of something that would satisfy.

Countless small stones lay everywhere about him. The light cut through the shadows, and suddenly he saw innumerable loaves of bread! Like manna from heaven, delicious little rolls of bread. And he remembered: So many good people were out of work. Hungry babies cried themselves to sleep at night. Children had become beggars on the streets. Every woman felt the budget crunch at the grocery. The working man was caught between the recession and the tax collectors.

He could hear the soft Whisper without straining: "So do it! . . . Hard rock into soft bread." And anything else that they might need. Like Moses in the wilderness . . . the people would gladly follow him. Loaves of bread or piles of stone? He knew the truth of human need. People cannot live on bread alone, certainly not bread from stone. The hunger returns day after day, and it always cries for more and more. He knew the deception of uncalculated greed.

The Word of God includes the need for bread, but bread alone rises deaf to the summons of the Word of God. Only the Word satisfies the gnawing emptiness deep inside. . . . Only the Word reaches all the way down into the dark recesses of hidden impoverishment that starve to be made whole. He knew the joy of grace received. Bread from stone? It could not be done. The greatest wonder for heeding humanity's hunger was the Word of God.

From wilderness wandering to the land of promise he stood atop the pinnacle of the Temple of God. The wind blew around him, occasionally flapping his robe like claps of thunder in the distance. Standing between heaven and earth afforded him a sense of human invincibility and divine majesty. When he looked down, momentarily a dizzying sight, crowds of people moved in miniature beneath him. The little dots trailed noiselessly through the courts and corridors of the Holy Place.

Malachi had prophesied that the Messiah would appear suddenly at the Temple. Steady and clear the Whisper pierced the humming of the wind: "Step down from the sky. God will protect you. The angels of God will not allow anything to hurt you." If he stepped out in faithfulness to the promises of God, when he did not fall but slowly descended . . . every eye would see him, every tongue would praise him, every knee would bow before him. All would confess that he was the Christ, the Son of God. He could drop from heaven to earth without a scratch, not just once but anytime he chose to do so. He could convince "the doubting Thomases" in the world the truth of his identity. God would honor God's Word and protect God's Son, giving him power over all the forces of nature. Nothing could harm him.

Was it the test of faith for him? Or was it God who would be put to the test? . . . Would he allow God to preserve him as the singular witness to the power of the Almighty? Or would he obligate God to fulfill the Scriptures to protect him from the destruction of chaos? The truth dangled in front of him: The feat would be a test of God's faithfulness rather than of his faith, a spurious test of self-serving under the disguise of serving God.

The brisk breeze whistled round him, and looking down almost sent him spinning. Cleareyed, nonetheless, he saw the truth of it: "You do not put God to the test." So he turned away from the heights of the spectacular to return to the court below, but the climb down proved more difficult than the climb up had been.

The cool of the mountain air was refreshing, and the view simply magnificent. He surveyed all the kingdoms of the world in their power and glory. Wherever the horizon touched kingdoms without number, Imperium Rome already ruled and plundered. A subservient king or appointed governor exercised authority under the banner of the empire. The legions of Rome had not only conquered these lands but had enforced the power of Caesar over them.

In every place the story was the same: Troops had pillaged house after house, taking whatever they had wanted. Onetime productive men had been crippled and scarred because of the arrogance of Roman soldiers, whether drunk or sober. Countless young women had sold themselves for the profits of prostitution to service the Roman army. Whatever went wrong or whoever got hurt involving the occupying Forces, the local authorities knew to look the other way.

Of course, he understood the truth of military occupation and political subjugation. Caesar had "pharaohed" the Israel of God into another Egypt. What could he do? Whatever he failed to do in Israel, he certainly could not accomplish among the kingdoms of the world. The unguarded Whisper promised: "You can have them all." But how? The Kingdom of God must displace the rule of Rome: kingdom against kingdom, army against army, sword against sword. The Zealots would hear his charismatic call, and they would follow him. He could liberate Judah and every other nation from the tyranny of Roman rule to the justice of the rule of God.

The nagging problem remained: Would the violence of conquest contradict the worship and service of God? The truth frustrated his sense of compassion. If he mobilized an army and established peace with the sword, the means to the Kingdom of God—OVERWHELMING FORCE—would contradict the goal of the rule of God—JOYFUL RECONCILIATION. Since the rule of God must conform to the way of God, he made his decision. He would not bow down and worship the god of this world, the power of "might makes right." He shouted angrily, "Get behind me, Satan." He would live in the worship and service of God, a servant to the way of love. Although he would never resort to the power of violence, he would risk becoming its victim. And his eyes brimmed with tears.

What does it mean to trust in God? Since temptation is in itself a beguiling lure that distorts faith in God, the temptation narratives clarify the variations in the temptations that Jesus encountered in his life and enable us to discern the distinctive response of trust with which he overcame each of them. Jesus recognized temptation, regardless of its appeal and disguise, and he tenaciously remained faithful to God. Trust in God is the distinctive and appropriate response to temptation. While obedience is sometimes elevated as the essential characterization of Jesus' relationship to God on the basis of selected New Testament texts, the deeper reality that transcends the ambiguity of life is ongoing trust in God, which includes obedience insofar as obedience expresses the more complex action of continual reliance on God. Indeed, Jesus' response to temptation through specific scriptural texts can be construed as acts of obedience, but the capability of Jesus to use Scripture to articulate his trust in God is an act of creativity that the category of obedience cannot contain but trust can. Therefore, Jesus confronted temptation with unshakable trust in God that included nonetheless the discipline of obedience.

The purpose of this chapter is to explore what it means to trust in God. The temptation not to trust God occurs at the intersection of the everyday choices of life on the journey of faith, and the context in which temptation happens is the dynamic arena of creation, more so, the abiding goodness of the creation of God. Beyond an examination of the temptations of Jesus, the identification of approximate corresponding forms of evil clarifies and accentuates the difficulty of living continually with trust in God. The problem of evil in all its forms must be addressed in the formulation of the understanding of providence and not afterwards, a way of understanding God's providence that a narrative approach requires. Jesus demonstrates that a person can live faithful to God in this broken world and experience within it the fulfillment of life. The possibility of living in a positive relationship with God nonetheless requires the ongoing nurture of spirituality.

The Experience of Providence:
The Goodness of Creation

After his baptism but before the beginning of his public ministry, Jesus retreated into the wilderness for forty days of fasting and praying, subsequently confronted with temptation. Throughout his confrontation with temptation Jesus continued resolutely to trust in God. The experience of providence that characterized his encounter with the Tempter extended the experience of providence at his baptism: Jesus knew himself as a blessed child of God in "the goodness of creation." So he affirmed the goodness of his creaturely existence within the boundaries of human finitude that God had established in nature and history, and, simultaneously, the authentic fulfillment of his life within these very boundaries. Creation is a risk for God, because it can be corrupted, exploited, and suffer unattended, but it is not in and of itself evil. Though not unqualified, creation retains the continuing affirmation of the good work of God.

The Genesis story of creation is a literary masterpiece, a hymn that heralds the goodness and grandeur of all the works of God in creation, each pivotal act concluding with the declaration: "God saw that it was good" (Gen 1:22, 25b, 28). With the creation of humanity that completed God's creative activity, "God saw everything that he had made, and indeed, it was very good" (1:31). Despite the fallenness and waywardness of humanity, the affirmation of the goodness of creation remains. In 1 Timothy 4 the Apostle Paul explicitly affirmed the goodness of marriage and the enjoyment of food, two essentials in the givenness of creation for the benefit of humankind. Paul summoned the Christian community to gratitude for creation: "For everything created by God is good, and nothing is to be rejected, provided it is received with thanksgiving; for it is sanctified by God's word and by prayer" (1 Tim 4:4-5; also, Rom 14:1-23).

What does the goodness of creation mean in a world distorted with the complexity and accumulation of human sin? The work of a master craftsman always begins within a specific context, a production for some particular purpose. A noncontextualized standard is simply nonexistent. So a creative act or useful production is good because of the goal for which it is prepared and to which it corresponds.[1] Thus creation remains good on the basis of the intention of God. God sees the work of creation and says, "Very good." We humans cannot make this comprehensive judgment, because humanity belongs within the historical movement of creation as creaturely existents. From our perspective much of creation is not positive and good but negative and destructive, senseless and savage. That the goodness of creation endures despite the elements that defy the good frees us to praise its Creator without paralyzing anxiety and over-whelming doubt. Since the creation story ends with God's affirmation of "very good," we are invited to celebrate the gifts of creation and to protect the abundance within creation. Therefore, God's evaluation of "good" invites the human response of "joy."

Though we see the meaningless and the reprehensible, the contra-dictions and the brutality in the history of creation—the negative experiences with the inevitable question of "Why?"—only the Creator can invalidate the overall goodness of creation in conjunction with the divine purpose. We enjoy the gifts of creation, and we endure its catastrophes. We withstand suffering, and we wrestle with questions in an effort to understand, but the intention of God and the characterization of creation remain "good," sometimes, "very good." Every "Why?" that we voice legitimately questions this goodness gone awry, but the context of the question remains the goodness of creation within which the "Why?" occurs, an agonizing question sometimes uttered with the blurred vision of tears and grief. The goodness of creation enables us to struggle with

---

[1]Claus Westermann, *Creation*, trans. John C. Scullion (London: SPCK, 1974) 61.

the question "Why?" in the context of the tragic: enduring disaster without giving-up, suffering with those who suffer, and persevering in the midst of other questions after the "Why?" If goodness refers to the purpose of creation, this goodness remains qualified, because we experience creation as adversary as well as friend.

An essential mark of the goodness of creation is the blessing of God, a mercy that continues beyond the Fall. Though blessing is an often overlooked mode of God's action in the world for the benefit of humanity, the history of Israel discloses that the God who saves is concurrently the God who blesses. Blessing applies to all the structures of a dynamic creation established for ongoing human existence in the mystery of life. The Priestly Document of Genesis 1 affirms a concept of blessing that has the widest meaning anywhere in the Bible: the blessing of all living creatures (1:22), the special blessing of human beings (1:28), and the blessing of the Sabbath, a holy day (2:3). Since blessing discloses that God has a friendly disposition toward the world, Walter Brueggemann concludes: "The blessed world is the world God intended. Delighting in creation, God will neither abandon it nor withdraw its permit of freedom."[2] The blessing of God maintains the goodness of creation, and humanity lives in the continuing grace of this great blessing.

The Temptations of Jesus

The temptations of Jesus were temptations to reject the goodness of creation of which he was a part and therefore the goodness of his creaturely place within it, that is, to deny the appropriateness of his finitude in the pursuit of his vocation as well as to repudiate the contingency of history as the actual arena for the gracious activity of God. Over against these temptations, Jesus affirmed his creaturely place and finite existence as

---

[2]Walter Brueggemann, *Genesis*, Interpretation Commentaries series (Atlanta: John Knox Press, 1982) 37. Cf. Claus Westermann, *Blessing in the Bible and the Life of the Church*, trans. Keith Crim (Philadelphia: Fortress Press, 1978) 1-14, esp. 6. "[Blessing] is primarily the power of fertility, an understanding of blessing that remained constant through the centuries. This is the specific meaning in Genesis 1:22, 28" (18). Since blessing in Genesis 1:22, 28 represents God's blessing of genealogies, "Blessing is realized in the succession of generations" (30).

dimensions of the blessing of God within the goodness of the history of creation. Jesus echoed the affirmation of God on the sixth day of creation: "God saw everything that he had made, and indeed, it was very good" (Gen 1:31). Jesus already knew and continued to affirm that the blessing of God in the fulfillment of life can occur in this world corrupted with suffering and sin.

Temptation is almost always subtle, the temptations of Jesus remarkably so. It is not so much the repudiation of the will and purpose of God as it is the distortion of it. The three temptations of Jesus in Matthew and Luke are variations of the same temptation, but precisely these variations with different settings and distinctive nuances clarify the subtleties of temptation and the corresponding definitions of "trust in God."

Finitude and Need

The tempter came and said to him, "If you are the Son of God, command these stones to become loaves of bread." But Jesus answered, "It is written,
　'One does not live by bread alone,
　　but by every word that comes
　　　from the mouth of God.' " (Matt 4:3-4)

The temptation to turn stone into bread taunted Jesus to miscalculate the need of humanity as well as his own ability. Beyond the physical requirements necessary for life, the deepest need of humanity requires more than all forms of bread. The gnawing need of lonely humanity is for God, for the Word of God, for the Word of grace who is God. Jesus did not misinterpret his need for food nor for the sustaining Presence of God in his life. Neither did he misconstrue the needs of the people to whom he would minister. Trust in God requires a self-reflective understanding of personal needs. Jesus was hungry, and he did need bread. The people were hungry, and the people needed to be fed. Yet the necessity for bread, while essential for human life, is not the ultimate need of humanity. We dare not ignore the need for bread, but the multiple requirements necessary to sustain physical life are not the deepest needs that we have. Although bread is requisite for life, meaningful life is rooted in the Word of God, the Word that affirms our daily dependence on numerous forms of personal subsistence. Beyond all forms of bread, however, Jesus recognized that the deepest need of humanity is for communion with God.

What did Jesus do? Did he weigh the importance of the Word of God over against the need for bread to determine his response? He faced the challenge of widespread hunger, sometimes because of a poor harvest but more often because of greed and exploitation: Everybody wanted his cut —from the Temple authorities to the tax-collectors to the free lancing protection of Roman soldiers. Did Jesus choose personal salvation over social transformation? Could he not remember the faces of emaciated children in the arms of their helpless parents in both town and country? Would he have forgotten the children turned beggars up and down the major streets of every city? Had he chosen the power of the Word over the need for bread?[3] For the hungry and thirsty, for the impoverished and oppressed, before they can hear the summons of God's Word, God must hear their cries of suffering. For children and others fated with malnutrition, the Word of God must take the form of bread before it can become the life-giving Word that nurtures the depths of their unique human need. Is there any authentic spirituality that does not acknowledge the necessity of daily bread?

Ever seductive, the temptation nonetheless is even more subtle: The temptation to turn stone into bread slyly suggested to Jesus to minimize the limits of his finitude and to misconstrue the uniqueness of his messianic calling. As the Son of God, he could have bread from stone, without work and without cost, without sweat and without labor. Yet Jesus chose reality as his life stance. He knew that bread comes from the difficult and time-consuming process of planting and harvesting, the careful and delicate task of grinding and baking. He understood the different and multiple stages in making bread. Jesus recognized that bread could not be had from stone. Examine the Gospels: Jesus performed many "mighty works," many miracles, but he never changed non-living objects into life-giving substance. He never transformed stuff devoid of life-giving potential into life-supporting resources. Contrary to the promise of such an apparently ordinary sin, Jesus affirmed the goodness

---

[3]C. S. Song, *Jesus, The Crucified People* (New York: Crossroad Publishing Co., 1990) 168, answered negatively: "For [Jesus] the word is not the Word of God until it makes the sick person well, comforts those in sorrow, empowers the weak and defends the victims of injustice."

of his finitude with its essential limitations in the context of living by the Word of God.

Stone cannot be made into bread: That is an illusion. Only those people well-fed with bread believe that bread can be had from stone, only they have the luxury of such an illusion. For the masses of the hungry throughout the world the shortage of bread is so real and life so hard that an illusion offers nothing, neither bread nor the Word of God—only stone.

Communion with God orients us to participation in the Kingdom of God, an orientation of life that distinguishes between needs and wants. We tend to confuse wants and needs, because our needs are so tightly wrapped in our wants that we require the help of Jesus to enable us to distinguish between them. The providence of God focuses on the needs of all instead of the wants of the few. Though he could not turn stone into bread, Jesus can turn the hardness of heart into the generosity of compassion. He works to awaken those with religious and political power to turn with open hearts to establish opportunity and eliminate oppression that deprive the hungry of bread, ultimately to provide education and employment to enable workers to earn enough to buy bread for themselves. Yet Jesus refused to be seduced into economic messianism, and he faced opposition, slander, and increasing danger every day of his life. The miracle of Incarnation cannot be exchanged for an economic illusion: The Word did become flesh, but stone cannot become bread.

Finitude and Vulnerability

Then the devil took him to the holy city and placed him on the pinnacle of the temple, saying to him, "If you are the Son of God, throw yourself down; for it is written,
'He will command his angels
concerning you,'
and 'On their hands they will
bear you up,
so that you will not dash your
foot against a stone.' "
Jesus said to him, "Again it is written, 'Do not put the Lord your God to the test.' " (Matt 4:5-7)

The scene shifts from the barren solitude of the wilderness to the hustle and bustle, buying and selling, bartering and gossiping of the market place of Jerusalem—the Holy City, none like it among all the cities of the world, the place of the Temple of God. Devout Jews of every nation planned to travel to Jerusalem on a sacred pilgrimage to worship in the Temple. Yet the city of David, the national and spiritual center of all the people of Israel, chaffed under the occupation of Roman troops maintaining colonial rule. If Jesus leaped from the pinnacle of the Temple and stepped uninjured on the court below, he would identify himself as the Messiah; and because he was invulnerable, the Romans would abandon the city of Jerusalem and all Judah without the loss of a single Jewish life!

This second temptation to leap from the top of the Temple and descend safely to the ground below enticed Jesus to ignore the creatureliness of his human existence. As the Son of God, he could drop from the top of the Temple straight down to the ground without being hurt. The Old Testament Scriptures confirm it! Yet Jesus recognized the poetic origin of the proof-text: "He will give his angels charge over you." And, "On their hands they will bear you up lest you strike your foot against a stone." This "promise" in Psalm 91 is a poetic song about the faithfulness of God rather than a prophecy about the coming Messiah. Jesus knew the difference between a song and prophecy, the futility of transposing poetry into prose. So he did not dare God to do it! Put plainly, Jesus knew that such action would be suicide. To leap from the heights of the Temple to the rock-hard surface below would be a foolish act that would break him to pieces. The uniqueness of his vocation did not mean the constant protection of God regardless of his decision-making and the circumstances of his life. Since humanness means the creatureliness of flesh and blood, Jesus refused to jump to his own self-destruction.

Follow the Son of God as he trudged to his cross. Blood spurt in hands and feet, flesh tore, excruciating pain wracked his body, when they nailed Jesus to the cross. *He did not have to give his body permission before he could bleed*! On the contrary with shouts and tears he died. Jesus would one day die in obedience to the will of God, a crucified Christ, but he refused to dare God to prevent his death on a short-cut to messianic grandeur. The promise of God does not mean unilateral intervention with a breath-taking miracle, but the assurance of God's

Presence among mostly anonymous people in their everyday struggle to be faithful to God.

Subtlety lingers in the temptation. The dream of almost every would-be prophet is to become a superstar, invincible and invulnerable, unequaled and unassailable. Conversely, Jesus accepted his personal vulnerability to suffering, pain, and death to be within the will and purpose of God. Risk and vulnerability belong to the gift of freedom. Beyond all freedom of choice, danger inheres in the freedom of human existence, which includes freedom *for* God. Choosing for God does not mean protection, because creaturely existence itself means vulnerability. The claim of freedom without such risk illegitimately tests the power and goodness of God. So Jesus accepted his personal vulnerability: He endured ridicule for his origins—a Nazarene, the carpenter's son! He knew hunger and thirst, frustration and fatigue, anger and disappointment, rejection and abandonment. He experienced vulnerability in relationships: vulnerable to the expectations of family and friends, vulnerable to criticism and attack from his adversaries, vulnerable to the misunderstanding and manipulation of the crowds, vulnerable to the betrayal and the desertion of the Twelve. Jesus was even vulnerable to God: In the agony of Gethsemane he prayed, "Not what I want but what you want," and he heard only the silence of God. Trust in God's providence does not mean protection from danger in the vicissitudes of human life. Trust in God's providence summons us to recognize the reality of risk and vulnerability and to deal with it responsibly, which is precisely what Jesus did: He refused to leap with blinded vulnerability from the parapet of the Temple of God.

Finitude and Power

> Again, the devil took him to a very high mountain and showed him all the kingdoms of the world and their splendor; and he said to him, "All these I will give you, if you will fall down and worship me." Then Jesus said to him, "Away with you, Satan! for it is written,
> 'Worship the Lord your God,
>   and serve only him.' " (Matt 4:8-10)

The third temptation enticed Jesus to see himself as the deliverer of his people and all the nations of the world suffering under the yoke of Roman rule. The situation was not unlike the suffering and the bondage of the people under Pharaoh in Egypt, and God called Moses to become the deliverer of his people. The appeal to become a military leader, "a prophet like Moses," could summon Jesus to action because of his great compassion for people living under the adversity of military subjugation. The subtlety of the temptation is captivating: Through his charismatic leadership and vision of the Kingdom of God, he could mobilize an army, drive the Romans from the land, and eliminate the injustice of oppression. The Tempter showed Jesus all the kingdoms of the world with their breath-taking glory, promising, "All these I will give you . . ." (Matt 4:8-9).

The offer of power and glory in a noble and righteous cause is almost irresistible. The people languished under Roman power. They lived in unnecessary hardship because of brutal colonial rule. They bartered their heritage and their faith to survive the blasphemous occupation of the Holy City. What a promise! All the nations of the world freed to the peace, justice, and well-being of the Kingdom of God. The temptation is less covert than those preceding it, because it offers a permanent solution to the problem of the cruelty of oppressive force as well as merciful relief for the impoverished and dispossessed masses. It provided an opportunity for all liberated people to embrace the Kingdom of God. The temptation to use all power at his disposal to implement the will and way of God had God's historic authorization in the liberating work of Moses for the sake of a captive people.

The offer came, then the condition: "If you will fall down and worship me." Jesus rejected this temptation with extraordinary though often unrecognized insight in this episode and throughout his ministry: The power of the Kingdom coming must be consistent with the power of *Abba* loving. Jesus knew that you belonged to the power that you served, that you could be blinded with the glory that all kinds of power offered you. The cost was incalculably higher than the gain: Conscience must be tailored to the garments of power, the special fit of the most regal position. Freedom must be defined in terms of security, the continuing preservation of the vision of glory. Truth must be shaped to support the system, the true believers its faithful facilitators and its worthy benefactors. Ethics must be construed to authorize control, doing things according to "the will and way of God."

Jesus rejected the inducement to political supremacy with sharp defiance. He had a political theology, but its seamless fabric was a peasant's robe, a vision more lofty than mountains high but viewed from the bottom side of history's power and glory. Despite the intoxicating thrill of almost incalculable power, Jesus knew that it could not be done. He could not and would not pick up the sword. Compassion for the oppressed did not justify hatred of the oppressor. Revolutions against Rome had failed in the past. Any future Judean revolution—all the more powerful it might be, all the more destruction it would contain—any such war of independence would be futile and likely devastating. Jesus knew that the David of Judah could not defeat the Goliath of Rome. He anticipated what a Jewish war with Rome would mean: the fall of Jerusalem and the destruction of the Temple. That is exactly what happened in 66–70 CE. Did Jesus resist the temptation to become the liberator of his people and the merciful Lord over the nations because he knew that he could not succeed? No. As Jesus' response clarified, the issue hinged on the worship and service of God.

What does it mean to worship and serve the *Abba* God? It includes the renunciation of dominating power and overwhelming force as the way to accomplish the will of God. Jesus' use of threat and violence against his [?] enemies would confuse the variegated "kingdoms" of this world with the Kingdom of God. Precisely because the means to accomplish the will of God required consistency with the identity of God, the restoration of freedom could not be achieved through violence in the name of the merciful God come near. Jesus demonstrated an unmatched compassion for the plight of his people, but he resolutely affirmed the intention of God to resolve human problems without resorting to force. "Worship the Lord your God, and serve only him." Jesus refused any attempt to impose the "rule" of God on people. He trusted God completely and continually, living out his life in the light of the identity of his *Abba* God.

The subtle continuation of this temptation in the life and work of Jesus requires a distinction between "the love of power" and "the power of love." When the disciples argued about who would be greatest among them, Jesus said to them:

> The kings of the Gentiles lord it over them; and those in authority over them are called benefactors. But not so with you; rather the greatest among you become like the youngest, and the leader like one who serves. For who is the greater, the one who is at the table, or the one who serves? Is it not the one at table? *But I am among you as one who serves.* (Luke 22:25-27)

Unlike the Gentile lords who could demand submission because of their ability to use force, Jesus revealed the power of God as the power to serve. Beyond the distinction between "the love of power" and "the power of love," the critical issue remains the definition of power. Only in the concreteness of Jesus' words and deeds, of the serving self-expenditure of love enacted in him, does "the power of love" attain concrete definition. Apart from the definition that Jesus provided through his teaching and ministry, "the power of love" remains only a slogan subject to a variety of opportunistic interpretations.

Trust in the providence of God is preeminently difficult at this point due to the tendency to confuse the power of God with the power of force, expansive power stretching to control. The vision of the Kingdom of God can be used to reinforce this misunderstanding, for it can suggest without qualification that the power of God is the power to rule and overrule. The temptation is so subtle: It seems to be simply the affirmation of the sovereignty of God! Yet the unspoken but definitive character of the third temptation is the use of force, of dominating power, of destructive violence in the name of God allegedly to establish the rule of God. These worldly tools are the weapons of the demonic, and whoever uses such weaponry, even mistakenly, falls immediately under its control. Jesus vigorously repudiated this temptation to distort his worshipful service to God and, ultimately, nothing less than the falsification of the very identity of his *Abba* God.

Conversely, Jesus revealed that the power of God is not expansive power but serving power, the power of self-expenditure. Expansive power is the power to possess, to manipulate, to overwhelm. Such dominating power is not really the power of God, because it is the power of coercion and conquest. The temptation of the pride of power may disguise itself with benevolence, but the exercise of expansive power eventually becomes visibly malevolent. For the sake of command and control, those who succumb to the pride of power stretch to dominate everything within their reach and to protect all they have and hold. Any confrontation with the representatives of expansive power is dangerous, because its proponents will respond with some form of force, and, if necessary, deadly violence.

When the pride of power embraces the pride of virtue and religion, it becomes all the more dangerous, because it claims the authorization of God for its right and destiny to dominate and control. The pride of power in religion structures everything on the basis of self-serving significance, and it neutralizes all expressions of potential opposition. Fearful of anything other than conformity, its proponents select, define, and propagate the values and truth that everyone must accept and support. Loyalty to the established leadership becomes the test of fidelity to the truth. The pride of religion fueled with the pride of power has an insatiable appetite for domination and control that excludes tolerance in the name of God. In this context—this ungodly context—the meaning of "the providence of God" receives its definition and form in service to the continued success and security of those in power. Precisely because providence means "the will of God," those at the peak of this high and lofty Tower of Babel, "making names for themselves," define the providence of God from the top down. Will Campbell has captured the mindset of the pride of power in religion with frightening accuracy: "God told me and I'm telling you and if you don't do like God told me to tell you to do I'll tell God and He'll tell me to get you and I will."[4]

Whether primarily political or essentially religious, the use of expansive power to gain and exercise control is ungodly, because its proponents skew the worship and service of God. The power of the *Abba* of Jesus is the power of self-expenditure, of self-giving. So Jesus exercised the power of God, serving power, a peculiar power never without ambiguity, because serving power does not dominate, threaten or impose violence. The power of this God is the scandal of the strength of weakness.

Trust in God

In the temptation narratives Jesus confronted the range of temptations that victimize humanity. With great insight and forthrightness he sought the will of God, and he did it. He demonstrated and defined "trust in God," which is seldom self-evident but frequently anxiety-producing. Such anxiety causes us to doubt God's providence, the affirmation and fulfillment of life within the boundaries of the goodness of creation. Although trust in God is a great adventure in simplicity and complexity,

---

[4]Will Campbell, "Personal Perspective 1," *Christianity and Crisis* 44 (1984): 463.

we fail to accept God's care and strive to establish our own means of security.

Trust in God means to accept our human limitations, our finitude, our creatureliness, and to acknowledge our multiple human needs. Our physical needs are necessary for survival and our community needs essential for personal well-being, survival needs and relational concerns that cannot be restricted to any single tribe of humanity. Spiritual resources do not substitute for everyday needs. On the contrary, authentic spirituality engenders a worldly compassion for those destitute and needy. Beyond our requisite needs, however, the depth of need for all humanity is for life-giving communion with God, our Creator, Provider, and Guide.

Trust in God means to accept our human limitations, our finitude, our creatureliness, and to acknowledge the inevitability of life's vulnerability. The difficulty is to discern the difference between appropriate vulnerability that God can address and bless and the illegitimate risk that dishonors the name of God. Of course, whether one is vulnerable or not in a specific situation sometimes lies beyond the choice of the faithful son and daughter of God. The problem becomes how to relate to this imposing, unwanted given wherein we are vulnerable, which inescapably requires some kind of response.

Trust in God means to accept our human limitations, our finitude, our creatureliness, and to acknowledge the forces that besiege us with unyielding and increasing pressure in the crossroads of life. Beyond the consistency of ends and means, beyond the logic of priorities and their actualization, we wrestle with forces that seemingly dictate only one possible response to alleviate the problems and pain of life, a response contrary to the appropriate character of genuine service to God for the benefit of humanity. So we struggle resolutely for a worshipful posture with its accompanying energy to enable us to maintain our balance that depends unequivocally on the Presence of God.

All of these temptations confronted Jesus with his limitations, his finitude, his creatureliness, and they offered quite unintentionally the dramatic opportunity in his freedom for God to be completely and genuinely human. Jesus overcame temptation with "fundamental trust" in the midst of uncertain reality, always walking with his face in the wind.

The Mystery of Evil

Evil is a mystery. Evil is not a problem that can be solved but a mystery that transcends human understanding. We can identify three forms of evil, forms that the temptations of Jesus approximate: sin, chaos, and the demonic. The lines between them are blurred, a blurred overlapping that defies anything more than a certain conceptual description: In any case the description of the mystery of evil is not its explanation.

Sin

Sin is a uniquely human predicament. We all sin, and therefore we are all sinners. Perhaps the best way to characterize human sin is to locate it in our common human experience, though sin itself remains an intruder and distortion that does not belong to the definition of humanness, whether individual or corporate. Each person through growth and corresponding self-awareness attains a point and reaches a stage where the polarity of freedom and finitude occasions anxiety, an insecurity that lacks the stability of a centered existence. With the heightening tension between freedom and finitude, the insecurity of an unanchored existence, anxiety intensifies. What does a person do? How does the person respond? Attempting to transcend the conflict between freedom and finitude, unable to cope with its attending anxiety, the self turns in to itself to gain stability within the self and falls into self-centeredness, the sin of egocentricity. Whenever we turn inward in search of self-security, whether we are aware of it or not, we turn away from the One who is the origin of the self and the source of security for the self, the One transcending the self inside out and to Whom the self should respond in trust, namely, God. The centered self is lost in a conceptual idealism never achieved, and self-centeredness is found in the existential plight of personal estrangement and self-contradiction. Sin is the fate of everyone of us. Though sin is not necessary, it is inevitable, but each one of us remains responsible.[5]

---

[5]Reinhold Niebuhr, *The Nature and Destiny of Man*, 2 vols. (New York: Charles Scribner's Sons, 1941) 1:178-86, 186-203, 241-44, 251-60. The advantage of the interpretation of sin in existential categories is its emphasis on the individual self in relationship to God. As critics have noted, this pattern of interpretation is much too individualistic and too directly focused on God. Sin actually occurs in the relational

The first temptation of Jesus to turn stone into bread in order to satisfy his immediate hunger addressed his vocation as well as his need, and it models the temptation of individual sin. Jesus confronted the universal human requirements for life (ever increasing in number and price), a temptation focused one on one, but he did not succumb to it.

Chaos

Chaos is an element in creation that threatens human life in the world. What distinguishes chaos from sin on the one side and the demonic on the other? God creates order out of chaos, which locates chaos always ever present on the boundaries of creation. The randomness of chaos within creation would include all the destructive forces that we call natural evil. We humans are always vulnerable to the unexpected and explosive violence of chaos in the form of natural disaster. Indeed, the dysteleological elements in creation precede human existence, but the destructive forces in creation become natural evil in the context of human life in the world. So we name these random elements that destroy human life and habitation "natural disasters": earthquakes, tornados, hurricanes, blizzards, drought, floods, forest fires, volcanic eruptions, mountain slides.

Human sickness and disease are another form of chaos that constantly afflict and destroy human life: polio, small pox, typhoid fever, cholera, spinal meningitis, lupus, leprosy, blindness, deafness, muteness, congenital heart disease, deformity, retardation. Chaos destructive of human life occurs in all kinds of illness—some typical, others rare; some manageable, others terminal. Illness can be as random and unpredictable as a tornado or hurricane, and just as deadly.

Since chaos exists, at least in part, on the frontiers of creation, when we violate these "natural boundaries" that impinge on our finitude, various degrees of self-destruction occur. The abuse of the limitation of our human creatureliness unleashes the ruinous force of chaos against us. Certainly the chaos of a natural disaster or some deadly plague can

patterns of life through socialization with other persons. See Marjorie Hewitt Suchocki, *The Fall to Violence: Original Sin in Relational Theology* (New York: Continuum, 1994), for a very different perspective that serves at least as a corrective to an existentialist concentration of sin and fallenness.

suddenly explode with devastating consequences for an individual and community without their culpability, but the violation of the limits of healthy human existence unleashes chaotic disintegration, short-term and long-term alike. The classic case of the violation of the boundaries of creation in willful self-destruction is suicide. Though less obvious but more dangerous, the ecological crisis confronts us with another expression of willful and reckless self-destruction. Through various forms of individual and corporate sin, we risk the ruination and disintegration of all life on this Earth—the devolution of planetary life *from order into chaos!* As the crisis continues and intensifies through human apathy, carelessness, and greed, the blatant assault on the Earth's ecological systems constitutes a terrifying form of planetary suicide, a generational legacy of deadly chaos to our children and grandchildren. Thus chaos has at least three reference points: natural disasters of various kinds, human illness and birth-bound brokenness, and the individual and corporate violation of the boundaries of authentic human existence.

The second temptation of Jesus to leap from the top of the Temple enticed him to see himself as "the exception" for whom the obvious danger of such behavior did not apply: He could violate the force of gravity as it applies to heights from which humans can leap to a hard surface below without self-destruction. Jesus knew himself to be an exception in his vocation under God but not an exemption from the vulnerability of human creatureliness. Beyond the chaos of natural disaster in the randomness of creation and of innumerable illnesses that threaten human life in the world, Jesus realized that the embrace of chaos in violation of the legitimate boundaries of human existence within the good structures of creation would be foolhardy and mean certain death.[6]

---

[6]The interpretation of the second temptation in Matt 4:5-7 (the third temptation in Luke 4:9-12) in terms of chaos is my own proposal. The temptation addressed Jesus at two levels, his messianic vocation and his human creatureliness. That succumbing to this temptation would mean suicide presupposes the genuineness of his humanness, which affirms a humanity limited like all others to the givens of creaturely existence.

Cf. Karl Barth, *CD*, IV/1: 259-64. Barth prefers Luke's ordering of the temptations, which makes the third and climactic temptation to leap from the top of the temple "the most astonishing of all" (262). This temptation "consists in the demand to commit an act of supreme, unconditional, blind, absolute, total confidence in God—as was obviously supremely fitting for the Son of God" (263). He argues that this temptation is "something worse and just as demonic" as the temptation to totalitarian dominion over all the world

The Demonic

The demonic is the collusion of chaos and sin. Of the three modes of evil, the demonic is most elusive and deceptive. So how do you recognize it? The destructiveness of the demonic is so overwhelming that the category of chaos cannot contain it. Often larger than chaos, the demonic is more ominous and devastating than a tornado or hurricane, a plague or earthquake. Human sin and human responsibility are practically indefinable in the darkness of the demonic. The sin and responsibility of humanity can hardly begin to be stretched across it, and chaos cannot contain its seemingly bottomless depths. It usually dwarfs human sin and natural disaster. Unlike the randomness of chaos, moreover, the demonic can be selective and calculating. While chaos simply erupts and destroys where it happens, the demonic can target its victims. It can twist chaos into a perversity beyond the chaotic and wrest chaos inside the borders of the demonic domain. The demonic is always a killer, almost always a mass murderer of some kind or the other. Its names are legion: Auschwitz, Nagasaki, the Gulag, Khmer Rouge, Jim Crow, *apartheid*.

Though not without appropriate criticism, Karl Barth provides the most sober and incisive analysis of the demonic in modern theology, what he called *das Nichtige*, Nothingness.[7] Barth does not distinguish chaos

---

(263), the climactic temptation in Matthew. Though I disagree with Barth's interpretation of the temptation to leap from the top of the Temple, he can make a case for a christological understanding of it. However, the temptation to totalitarian dominion is more disastrous for the people of the world under the weight of subjugation and oppression. Barth's Christocentrism distorts his judgment here, and what "Christocentrism" actually means.

[7]Karl Barth, *CD*, III/3: 289-368. I do not claim that Barth's interpretation of the origin and destruction of Nothingness is valid, only the description of the power of Nothingness in conjunction with the ongoing movement of human history. Barth's identification of Nothingness with chaos issues in part from his understanding of Genesis 1:2, one of the most difficult and disputed aspects of Barth's theology (*CD*, III/1: 101-110). Since "the world was fashioned and ordered by God in time," everything else "belongs only to the nonrecurring past of commencing time," i.e., chaos (101-102). "That which is ungodly and anti-godly has been rejected and has disappeared, and therefore only as a frontier of that which is and will be according to God's decision and actions" (102). "In v. 2 there is absolutely nothing as God willed and created and ordained it according to v. 1 and the continuation. There is only 'chaos' " (104).

from the demonic, but the difference between the second temptation to leap from the top of the Temple and the third temptation to pursue domination through conquest accounts for the distinction that I am compelled to draw. Whenever we violate the creaturely boundaries of human existence, whatever the measure of intentionality, we unleash the destructive violence of chaos into human life. However, human action differs sharply in relation to chaos on the one side and Nothingness on the other. Whether intentional or suspected, through deception or clarity, with deliberation or passivity, human activity in relation to Nothingness is less violation and more cooperation. Nothingness, I would argue, always entails some measure of human concurrence, human complicity, human acquiescence in the actualization and ascendency of demonic evil. Beyond the destruction of chaos through the violation of the boundaries of human finitude, Nothingness lures us in its drive to dominate, victimize, oppress, and destroy authentic human existence. Unlike chaos, Nothingness presupposes the pervasive reality of human sin, indeed, thrives on it. Therein, Nothingness strives to become systemic, which makes it less obvious but more destructive.

Genesis 1:2 portrays a world that was "negated, rejected, and left behind in [God's] actual creation, i.e., in the utterance of His Word" (p. 108). This sphere is real in its absurd way, but a sphere that has no existence, essence, or goodness. "This ugly realm did exist." From the perspective of v. 1 "it is the epitome of that which *was*. The state of chaos portrayed in v. 2 is . . . the past of the real cosmos created by the Word of God" (108). Originally and definitively superseded and obsoleted, Barth says, "It is only behind God's back that the sphere of chaos can assume this distinctive and self-contradictory character of reality" (108). Yet the creature can in "inconceivable rebellion" look past the Word of God back to the past, "to this state of chaos; loving what God hated in His love as the Creator, and thus drawing upon itself the wrath instead of the love of God the Creator. The primeval waters and darkness, the *tohu wa-bohu*, can become to it an acute and enticing danger" (108-109).

The cosmos can become to the creature "a pathless, barren, monstrous and evil cosmos," a risk God has taken in the creation of a freedom distinct from the freedom of God. "It is not by the use but the misuse of this freedom that man can look back and return to that past and conjure up the shadow of Gen 1:2, thus enabling that past to defy its own nature and to become present and future. . . . That chaos can also become present and future cannot alter the fact that it is essentially the past, the possibility negated and rejected by God" (109).

Barth locates chaos and Nothingness in Gen 1:2, and he does not distinguish between them. Therefore, Barth obscures the difference in human responsibility for chaos and Nothingness as well as the kind of human response one makes to each.

What is Nothingness? It is not simply nonbeing, essential in the act of creation. The shadowside of creation is the legitimate "No" that corresponds to God's creative "Yes." Nothingness is the constant resistance and hostile opposition to God's intention and provision for creation. It is the vicious, malevolent, alien, murderous adversary of God. Utterly inimical to God and creation, Nothingness must not be confused with the shadowside of creation.[8] The shadowside includes progress and limitation, growth and decay, clarity and obscurity, beauty and ashes, value and worthlessness, beginning and end, success and failure, laughter and tears, youth and age, gain and loss, birth and death. The shadowside of creation corresponds to *meonic* nonbeing that the creation of finite being inevitably involves. However, *oukonic* nonbeing is innately, intrinsically, inimically hostile to God and God's creation. Unlike *meonic* nonbeing, *oukonic* nonbeing lacks any positive dimension: It is purely negative, absolute nonbeing, radical evil. *Oukonic* nonbeing is Nothingness.

Conversely, the shadowside belongs to the goodness of creation, and the providence of God does not exclude but includes the harmony of life's contrasts. Yet the shadowside of creation remains most vulnerable to the threat of Nothingness. Sin, the concrete form of Nothingness in human life, turns the shadowside of creaturely existence into terrifying experiences of Nothingness, and we wrongly judge the distorted experiences of the shadowside to be evil in and of themselves. Thus Nothingness nightmares death into Death. Lurking behind and within the shadowside, Nothingness twists the negative dimension of the goodness of creation and human existence into shocking instances of demonic evil. In our sin, however, sometimes we sense something more, much more— more frightening, more savage, more deadly, more maddening than what we ever thought to be conceivable. In the light of Jesus Christ we recognize this vast, immense, alien *more* to be the undermining and overwhelming provocateur of Nothingness that dominates us all from time to time, its victims and its servants.

Yet Nothingness is first and foremost the adversary of God, assaulting God through humanity. In our sin we reject the goodness of God in creation and refuse gratitude to God for the gift of life. Accordingly,

---

[8]Karl Barth, *CD* III/3: 296-97. The shadowside of creation is an expression of the goodness of creation in its developmental stages and contrasting elements. However, Barth does not use the category of *meonic* nonbeing to describe it.

Nothingness turns our inevitable death into an intolerable and unbearable, suffering-laden and life-destroying fate that disclaims and defames the goodness of God. Through the negation of the creature, moreover, Nothingness seemingly negates the goodness of creation and thereby the Creator God.

The origin of Nothingness is significant, but it is not so significant as its destruction. God knows Nothingness and its terror over humanity, and Barth is eloquent in his characterization of God's advocacy of humanity against the assault of Nothingness:

> [God] would rather be unblest with His creature than be the blessed God of an unblest creature. He would rather let Himself be injured and humiliated in making the assault and repulse of Nothingness His own concern than leave His creature alone in this affliction. . . . He intervenes in the struggle between Nothingness and the creature as if He were not God but Himself a weak and threatened and vulnerable creature. "As if"—but . . . in Jesus Christ, He actually becomes a creature, and thus makes the cause of the creature His own in the most concrete reality and not just in appearance, really taking its place. This is how God Himself comes on the scene.[9]

The God of grace is the primary victim and the relentless enemy of Nothingness. While Nothingness has power over humanity, Nothingness cannot withstand the God who became a human creature like us and confronted it. Nothingness could not destroy this victim. The God of grace became one with us, a threatened, ruined, and lost creature to judge and destroy Nothingness.

At this point Barth poses a dialectical perspective on the subjugation of Nothingness. In this historical and eschatological dialectic the final word must be the first word: Nothingness can be interpreted only in retrospect of its judgment and destruction already accomplished through Jesus Christ and only in prospect of the revelation of its refutation and termination in the future of Jesus Christ. In utter seriousness the Christian must affirm: "If Jesus is Victor, the last word must always be secretly the first, namely, that Nothingness has no perpetuity."[10] In the meantime

---

[9]Ibid., 358.

[10]Ibid., 364. Barth said: "Nothingness is the past, the ancient menace, danger and destruction, the ancient non-being which obscured and defaced the divine creation of God

Nothingness can retain "its semblance of validity only under the decree of God," only through the permission of God. Although Nothingness has been judged and destroyed through Jesus Christ, God permits Nothingness to retain its semblance of power and devastation, its semblance of significance, but Nothingness exists and functions under God's control. The triumph of God over the dominion of Nothingness has already happened, but it is not yet recognizable. Thus God permits us to be prey to Nothingness until the hour strikes that will reveal the destruction of Nothingness in the victory of Jesus Christ. Barth concludes:

> In this already innocuous form, as this echo and shadow, it is an instrument of His will and action. He thinks it good that we should exist "as if" He had not already mastered it for us—and at this point we may rightly say "as if."[11]

Eloquence and insight notwithstanding, Barth understates the power of Nothingness and overstates God's subjugation of Nothingness. Does God think that it is *good* for us to live "as if" God had not already mastered Nothingness for us? Of course, the eschatological perspective is crucial. Nothingness has been judged in the death of the crucified Christ, and death in Nothingness has been overcome. Not even death can separate us from the God who has endured death for us![12] *Nevertheless—*

---

but *which is consigned to the past in Jesus Christ,* in whose death it has received its deserts, being destroyed with this consummation of the positive will of God which is as such the end of His non-willing. *Because Jesus is Victor, Nothingness is routed and extirpated.* . . . It is no longer to be feared. It can no longer 'nihilate.' But obviously we may make these undoubtedly audacious statements only on the ground of one single presupposition. . . . a backward look to the resurrection of Jesus Christ and a forward look to His coming in glory, i.e., the look of Christian faith as rooted in and constantly nourished by the Word of God" (363, italics added).

[11]Barth summarizes his perspective: "Nothingness has its reality and character, and plays its past, present and possibly future role, as the adversary whom God has regarded, attacked and routed as His own enemy" (366). " . . . no true or ultimate power and significance but only a dangerous semblance of them are to be attributed to the existence, menace, corruption, disturbance and destructiveness of Nothingness as these may still be seen. . . . only an echo, a shadow, of what it was but is no longer" (367). "The defeated, captured and mastered enemy of God has as such become His servant," though a strange servant (367-68).

[12]Jürgen Moltmann, *The Trinity and the Kingdom* (New York: Harper & Row,

Nothingness ranges as wide and as deep through the structures of creation and the movement of history as it did before the coming of Christ. Nothingness has not been destroyed and relegated to the past. Does God now control Nothingness? In the exploding population of today's world, the nihilating force of Nothingness has not diminished but radically increased with the scientific advances of modern technology. The power of the demonic and the deceit that claims to control it constitutes a staggering threat heretofore unknown in the history of humanity. Has God already reduced Nothingness to only an echo or shadow of what it was but is no longer? Despite the depth and power of his analysis, Barth's perspective is skewed: That *"Nothingness has no perpetuity"* is an affirmation that lingers on the horizon of the future, a future that has not yet become present.

The Japanese businessman concluded his presentation with a stunning statement about America and Japan. He stated the obvious: The United States had dropped not one but two atomic bombs on Japan to end World War II, the first on Hiroshima and the second on Nagasaki. The bombing of Nagasaki, hardly a military target, he opined, was American revenge for the surprise Japanese attack on Pearl Harbor at the beginning of the War. Like many of today's Japanese leaders, did he intend to recast the role of Japan in World War II from villain to victim?

The end of World War II in the Pacific is a story of sudden tragedy if not senseless savagery. On 6 August 1945, at 8:15 A.M., a high-flying American B-29 dropped the first atomic bomb on Hiroshima, Japan, which destroyed about four-and-one-half square miles of the city. More than 122,000 died and at least 30,000 were severely injured. The "Little Boy" atomic bomb decimated Hiroshima, using uranium as its fissionable material. On 9 August 1945, another B-29 left the Tinian air base for

---

Publishers, 1981) 34, 228, n. 40; and Jürgen Moltmann, *God in Creation: A New Theology of Creation and the Spirit of God* (New York: Harper & Row, Publishers, 1985) 87-88, 334-35. n. 29. In both these books Moltmann refers to and appropriates Barth's understanding of Nothingness, but not uncritically. Likewise, Eberhard Jüngel, *God as the Mystery of the World* (Grand Rapids: Eerdman's Publishing Co., 1983) 215-25. Jüngel interprets the cross of Christ as the place where God has overcome Nothingness. However, neither Moltmann nor Jüngel explores the category and power of Nothingness like Barth, but both understand the cross to be the event wherein God overcomes Nothingness and gives Nothingness or death in Nothingness a place in the life of God.

Kokura, Japan, its first target. Already an arsenal in 1933, the city had attained a strategic position as an army base, but heavy cloud cover turned the plane from Kokura to Nagasaki, a less significant target. The second atomic bomb fell on Nagasaki at 11:02 A.M.—three days, two hours, 47 minutes after the bombing of Hiroshima. The "Fat Man" atomic bomb, an improved design using plutonium as its fissionable material, destroyed about one-and-one-half square miles of the city, and at least 73,000 persons died and an equal number of people were severely injured.[13]

The use of the atomic bomb on Japan had a military rationale: A massive strike of unparalleled proportion could force a Japanese surrender without bloody battles from island to island in order to force a reluctant and costly Japanese retreat and eventual surrender, a strategy that would save the lives of thousands of American and Japanese soldiers. The argument applies to Hiroshima, but Nagasaki . . . ? Two different kinds of atomic bombs, the bombing of a less important second target, only a three-day interval in between—was the bombing of Nagasaki necessary to end the War with Japan, or was it in part an act of revenge for the surprise Japanese bombing of Pearl Harbor?

On the evening of 7 December 1941, only hours after the Japanese had destroyed the American naval fleet anchored in Pearl Harbor, the arrest of Japanese Americans connected to the government of Japan had

---

[13]*Hiroshima and Nagasaki: The Physical, Medical and Social Effects of the Atomic Bombings*, ed. The Committee for the Compilation of Materials on Damage Caused by the Atomic Bombs in Hiroshima and Nagasaki, trans. Eisei Ishikawa and David L. Swain (New York: Basic Books, 1981; Japanese, 1979) 21-29, 30-31, 113-15. The statistics on Hiroshima's dead and injured are based on the investigation of causalities until 10 August 1946, and the statistics on Nagasaki until 31 December 1945. This massive document specifies that the death toll at "the end of 1945 totaled 140,000 (+10,000) in Hiroshima and 70,000 (+10,000) in Nagasaki" (113). The massive destruction of these bombings and the long-term consequences for the physical health and psychological well-being of the "survivors" is overwhelming and extensively documented in this volume. Photographs are vivid. Cf. *Hiroshima and Nagasaki: A Photographic Record of an Historical Event*, sponsored by The United Nations Staff Recreation Council, Photo Exhibit in the UN, 1978. The pictures were presented by the cities of Hiroshima and Nagasaki "33 years after the atomic bomb disaster in these two cities." For a moving account from a Japanese Christian physician who survived the bombing of Nagasaki, see Takashi Nagai, *The Bells of Nagasaki*, trans. William Johnston (Tokyo: Kodansha International, 1984: Japanese, 1949).

already begun. The hysteria in the United States about "a fifth column" proved especially strong on the West Coast, where the rhetoric of otherwise responsible commentators and editorial writers made all Japanese Americans "the enemy." After its creation on 18 March 1942, the War Relocation Authority uprooted 120,000 Japanese Americans, deprived them of most of their personal possessions, and imprisoned them for the better part of three years.[14] The evacuees had about six days to dispose of their property and to bring only what they could carry to control centers, where each family registered and received a number. "Henry went to the Control Station to register the family," remembered Monica Sone. "He came home with twenty tags, all numbered '10710,' tags to be attached to each piece of baggage, and one to hang from our lapels. From then on, we were known as Family #10710."[15]

The Japanese Americans were sent to ten different relocation sites called "evacuation camps" but actually more like humane concentration camps, which were "deliberately placed in God-forsaken spots in alien climes where no one had lived before and no one has lived since." These places of confinement were ringed with barbed wire, spot lights, and guard towers manned with armed soldiers. Families were housed together in barracks divided into small rooms, none with running water. While the entire camp lined up three times a day for "communal feeding in mess halls," families seldom ate together, which had a destructive impact on the relationship of parents with their children. By the War's end, the population of the camps had declined to about 44,000 inmates. Although more than two-thirds of these Japanese Americans eventually returned to the Pacific West Coast after the War, many thousands had lost their shops, homes, and farms. For years historians have cited $400 million as an estimate of the property loss of Japanese Americans, but the figure is a postwar invention: The actual loss was many more hundreds of millions of dollars.[16]

---

[14]Roger Daniels, *Asian Americans: Chinese and Japanese in the United States Since 1850* (Seattle: University of Washington Press, 1988) 231, but in the context of 199-282.

[15]Ronald Takaki, *Strangers from a Different Shore: A History of Asian Americans* (New York: Penguin Books, 1989) 393-94, 399-403.

[16]Daniels, *Asian Americans*, 225-28, 231, on the camps; and 290-91, esp. n. 8, on the estimate of property loss.

The incarceration and robbery of the Japanese Americans in less than six months after the aerial assault on Pearl Harbor unquestionably denotes the rage and the fear of Americans against all Japanese, including Japanese Americans. The correlation of these two events is not speculative but self-evident, and it constitutes a disgraceful stain on American history.[17] Whether or not the bombing of Nagasaki qualifies as revenge for Pearl Harbor is an entirely different question, however, which cannot be answered on the basis of the government's fear of the collaboration of Japanese Americans with the Empire of Japan.[18]

---

[17]The impact of World War II on Japanese Americans marked a turning point in their history. Japanese America was simply destroyed, though some of the pieces would be put together again. Relocation remains *the* crucial event in Japanese American history. The phrases—"before the war" and "after the camp"—punctuate the life story of almost every mainland Japanese American family. "On the basis of one executive order a whole community, the West Coast Japanese, was ordered from its homes and confined without a trace of due process . . . judged guilty, deprived of much of their real property, and incarcerated, some for more than three years, merely by reason of their ancestry" as Japanese American (Daniels, *Asian Americans*, 228).

When the Carter administration appointed a Commission on the Wartime Relocation and Internment of Civilians conducted hearings across the country in 1981, some of the bitterness of Japanese Americans during the war years resurfaced. "Long pent-up tears were shed in public and formerly whispered accusations were spoken aloud. . . . [T]he relocation of Japanese Americans continues to affect lives that did not exist when it occurred" (Ibid., 282).

[18]Actually 33,000 Japanese Americans served in the U.S. Armed Forces during the war in Europe and the Pacific, and they distinguished themselves with great courage, heroism, and causalities. See Takaki, *Strangers From a Different Shore*, 399-403: The 100th Battalion of 1,500 Hawaiian Japanese Americans fought in northern Africa and then in Italy, 300 killed and 650 wounded. They were called "the Purple Heart Battalion." The 100th was merged with the 442nd Regimental Combat Team composed of Japanese American soldiers from Hawaii and the internment camps on the mainland. In heavy fighting in Italy and France they suffered 9,486 causalities, 600 killed. They earned 18,143 individual decorations—Distinguished Service Crosses, Silver Stars, Bronze Stars, and more than 3,600 Purple Hearts. The 442nd was probably the most decorated unit in United States military history" (402).

In April 1945 Captain Daniel Inouye lost an arm in an assault on German troops on Mount Nebione in northern Italy, which ended the war for him, and two weeks later the war in Europe ended for everyone. On his way home to Hawaii in 1945, Captain Inouye tried to get a haircut in San Francisco. "Entering the barber shop with his empty right sleeve pinned to his army jacket covered with ribbons and medals for his military heroism, Captain Inouye was told: 'We don't serve Japs here' " (403). Japanese

Since Japan had never experienced defeat in all its recorded history, the difficulty of the Japanese government to terminate military action through surrender constitutes a crucial component in the interpretation of events concluding World War II.[19] The bombing of Hiroshima on August 6 had shaken the Supreme Council for the Direction of the War, but it did not break the bitter stalemate between the military faction and the peace group within the small Supreme Council or the larger Japanese Cabinet. Prime Minister Suzuki and Foreign Minister Togo favored accepting the Allied terms of the Potsdam Proclamation, but War Minister Anami and key military leaders opposed it. When the Cabinet began its meeting on August 9 the announcement of the fate of Nagasaki did not crack the deadlock. Late that night, Emperor Hirohito convened the full Cabinet for an unexpected meeting in a large bomb shelter. He listened patiently to their debate, but at 2:00 A.M. the Emperor shocked the Cabinet with his advocacy of the acceptance of the Allied terms of surrender. Before dawn on August 10 each Cabinet member had signed a statement ratifying the Potsdam Proclamation on the condition that it would not compromise "the supreme power of the Emperor."

The Allies relayed their response to Japan on August 12 but the Cabinet slid quickly into the same impasse of three days earlier. Meanwhile, a group of younger officers planned a *coup d'etat* to continue the War, but their desperate plot failed. On August 14 Hirohito convened the Cabinet again and asked for their agreement with his conclusion not to continue the War but to accept the terms of surrender in the Allied proposal. At noon on August 15 Emperor Hirohito broadcast on radio nationwide the Imperial Rescript of Japan's unconditional surrender, and he referred directly to the bombing of Hiroshima and Nagasaki:

> The enemy has begun to employ a new and most cruel bomb. Should we continue to fight, it would not only result in an ultimate collapse and obliteration of the Japanese nation, but also it would lead to the total extinction of human civilization. This is the reason why We have

---

Americans helped to win the war, but they lost the war of prejudice at home, especially on the West Coast.

    [19]See Keith Wheeler, *The Fall of Japan* (Chicago: Time-Life Books Inc., 1983) 88-172, esp. 152-66.

ordered the acceptance of the provisions of the Joint Declaration of the Powers.[20]

Under the massive destruction of mushroom clouds over two former Japanese cities, Emperor Hirohito acted resolutely to end the War. Did the Emperor's decision to surrender validate the American military strategy to use two atomic bombs in rapid succession to ensure Japan's capitulation?

World War II in its entirety, the events at its beginning as well as those at its ending, confront us with the devastating power of Nothingness in less than a decade of global history. The inability of the collective leadership of Japan to accept defeat after the bombing of Hiroshima complicates any analysis of hidden motives in the strategy of the American high command to the end the War. Regardless of the military rationale for dropping atomic bombs on Hiroshima and Nagasaki—action several military and civilian leaders considered unnecessary—many Americans undoubtedly did feel a measure of vengeful satisfaction in the nuclear bombing of Japan as retaliation for the Japanese surprise attack at Pearl Harbor on 7 December 1941. However, the correlation of the military strategy to drop a second atomic bomb on Nagasaki with a sense of revenge for the Japanese aerial bombardment of the Pacific Fleet at Pearl Harbor remains a subjective impression rather than an objective conclusion. If an element of revenge informed the American decision to use the atomic bomb against Japan, it included *both* Hiroshima and Nagasaki.

The continuation of the War in the Pacific would have meant death for thousands of American troops plus even more Japanese soldiers and civilians. The bloody battle for the island of Iwo Jima indicated how many hundreds of thousands would die in an American invasion of Japan. Thus the charge of revenge loses much of its force in the light of the military strategy to strike Japan quickly with a second atomic bomb before the Japanese had time to recover their balance from the first, forcing an immediate surrender. The strategy did end World War II, but the question of revenge does not change the devastation and death in the wasteland of onetime Hiroshima and Nagaski.

The Pacific theater of the World at War shifts to another scene in Southeast Asia twenty-five years later, when the United States did

---

[20]Ibid., 165-66.

confront the question of motive contained in its military strategy. Americans learned a painful lesson in the infamous War in Viet Nam. The best of motives can perish in the self-destructive quicksand of incalculable violence. The aerial bombardment of South Viet Nam, North Viet Nam, and, yes, Cambodia lies unprecedented in the history of war: The United States dropped more bombs in the Viet Nam War than all the bombs exploded in the entirety of World War II: five tons of bombs per Viet Cong soldier. The Vietnamese and Cambodian dead numbered nearly a million. The specter of defeat blinded a government of the people to the betrayal of its own national ideals, and the patriotic pledge of "Peace with Honor" rushed the senseless sacrifice of its available young men to the salvaging of national pride. Theologically stated: Nothingness thrives in the deception and conflicts of the war-worn corridors in the history of power and glory. War combines sin, chaos, and Nothingness into a craving for bloody violence that defies the calculation of the wounded and the dead.

Though Nothingness may already be judged in Jesus Christ, nothing has apparently changed, not yet.

The Power of God

The fact that God creates out of nothing and brings order out of chaos should not obscure the reality of Nothingness and its overwhelming threat to every aspect of creation. Yet the enigma remains: How can Nothingness exist? Like chaos, Nothingness has always existed on the boundaries of creation and alongside everyone of us in our creaturely existence: Nothingness lurks behind and sometimes within chaos, but the threat of Nothingness usually dwarfs the danger of chaos. Whenever we break the sacred boundaries of creatureliness, refusing to accept our dependency, our finitude, our vulnerability, whenever we exploit, manipulate, and use other people to their detriment, if not their death, or whenever we only participate in a system that does so, we unleash the overwhelming destructiveness of chaos and of Nothingness to invade and plunder our lives. The essence and center of Nothingness is death: Death into Nothingness—absolute, unequivocable, final.

Overcoming Evil

Does the meaninglessness of the void of chaos or the destructiveness of the assault of Nothingness sometimes overshadow goodness of life and the creativity of God? Paul teaches in Romans 8:28 that "God works *in* everything for good" with those who love God and are called according to God's purposes. Whenever such meaninglessness and destruction does occur, God can bring some order out of chaos, some good out of even demonic evil. James H. Evans, Jr., says:

> Providence refers not only to God's *acts* in history but more accurately to God's work in history. . . . God, in African-American religious experience, *works* in history. To work is to accomplish something in spite of resistance.[21]

Yet God's positive work in the midst of chaos and God's personal action against Nothingness does not imply that a God-given pattern of mystery and meaning lay behind a catastrophic disaster or indescribable instance of demonic destruction from the outset, a charade that reduces the destructiveness of chaos and the desolation of Nothingness into some sort of disguised blessing of God. Darkness remains darkness, pain remains pain, death remains death. All the pious platitudes and sanctimonious superstition of the smiling merchants of faith cannot change the truth of it. The mystery of evil does not exist to highlight the mystery of God. Rather, the mystery of evil stands overagainst and mocks the mystery of God. Though evil may sometimes be turned to help advance the work of God, contrary to its intention, the mystery of evil is not the work of God whatsoever—not the discipline of God, not the strange work of God, not the left hand of God. No, God does not particularize evil to enable us to praise God in the painful experience of demonic power. On the contrary, the mystery of evil is most visible in those circumstances where God seemingly does little or nothing to protect the goodness of creation against the awesome threat of Nothingness that assaults all aspects of creaturely existence.

---

[21]James H. Evans, Jr., *We Have Been Believers: An African-American Systematic Theology* (Minneapolis: Fortress Press, 1992) 75.

In every situation of dramatic human need with its historic as well as its transcendent limits and possibilities, does God always do the most and best God can do? An earlier affirmation can become an urgent question, and the joyful praise of God can turn into an angry protest against God. The laments and complaints hurled at God in the anguish and travail of the Psalms remain an essential part of the prayerbook of the church. Has God created a world within which the randomness of chaos proves far more destructive and uncontrollable, ghastly more deadly and unpredictable than the declaration of the goodness of creation would seem to allow? Do the horrors of Nothingness in its sometime insidious cannibalism and oftentime indescribable rampages negate all semblance of justice that otherwise ought to characterize a world wherein the God of love creatively and constantly works? Has God conceded far too much of God's power to this relatively[!] independent world—an arena for an inhumane humanity fixated on variations of gladiatorial combat, a stage for an incalculable multiplicity of the whirlwinds of chaos, and a carnival of irresistible lures of evil so monstrous that only Nothingness fits its facelessness? Faith's confession that God always does the most that God can do dies the death of soundless pity lightyears beyond the ridicule and scorn that drapes all surges of lament and complaint with the unseen dust of memory long forgotten. The simpliest question is the most difficult: Where is God? This question compels us to return to the story of Jesus.

Beginning a New Humanity

The temptation narratives constitute the rudiments of a Second Adam Christology. Affirming the goodness of God's creation and thereby his own creaturely existence, Jesus accepted with humility and gratitude the limitations that God has established in creation. He did not just affirm the limitations in the goodness of creation, because he celebrated the joy of his creaturely existence. He affirmed and enjoyed the theater of creation to which he belonged and of which he was a part as a source of delight in the fulfillment of his vocation. The distortion of sin, the danger of chaos, and the terror of Nothingness did threaten Jesus, but because he exercised his freedom for God, these did not and could not penetrate the definition of his genuine human existence. The way Jesus lived his life, whereby Nothingness did not perforate his living, is precisely the new life God initiated with him *before* his cross, and through him God establishes this life in a new humanity *after* his cross. Thus the possibility of a new humanity apart from the desolation and devastation of Nothingness begins with and through Jesus. The Gospels implicitly undergird my conclusion, because, despite Jesus' embrace of John's "baptism of repentance," they do not ascribe to Jesus any sense of guilt or sin. John A. T. Robinson says: "It is so universal a mark of saintliness, from Paul onwards, that the saint sees himself as 'the chief of sinners,' that the omission cannot but strike us." Against those who would argue that the church has simply written the sinfulness of Jesus out of the Gospels, Robinson responds: "But the remarkable thing is that its absence is not emphasized or defended—but simply passed over in silence. It is an astonishing omission."[22]

When Jesus walked out of the wilderness, tempted but not fallen, the Kingdom of God had begun with him and now comes through him for us.

Conclusion

Spirituality, the life-style of trust in God, begins with God surrounding us with grace and responding to our needs. Although many words are available to name our common human brokenness, Henri Nouwen considers "loneliness" the best expression of the depths of human need, the universal human woundedness that theology and ministry should address. Yet he surprisingly concludes: "The Christian way of life does not take away our gift of loneliness; it protects and cherishes it as a precious gift."[23] Why? The separation and incompletion that we all feel, our inevitable lonely condition, reveals our need for God, for grace, for a future in God's grace. This loneliness identifies for us the necessity of the

---

[22]John A. T. Robinson, *The Human Face of God* (Philadelphia: The Westminster Press, 1973) 97.

[23]Henri Nouwen, *The Wounded Healer* (Garden City NY: Doubleday & Company, 1974; 1972) 84. Though several eminent names and their approaches to spirituality are available, e.g., Thomas Merton, Frederick Buechner, Annie Dillard, and Matthew Fox, I would be remiss if I failed to refer specifically to Martin E. Marty, *A Cry of Absence: Reflections for the Winter of the Heart* (San Francisco: Harper & Row, Publishers, 1983).

cultivation of spirituality in the life of faith, because spirituality nurtures our trust in God.

Any sort of spirituality requires the sustaining Presence of God in the life together of a community of faith. What nurtures and sustains the continuing concern for authentic spirituality, for Presence? The worship of God in the service of the Word, the cleansing of baptism, and the celebration of the Eucharist. Worship enlivens spirituality. The Word of God in Jesus Christ calls us to mercy and grace, the forgiveness of sin and the empowerment of faith. The Word of God happens in the reading of Scripture, through prayers of praise and petition to God, with music resounding through the church historic, and uniquely in the proclamation of the Word of God today. Thus the celebration of the Word of God is a congregational event.

The gathering of a community of brothers and sisters together in Jesus' name often includes the incorporation of new Christians into the fellowship through the initiation of baptism. These newly acknowledged children of God who commit themselves to the Way of Jesus Christ are members of a family not bound together with flesh and blood but the gift of grace. So the worshiping life of the church intentionally nurtures a spirituality of familial relationship, because the church is at its best the family of God.

Worship anchors spirituality in the memory and hope of Jesus Christ crucified. The celebration of broken bread and a shared cup nurtures Christian spirituality with the blessing of memory and the promise of hope for life in the eternal tomorrow of God. Memory—God has come to us in the person of Jesus Christ, revealing love that is costly but free. Hope—Jesus Christ offers us the experience of meaning here and now and the promise of resurrection yet to be. We celebrate Christian hope with ordinary bread and the vineyard's wine. Therefore, the feast of the Eucharist nurtures a spirituality of creation, because bread and wine remind us of our lifelong need for the bounty and productivity of this good Earth. Such an ecclesial spirituality contains profound social, political, and ecological concerns.

Chapter 4

The Elusive Promise of Joy

A BEAUTIFUL SATURDAY AFTERNOON IN JULY. The people entering Highland Church did so in the festive delight of a wedding. Once inside the sanctuary the celebration wrapped itself in the sacred without diminishing the excitement of this special day. The sanctuary reached skyward with great beams lifting a vaulted ceiling. Stained glass windows shined with bright reminder of events in the life of Christ. The four robed ministers who faced the congregation reminded everyone that the bride and groom had multiple connections in the larger life of the church. James and Andy, groom and best man, waited at the altar, and the entire wedding entourage happily took their places alongside them, including the groom's son and the bride's daughter, both university students. Organ music piped the joy of the occasion and at the appropriate moment majestic sound signaled the appearance of the bride. Wearing a striking white hat and gorgeous white dress, Cannan moved down the aisle for the sharing of public vows. The beauty of the bride and the brightness of her smile matched the brilliance of the stained glass dance of summer sunshine. The bride and groom had each gone through the painful death of a previous marriage in divorce. Now they chose the union of marriage again with the risk of togetherness and the promise of love, the risk and promise of joy.

Prayers offered and vows begun, the youngest of the ministers read Scripture from John 2 and gave a brief meditation:

> There was a wedding at Cana in Galilee. Jesus' mother was there, and Jesus also was invited to the marriage along with his disciples. When the wine gave out the mother of Jesus said to him: "They have no wine." And Jesus said to her, "O woman, what does this have to do with me. My hour has not yet come." His mother said to the servants, "Do whatever he tells you." Now six stone jars were standing there, for the Jewish rites of purification, each holding twenty or thirty gallons.

Jesus said to them, "Fill the jars with water. And they filled them up to the brim. Then he said to them, "Now draw some out, and take it to the headwaiter." So they took it. When the headwaiter of the feast tasted the water now become wine, he called to the bridegroom and said to him, "Everyone else serves the good wine first; and when men have drunk freely, then the poor wine; but you have kept the best wine until now."

The Gospel read, the Pastor offered his meditation:

Sometimes the wine does run out. Sometimes the joy that you had earlier planned and tasted for a time inexplicably runs dry. Early dreams can become broken dreams and cut short the joy that we had claimed. The music stops. The wine is gone. The celebration ends. The common wisdom for such a time is to accept our losses, to savor our best memories, and to move on to live in a new day. But often we are unable to get beyond the pain of yesterday and to anticipate something new tomorrow. Sometimes, however, the most amazing surprises happen along the way. The most astonishing of all surprises is the power of our God to bless lives and to strike up a completely new party.

Before he began his ministry, Jesus with his mother and his disciples were guests at a wedding. At this wedding for an unnamed man and one woman the wine ran dry. Jesus changed things. When the shortage happened, the mother of Jesus told him: "Son, we need to do something." And Jesus said to her what translates into today's English something like, "Mother, I can serve no wine before its time!" Not in our time. Not according to our design. Not on the schedule of our minds. Rather, what we almost always realize in retrospect, we know as the right time. Sometimes the ultimate surprise of a new beginning is the unexpected vitality of beginning again, a deeper and richer joy than had ever been before.

Cannan and James, we celebrate with you today in a way that words cannot express, which warm embrace can only suggest. We celebrate with the deepest thanks for what our God has given you whom we love, this grace of a new beginning. We give thanks especially that what is best and richest has been saved until now. We who love you charge you today in the name of the Christ of the wedding feast always to dance together under this mercy. Savor this moment. Treasure this joy. Guard it, grow it, and give it to one another. And as you are able, offer it to others who are thirsty like you for such a hope and such a grace.

May you be aware today that one Guest is among us who is happier than us all, and happier even than the two of you. The One who has given this grace of a new beginning that tastes better than everything before dances with arms around you, and invites you in the rest of your days to dance together as one, for the sake of grace and to the glory of God. Amen.[1]

The purpose of this chapter is to explore the multifaceted experience of the providence of God that characterized the Galilean ministry of Jesus. Three aspects of God's provision for us characterized Jesus' ministry and remain of central importance for us today: compassion, prayer, and miracle. These three themes are inextricably intertwined together, but the significance of each warrants explicit and careful analysis. Since the experience of joy is fundamental to the celebration of the providence of God in our lives, the elusive promise of joy informs the exposition of compassion, miracle and prayer.

The Experience of Providence: *Joy*

Unlike the disciples of John the Baptist, the disciples of Jesus did not fast. On the contrary, the Jesus movement exhibited festive celebration. Eating and drinking with Jesus, listening and responding to Jesus, following and learning from Jesus—all these Jesus experiences evoked joy. Fasting would come after the banquet, when Jesus would be taken away, but not before. Did the celebration of life and the freedom from life's burdens make sadness in the presence of Jesus an existential impossibility? No, that says too much. The tragic dimensions of life gleaned earlier in the Gospel traditions require a more sobering interpretation of the celebration of life in the company of Jesus. It is more accurate to speak of the existential possibilities in the festive circle of Jesus: The

---

[1]Paul Duke, "Marriage Meditation," Highland Baptist Church, Louisville KY, July 1988 [Adapted].

experience of the otherwise everydayness of life in the company of Jesus occasioned the ever occurring possibility of joy.

A difficult but essential distinction between "happiness" and "joy" is necessary. Unlike the lightness of happiness with its contrast of sadness, the depths of life that nurture joy provide a place for pathos. The very presence of Jesus evoked a life-stirring sense of joy that did not require "momentary forgetfulness" of the hardship and pain that so frequently accompany life. Rather, the joy of Jesus in the midst of the often tragic context of life rooted in his *Abba* experience that radiated from within him outward to encircle all those in his company. Accordingly, the *Abba* experience of Jesus, utter realism for him, often made the Jesus experience of his companions a surging surprise of joy. Everything changed, though sometimes everything appeared the same. In the presence of Jesus the elusive promise of joy rushed over the drabness of everyday life and deep down the crevices of lifelong brokenness. Laughter washed the colors of ordinary existence with a striking brightness, and gentle touch sparked healing in the inaccessible depths of twaddled alienation.

Providence takes a new and dynamic form in the activity of Jesus: The ever occurring possibility of the surprising experience of joy. Since the promise of joy is awash with the overflowing compassion of God, Jesus embodied an unmatched compassion for people in need, indeed, for all needy people. The provident care of God happened around Jesus in parable, prayer, and miracle. In fact, Jesus himself becomes the parable of God.

Part One: Compassion

Since providence endeavors to understand and interpret the mode of God's activity in the movement of human history and in the journey of each person's life, what does the activity of Jesus in Galilee tell us about God's involvement and investment in the world in which the Nazarene lived? The first word is *compassion*. The promise of joy bloomed in the company of Jesus with the surprise of desert flowers and the fragrance of gentle compassion.

The Lawyer's Questions

In Luke 10:25-28 a scribe put a question to Jesus: "Teacher, what must I do to inherit eternal life?" Jesus posed a counter question: "What is written in the law? What do you read there?" Learned in Torah, the scribe answered: "You shall love the Lord your God with all your heart, and with all your soul, and with all your strength, and with all your mind; and [love] your neighbor as yourself." While combining Deuteronomy 6:5 and Leviticus 19:18, the form of the lawyer's response accentuated the unity of the two as one. The love commandment is singular and theocentric, because the love of neighbor presupposes the love of God. Jesus said to him, "You have given the right answer; do this and you will live."

The scribe posed another question to Jesus: "Who is my neighbor?" Though not necessarily insincere, he disclosed that he did not know the meaning of the commandments that he could otherwise recite quite accurately. How could the lawyer understand the love of God apart from the love of neighbor? Why did he not ask: "Who is 'God'?" "What is 'love'?" "What does 'do this' mean?"

The lawyer assumed that he knew the answer to the question, "Who is God?" He thought that he had the answer to the question, "Who am I that I should love my neighbor as myself?" He had only one unanswered question, "Who is my neighbor?" The parable showed, however, that the lawyer did not understand who he is, he did not know who God is, and he did not realize where the Presence of God is to be found. So the lawyer's question—"What must I do to inherit eternal life?"—a question that he himself could answer from the Law, occasioned a self-justifying question, "Who is my neighbor?" Jesus answered with a parable.[2]

The Parable of the Compassionate Samaritan

Jesus accepted the challenge of the scribe's question, but he rearranged questions and answers with unexpected creativity, telling a story. "The parable of the Compassionate Samaritan" is one of the most significant

---

[2]Karl Barth, *CD* I/2: 417.

Gospel narratives for understanding the providence of God. It seems obvious enough, but the subtleties in this overfamiliar story of Jesus contain surprises, then and now.[3]

Scene 1: A Traveler

An unidentified man, probably an Israelite returning from worship in the Temple, journeyed down the treacherous road from Jerusalem to Jericho. He came "down" from Jerusalem because the Jericho Road dropped 3,600 feet in only seventeen linear miles to Jericho. About a day's journey, the road followed a desolate terrain with sharp turns that provided hiding places for would-be robbers. A gang of thieves brutally attacked the traveling man. The savagery of their murderous deed left him half-dead. The robbers stole his goods and stripped him of his clothing, slashing and bashing him in the assault. They struck him on the head and beat him unmercifully. Naked, bruised and bloody, less alive than apparently dead, they left the man lying in the ditch beside the road.

The listeners, all Jews like the Teller of this tale, understood immediately what had happened, what could happen to any one of them on the dangerous Jericho Road. This initial scene in the story puts all the listeners inside the ditch alongside the victim, waiting.

Scene 2: The Priest and the Levite

A priest came "down" the road from Jerusalem enroute to Jericho. Traveling from Jerusalem, he probably had completed one of two of his

---

[3]The literature on "the parable of the Good Samaritan" is extensive. See the volume of essays in *Semeia* 2 (1974). Cf. Peter Rhea Jones, *The Teaching of the Parables* (Nashville: Broadman Press, 1982) 234-41, for a wealth of resources in his "Notes" concluding his treatment of the parable.

See Robert Funk, "The Old Testament in Parable: A Study of Luke 10:25-37," *Encounter* 26 (1965): 260-66; also, Funk, "The Good Samaritan as Metaphor," *Semeia* 2 (1974): 77-81. Cf. Walter Wink, "The Parable of the Compassionate Samaritan," *Review & Expositor* 76 (1979): 208-14.

See Helmut Gollwitzer, *Das Gleichnis von Barmherzigen Samariter* (Neukirchen-Vluyn Kreis Moers: Neukirchener Verlag, 1962). Funk and Gollwitzer have significantly influenced my interpretation of the parable.

annual sabbath-to-sabbath services in the Temple for the year. When the priest saw the lifeless stranger lying beside the road, he went completely to the other side. The priest would not risk contact with a corpse that would make him unclean. Why not? Was he not a good and decent man? Did he lack ordinary human sensitivity for a brutalized victim of thieves? Had tragedy become so commonplace to him that this man's plight did not touch him? On the contrary, he reacted within the restraints of the practice of his profession. If the priest had walked within four cubits of the victim, a distance necessary to determine whether or not the man actually lay dead, a lifeless corpse would make him unclean. In fact, the Law instructed priests to avoid contact with the dead altogether, except for close kin (Lev 21:1-4). Questions are left unanswered here. Would the priest be required to destroy the tithes he had collected if he became unclean? Would he have to return to Jerusalem for ceremonial cleansing? Did he think the plight of the victim meant that he did not live under the blessing of God? What kind of claim would the prostrate man make on the priest? If he were dead, would the priest have to pay for his burial? If alive, would the priest be obligated to care for him, penniless though the victim might be? Does the Teller of the story intend to suggest that the priest acted out of the possibility of inconvenience? Whatever the priest did for the (half-dead) man beside the road, he would inevitability experience some interruption: It would at least cost him time and money. If the man lay dead, the corpse of a stranger would make him unclean that would complicate his life and compromise his identity, soiling his religious self-esteem and public prestige alike. The priest would not risk himself for the sake of the wounded man. So he walked to the other side.

Then a Levite came along, his direction untold. He may have gone nearer to see the victim more carefully, but he too continued his journey, retreating to the other side. The Levite faced a similar problem as the priest, but less severe. The Levites formed an inferior clergy who served in the Temple, a step down from the priests though a step up from the common people. They could not take part in the offering of sacrifice, but they served as repairmen, musicians and Temple police. Unlike the priests, however, the Levites only had to observe ritual cleanliness during their scheduled service in the Temple. Yet the Levite felt a threat to his sense of clerical importance because of the possible defilement from this maybe-dead man. Like the priest, he left the bloody body unexamined and retreated to the other side of the road. From the viewpoint of the wounded man beside the road, neither cleric had compassion.

In the ditch with the victim the listeners saw the priest and the Levite pass without any attempt to help. They divided into two groups: Those sympathetic with the dilemma of the priest and the Levite felt misrepresented and misunderstood. Those excluded from the religious establishment felt vindicated and absolved. Now they all anticipated the conclusion of the anti-clerical critique.[4]

Scene 3: A Compassionate Samaritan

A Samaritan came along, he too saw the beaten victim, and he felt the deep stirring of compassion. The turn in the parable shocked Jesus' listeners, because they anticipated a layman who would recognize his neighbor in the half-dead man, which would complete the anti-clerical critique. But a Samaritan! The introduction of a Samaritan into the story staggered everyone with utter disbelief. Now the religious outcasts had to see themselves receiving help from a hated enemy. The twist in the parable alienated them from the story as much as the portrayal of the priest and the Levite had estranged those who belonged to the religious establishment. The Samaritan was a layman, but he was a non-Jew, a mortal enemy because he was a despicable and detestable half-brother.

The Samaritans were hardly more than Gentiles. When the Northern Kingdom fell to Assyria in 722 B.C.E., about half of the aristocrats were deported to various parts of the Assyrian empire and other conquered people were relocated in Samaria. A history of intermarriage compounded theological differences with "the Jews," an exclusive reference that referred only to the tribes of Judah and Benjamin in the former Southern Kingdom. The Jews considered the Samaritans as mongrels and half-breeds, almost Gentiles. They cursed them publicly in the synagogues. They prayed the Samaritans would not share in eternal life. They would not believe the testimony of a Samaritan under oath. The Jews would not accept Samaritans as children of Abraham, and they excluded them from worship in the Temple. A Jew might do business with a Samaritan

---

[4]Funk, "The Old Testament in Parable," 260-61; "The Good Samaritan as Metaphor," 79.

merchant, but he would not eat with him or use dishes in common with him. The Jew would not allow a Samaritan to touch him, much less accept a service from one. The Jews intensely despised the Samaritans: When going from Galilee to Judah, the Jew would cross the Jordan River, travel around, and recross the Jordan into Judah rather than go through Samaria.[5]

At the time of Jesus the enmity between the Jews and Samaritans had become bitter. Hostility and hatred centered especially around "the Temple." Although the Samaritans accepted the Law of Moses, they worshiped in their own Temple on Mount Gerizim. In 128 B.C.E. the Jewish King John Hyrcanus destroyed the Samaritan Temple. The Samaritans retaliated when they could: One infamous night during the Passover about 7 C.E., Samaritans entered the Jerusalem Temple and scattered human bones around, which desecrated the Holy Place. The Temple of each alienated and embittered the other. The circle of neighbors did not include a Jew for a Samaritan or a Samaritan for a Jew. *Above all a Jew would not accept help from a Samaritan.* They were mortal enemies.

Yet this Samaritan overcame his enmity and had compassion, indeed, lavish compassion. Such compassion required vulnerability, for compassion is a verb, "doing heartfelt mercy."

> The Samaritan *saw* him . . . and *went* to him;
> He *bound up* his wounds, *pouring* on oil and wine;
> He *set* the man on his animal to ride;
> He *brought* him to an inn;
> He *cared* for him through the night;
> He *gave* the innkeeper two silver coins to take care of him, now penniless;
> He *promised* to *return* and to *repay* all future expenses.

Without concern for himself the Samaritan stopped, got down in the ditch, and examined the anonymous man half-dead. He tended his wounds gently and carefully. Then he wrapped him in his own clothing,

---

[5]Wink, "The Compasionate Samaritan," 210-11. He admits that the specific characterization of the Samaritans are late but reflect nonetheless "established attitudes and practices," 211.

dirt and blood notwithstanding, lifting him out of the ditch. He set him on his donkey to ride, walking at his side. He took him to an inn and cared for him throughout the night. When he left the next day, the victim clean and his wounds treated, the Samaritan paid the innkeeper for continuing care, and he promised to return and to pay for all expenses incurred in the recovery of the victim. Jesus underscored the extravagance of the Samaritan, who acted without any anticipation of reciprocity. Unlike the priest or the Levite, the Samaritan could not require any repayment of expenses, because his oath was not accepted in a Jewish court.

Interpretation

The lawyer asked the question, "Who is my neighbor?" If Jesus had intended to answer the lawyer's question as he had asked it, he would have concluded with the question: *"Which one of the three recognized his neighbor in this needy man whom God threw at his feet for him to love?"*[6] Which of these three acknowledged the man in the ditch as his neighbor? The priest, the Levite, or the Samaritan? However, Jesus reframed the lawyer's question, from neighbor as object to neighbor as subject, a shift from "Who is my neighbor?" to "To whom will I be a neighbor?" The lawyer had to ask: "Will I do as the Samaritan and become a neighbor to anyone in need, including my enemy?" The neighbor is not primarily an object for the lawyer to define, who to include and who to exclude, a task that distinguishes neighbors from nonneighbors, but any needy person whom he might encounter, even an enemy. Jesus required the lawyer to reverse his concern—from searching for the person who would qualify as his neighbor to an examination of whom he would be willing to love as neighbor. When the scribe identified the Samaritan as the model for the love command, Jesus charged: "Go and do likewise." Jesus taught that in the perspective of the Kingdom of God even an enemy is your neighbor, a revolutionary extension of Leviticus 19:18. Love of neighbor could mean doing mercy with your enemy. Gustavo

---

[6]Gollwitzer, *Das Gleichnis von Barmgerzigen Samariter*, 56-57 (italics added). Many interpreters either concur or follow Gollwitzer on this point, e.g., Wink.

Gutiérrez puts the issue sharply: "The neighbor was the Samaritan who *approached* the wounded man and *made him his neighbor.* The neighbor . . . is not the one whom I find in my path, but rather the one in whose path I place myself, the one whom I approach and actively seek."[7]

The shift from object to subject thus far, demanding as it may seem, remains insufficient. Though not without value, considerable value, something is amiss in this pattern of interpretation. What is it? "To whom will I be a neighbor?" translates into, "Will I be a neighbor to anyone who needs neighboring?" The shift of neighbor from object to subject can very quickly shift back to neighbor as an object: "Will I define my neighbor to include my enemy?" In this framework the lawyer responded on the basis of his willingness to specify which of the three travelers had recognized his neighbor, which of the three had broadened his definition of neighbor to include anyone in need, even his enemy. The compassionate Samaritan who neighbored a bitter enemy personified the example the lawyer should emulate. Within this scheme of interpretation Jesus essentially answered the question as it had been asked, and the lawyer remained an engaged inquirer who continued to answer Jesus' questions correctly. The shift of neighbor from object to subject is ultimately so minimal that the lawyer's identification of "neighbor" becomes an object again: "My neighbor" includes "my enemy." The parable is a powerful example story, the exegesis of what Jesus intended in his earlier summons: "Love your enemies" (Luke 6:27b). Can a parable ever be reduced to a proposition?

Yet the question that Jesus actually asked required far more than an all-inclusive definition of "my neighbor." The shift is more subtle, more radical, and all the more important. The subtlety may seem slight, but only seemingly so. Through the parable Jesus entirely redefined the question, "Who is my neighbor?" Jesus asked, *"Which of these three, do you think, proved neighbor to the man who fell into the hands of the robbers?"* The question required the lawyer to move from the posture of an observer to the plight of the victim, beyond an observer's evaluation

---

[7]Gustavo Gutiérrez, *A Theology of Liberation* (Maryknoll NY: Orbis Books, 1988; 1973) 113, shows how powerful an all-inclusive definition of "neighbor" to include anyone in need, even "my enemy," can be. Cf. Jones, *Parables*, 227-28, who thinks the "tension" between the lawyer's questions and Jesus' question can be overdrawn, and he concludes that Jesus did answer the lawyer's question essentially as he asked it.

of the Samaritan's compassion and beyond an all-inclusive definition of neighbor. Who does the wounded man identify as the neighbor whom God commands him to love as himself? Certainly not the priest nor the Levite, because they did not respond with mercy to the brutalized man who desperately needed the mercying of a neighbor. Jesus' reformulation of the question required the lawyer to answer from the perspective of the half-dead man: *The wounded man is the one who identifies the neighbor.* The scribe must see through the eyes of this half-dead man in the ditch in order to identify the one who proved to be a neighbor to him. Only the view from the ditch enabled the lawyer to answer Jesus' question as he now asked it.[8]

That the lawyer would have to see himself inside the ditch in order to answer Jesus' question is convincing and compelling, but the rationale does not hinge on a single turn: Did the lawyer locate himself in the ditch because of his initial identification with the wounded man? Must the lawyer see himself in the ditch because of the way Jesus had reformulated the question? Could the lawyer find himself simultaneously in the ditch and outside the ditch throughout the telling of the parable? Each and all these questions would locate the lawyer in the ditch.

So Jesus shifted the issue *decisively* from the neighbor as an object to the neighbor as subject. As long as the neighbor remained an object to be defined, the issue continued to be the limits of the appropriate definition of neighbor, which included the redefinition of neighbor to encompass an enemy. Moving the issue from object to subject, from the observation of the travelers to the vantage-point of the victim, Jesus took the issue entirely out of the lawyer's hands and dramatically relocated the lawyer himself in the parable. Jesus put him in the vulnerable position of being able to see himself as wounded and in need of help, which required him to shift from the perspective of the helpful neighbor to the plight of the helpless victim. Before the scribe could step back and judge the three travelers, he had to hear Jesus' question inside the ditch, because the singular viewpoint of the half-dead man enabled him to see who "proved neighbor to the man who fell among robbers."

---

[8]Funk, "The Good Samaritan," 78-79. The location of all the hearers of the parable in the ditch (Funk) plus the recognition of Jesus' reformulation of the lawyer's question (Gollwitzer) come together to frame the parable with a depth of meaning that is both profound and compelling.

The dramatic conclusion of the parable left everyone holding their breath. Unable to say the name of the mortal enemy, "Samaritan," the lawyer answered: "The one who showed mercy on him." The question of Jesus required the lawyer to connect two words that he thought constituted a contradiction: Samaritan and neighbor. Why did he choke on the word Samaritan? Shock at the turn of the parable? The lawyer choked because he, like everyone else, had initially identified with the victim, and he did not want nor would he accept the service of a Samaritan. The unwillingness to speak the name Samaritan, a word that Jesus used comfortably in the parable, reflected the contemptible thought of himself as a victim who would never accept the mercy of a Samaritan. Contrary to popular piety and charitable good will, the parable does not focus on the example of the good Samaritan, admirable as it is. The parable concentrates on the surprising exchange, the shocking encounter between the Samaritan and the wounded Jew: The Samaritan overcame victimization and responded with compassion, and the Jew abandoned racial hatred and accepted the help of a bitter enemy. Unlike the victim in the ditch who remained passive, however, the lawyer faced a decision: Would he see himself as the victim, helpless but accepting the help of the compassionate Samaritan? The radical shift located the lawyer in the parable with the victim so needy that he would accept mercy from a hated enemy. All who really are victims, all who are truly disinherited and dispossessed, all who are on the edge between life and death—all welcome mercy whenever and from whomever it comes. The parable is not in the first instance an invitation to become "a good Samaritan" but to see oneself as the victim in the ditch who needs the mercy of a neighbor. Then and only then can one hear the summons of the text: "Go and do likewise."

Contemporary Theological Reflection

The purpose of the parable was to answer the lawyer's question, "Who is my neighbor?" Yet this question remained in the context of the lawyer's prior question: "Teacher, what shall I do to inherit eternal life?" He answered his own question from the Law with the twofold commandment to love God and his neighbor. One dimension of the parable is a prophetic expose of the failure of religious life centered in the Temple to nurture the love of God. When the priest and the Levite did nothing to help the apparently-dead but maybe-alive bloody body on the side of the road, the lack of love for their neighbor exposed their lack of love for God. Though the worship of God is essential to the love of God, the love of neighbor becomes the test for determining whether or not the activities in the Temple constitute the genuine worship of God. The failure of these priestly figures to practice love of neighbor exposed their devotion to religion instead of the love of God. The prophetic critique of the Temple was certainly a central element in the parable.

An Obvious Judgment?

Generally we judge the Priest and the Levite to be calloused and uncaring persons, but we are too harsh in our criticism. They did not know who or what the wounded man was: a Pharisee or tax-collector, an outcast or Samaritan, a robber or Roman soldier. As tutors of the spiritual life, they had to live within the structures of their religious responsibilities. The problem of the love of neighbor, however, cannot be solved through ecclesiastical calling or friendly benevolence. Since the parable is as familiar to us as a worn penny of little value, we rush through it or glance over it without seeing the extravagant investment of the Samaritan. Conversely, Jesus accentuated the Samaritan's costly response, a response that conveys no limit to the self-expenditure the Samaritan was willing to make. The parable magnifies the limitless compassion of the Samaritan.

The parable is so overexposed and culturally-defined as a notable example of winsome charity that the reader remains blind to the extent of the Samaritan's service and the extravagance of his compassion. Since we balance our love of neighbor with appropriate concern for our own needs, we assume that the Samaritan measured his mercy for the wounded man with similar realism. We think that he only did what anyone of us would do! Accordingly, the failure of the priest and the Levite strikes us as heartless and hard. We assume that they could have stopped with assistance for the brutalized man without risking their position, neglecting important responsibilities, minimizing other relationships, or sacrificing essential resources. We would never respond like the priest and the Levite, because we would offer some charitable assistance like the good Samaritan. Our assumptions prove false.

Did the Samaritan act in comfortable accord with his own needs? Did he stop and consider his needs at all? Did he indicate an awareness of his own limitations? On the contrary, he did not calculate his compassion for the anonymous victim with a corresponding concern for himself. When the priest and the Levite responded on the practical basis of position and responsibility, they reacted with everyday realism. Overfamiliarity has made us oblivious to the extravagance of the Samaritan's compassion. He stopped without concern for the danger of robbers. He remained unhurried in his mercy. He accepted without hesitancy this unexpected responsibility, and he changed his plans to care for the unidentified battered man. He took him to an inn and nursed him through a restless night. Before he left the next day, he paid in advance for the man's extended care and accepted full responsibility for the payment of all future expenses. The Samaritan did not respond in the light of his limits: He acted on the basis of the victim's needs. Which one of us has the flexibility and the resources to make this kind of compassionate commitment?

An Impossible Task

Now we must ponder the question anew: "Who is my neighbor?" "Who is the neighbor whom I should love as myself?" We do not need the parable of Jesus to open our eyes to the suffering in the world or to tell us how to make some kind of compassionate response. "Who is my neighbor?" is not an entirely unanswerable question. A litany of those in need of neighboring confronts us:

> hungry people and street people, some mentally ill;
> single mothers and fatherless children;
> the homeless and the inadequately housed;
> the illiterate and uneducated, the jobless and unskilled;
> the sick—some in hospitals, many homebound, others in nursing
>   homes;
> neglected minorities and the marginalized in ghettos;
> wayward youth and guilt-scarred parents;
> lonely executives and suicidal achievers;
> professionals trapped in meaningless work and criminals in
>   overcrowded prisons.

Some of these have names that we know and faces that we recognize. If the compassionate Samaritan is the model of the love command, which one of us can "Go and do likewise"? Who has the resources and flexibility of the compassionate Samaritan? Is he anything more than a character in a story? Unlike Jesus' parabolic Samaritan, we are real people. We have family commitments, job responsibilities, full schedules, limited bank accounts, legal restraints, and spiritual needs. And, yes, we suffer from conflict, loneliness, burdens, anxieties, and fears that threaten our hope for life in the everydayness of human existence. Can we ever in good conscience pass by on the other side? Can we sometimes alert agencies that are equipped to provide appropriate relief? Can we work for social and political change that makes all kinds of roads safe to travel? The problem is critical: As we care for one half-dead man, we are unable to tend to the others only half-alive all around us. The parable confronts us with "an impossible task." *Who* is *my* neighbor? Common sense and reasoned priorities flail uselessly in the face of the parable. The Samaritan acts with extravagant compassion, he is prodigal in his care, and he lavishly befriends an enemy.

The excessive love of the Samaritan who embodies compassion staggers the ordinary, indeed, the extraordinary human capability to respond. So the enlarged responsibility to neighbor both friends and enemies in need becomes insurmountable. The apparently possible but realistically impossible task confronts any one of us with our limits: Who has the ability, the resources, the time, or the will to do mercy with every half-dead person found on any of our short streets? The parable discloses a neighbor whom you and I most often cannot be. In fact, the command to "love my neighbor as myself" becomes God's judgment against each of us. The inability to be neighbor to the half-dead all around any one of us makes self-acceptance difficult, if not impossible. Jesus puts each of us in this quandary, in a position of overwhelming expectation that engenders inevitable self-reproach and damaged self-esteem. Is such self-recrimination and self-condemnation appropriate? Do we not need to recognize our limitations and restrict our responsibility to manageable and realistic limits? Yes, that is the healthy perspective. The problem remains, nonetheless, because this healthy perspective is much less than the uncalculated compassion of the Samaritan—at least slightly more charitable than the priest and the Levite but infinitely less than the unlimited mercying of the Samaritan.

The Claim of the Parable

"Go and do likewise"? This kind of neighbor can only be a character in a story. Where else can a compassionate Stranger be found? I am not able to do mercy like this Samaritan nor do I know anybody who is. Beyond the "narrative world" of the parable into the "real world," the truth of it is: I need a neighbor. I need a neighbor to love me and to enable me to love myself. "Love your neighbor as yourself?" The lawyer's question is everybody's question: Who is my neighbor? *Why*? *Because we do not begin with love to give but with the need for love.*[9] Precisely at this point the human situation itself compels us to acknowledge Jesus' reformulation of the lawyer's question that relocates the scribe and everyone else in the ditch. Jesus required the lawyer to see himself in his need, a dramatic reversal of the position and condition of the inquiring scribe prior to the parable. When God commands us to love our neighbor, the

---

[9]Arthur C. McGill, *Suffering: A Test of Theological Method* (Philadelphia: The Westminster Press, 1982; 1968) 107. Although I cannot find anyone who is as explicit as McGill on this point, the insight that we begin with "the need for love" instead of with "love to give" dovetails with the perspective of Gollwitzer and Funk. I suspect Karl Barth, *CD* I/2: 417-19, has influenced McGill, but he does not provide any documentation.

Since McGill thinks we begin in our need for love, the continuing experience of the compassion of Christ is essential for our appreciation of the parable. However, note Wink, "The Compassionate Samaritan," 213: "Jesus assumes that such compassion is within our reach." Whoever responds to the "permission" of the parable may embrace the Samaritan as a friend, *may* love him. If so, the continuing response of gratitude becomes "natural" (212). How? "Abandoning our presumed virtue, our anxiety about earning eternal life, and our pretended self-sufficiency, and learn to see ourselves as wounded and helpless, desperate for the healing God who reaches us from below, from things hidden and repressed, and through those outside the safe borders of our arranged lives" (213). Wink follows Howes and Moon, who say: "When some aspect in us once accepts wounds and tries to assimilate and transform them, it becomes in us a Samaritan to help hurt parts both in us and in other people. This inner helper remembers what hurts are like, and what it is to be healed. And *this Samaritan in us, this healing principle, matures* by the facing of wounds, small as well as large, without repressing the anguish of them . . ." (213), citing Elizabeth Howes and Sheila Moon, *Man the Choicemaker* (Philadelphia: Westminster Press, 1973) 58-59. Though a psychological perspective is undoubtedly of some help, the very concept of *a Samaritan healing principle* is essentially contrary to the intent of the parable. Compassion originates primarily out of continuing Christian experience rather than some capacity "within our reach."

neighbor is not just any helpless victim on the side of the road. The neighbor is the one who proves to be neighbor to us! The parable does not confront us with the demand of an impossible task but with our need for a compassionate Samaritan. We need a neighbor, to say it again, for we do not begin with love to give but with the need for love.

Jesus' reformulation of the lawyer's question does more than relocate all of us in the ditch and expose the inability of anyone of us to function like the compassionate Samaritan. Through the parable Jesus confronts us with his assessment of the desperate need of humanity, a condition reflected in the self-contradiction of the question, "What *must I do* to *inherit* eternal life?" The point of the parable is that *we can do nothing* but *acknowledge our need* and *accept the mercy* of whoever offers it. The point evokes fundamental questions: Is the parable too negative in its presentation of the human condition on the journey of life? Does Jesus really intend to repudiate the human potential in the lawyer's question, "What must I do . . . ?" Should we not have a more positive perspective on life for the sake of a healthy self-esteem and wholesome relationships with others? If the intention of the parable is not to summon us to "Go and do likewise" but to see ourselves in our brokeness and woundedness, the application of the parable is more radical in its estimate of our neediness than in its demands on our neighboring! We are beaten, bloodied, and bruised sooner or later by the pounding of life, which robs us of all joy and leaves us half-dead in a roadside ditch, utterly helpless and entirely alone. When the pain of life strikes us, "Who is my neighbor?" becomes an entirely different question. The one who proves to be neighbor to us in our need is the one God commands us to love as ourselves.

The Samaritan was the neighbor about whom the scribe was asking but did not know. The lawyer needed to see himself ravaged with the assaults of life and lying helpless beside the road. The scribe did not see his own helplessness and thus the Samaritan as his only helper. Yet he was summoned to do what the Samaritan did: to live under mercy and to do mercy, especially with his enemy. Since the lawyer did not recognize his neighbor nor understand what doing mercy means, why did Jesus summon him to "Go and do likewise"? The summons is grace before it is demand. The compassionate Samaritan, the neighbor who offered help, stood close to the lawyer, but he confronted him with his need as he extended to him his help. The lawyer, however, could not let go of his superiority to the Samaritan and acknowledge the desperate neediness in his own life; correspondingly, he could not accept the gift or the summons of the storytelling Nazarene. This neighbor made his claim only after he extended his offer. "Go and do likewise" means "Follow me." That is, you can do compassion only if you have accepted compassion.[10]

Who is the compassionate Samaritan? As in other parables of Jesus, the story of the compassionate Samaritan is a parable about the coming of the Kingdom of God. Within the telling of the parable, the Teller of the tale becomes a parable himself: Jesus of Nazareth is the parable of God.[11] He incarnates for us and offers to us the extravagant compassion

---

[10]Barth, *CD* I/2: 419; Gollwitzer, *Das Gleichnis von Barmgerzigen Samariter*, 68.

[11]Directly or indirectly interpreters almost always raise the question: What is the relationship of Jesus to the parable of the Compassionate Samaritan? Karl Barth says: "Well, it is Jesus Christ who gives the summons, and we cannot abstract Jesus Himself from the summons that He gives" (*CD* I/2: 419). Barth sees the good Samaritan "incarnate" in Jesus Christ.

Conversely, Walter Wink, "The Compassionate Samaritan," 214, says: "The parable itself is totally non-christological," because the Samaritan's compassion does not spring "from faith in Jesus." However, "the preceding verses in Luke are the most august Christological statements in the entire Synoptic Gospels (10:21-24)." He considers Luke's meaning clear: "The one who knows God as an Abba, who knows himself or herself unequivocally as God's child, is freed from anxiety about 'eternal life,' for 'eternal life' has already begun, the kingdom is already dawning. . . . When Samaritans help Jews, when Jews abandon racial hatred and embrace their foes—the kingdom of heaven is in the midst of you! (17:21)." Unknown to the lawyer, Jesus offers him in this moment the eternal life that he seeks and that Jesus reveals.

Funk, "The Old Testament in Parable," 263, asks: "does Jesus appear in the *field* of the narrative picture?" Jesus is "the physician, healer, shepherd who moves to the side of the destitute, tax-collectors, prostitutes, sinners. . . . Jesus stands behind the Samaritan," one who lives in the "world" of the parable or under its "logic." If Jesus does move to God's side, acting out the righteousness of God, "then it could be said that Jesus hovers behind the Samaritan also in the sense that he is the one whom his hearers could not expect and from whom they wanted no help, that is, so long as they refuse to be victims and allow themselves to be helped by the alien. In that case the parable is Christological . . ." (263). If the hearer "sees" what the Samaritan "sees," he is invited to follow Jesus, which means Jesus " 'appears' in the penumbral field of the parable as one who qualifies the situation" (264). Again, the parable is Christological. What frees the Samaritan to act with compassion? "The field intended by the parable. . . is qualified by the one speaking, by Jesus as the incarnate word. This word must be love as event. . . . God's love as event which gives the Samaritan in the narrative picture this freedom, the freedom to risk all, to proceed with his love unhurried, deliberately" (266).

of God, coming in radical self-expenditure to all of us ditched and half-dead: "God is love."

A Concluding Word

The parable of the Compassionate Samaritan tells us of the lavish love of God for us in Jesus Christ. The fundamental problem of humanity, of all of us, is to identify with the half-dead man on the side of the road—always wounded, always needy. The great difficulty of humanity is in appreciating the one who loves us and gave his life for us—Jesus Christ, a crucified derelict on a cursed Roman cross. He comes to us where we are, wayward and wounded, and he embraces us with the firm strength and gentle touch of compassion. The Nazarene appears powerless among the conventional powers of this world, but he is uniquely powerful in the love that he offers to humanity—caring for us on a journey toward healing that includes the promise of eternal life. So God has come to humanity in the compassionate Samaritan, Jesus of Nazareth. And God exercises providence in the world, at least in part, by opening the eyes of those who have accepted the mercy of the Samaritan Son, empowering us to use the resources God has given us to provide for them.

Part Two: Prayer

If providence begins with our human need and the compassion of God, prayer acquires an importance that we tend to minimize or ignore: Prayer proves essential to the life of the person and community seeking the provision of God. So we turn to the Model Prayer, the prayer Jesus has given us to guide us in our praying. The multiple expositions of the Model Prayer available today would seem to render another treatment even less than unnecessary. What else can be said? Certainly nothing new. Yet the providence of God requires continuing attention to the place and efficacy of prayer, and the Model Prayer is the appropriate place to begin.

Preface to Prayer

The Gospels provide two recountings of the Lord's prayer. Matthew includes Jesus' perspective on prayer in the Sermon on the Mount, which locates prayer within the personal relationships and ethical vision of the Kingdom of God. In Matthew 6:5-8 Jesus underscored two points prior to giving the Model Prayer: privacy and reverence. First, Jesus instructed his listeners not to pursue prayer in public places in order to gain the admiration of observers. Against such hypocrisy he charged:

> Whenever you pray, go into your room and shut the door and pray to your Father who is in secret; and your Father who sees in secret will reward you. (Matt 6:6)

Does Jesus repudiate public prayer? On the contrary, Jesus himself prayed in public and affirmed the place of prayer in worship. Yet communion in private prayer is the essential undergirding of prayer in public worship. Against hypocrites who prayed in public in order to impress others with their piety, Jesus advocated the nurture of authentic piety in solitude. Privacy does not guarantee the authenticity of prayer, because the person who seeks God in solitude may still do so in order to impress God or himself with the spiritual discipline that gives proper attention to the appropriate place to pray. *Self-deception runs deep in the life of faith, public and private.* Yet solitude in prayer does offer a better opportunity for reflective confession of sins and for exploration of neediness under God.

Second, Jesus warned against the temptation to use prayer to manipulate the response of God.

> When you are praying, do not heap up empty phrases as the Gentiles do; for they think that they will be heard because of their many words. Do not be like them, for your Father knows what you need before you ask him. (Matt 6:7-8)

Although Jesus devoted considerable time to prayer, he stressed that we do not pray to inform the *Abba* God of our needs. Instead, we listen for

God to clarify what our genuine needs really are. Does such listening eliminate ongoing petition in prayer? In Gethsemane Jesus himself prayed to God three times for the removal of the cup of suffering. A continuing conversation in prayer may be necessary to discern our needs and God's will. Perhaps the primary point for initial thinking about prayer and provi-dence occurs with Jesus' observation: "They think that they will be heard because of their many words" (Matt 6:7b). The temptation is to think that the person who prays can voice a specific request to God according to a certain formula or in a particular posture that requires God to grant the petition of his or her prayer. Prayer does not inform God, and neither the content nor the method of prayer can coerce God. Although prayer does contain petitions, Jesus insisted that the pattern of our asking does not dictate the mode of God's response.

Jesus' instructions in Matthew 6:5-8 are certainly not contrary to the request of the disciples in Luke 11:1. "Lord, teach us to pray as John taught his disciples." While the disciples already knew prayers for recitation in synagogue services, they wanted the Teacher to give them a prayer that would summarize his unique vision and commitments, as John apparently did for his disciples. They came with their request after Jesus had concluded one of his lengthy prayer retreats alone with God. So they expressed the longing to learn to pray in conjunction with a specific prayer that would express their discipleship in following Jesus. Therefore, the question of how to pray embraced their concern for authenticity in devotion as well as for specificity in content, and the Model Prayer guides both concerns.

Relationship and Petitions: The Model Prayer

The Lord's Prayer seems to be preeminently a prayer of petitions, a prayer of asking. The context of the prayer in Matthew and Luke significantly qualifies this otherwise dominant impression. The prayer of asking must be set within the prayer of meditation, and the prayer of meditation is preeminently a relational experience. The characterization of the Presence of God in prayer will vary according to a person's cir-cumstances or disposition, but the point nonetheless remains: The prayer of meditation is the atmosphere in which the prayer of asking breathes. Since our prayers of petition do not inform, coerce, or persuade God to do something God would otherwise not do, prayers of petition shaped in the habits of the heart are nevertheless relationally appropriate. Peter Baelz offers a uniquely wholesome perspective: "Perhaps we ought rather to think that our asking in faith may make it possible for God to do something that he could not have done without our asking."[12] Therefore, the Model Prayer with its multiple petitions remains preeminently a relational event, petitions included, but our investment in asking affords God opportunities that would otherwise be unavailable.

The Beginning of Prayer

The beginning of the Model Prayer is the heart of the prayer: "Our Father." We experience God as *Abba* through our relationship to Jesus, who has named God *Abba*, the Motherly Father, a compassionate Presence who is always "Thou." Actually we cannot ever speak exclusively about God without in some sense speaking to God. When the Christian does speak about God, employing the nominative instead of the vocative, she does so with the awareness that the nominative replaces the vocative for the sake of theological reflection. Yet the only posture appropriate to God is to address God. Karl Barth says: "Father as a vocative, whether expressed or not, is the primal form of the thinking, the primal sound of the speaking, and the primal act of the obedience demanded of Christians."[13] When we use a phrase such as "Perfect Parent" to speak of God, we do so because we have learned to address God, despite its awkwardness, with this mode of address. The parental image refers to the Thou whom we know as the *Abba* God, and it means thinking and feeling the mothering/fathering Presence of God. Since misunderstanding inevitably occurs through the exclusive use of masculine

---

[12]Peter R. Baelz, *Prayer and Providence: A Background Study* (New York: The Seabury Press, 1968) 118. Though prayer does not function in a mechanical way, Baelz believes that a petition to God remains "in some way instrumental in bringing about [an] occurrence, that had I not prayed as I did what happened would not have happened" (115). Again: "we are setting the prayer [of petition] in the context between man and God which is all-embracing, and we are affirming that within the particularity of this context, at this particular juncture of events here and now, this particular prayer is a significant factor in shaping what follows after" (116).

[13]Karl Barth, *Church Dogmatics, The Christian Life*, IV/4: *Lecture Fragments*, trans. Geoffrey Bromiley (Grand Rapids MI: Eerdmans Publishing Co., 1981) 51.

images and male pronouns—even in prayer—the choice of language to address God should include feminine imagery drawn from the biblical traditions. The Scriptures offer a wealth of images for addressing God in liturgical celebration and corporate prayer. The issue is not simply the use of inclusive language but the vision of God in the best of church tradition that our language portrays.

Relationships in the First Petition

"Hallowed be your name" is the first petition of the prayer. What does it mean? The "hallowing" of the name of God is the affirmation of God's Godness and our creatureliness. The petition accentuates the freedom of God: God is God and not a human being, the Holy Other who chooses in divine freedom to be for humanity—as a ruler to his subjects, as friend to a friend, as a father and mother to son and daughter. God is YHWH, "I am who I am." God is Emmanuel, "God with us." God is *Abba*, "the Motherly Father." However, the sense of God as ruler and the followers of Jesus as subjects has been transformed through the friendship of Jesus into a community of sons and daughters, a family of brothers and sisters.

The freedom of God is a freedom for humanity and a freedom with humanity. God wants us to be free. Yet our freedom comes through faith in God and not through turning from God, which always means bondage. The deepest need of humanity is the need for God—the God who creates us, the God who accompanies us, the God who names us children. God wants all children to taste and enjoy the fulfillment of freedom, the gift of sonship and daughterhood within the freedom of the family of God. Indeed, the name to be "hallowed" is *Abba*, the self-revelation of "I am who I am" who has come to be "God with us." We are not subjects to be ruled but children who are loved. The petition nonetheless is to God, that God would hallow God's own name. We do not. We suffer a profound ambivalence about the place of God in our lives, an ambivalence that desecrates the name of God in the world and that profanes the name of God in the church. So we pray to God to hallow the name of God. Thus the first petition in our relationship to God, "Hallowed be your name," is at least in part a confession of sin.

All the petitions of the Lord's Prayer are concerned with the Kingdom of God that Jesus embodied and proclaimed. The second and third petitions—"Your Kingdom come, your will be done on earth as it is in heaven"—magnifies the theme of the Kingdom of God, an eschatological theme personalized and hallowed in the company of Jesus, a vision of the coming Home-Coming of God. These two petitions express a longing for the Kingdom of God, for Kingdom life here and now. So this longing for the way and will of God refers to the present as well as the future. The longing of the heart becomes a continuing commitment to the relational and ethical vision of the power-of-*Abba*-ruling already anchored in the coming of Jesus.

Relationships in The Fourth Petition

"Give us this day our daily bread" is a petition that corresponds to our primary needs—physical, emotional, and spiritual needs. The three preceding petitions focused on God: *your* name, *your* Kingdom, *your* will. At this point the Model Prayer turns from preeminent concern for God's cause to primary concern for the cause of humanity: give *us*, forgive *us*, do not test *us* but rescue *us*. The shift from petitions focused on God to petitions oriented to humanity is more significant than it may seem, because each of the remaining three petitions puts the disciple who prays face to face with her needs, which requires a posture of receptivity. Though we humans do not live "by bread alone," we do require "daily bread." Without attention to the material needs of "hungering" human existence, we would die. So the petition for "daily bread" broadly encompasses everything human existence requires, from food and clothing to parents and children to trusted neighbors and good governments. Yet the prayer is for "daily" bread, what one needs for today. Beyond the legitimate hunger for all kinds of needs essential to life, however, we are vulnerable to an illegitimate hunger driven with an insatiable appetite for the accumulation of things and the power these can bring. Prayer cannot be used to justify "wants" of any and every kind under the guise of the promise of prayer. "Give us this day our daily bread" sets limits on the quality and quantity of needs for which we legitimately pray.

    Within this petition for "daily bread" the Model Prayer takes the form of intercession: "Give *us* this day *our* daily bread." Wrapped in the "us" and "our" are ever expanding circles of intercession for the multiple needs of family and friends, ultimately for all needy families and for every sojourner whose faces God can see though we cannot. The petition as intercession becomes a plea for mercy and a mandate for justice, because vast numbers of people live and die "without bread," all alone. The fourth petition summons us to gratitude and simultaneously to work for elementary justice in behalf of the hungry, the homeless, the dispossessed. The prayer for provision of God includes unnumbered masses of people, and the extent of God's care depends largely on the compassion of those who have for those who have not.

Difficult Relationships in the Fifth Petition

"Give us each day our daily bread. And forgive us our sins, for we ourselves forgive everyone indebted to us" (Luke 11:4). Without bread, we die. Without forgiveness, we cannot survive. Accordingly, the little word "and" hangs between and holds together the prayer for "daily bread" with the prayer for "forgiveness." Matthew 6:12 phrases this petition differently from Luke 11:4, perhaps a more liturgical rendering: "And forgive us our debts, as we also have forgiven our debtors" (6:12). Then Matthew adds a sharp qualification not found in Luke, where Jesus says: "For if you forgive others their trespasses, your heavenly Father will also forgive you; but if you do not forgive others, neither will your Father forgive your trespasses" (6:14-15).

What are we to make of the fifth petition? Unlike the other petitions, this one has two parts, "forgive us" and "we forgive." Does this two-part petition mean that God's forgiveness of our sins depends upon our forgiveness of those who have sinned against us? Some answer negatively: "God's pardon is not conditional upon ours."[14] The issue is the sincerity of our praying or the credibility of our living. Forgiveness moves from God to us and from us to others. Conversely, others answer the question positively: "There will be no divine forgiveness for those who harbor grudges."[15] Our forgiveness is conditional at least to the extent of our willingness, if not our ability, to forgive another. A third viewpoint: On the basis of the relational Presence of the *Abba* God through whom we experience life as the children of God, a different and surprising interpretation transcends both these alternatives. This petition

---

[14]Jan Milic Lochman, *The Lord's Prayer*, trans. Geoffrey W. Bromiley (Grand Rapids MI: Eerdmans Publishing Co., 1990) 121.

[15]Robert Hammerton-Kelly, *God the Father* (Philadelphia: Fortress Press, 1979) 76.

does not contain a conditional qualification but "a joyous cry of certitude: our sins are forgiven. We know this is so because we are forgiving toward each other."[16]

Does the affirmation of providence require us to make a commitment to any one of these interpretations? Since the conjunction "and" connects the petition for "daily bread" with the petition for "forgiveness," the provision necessary for bodily health and the posture essential for spiritual well-being are appropriately interrelated. The lack of provision for daily needs can stimulate anger and frustration: "Why am I denied daily bread?" The loss of confidence in the forgiveness of God can nurture guilt and blame: "What have I failed to do, which denies the comfort and assurance of God's pardon for me?"

A Mandate in Parable

At this point we face the question of the compassion of God, indeed, the mercy of God. Unlike Luke, Matthew warns that the forgiveness of God hinges on whether or not we have a forgiving attitude toward others. Matthew recounts a conversation between Jesus and Peter about the proper limits of forgiveness. Peter asked: "Lord, if my brother or sister sins against me, how often should I forgive? As many as seven times?" Jesus said to Peter, "Not seven times, but, I tell you, seventy times seven" (Matt 18:21-22). Jesus essentially moved Peter's generous limit of seven times to the limitlessness of seventy times seven. Then Jesus told "the parable of the Unmerciful Servant" (18:23-35). The story unfolds in three scenes and concludes with a warning strikingly similar to Matthew 6:14-15.

Scene 1: The Mercied Servant. A powerful king decided to settle his accounts with his servants. One insolvent debtor could not pay his debt of ten thousand talents, and the king prepared to sell him, his wife and children, and all his goods to write off the debt. The servant pleaded, "Have patience with me, and I will pay you everything." The king felt great compassion for the indebted servant and forgave his debt entirely.

Scene 2: The Mercied, Unmerciful Servant. When the debt-free servant sought out a fellow servant who owed him a hundred denarii, a

---

[16]Edward Thornton, "Lord, Teach Us to Pray," *Review & Expositor* 76 (1979): 235.

pittance compared to the debt the king had forgiven him, he grabbed him by the throat and demanded immediate payment. This servant pleaded, "Have patience with me, and I will pay you," the selfsame plea that the first servant offered the king. However, the forgiven servant refused to practice the forgiveness that he himself had already received, and he threw his fellow servant in prison "until he would pay the debt."

Scene 3: The Mercied Servant Unmercied. Other servants saw the greatly forgiven servant refuse to forgive the piddling debt of his fellow servant, and they felt such outrage that they reported the entire story to the king. Furious, the king summoned the forgiven but unforgiving servant, retracted his earlier decision to forgive him for his great debt, and threw him in prison "until he would pay his entire debt." Jesus concluded the parable with the charge: "So my heavenly Father will also do to every one of you, if you do not forgive your brother or sister from your heart" (18:35).

The parable seems to reinforce the conditional character of God's forgiveness. God will not forgive us unless we are forgiving toward others. In fact, the parable seems more demanding than the Model Prayer on the imperative of practicing forgiveness. The affirmation of the necessity of a forgiving attitude toward others in Matthew 6:14-15 becomes a mandate of limitless forgiveness in Matthew 18:35. Apparently God will rescind the forgiveness of any disciple who does not practice unlimited, heartfelt forgiveness toward brothers or sisters in Christ. To be cut off from God and God's forgiveness is completely contrary to the experience of joy in the life of the blessed child of God. The assumption seems to be: Whoever experiences the great forgiveness of God can practice heartfelt forgiveness for the lesser wrongdoing of one's brother or sister. How does this process happen? Through *a new perspective*: God always forgives me for greater sins than the lesser sins for which I must forgive my brother or sister who has wronged me. Through *a new attitude*: The forgiveness of God to me evokes a new willingness to forgive my brother or sister for sins against me. Through *a new empowering*: The energy of the forgiveness of God in me enables me to forgive all those who have wronged me. Are these three new resources enough?

The Painful Problem

Sometimes the pain of life is so deep that the capability of forgiving the wrong doer who caused the pain is not only positively lacking but negatively depressing. The possibility of forgiving another for some devastating wound seems abhorrent. Worse, even the consideration of forgiveness is already in itself complicity with the evil done, which God as God must also oppose. In some circumstances all human decency is heavily weighed against any possibility of actual forgiveness. Sometimes the only positive element is a fleeting awareness of the need to forgive, not for the benefit of the wrongdoer but for the one wronged—an entanglement in which the will of the injured person barely senses the importance of forgiving the other for the sake of the continuation of the person's own life. Only a flickering candle toward forgiveness in the darkness of ever present pain and recurring rage, only a slight inclination constitutes the full measure of the energy to forgive that the experience of God's forgiveness can engender. The promise of the power of forgiveness of "my brother" or "my sister" because of God's forgiveness of "me" hardly sparks the light of life at all. The providence of God for the shattered life, life that hardly feels like life, has recognizable self-destructive form, but the promise of the provision of God is so slight that the wounded person trapped in self-destructive unforgivingness finds nothing within the torn self or in the memory of God to enable the turn toward life-affirming forgiveness.

The parable of the Unmerciful Servant proves hopelessly punctiliar and inexplicably one-dimensional. Limitless forgiveness is not a human possibility, at least not in this fallen world. Continually doing mercy is not a human capacity, certainly not in the midst of the swirling ambiguity and tattered complexity of the real world. In these circumstances the experience of God is not so memorable as negligible, and the touch of God is not so transforming as unfeelable.

What then is the purpose of Jesus' parable? Both servants, when last seen in the parable, remain incarcerated "until he would pay his entire debt." The judgment of the compassionate king against the overwhelming indebtedness of the first servant, a debt forgiven earlier but now re-instated, is essentially less negating than his initial judgment. The king does not impose his earlier decision to sell the servant, his wife and children, and all his goods; rather, the king subjects his once-forgiven but unforgiving servant to the same judgment this mercied but unmerciful servant has directed against his fellow-servant. Unlike the earlier decision to terminate the relationship with the insolvent servant, *the king chooses to preserve his relationship negatively.* He jails the servant "until he would pay his entire debt." The parable ends with the unmerciful and un-mercying servant again in need of mercy and mercying that he had denied his fellow servant. Jesus concluded the parable with the threat of judgment, unless Peter and all like him do not practice unlimited and heartfelt forgiveness.

The Power of Forgiveness

The problem with the parable and its accent on the compassion of God is the problem of "how." How can I do mercy and practice heartfelt forgiveness? Matthew does not answer this fundamental question, at least not clearly or directly. The Gospel of Luke may offer the best answer, perhaps the only answer. On the cross Jesus cries: "Father, forgive them; for they do not know what they are doing" (23:24). Jesus does not say, "I forgive you; for you do not know what you are doing." Why not? He is the one hanging in pain on a Roman cross. He is the rejected one. He is the victim. He has offered God's forgiveness before, why not do so now? When Jesus cries, "Father, forgive them," does he mean: "Father, you forgive them because I cannot"? Has he reached the limits of his forgiveness? Can he not in this tragic, unbearable moment find enough compassion within himself to forgive his enemies?

Jesus cried to the *Abba* God to continue to forgive those around him in his dying as God had forgiven those in his company during his living. Why does he not do so? Limitless forgiveness is not an intrinsic human possibility, not even for Jesus. As he has lived out his life, always receiving himself from God and giving himself to God, he comes to death still receiving himself from God and giving himself to God. The crucified Nazarene knows: Limitless forgiveness is God's possibility. Only the continual receiving of life from God and the surrendering of life to God creates the radical possibility of living and dying within the compassion of God. Sin does not belong to the definition of humanness; cor-respondingly, the capacity of heartfelt forgiveness, the resources for the limitless forgiveness of those who sin against us, lies beyond the givenness of our humanness.

God must forgive "us." God alone can lovingly turn us toward receiving life from God and surrendering life to God, saving us from sin's distortion of our humanity and healing us with a forgiveness beyond the reach of our human vulnerability. Forgiveness is not a human possibility but God's possibility, God's grace working on us, in us, and through us. Sometimes the gift of grace is only a flickering touch of light in the darkness—unsteady, dim, momentary, hardly light. Grace must do its work, grace doing the work that we cannot do but that must be done to us, in us, and through us, because limitless forgiveness is not a human possibility for anyone of us. So we take refuge in the cross of Christ with the forgiveness that he offers to us and toward others for us, receiving life from him and surrendering life to him, always with the possibility of God's forgiveness through him extended to us—and from us, however slightly, to others. The continuing movement of life received from God and surrendered to God, of forgiveness offered to us and extended from us, is a movement never simply done but lived daily for its ongoing doing.

A Concluding Petition

The sixth petition, "and do not bring us to the time of trial," is a plea for the sustaining Presence of God in the inevitability of the trials of life. These are not tests that God has laid upon us but trials that happen to us in life. The prayer is partly for the clarification of faith that enables us to avoid misunderstanding the troubles and pain of life. So we continue the petition, "but rescue us from evil." The life of faith is perilous with its constant threats and ever fearful entrapment in evil. Here one must trust the *Abba* God and hope in the future of God. Strength in the face of trials and trust in the power of God, ultimately taking us beyond all forms of evil, constitute the promise of Christ on our journey of faith.

"The Lord's Prayer" models authentic prayer for us, instructing us and guiding us in the relational experience of communion with God, the *Abba* of Jesus. The petitions of the Model Prayer establish the agenda and the boundaries for discerning the appropriateness of the requests that we voice to God in prayer, but the parameters of petitioner prayer are hardly self-evident. A thoughtful understanding of the petitions within the prayer that Jesus continues to teach us to pray should nurture maturity and realism in our prayers to God.[17] We ask, search, and knock, we who are poor in spirit, who mourn, who long for righteousness, who are meek and live through mercy, we who are the children of God. The journey toward the Kingdom of God, our eschatological dreaming of the coming Home-Coming of God, always requires the reach of prayer with the One who accompanies us in our shared "pilgrims' progress."

---

[17]See H. H. Farmer, *The World and God: A Study of Pray er, Providence and miracle in Christian Experience* (London: Nisbet and Co., 1935) 127-44, 260-74. Farmer affirms the importance and appropriateness of petitionary prayer (137-44), but he acknowledges the limits of the prayer of asking. The praying person knows "Such limitations on prayer, which spring from the nature and purpose of God and which therefore are not rightly called limitations at all . . ." (267). The Christian who continues to experience the transforming presence of Christ in his or her life will gain the insight of love for what things he or she ought to pray. Most Christian people do instinctively recognize certain limits to their prayers, and they have always done so. They pray for recovery from pneumonia but not for the growth of a new limb after amputation. They pray for rain but not for the upstanding of crops dried and dessicated on sun-parched ground. They pray for a loved one's safety but not for resuscitation after he has been killed. Those who participate regularly in public worship know that the prayers of petition and intercessions within the life of the church in behalf of others frequently end with a slight echo of Gethsemane: "If it be your will." Farmer argues: "The source of these distinctions [between appropriate and inappropriate petitions in prayer] can be found only in the fact that there is given to mankind, and supremely to the man whose inner life is being cleansed and reconciled to God by Jesus Christ, an insight into those limits which the divine love has itself set, *at least for the time being*, upon the open possibilities of this world in any situation" (268, italics added). While Farmer does speak of the limitation of God, he qualifies himself with the thought "at least for the time being." He continues: "These are what may be called hygienic limits to prayer defined by the divine purpose of fashioning human personalities in love, and it is the Christian's calling . . . to be increasingly able to discern what they are in each situation as it arises."

Christians draw the limits in different places, but, I think, the decision not to pray or not to continue in prayer with a specific peition is the negative side of the positive purpose to discern the will of God. Farmer does not address the question of the self-limitation of God, but he speaks of "limitations which spring from the nature and purpose of God" and limits that remain "at least for the time being." He works with a sense of limitations in the structures of creation in the movement of human history, which entail some sense of the self-limitation of God. Although Farmer remains cautious, the story of temptation indicates that Jesus had "a very clear insight into what we have called the hygienic limits of the possible from the point of view of God's saving purpose, . . ." e.g., turning stone into bread (269, n. 1).

Unanswered Prayers?

Are there unanswered prayers? The question is put essentially and perhaps exclusively to petitionary and intercessory prayer. The easiest response is to declare: "God answers all of our prayers: sometimes positively, sometimes negatively, sometimes partially." The problem remains, because the investment in prayers of petition and intercession denotes some impact of the one who prays on the response of God. The question helps us to reflect on the meaning of the Presence of God, beyond God's response to our prayers to the mode of God's Presence with us in our praying.

February 1984. Friday morning. I looked out the door of Norton Hall toward Alumni Chapel and debated whether or not to attend the service that had already begun. I should go, I thought. An important denominational official would be preaching. I was late, so the congregational hymn and probably the choral anthem would have already been sung. The hymns affirm too much and qualify so little. I decided to go, and at the same time I retreated deep inside myself. The depths of solitude within did not offer any warmth, only familiarity. But everything was so fragile that even the cold familiarity of grief seemed comfortable. The cobble-stone walkway toward the chapel already lay under a soft blanket of snow, but traces of earlier footprints remained without anyone else in view. The snow fell rapidly in saucered, billowing flakes. Trees stood stark and black and skeletal, shimmering with white ribboned lines of delicately fashioned lace. Cloudy but clear. A haunting beauty. I walked alone, alone with myself. I had retreated so deeply inside myself that I was aware of nothing but the landscape and my inward isolation. From somewhere far behind me I heard someone call my name. As I turned, a hand touched my elbow—a young man, obviously a student. He introduced himself, but I did not hear his name. "Dr. Tupper," he said, "my father is dying, and I would like to make an appointment to talk with you." I accepted his intrusion and slowly surfaced from the depths of silence. My father had died when I was a seminary student, and two of my professors had been helpful to me. I did not want to be unkind to the young man.

"Walk with me to chapel. There's not much that I can tell you in my office that I cannot do so now." So I talked about grace. The words rolled out for his benefit and not for mine. Essentially I told him: "God always provides at least a small window for grace to shine through, regardless of the circumstances." We had arrived at Alumni Chapel and stood together in the foyer. I thought the conversation had ended. Then he turned slightly away from me and said: "I prayed every day for that baby, but the baby died. *God gave me a stone.*"

Suddenly I realized that the young man had not interrupted me primarily because of his grief for his dying father. He and his wife had lived with the joyous expectation of the birth of a child whom they would love as father and mother, a baby who would be the good gift of God. Despite their joys and hopes and prayers, the baby died; hence the conclusion: "God gave me a stone." Cold words. Hard words. He repeated himself: "God gave me a stone." I said something else about God and grace that I later could not recall. I think that I more or less repeated what I had already said. I had remained mostly disengaged. Unexpectedly he startled me to a level of awareness that demanded more attention than I had given or that I could quickly muster. He walked to the stairway to the balcony on one side of the foyer. When I saw that the guest preacher had already begun, I went up the stairway on the other side. My thoughts were jumbled and my feelings anxious and uncertain. The weight of the young man's words raced forward in my mind and inexplicably frightened me. When I located a seat in the back of the balcony, I looked around until I found him on the side. Near the conclusion of his sermon, the chapel speaker referred to the death of his grandfather in retirement and his father much earlier, concluding: "God will not take me before He has finished his work with me." The preacher's words struck the young man badly. I could see that much. I knew that I needed to talk to him. When the service ended with prayer, I looked to the place where he had been sitting, but the young man had gone.

Though the student had introduced himself, I could not remember his name. Actually I had never really heard it. I tried to locate him through the office of the Seminary Pastor (how many students whose father was dying had recently lost a baby?), but I could not find him. I never saw him again. If I had found him, what would I have said to him? First, I would have told him that God did not intend for his baby to die. God does not control the variables in pregnancy nor the contingencies in child birth. *God did not give him a stone.* God did not *take* his child. The death of any little child is contrary to the will of God. Second, I would have said to him that God suffers with him and his wife in the loss of their child, sharing the deep regret and sadness of the death of their new-born baby. Third, I would have pointed him beyond the Gospel of Matthew to the Gospel of Luke, because Luke's rendering of the words of Jesus is significantly different from Matthew's statement. In Matthew's presentation of the Sermon on the Mount, Jesus said:

> Ask, and it will be given you, search, and you will find, knock, and the door will be opened for you. For everyone who asks receives, and everyone who searches finds, and for everyone who knocks, the door will be opened. Is there anyone among you who, *if your child asks for bread, will give a stone*? Or if the child asks for a fish, will give a snake? If you then, who are evil, know how to give good gifts to your children, how much more will your Father in heaven give good things to those who ask him! (7:8-10)

The words of Jesus did not help the young almost-father. On the contrary, he framed the death of his child and the rage of his grief with Jesus' own words: "God gave me a stone." The crisis of his faith in the *Abba* God of Jesus occurred because of his faithfulness to this God in prayer: "I prayed every day for that baby, but God gave me a stone." "Give us this day our daily *bread*" is a specific petition that would include the prayers for a healthy mother-to-be and the child she carried. The correlation of the petition for daily bread in the Model Prayer and the affirmation of Jesus, "Is there anyone among you who, if your child asks for *bread*, will give a stone?" is certainly not contrived. The prayerful expectation would be for bread, the good gift of God. Indeed, Jesus emphasized, "How much more will your Father in heaven give good things to those who ask him," beyond the capability of any father and mother "who are evil [but] know how to give good gifts to [their] children." Even without the correlation of Matthew 6 and 7, on the basis of Matthew 7:8-10 alone, the implications in the situation of this young almost-father remain quite devastating. If the young man's prayer was answered precisely in the context of Matthew 7:9, God answered his prayer negatively and gracelessly.

The better judgment is to recognize that God did not and could not answer his prayer. Within the tragedy of this young family God could hear but could not answer their prayer. They anticipated the pain of childbirth, but the prayer God could have answered would have been a prayer to help them bear the pain of a child's death. It would have been

a different prayer with a different kind of potentially positive answer. So
I would have referred him beyond the Gospel of Matthew to the Gospel
of Luke. Why? Luke renders the words of Jesus differently, and corrects
or clarifies the parallel saying of Jesus in Matthew. Luke reads:

> Ask, and it will be given you; search, and you will find; knock, and the
> door will be opened for you. For everyone who asks receives, and
> everyone who searches finds, and for everyone who knocks, the door
> will be opened. Is there anyone among you who, if your child asks for
> a fish, will give a snake instead of a fish? Or if the child asks for an
> egg, will give a scorpion? If you then, who are evil, know how to give
> good gifts to your children, *how much more will the heavenly Father
> give the Holy Spirit to those who ask him*! (11:9-13)

Of course, the parable of the importunate friend (Luke 11:5-8) who
receives late night provision for a guest solely through his persistence
contains its own problems, located as it is between Jesus' instructions
about the Model Prayer that precede it and these affirmations of Jesus
that follow it. The words of Jesus in Luke about asking and receiving
nonetheless are significantly different from Matthew: "If you then who
are evil know how to give good gifts to your children, *how much more
would the heavenly Father give the Holy Spirit to those who ask him.*"
The only gift that God ultimately promises to give us in our need is the
gift of Presence. Experiential exegesis requires us to move from Matthew
to Luke to understand what God offers to us. It is a good gift, Presence,
though perhaps unrecognized, maybe not entirely satisfying. Yet the God
of grace promises the good gift of Presence to those who ask. When other
gifts come, we receive them gratefully, but the only gift that we can
finally expect on the basis of the promises of God in the story of Jesus
is the gift of Presence, the Presence of the Holy Spirit. Therefore, fourth,
I would have covenanted to pray with him for the Presence of God to
give strength to him and his wife to bear the pain of the death of their
baby and to hope for the joy of another child who might yet come to be.
I would have tried to direct him to the final petition of the Model Prayer
in Matthew as the petition corresponding to his need: "Do not bring us
to the time of trial but rescue us from evil" (6:13). Finally, I would have
attempted to help him and his wife get into family counseling to find
ways to address their grief. So many, "I would have . . . ," but I could
not.

The experience of the Presence of God takes different form in different circumstances with different people. The experience of the Holy Spirit can occur in the heart-warming Presence of nearness. There are moments when the vision of the Kingdom shines brightly, when the Word of God sounds clearly, when the Presence of God touches deeply. The Presence of God is mediated to us in a variety of ways: through the Christian community, through friendship, through the reading of Holy Scripture, through prayers, through the touch of another, through memory of different days, through hope for a future yet to be. Sometimes Presence radiates joy.

The Presence of God in the midst of tragedy, within the crisis of the providence of God, takes a different form. The Presence of God in the midst of tragedy, within the crisis of the providence of God, takes different form. One metaphor that evokes imagination and contemplation is "the silence of God." The Presence of God in the valley of shadows sometimes comes in the silence of God. The characterization of the silence of God refers to Presence that you cannot see, touch, or feel; a relationship where the Word is unspoken, nothing said and nothing heard; a relationship, God unseen and god unaware, when faith simply accepts the Presence; a relationship, sometimes a thundering silence, when you know to faith the Presence. The silence of God is a significant and appropriate mode of the Presence of God in the shadows.

Sometimes the most appropriate metaphor is "the absence of God," though absence is never unqualified: God is present as the One who is absent.[18] Dietrich Bonhöffer alluded to this meaning of Presence. "God lets himself be pushed out of the world on to the cross." God is the crucified God, "weak and powerless in the world."[19] The metaphor of the silence of God cannot contain the awareness that Bonhöffer describes but points beyond itself to the metaphor of Presence through absence. Here theological reflection struggles with the edges of language. The depth of awareness of God beyond silence upon silence is absence. The Presence

---

[18]See Eberhard Jüngel, *God as the Mystery of the World* (Grand Rapids MI: Wm. B. Eerdmans Publishing Co., 1983) 57-63, esp. 61-63. I am indebted to Jüngel for this conceptualization of the Presence of God, but I consider it one of the modes of God's Presence rather than the normative experience of God in the world.

[19]Dietrich Bonhöffer, *Letters and Papers from Prison*, ed. Eberhard Bethge (New York: The Macmillan Company, 1971) 360. See below, chapter eight.

of God as the One who is absent does not mean that God is *only* absent. On the contrary, God is actually present as the One who is absent, the God pushed out of the world on to the cross is the God who comes to the world in the death of the Crucified. The God who is, this God is not the do Anything, Anytime, Anywhere kind of God, the rescue God who is allegedly always available to the religious person. No, the God who is, the God "weak and powerless in the world," is the "God who lets himself be pushed out of the world on to the cross": The absence of God in the death of Jesus becomes the place of the Presence of God through Jesus crucified dead. The experience of the God who is present as the One who is absent does not mean that God is only absent or that the Godward person is simply unattending. The dead Jesus mediates an inclusive Presence through his death of Godforsakenness to others Godforsaken. The image of Presence through absence allows sharper definition: The interval begun in taking the lifeless body of the Nazarene down from the cross for burial in borrowed tomb constitutes a most poignant moment wherein God is present as the One who is absent. Jesus died God-forsaken, but he did not die Godforgotten. In the company of the dead Jesus, after his death cry from the cross but before the discovery of his empty tomb, the Christian in the darkness of an unwelcome Sabbath experiences relief through the Presence of God that the dead Jesus mediates: God did not forget him, and God has not forgotten me. While this sense of Presence through absence is not exhaustive, the awareness of the Presence of God as the One who is absent comprises a dimension of Christian experience. Beyond the silence within silence, Presence that lacks the measure of silence nurtures another sense of Presence, that God is present as the One who is absent. In silence piled upon silence, of silence turned through silence, with silence sinking with silence, the Presence mediated through the absence of God becomes . . . almost . . . palpable.

Part Three: Miracle

In the story of Jesus the mystery of the providence of God converges with the vision of the Kingdom of God, already arriving in the ministry of Nazarene. How did Jesus respond to the crises and troubles of the people whom he encountered? Oftentimes with a miracle that resolved their crisis or overcame their trouble. If God is God, can God not choose to deliver anyone of us from tragic adversity through a miracle? Can God not do for us what Jesus did for his contemporaries? Any attempt to understand the providence of God in the story of Jesus must wrestle with the category of miracle. In fact, the juxtaposition of compassion and prayer requires an exploration of the response of God to human need in terms of miracle. Our questions continue: Is a miracle always a possibility? Under what circumstances can we pray expectantly for a miracle? If God does not work a miracle, why does God not do so? If God answers our prayers with a miracle, how do we recognize it as the action of God? Since God is the God of compassion who hears and responds to our prayers, the affirmation of our investment in God through prayer occasions possibilities for God toward us that otherwise would be unavailable. Among these possibilities we affirm at least in principle the opportunity for a miracle, but our affirmation evokes the restlessness of previously unanswered questions.

The Necessity of the Category of "Miracle"

The whole of biblical history speaks of miracles, the mighty acts of God. These "signs" and "wonders" constituted disclosure situations, the manifestation of a mysterious depth in a situation of need that disclosed the saving Presence of God. In the biblical traditions, therefore, miracle is not a scientific category but a religious category.[20] Two problems persist: (1) Rationalistic reductionism that accentuates the essential similarity of all human events, continuity at the expense of discontinuity, strips miracle of the unusual Presence of God in circumstances of dramatic human need. (2) An unreflective literalism that concentrates exclusively on the uniqueness of divine activity, discontinuity at the expense of continuity, rips the miracles of God from the fabric of genuine human experience. Actually

---

[20]See H. H. Farmer, *The World and God*, 107-127, 145-179; and Eric C. Rust, *Science and Faith: Towards a Theological Understanding of Nature* (New York: Oxford University Press, 1967) 287-300.

both these approaches tend to view miracle as a scientific category that entails the overruling of the statistical probability of "natural law." A critically-informed biblical realism is a better approach, I would argue, because it understands miracle as a religious category that embraces the space/time continuum with specific descriptive points of reference.

The Identity of Jesus as a Miracle Worker

The identity of Jesus as a miracle worker is indisputable in every layer of the New Testament traditions. All the Evangelists tell the stories of the mighty acts of God in Jesus' activity in a fashion congruent with the distinctives of each Gospel. Precisely at this point a critically informed perspective has something important to say: The crux of the ministry of Jesus centered in his proclamation of the inbreaking Kingdom of God, and the miracles of Jesus happened in conjunction with his message of God's gracious rule already dawning in his ministry. The mighty works of Jesus are not central in themselves but belong within the center of Jesus' embodiment of the Kingdom of God. So the Synoptic Gospels set Jesus' miracles in the context of his proclamation and activity in behalf of the coming Kingdom of God, because his miracles remained "indicators" of the truth of his proclamation of God's salvific rule. The Kingdom of God proves to be the primary category, the miracles the dependent category. The most numerous and significant miracle stories of Jesus focus on healing.

Biblical realism recognizes nonetheless limits in the miracle-working activity of Jesus. First, the absence of faith limited what Jesus could do. So says Matthew 13:58: "And he did not do many deeds of power there, because of their unbelief." Yet the issue hinged not so much on the great measure of faith but its authenticity (Matt 17:20). Second, the miracles of Jesus constituted "preliminary signs" of the truth of his mission for the sake of the Kingdom of God (Matt 11:2-6), but less than an unambiguous authentication of the truthfulness of his message. Third, Jesus refused to present "a sign from heaven" (Mark 8:11-13) because such a sign would render faith superfluous and, more importantly, because such a sign from heaven belonged to the prerogative of God alone, beyond the scope of Jesus' own unprecedented ministry. Fourth, only God's exaltation of Jesus "on the third day" instilled fearless and enduring faith in the disciples who had witnessed his ministry. The miracles of Jesus himself did not do so.

Beyond Historical-Critical Interpretation

With the historical and cultural distance of the modern world from first-century Palestine how does a responsible, critically-informed realism interpret the miracles of Jesus? Since we have lost the "narrative innocence"[21] of antiquity, indeed, of pre-modern historiography, "a second naiveté" is sometimes essential for hearing the story of God in the stories of Jesus.[22] Unlike the mindset that interrogates a Gospel narrative for the sake of its historically-warranted truth, a second naiveté listens to a Gospel story in order to understand its narrative meaning.

A second innocence, as I understand it, has undergone a heightening of critical consciousness that prohibits the use of the Jesus stories for ideological purposes and recognizes a surplus of meaning in these stories that transcends all critical interpretation. The narrative depths of meaning that a second naiveté encounters in the Jesus stories generally and the miracle stories particularly rearrange the line of inquiry.[23] The first question should not be: "Did Jesus perform these miracles?" but "What do these miracle stories mean for the people who witness to these mighty works of Jesus?" The second question follows: "What is it in the activity and ministry of Jesus generally that corresponds historically to these miracle stories?" Only after the first and second questions are asked and answered does the third question become an issue: "Which mighty works did Jesus actually perform?" Perhaps better: "Which rendering of a specific miracle among the Gospels has the strongest claim to historical veracity?" Although this pattern of interpretation does not assume a positive or negative verdict from the outset concerning the particulars of a miracle story, it does provide a frame of reference for understanding the

---

[21]Edward Schillebeeckx, *Jesus—An Experiment in Christology*, trans. Hubert Hoskins (London: Collins, 1979) 79.

[22]Paul Ricoeur, *The Symbolism of Evil*, trans. Emerson Buchanan (Boston: Beacon Press, 1967) 351. In addition, see Mark I. Wallace, *The Second Naiveté: Barth, Ricoeur, and the New Yale Theology* (Macon GA: Mercer University Press, 1990) 51-85, esp. 70-71.

[23]Schillebeeckx, *Jesus*, 79-80, poses this pattern of interpretation and inquiry.

selection, the sequence, and the significance of the miracles of Jesus in the trajectory of each Gospel tradition.

Case Study I: The Feeding of the Five Thousand

The only specific miracle of Jesus included in all four Gospels is the feeding of the five thousand: Matthew 14:15-21; Mark 8:34-44; Luke 9:12-17; and John 6:5-13. *Question 1*: What characterized the activity of Jesus that made this miracle so important and so memorable? Jesus had compassion for needy people: "As he went ashore, he saw a great crowd; and he had compassion for them, because they were like sheep without a shepherd" (Mark 6:34a). In this single story of feeding the five thousand, the Gospels all say: Jesus comes with great compassion to help those in dire need. Through miracles of help and healing the One sent from God embraced the needs of others and expended himself in their behalf. In this way the story of Jesus enacts the story of God, the God of overflowing compassion.

Question 2: To what in Jesus' life and ministry does the feeding of the five thousand recall? First, Jesus was the friend of tax collectors and sinners. He offered his acceptance through table fellowship to all the low-classed, outcasts and the marginalized of society. In fact, Jesus "de-classed" himself through eating with them, announcing in word and deed that the good news of God is offered to sinners. At a dinner for tax collectors at the house of Levi the tax collector, Jesus demonstrated that sinners are invited to the great eschatological feast of God (Mark 2:15-17). This fellowship with Jesus broke down barriers of isolation and pre-viewed the radical acceptance of God for anyone who received Jesus. Unlike foxes with holes and birds with nests, Jesus could not claim any place of his own, but he and his disciples apparently never lacked any necessities. Why? He accepted the welcome of sinners and offered the Welcome of God. Where did Jesus do so? Around the table, eating and drinking openly with publicly identified sinners. The feeding of the five thousand evoked the continuing memory of this unprecedented embrace of Jesus with God's own great love for those otherwise outside the circle of "the righteousness of God." So Jesus would attend a meal as a guest, but sometime during the meal he would become the host: Through the acceptance of his presence he would host the celebration of the eschatological banquet of God in advance. A meal with Jesus became, through his initiative, a feast with God.

Second, that Jesus accepted sinners through a shared meal is not the only memory that the feeding of the five thousand conveyed. The disciples would remember countless meals where Jesus would bless and break bread for all present. An ordinary meal with Jesus always included gratitude to God for the gift of life and for the good gifts of God necessary to sustain life. The miracle story stimulated the ongoing memory of Jesus' attitude of gratitude whenever they ate together: Jesus "looked up to heaven, and blessed and broke the loaves, and gave them to the disciples, and the disciples gave them to the crowds" (Matt 14:19).

Third, the story of the feeding of the five thousand especially reminded the followers of Jesus of his Last Supper with the Twelve: "While they were eating, Jesus took a loaf of bread, and after blessing it he broke it, gave it to the disciples and said, 'Take, eat; this is my body'" (Matt 26:26). This Passover became Jesus' farewell meal with his disciples, the Last Supper to be celebrated thereafter as the Lord's Supper. Whenever the followers of Jesus celebrated the Supper, the Eucharist, they would remember the fellowship that Jesus had established and his promise of future fellowship in the Kingdom of God. Of course, these memories of Jesus concretized in the feeding of the five thousand became so intertwined that the church could hardly remember one without the other: acceptance in fellowship, companionship at the table, and anticipation through memory of the hope for the Kingdom of God.

Question 3: Did the miracle of the feeding of the five thousand occur? Yes. The story is not difficult to tell. Jesus intended to retreat from the multitudes for rest, but the crowds followed him to the countryside. Jesus welcomed them, teaching and healing. Near the end of the day the disciples told Jesus to send the crowds away to nearby villages to buy food. Instead, Jesus instructed the crowds to sit down in groups. Then he took the five loaves and two fish given him, looked toward heaven, blessed and broke the food, which the disciples distributed to the people. After all had eaten, the disciples collected twelve baskets of uneaten bread and fish. In the open air of the countryside [where else?] Jesus hosted a meal for everyone there through the multiplication of five loaves and two fish: the joyous celebration of the messianic banquet with an eschatological abundance of plenty.

The only critical question that remains concentrates on the "how" of the miracle: Was it a miracle of multiplication or a miracle of inspiration? When the interpreter stands inside the world of the narrative, seeing Jesus as host, the miracle of the feeding of five thousand is nothing less than a miracle of multiplication. When the interpreter stands between the narrative world of the text and the present-day reality of world hunger, witnessing exploding populations and staggering starvation, the miracle Jesus hosts for us is the compassion to share our daily bread with the countless masses of hungry people in our world. The irony is vivid: The interpretation of the miracle as a miracle of multiplication inside the narrative demands the understanding of the miracle as a miracle of inspiration in the contemporary world disclosed through the narrative.

What does the miracle of the feeding of the five thousand contribute to a contemporary understanding of the providence of God? This mighty work of Jesus happened in a historically-defined context with the resources available therein, which includes the faith of Jesus. He did not turn stone into bread to feed the five thousand. On the contrary, Jesus took five loaves and two fish given to him, and he blessed a multitude of people. The miracle presupposed some resources already available in the situation. Beyond the interpretation of the miracle story itself, the providence of God in this instance cannot be abstracted from the historical context in which the miracle occurred. In fact, the Gospels never present Jesus as a miracle worker turning non-living objects into life-giving resources. The transformation of possibility into actuality stamps the miracle of feeding the five thousand.

The significance of this miracle for the life of the church today seems almost obvious. First, within the congregational life of the church the followers of Jesus must remember their own neediness under God and for one another. The compassion of God in the story of Jesus reminds us of God's ongoing welcome and continuing acceptance that is ours through the company of Jesus. Second, the miracle summons the church to give away its own food to enable the Christ to bless the hungry people of our world, whether they are Jesus' disciples or not. Third, the miracle of "the loaves" informs the worshipping life of the church, public and private. The celebration of the Lord's Supper reminds the church of the eschato-logical banquet that Jesus extended to all sorts of sinners, which includes us, and the presence of Jesus through the Supper for the benefit of individuals and families in moments of great need, again, which includes us. The story of the feeding of five thousand is a story of the compassion of God, a story of provision and Presence.

Case Study II: The Healing of the Paralytic

Within the story of feeding the five thousand, the Gospels speak of Jesus' ministry of healing, the most numerous miracles that he performed: "he had compassion for them and cured their sick" (Matt 14:14); "he welcomed them . . . and healed those who needed to be cured" (Luke 9:11). The healing of the paralytic, a story told in all three Synoptic Gospels, is an instructive story of healing for understanding the providence of God. The story combines an instance of healing with Jesus' authority to forgive sin. The recounting of the healing in Mark 2:1-12 is striking and illuminating, but providence focuses attention on the story line of healing.

Scene 1: Jesus had returned to Capernaum after preaching and healing in various parts of Galilee. With fame spreading because of his good news and wonderful deeds, crowds coming from everywhere, Jesus could not enter a town openly without the crush of multitudes. So Mark implies that he slipped quietly back into Capernaum. The crowds nevertheless learned that Jesus was home, and they found him, gathering in the house to listen to him preach the word. The crowd crammed into the house and jammed the doorway, everyone wanting to see, some only able to hear, others milling around outside.

Scene 2: A small group arrived, four men carrying a paralyzed man on a pallet. The crowd-jammed doorway blocked their efforts to enter the house. The widespread enthusiasm for Jesus had prompted their journey to find him, but now the same enthusiasm made it impossible to get the crowd's attention to allow them inside the house. The constant surge of people back and forth reduced the notion of pushing their way through the crowd to utter impossibility.

Scene 3: Unable to enter the door, the four stretcher-bearers refused to leave, Jesus unreachable and the paralytic untouched. Instead, they went up the external stairway to the flat roof of the house—a roof composed of poles from wall to wall, smaller sticks woven together, the entire structure covered with matting and hardened earth. Tearing open the roof posed little difficulty and subsequent repair a minimum cost. The pallet-bearing friends of the paralytic cut open the roof, the falling debris created a hole in the crowd, and the rooftop "let's-do-it squad" lowered the paralytic down to Jesus below.

Scene 4: "When Jesus saw their faith, he said to the paralytic, 'Son, your sins are forgiven.' " Beyond the widespread news of healing power, Jesus now claimed the authority of God in forgiving the paralytic's sins. Against murmurings of blasphemy, Jesus fused the word of forgiveness with the word of healing, charging: "I say to you, stand up, take your mat and go to your home." Actualizing his own faith on top of the faith of his stretcher-bearers, the paralyzed man stood up, picked up his pallet, and walked through an opening sea of people in a once-jammed doorway to friends outside, walking home.

Questions and Answers

The questions that a second innocence puts to the healing of the paralytic are not difficult to ask or answer. (1) What does this story mean to those who remembered it? The activity of Jesus on behalf of the Kingdom of God included an overflowing compassion and special concern for those sick and suffering. That human health is a specific concern of God stamped the memory of the recipients and observers of Jesus' compassionate healing. (2) To what in Jesus' ministry does the healing of the paralytic recall? Jesus healed the sick. He forgave their sins and nurtured healing in their lives, the one none easier than the other, the one no more difficult than the other. (3) Did this particular miracle happen? The differing dynamics that converge in this very human story require a resounding affirmation: "Yes."

Beyond the interpretive questions of a second naiveté, the question of the significance of the healing of the paralytic for a contemporary perspective on God's providence is the more demanding line of inquiry. The features of this narrative accentuate the ordinary human situation as the context of an extraordinary experience of God's mercy. First, the family and friends of the paralyzed man constituted a network of concern who would not accept paralysis as his permanent condition. They believed in the possibility of his healing. Second, when they heard the Jesus-stories of God's good grace and the sick made well, they decided to make a venture toward healing: Jesus could, the stories said, heal the sick. They believed, at least enough to make them try. Third, they encountered an unexpected and apparently insurmountable problem: They could not even get into the door of the house where Jesus was preaching, much less catch his attention for their pallet-bound friend. Yet they did not quit. With imagination and determination, they decided to tear a hole in the roof and lower their paralyzed friend into the circle around Jesus.

Fourth, the friends of the paralytic decided the risk of the anger of the crowd and the interruption of the preaching of Jesus was worth the effort. If the Jesus-stories were true, despite their presumption, he would, if he could, heal their paralyzed "brother." Fifth, when Jesus saw "their faith" through the dust and dirt and debris, he turned to their paralyzed friend with confidence in his faith. Jesus instructed the pallet-laden, paralyzed man to get up, take his pallet with him, and go home. With the faith of friends above him and the faith of Jesus before him, he stood up in his own faith and walked home. The providence of God mediated through Jesus of Nazareth healed the paralyzed man, but God's opportunity for healing occurred in a remarkable series of genuine human decisions and actions stamped with understandable but surprising human activity and creativity. Here, clearly and unmistakably, the providence of God happened in concurrence with a dynamic historical context that maximized the faith of the participants and the uniqueness of Jesus' ministry.

From Gospel Narratives through Modernity to Understanding

When the interpreter of the biblical narrative enters the world of the text, he or she must "suspend critical judgment" and read with "a second naiveté." The task is to listen and see from inside the narrative, namely, the narrative depiction and definition of reality. How does the interpreter move out of the narrative world into the modern world of contemporary life with a reclaimed critical judgment informed by the wonder of the Gospel narrative? If the story has been heard and envisioned on its own terms, the depths of its contents will transcend critical reflection with enduring narrative meaning. Elements of continuity and discontinuity will inform critical assessment and narrative insight, but precisely what the interpreter leaves behind in the narrative world of the miracle story and what he or she brings back into the contemporary world, whether "modern" or "post-modern," will reflect the reciprocity of the life experience of the interpreter with the life experienced in the text.

Responsible narrative interpretation will accept the tension that such reciprocity entails. A hermeneutic of reciprocity will endure the scandal that dialogical interpretation occasions, moving back and forth between the biblical narrative and contemporary lived-experience, listening and learning through the conversation. Likewise, a hermeneutic of reciprocity will bear the scandal of particularity: Some miracle stories will attain greater credibility than others because of the life-experience of the interpreter, always experience communal in scope, and some stories will acquire greater importance than others because of the life-vision of the interpreter, again, communal in scope.

Moving into and out of the Gospel stories, reciprocity of interpretation occurs with variation. The "fit" of contemporary understanding cannot be specified in advance nor hammered out with finality. Is it possible to move through the miracles of Jesus in the Gospels to the experience of miracles today? I believe so. Nevertheless, the miracles of Jesus do *not* constitute the *model* for understanding God's response to the contemporary situation of human need. The story of Jesus feeding the five thousand with five loaves and two fish cannot resolve the tragic problem of starvation in the world today, but the miracle is certainly not irrelevant to the plight of the hungry nor the proper use of world resources. In addition, the most numerous miracles that Jesus performed involved various kinds of healing. Yet contemporary experiences of healing, indeed, miracles of healing, usually occur in the context of modern medicine. The miracles of Jesus are essential pointers to the providential activity of God in the world, but without precise correlation. Although the miracles of Jesus do not constitute the model for envisioning God's activity in the world, the Gospels extend and encircle our world within the horizon of the compassion of God.

Contemporary Narratives

The chasm that separates the memory of life in antiquity from the realities of life today is so radical as to seem unbridgeable. The sharp break that we feel is nowhere more intense than differing perspectives on miracle. Questions abound. Do miracles happen today? Can we identify events that essentially require us to speak of a miracle of God? What would characterize these numinous moments of deliverance or relief? All these questions and more confront theological reflection on genuinely human stories that evoke the suggestion or compel the affirmation of a miracle of God.

A Transforming Moment: James Loder

Of all the literature I have read, the convictional experience of James Loder evokes the affirmation of a miracle of God more than any other. Insofar as possible in the economy of telling his story, Loder himself best narrates the account of his experience of the life-giving Presence of God. He begins with scenic description:

> On Saturday, September 2, 1970, my wife, two daughters, and I set forth on a brief trip from our home in Princeton, New Jersey, to Quebec, Canada. The day was lifted from a travel poster. The sun glistened on the green, wooded hills lining the highway, and a gentle breeze from the east rippled the grass and pushed wispy clouds across a bright blue sky. The setting was in stark contrast to the scene that follows, although quite in keeping with its ultimate significance.[24]

About 4:30 P.M. driving north on the throughway near Kingston, New York, Loder saw a middle-aged woman standing near a disabled car, waving a white glove. Concerned for her safety alongside constant and rapid traffic, Loder stopped to offer assistance. He parked his camper about fifteen feet in front of her car and walked back to the simple problem of a flat tire on the left front wheel. As his wife Arlene chatted with the two stranded women, Loder attempted to lock a wobbly jack into the chassis on the left front side of the car, but without success. He moved over to the right front wheel looking for clues. Just as he knelt in front of the right front fender, he heard an ear-splitting screech of brakes. An older man who had never had an accident in his life had fallen asleep at that exact point on the throughway. He rammed the Olds from behind and shoved it over on top of Loder. Anticipating the impact, Loder kept his legs pushing from under the car to keep his head and shoulders in front of the bumper as the car drove him forward through the gravel. The

---

[24]James E. Loder, *The Transforming Moment: Understanding Convictional Experiences* (San Francisco: Harper and Row Publishers, 1981) 1.

Olds smashed into the rear of the family camper, but "fortunately" on the left side of the Olds. It stopped at an angle with enough space to rest his head and shoulders to the right of the point of impact.

Though injured, trapped with the Olds on his chest, Loder never lost consciousness. He called for help, his wife Arlene the only one able to respond—a slight woman, hardly over five feet tall. She prayed, "In the name of Jesus Christ, in the name of Jesus Christ," lifting with her hands under the bumper. As she began to lose her strength in lifting, she partially lost consciousness for a few seconds. When her head cleared, to her surprise, she had lifted the car. (She broke a vertebrae in her effort, but eventually recovered the full use of her back.) Loder says:

> As I roused myself from under the car, a steady surge of life was rushing through me carrying with it two solid assurances. First, I knew how deeply I felt love for those around me, especially my family. My two daughters sat crying on the embankment, and a deep love reached out of me toward them. The second assurance was that this disaster had a purpose. These were the words with which I repeatedly tried to reassure my wife and children: "Don't worry; this has a purpose."
>
> Walking from the car to the embankment, I never felt more conscious of the life that poured through me, nor more aware that *this life was not my own*. My well-being came from beyond my natural strength, and I lay down on the grass mostly because I thought I ought to.[25]

While he felt anger toward the driver responsible for the collision, "the flow of life" proved a stronger and quieter force. The most significant and memorable effect Loder felt was not pain or anger but the gracious nature of life that he was experiencing. Others stopped to help— state troopers, a clergyman, a physician. To Loder life was never in doubt, because he was being lived, he felt, by a life not his own. Life poured into him from a source of grace beyond the power of the accident to destroy him. While the ambulance took Loder to the hospital, Arlene refused to leave until the trooper promised to find his right thumb torn off in the accident.

---

[25]Ibid., 2-3.

At the hospital the crucifixes in the lobby and patients' rooms provided Loder the best account of his condition: In the cruciform image of Jesus physical pain converged with the assurance of life greater than death, a sense of promise in the midst of suffering. The surgeon said they would round off the thumb quickly in order to get him oxygen for his bleeding lung as soon as possible. Arlene telephoned her father, a clergyman near Chicago, finding him at church with congregational friends in prayer. They began to pray for him at once, just about the time Loder entered surgery. Unaware of their prayers, he felt the power of life from beyond him rush once again into his body. Loder described the moment as a sense of power that was not impersonal but originating from the awareness of Another who positively intended his well-being. With that intuition, the pain decreased. In the waiting room his older daughter Kim stopped crying and told her mother that Daddy was going to be all right.

As he entered surgery, Loder saw the tired faces of the surgical staff waiting for another grim life-against-death struggle. Loder happily assured them that he would soon be well. He remembers: "It did not seem inappropriate in that *joyful Presence* to invite the staff to join me in a hymn of praise before the surgery began."[26] Whatever their thoughts, the staff stood quietly as he sang a few bars of "Fairest Lord Jesus." The atmosphere nonetheless changed, and contagious humor turned into laughter and smiles. The surgeon rounded off and sewed up Loder's thumb. As visible evidence of what had occurred invisibly, Loder's bluish skin turned pink, which signaled the bleeding in his lungs had stopped and oxygen would not be needed.

Two days after the accident the surgeon cancelled plans to perform skin grafts on damaged areas of Loder's back, saying that he knew when to step aside and let God do the healing. The two women, themselves injured in the accident, became the Loders' friends, but James Loder

---

[26]Ibid., 4 (italics added). Several days before the accident Arlene Loder had written down some notes during prayer, which included a statement quite puzzling at the time: "Take the cup I have prepared for you" (5). James Loder does not explicitly correlate Arlene's prayer notes with his accident, but he suggests a connection of some sort. Any interpretation is necessarily retrospective and partly speculative. "The cup" has multiple and different meanings in Scripture and church tradition, e.g., Ps 23:5 and Mark 14:36. If applied to the accident—a significant "if"—"the cup" could address Arlene positively in the case of Loder's survival or his death. The cryptic line does not denote any form of historical determinism.

could never reach the driver of the car who had crashed into the Olds-mobile. The entire experience reshaped Loder's life. Though difficulties accompanied the affirmation of the depths of this remarkable experience, reflective and relational difficulties, James Loder accepted the integrity of his "transforming moment."

A Tragic Moment: L. D. Johnson

Unlike the life-changing story of James Loder, L. D. Johnson narrates a different story—a tragic story of the death of his daughter Carole in an automobile accident on 21 December 1962, the day after her twenty-third birthday. Like Loder, Johnson begins his story with scenic description.

> The day Carole was killed had an uneasy quality about it. We awakened to leaden skies and chill more penetrating than brisk-cold. There were suggestions we might have a white Christmas. Marion didn't like it; neither did I. Carole would be leaving Richmond, Virginia, at one o'clock, after classes were dismissed from Hermitage High School where she was in her first year as an English teacher. She would be driving home—four hundred miles to Greenville, South Carolina.[27]

Before breakfast they talked about the inclement weather and decided to call Carole to tell her the weather looked threatening and to ask her not to drive home but to travel by bus or train or plane. What else could you say to a twenty-three-old young woman who had been grown-up almost all her life, who had hitchhiked over Europe, and who was now a high school teacher in a city two states away? Marion called Carole to explain their concern about the long drive in bad weather. Carole assured her mother not to worry about her because she would drive carefully. Near Oxford, North Carolina, a tractor-trailer truck collided with Carole's small car and collapsed it into junk. She died in minutes. Someone told L. D. later that the only thing she said was, "It hurts so much."

Some fifteen years later L. D. Johnson still lived with the questions of his grief that his faith in God did not answer and with the mystery that even God's love could not resolve. In his poignant memoir, *The Morning*

---

[27]L. D. Johnson, *The Morning After Death* (Nashville: Broadman Press, 1978; Smyth & Helwys, 1995) 15.

After Death, he reflects on the agony of Carole's loss with the clarity and difficulty of a man of faith for whom questions remain. L. D. Johnson best speaks for himself. He asks the most elementary and the most difficult questions:

> If God is God could he not have kept the accident from happening? The slight alteration of any one of several contingencies would have produced another result. One twist of the wheel, a hundred yards ahead or behind on the road—a tiny, insignificant detail—ten ticks of her little Swiss watch—and she would have missed the truck that crushed out her life.
>
> I ask myself, *If I knew beforehand that such a loss was about to occur, would I not have arranged for those ten ticks or hundred yards?* Wouldn't you? Or would you say, "Sorry, I'd like to help but, you see, we've got rules"? Why didn't God intervene, just a little, just enough to slow her down or speed her up to get her past that icy spot at a time different from the truck's exact arrival? It is hard to think that God's purpose is better served by Carole's being killed. It is impossible for me to believe that God would not have spared her if he could, and I wonder why he couldn't.[28]

The theological issues in Johnson's questions are central to the conception of the providence of God. On the one side, he thinks in terms of a monarchical model of God's relationship to the world: God could have prevented the accident through "the slight alteration of any one of several contingencies." Again: "Why didn't God intervene . . . to get her past that icy spot at a time different from the truck's exact arrival?" On the other side, Johnson poses questions that reflect a sense of the self-limitation of God: "Or would you say, 'Sorry, I'd like to help but, you see, we've got rules'?" "I wonder why God couldn't [spare her]." A model of providence that operates on the basis of the self-limitation of God must distinguish in some fashion between abstract possibilities and real possibilities, a distinction that Johnson does not explore. Moreover, he does not reckon with the sharply deliminited number of variables in the ten ticks of Carole's Swiss watch, an exceedingly short time frame with the probability of accidental death correspondingly higher. That God

---

[28]Ibid., 101.

actively engaged the variables in this mishap but could not turn them away from tragedy is a painful assessment of her accidental death. Yet casualties in accidents happen everyday all over the world with God's active engagement but without God's intervention and deliverance.

Sixteen pages later, L. D. Johnson framed his question quite differently. Automobile accidents kill fifty thousand Americans every year, about half involving alcoholic beverages, others carelessness or recklessness. Yet some accidents just happen without such complicating factors. Johnson continued:

> That seems to have been the nature of Carole's accident. It was no less fatal and permanent than if we could have blamed somebody. Could God have prevented it? Yes, since he is God. Why didn't he? I do not know. I live with the mystery, knowing that what happened to Carole and her family is so much a part of the human tragedy as not to merit space in the obituary notices save in the tiny circles in which we all live our lives, experience our joys, and weep our tears. Does God rejoice and weep with us? Yes, I believe he does.[29]

Unlike what he had written earlier, Johnson then wrote: "Could God have prevented [the accident]? Yes, since he is God. Why didn't he? I do not know." The statement as it stands is self-contained, an affirmation of the mystery within which L. D. Johnson chose to live and die. Was he aware of the contradiction between this declaration and his statement sixteen pages earlier: *"It is impossible for me to believe that God would not have spared her if he could, and I wonder why he couldn't"*? I think so. Did he intend for his later statement to negate his earlier conclusion? I think not. *"It is impossible for me to believe. . . ."* remains, qualified to be sure. Yet it belongs within his theological grief as surely as his faith. He chose to live with the unanswered questions and the contradiction. I suspect L. D. Johnson felt the disquieting tension between the affirmation of the self-limitation of God on the one side and the hope for resurrection into the Kingdom on God on the other. The underlying question that proves so troublesome is whether or not a monarchical model of the providence of God proves necessary for the eschatological reality of the Kingdom of God. Eshatology notwithstanding, the story of

---

[29]Ibid., 116.

Carole Johnson converges with the stories of millions of others and confronts us with the question of the viability of the monarchical model of God's relationship to the world.

An Analytical Inquiry

Reflecting on these two very different stories, several questions come immediately to mind: Does God control specific weather patterns, at least smaller configurations within larger patterns? Does God determine with subtlety almost unrecognized the speed of an automobile or truck? Does God provide protection beyond the structural safety of a particular car? Does God regulate the possible intersection of two vehicles on an icy highway? Do the prayers of a father and mother have life-preserving impact on the specific circumstances of their children for whom they pray? These questions are all the more difficult because of the remarkable experience of James Loder. Do these two accidents present conflicting perspectives on the activity and availability of God? Did God work a miracle for James Loder but chose not to grant one to Carole Johnson? Miracle and providence converge on this point: Is a miracle always a possibility? Or again, under what conditions might a miracle occur?

L. D. Johnson's comment is my starting point: "The slight alteration of any one of several contingencies would have produced another result." The variables or contingencies in Loder's accident are numerous, but some are especially important: (1) The traveling of the Loders on the throughway in a timeframe of a stopped car and a woman waving a white glove for help: *contingency*. (2) The decision to stop and to provide assistance: *contingency*. (3) Unable to lock the jack into the chassis on the left front side, Loder moving over to the right front fender for clues: *contingency*. (4) A sixty-four-year old man going to sleep in his car at precisely that point on the throughway: *contingency*. (5) The screeching brakes and impact of the older man's car into the rear of the Oldsmobile, shoving it over on top of Loder, who remained uninjured and clear-headed enough to continue pushing his legs under the car to keep head and shoulders up in front of the bumper, dragging him forward through the gravel: *contingency*. (6) The angle of impact of the Olds into the family's camper fifteen feet away on the car's left side (where Loder had been working the jack shortly before, a position that would have crushed him dead), an angle that gave him space for head and shoulders:

contingency. (7) Arlene, the only one not injured in the accident, rushing to help, praying as she lifted the car off her husband: *contingency.* (8) Loder able to rouse himself out from under the car, injured but not fatally: *contingency.*

Precisely at this point in the indeterminacy of the accident—at this point and not before, alive instead of dead—Loder experienced "a steady surge of life" rushing through him. He felt a remarkable sense of the life-giving Presence of God, of grace. *God could grace him with surging life because the variables in this accident did not kill him.* Could this accident have happened with another configuration of contingencies that would have ended his life? Yes. The steady surge of life happened within him only after and in the context of a configuration of variables that had not already destroyed him.

Again, as L. D. Johnson said, "The slight alteration of any one of several contingencies would have produced a different result." Did the felt-love and deep-gratitude of Loder enhance his recovery? Yes. Did the prayers of family and friends in Chicago contribute to his well-being? Yes. Did Arlene prove to be the only human agent available to save her husband's life, praying as she did so. Yes. Did God predetermine this accident with its mostly joyous outcome? No. The provision of God happened moment by moment in conjunction with Loder's need: The temporal progression in the happening of the accident included life-destroying and live-giving variables, but in continuing response to God, through God's configurating interaction with all aspects of the event, the arrangement of the variables enabled Loder to survive, retrospectively, a miraculous event in the providence of God.

What happened to James Loder occurred with variables that did not kill him but permitted a stunning new experience of God, with the accident over and James Loder still very much alive. The disaster that befell Carole Johnson killed her almost immediately, her last words, "It hurts so much." Miracles do happen, the story of James Loder affirms, but a miracle is not always a possibility, which the tragic story of Carole Johnson makes painfully plain.

Conclusion

The great miracle that God has given to us is the gift of Jesus Christ. Accordingly, the miracles of Jesus throughout the Gospels indicate the transforming Presence of God in situations of dramatic human need, miracles of God's compassion that evoked spontaneous joy. Compassion, prayer, and miracle are inseparable themes in the providence of God for Christian life. The miracles of Jesus, especially his miracles of healing, are God's confrontation with the ever present problem of chaos and sin. Yet Jesus did not forfeit his creaturely identity but worked miracles as a graciously gifted, Spirit-filled, and prayerful man. The stories in the Story of Jesus radiate the compassion of God—the God who loves us, who hears and sees us, who continually endeavors to bless us. So we pray in our closets for compassion, for grace, in Jesus' name, because Jesus is the parable of God, the God of a vulnerable compassion.

Chapter 5

The Politics of Providence

ON 6 AUGUST 1945, an American B-29 called the "Enola Gay" dropped a bomb with a nuclear warhead on the Japanese city of Hiroshima. In a blinding flash of light, "dazzling white" (Mark 9:3a), the face of the earth and sky was radically and irrevocably changed, never to be the same again. The mushroom cloud rising mountains high above what had once been a thriving city marked a turning point in history for the future of humankind. Although a voice could not be heard from the cloud, the mushroom cloud contained a staggering message: *"This is the risk of the future, the power and possibility of the complete destruction of life on planet Earth."*

The secret of the Manhattan Project had been disclosed to powers weak and mighty in a world ravaged with war. Few churchmen and hardly anyone in the world of politics, certainly not President Truman and his political and military advisors, knew that 6 August 1945, on the calendar of the church was the day of the Feast of the Transfiguration. In fact, Vice President Truman knew almost nothing of the secret Manhattan Project to create the atomic bomb until the death of President Franklin Roosevelt on 12 April 1945.[1] Who could have suspected the coincidence of the explosive transfiguration of politics with the celebration of the Transfiguration of Christ on 6 August 1945? Transfiguration marked a turning point in history that can never be turned back to what had been before.

The Story of Jesus constitutes the definitive event in the Story of God, and the Transfiguration occasioned the decisive turning point in the story of Jesus. In its depths the Transfiguration of Christ is nothing less

---

[1]Jonathan Daniels, *The Man of Independence* (Philadelphia. J. B. Lippincott Company, 1950) 258-67, esp. 266; note 287-88. The author of this biography of Truman does not even mention the bombing of Nagasaki.

than a political paradigm.[2] Is there a politics of providence? Yes, because the providence of God occurs in the swirling historical movement of social and political processes wherein people live. The way God works in sociopolitical spheres requires reflection on the activity and goals, the responses and contribution of individuals within groups, small and large, as small as families in a community and as large as nations among nations. Events of fate and destiny happen to individuals, families, communities, and nations within the social and political dynamics of history. Since the endeavor to understand God's providence confronts issues and concerns embedded in social and political life, any proposal to interpret the provident activity of God must at least ask the question of a political theology.

The purpose of this chapter is to explore the politics of providence, but the attempt to sketch in the most elementary fashion the aspects of a politics of the providence of God may very well be an impossible enterprise, because it presupposes a Christian interpretation of history, which lies far beyond the limits of this essay. Despite the brevity of my analysis the theme of the providential activity of God in social and political life must be addressed.[3] Within the limitations of this essay, therefore, I

---

[2]See Paul Lehmann, *The Transfiguration of Politics* (New York: Harper & Row, Publishers, 1975) 96-97. As the Introduction to this chapter suggests, I am following the lead of Paul Lehmann, who interprets the Transfiguration of Christ as a theological and political paradigm. The thematic application of the Transfiguration to revolution (xiii, 103-226) proved to be ill-founded, however, which left Lehmann's incisive interpretation of the Transfiguration of Christ floundering in the typology of then-current revolutions. See, e.g., James M. Gustafson, "A Review of *The Transfiguration of Politics* by Paul Lehmann," *Theology Today* 32 (July 1975): 197-202

[3]The theologian working in the United States today has several programmatic alternatives for addressing the broad arena of politics. See John Howard Yoder, *The Politics of Jesus* (Grand Rapids MI: Wm. B. Eerdmans Publishing Co., rev. ed. 1994: 1972), a landmark in Christian ethics. In addition, see the Powers triology with a practical case study by Walter Wink: *Naming the Powers* (Philadelphia: Fortress Press, 1984); *Unmasking the Powers* (Philadelphia: Fortress Press, 1986); *Engaging the Powers* (Minneapolis: Fortress Press, 1992); *Violence and Nonviolence in South Africa: Jesus' Third Way* (Philadelphia: New Society Publishers, 1987). See Stephen C. Mott, *Biblical Ethics and Social Change* (New York: Oxford University Press, 1982), a major challenge to American envangelicals. Not to overlook, Glen H. Stassen, *Just Peacemaking: Transforming Initiatives for Justice and Peace* (Louisville: Westminster/John Knox Press,

intend to highlight the politics of providence in different and sharply delimited historical settings.

The paradigmatic event in the Synoptic Gospels that frames the discussion is the Transfiguration of Jesus. This occurrence marked the end of Jesus' mission in Galilee and the beginning of his journey to Jerusalem to confront the religious and political authorities with his claims, which included his bold action of judgment in the Temple. The analysis shifts subsequently from the Gospel narratives to an examination of three different contemporary narratives. These stories demonstrate the inseparability of the politics of providence from the fate and/or destiny of the advocates of social and political change as well as for those who potentially benefit from their work. These representative figures are Marian Wright Edelman, founder of the Children's Defense Fund in Washington DC; Archbishop Oscar Romero, martyred for the sake of the poor in El Salvador; and Langdon Gilkey, premier American theologian who has addressed the question of providence in his Christian interpretation of history and in a brief theological autobiography.

The Synoptic Gospels all narrate the story of the transfiguration, the Gospel of Mark the most apocalyptic and most vivid.

> Six days later, Jesus took with him Peter and James and John, and led them up a high mountain apart, by themselves. And he was transfigured before them, and his clothes became dazzling white, such as no one on earth could bleach them. And there appeared to them Elijah with Moses, who were talking with Jesus. Then Peter said to Jesus, "Rabbi, it is good for us to be here; let us make three [tabernacles], one for you, one for Moses, and one for Elijah." He did not know what to say, for they were terrified. Then a cloud overshadowed them, and from the cloud there came a voice, "This is my Son, the Beloved; listen to him!" Suddenly when they looked around, they saw no one with them any more, but only Jesus. (Mark 9:2-8)

1992), especially the innovative interpretation of the Sermon on the Mount.

The Experience of Providence:
Sociopolitical Transformation

The Transfiguration of Jesus occurred between the confession of Jesus as the Messiah at Caesarea-Philippi and the turn of Jesus to Jerusalem for confrontation with his adversaries during Passover. Furthermore, the Transfiguration of Jesus happened between the first and second passion predictions of his suffering and death, the murderous reaction of his religious and political opposition. The narrative of the Transfiguration with Moses and Elijah accentuates the interpenetration of political and religious issues, social and economic concerns that each faced as the prophets of God: The presence of Moses and Elijah at the Transfiguration of Christ already suggests the political dynamics in this singular event.

That the Transfiguration on a mountain top happened simultaneously with the Feast of the Tabernacles contextualizes its significance for the vocation of Jesus. As God had acted in the social and political arena of Israel in the past, God would continue to do so for the well-being of the children of Abraham in the future. Through Israel and its Christ God willfully and continually works for the healthy life of all people, Jew and Gentile alike. The Christian appropriation of the Hebrew scriptures as the Word of God is the tacit recognition that the story of Israel is crucial for a Christian understanding of providence. Thus the politics of God continues beyond the days and deeds of Moses and Elijah to the words and way of Jesus through his church.

The interpretation of the providence of God cannot be concentrated on the life of the individual person but requires an understanding of the social and political context in which every person lives. Gustavo Gutiérrez has addressed the fundamental responsibility of the Christian community:

> Every attempt to evade the struggle against alienation and the violence of the powerful and for a more just and more human world is the greatest infidelity to God. To know God is to work for justice.[4]

---

[4]Gustavo Guitiérrez, *A Theology of Liberation: History, Politics, and Salvation* (Maryknoll NY: Orbis Books, 1988; 1973) 156.

Thus, the characterization of the providential activity of God must include the social, economic, and political processes that inevitably shape each human life within its particular communal setting. Persons in communities of every configuration are summoned to respond to the problems and crises that the community faces, working to engage the problems and to resolve the crises, whether the specific guidance of God is sought or not.

The aspects of providence discussed thus far include the importance of the sociopolitical currents that move people and shape the limits of God's providential care: the mandate of King Herod to kill all potential rivals to his throne; the Roman rule and military occupation of Judah; the orders of the Roman governor Pilate to murder a group of Galileans preparing sacrifices in the Temple; the economic deprivation and hardship of the marginalized people of the land; the ever present plight of the poor; the mobilization of guerrilla activity among the Zealots to drive the Romans from "the land of promise"; the collaboration of Jewish harlots and tax collectors with the hated Roman authorities for monetary gain. In these situations of biblical history the providence of God aims to nurture blessing in the experiences of each person in the context of the corporate structures of life—political opportunity, economic necessities, racial equality, social responsibility, and religious toleration. Within these corporate structures providence is most noticeable through its limits and inadequacies.

The necessity for a politics of providence can be argued on the basis of the story of providence in the history of the people of God chronicled in the pages of biblical history. Yet the contemporary problem of discerning with even minimum insight the work of God in regional, national, and international arenas proves almost impossible: None of us has the capacity for envisioning the activity of God for the well-being of humanity through countless centuries in thousands of countries with millions of communities for billions of people, always amid the swirling mix of social, political, and economic concerns. Are any criteria available for assessing some measure of the accomplishment of the purposes of God in the staggering complexity of the human story, from farms and villages through neighborhoods and cities to nations among nations? Two criteria are fundamental for a providential perspective nurtured in the biblical traditions and broadened to include an enlightened humanism: *The criteria are justice and peace.*

The experience of providence of God in the Transfiguration of Jesus the Christ is the intention of God to generate the transformation of socio-political processes through the Christ on the way to the Kingdom of God, which at least means approximations of justice and peace. The activity of God through people in the past and the anticipation of people for the promise of the future intersect in the present, an intersection of the past with its limitations and the future with its possibilities for creative transformation in the present.

Part One: Messianic Politics

The providence of God in the Transfiguration of Jesus points to the necessity of messianic politics and the rejection of political messianism. The vision of the Kingdom of God requires the political agenda of justice and peace, the advocacy of justice for the powerless, the poor, and the marginalized through nonviolent confrontation with systems of exploitation and oppression—systems that threaten any significant opposition with deadly force. Therefore, the path of Jesus moved from the Mount of Transfiguration to a confrontation with his adversaries in Jerusalem who rejected his vision of the Kingdom of God and the authority from God that his message implied. *Caution*: The transfiguration of politics in the light of the Transfiguration of Christ inevitably means confrontation and suffering.

Movements in Transfiguration

Mark locates the Transfiguration of Christ at the center of his Gospel, because it constitutes the turning point in the story of Jesus, the end of his Galilean ministry and the beginning of his journey to Jerusalem. What kind of Messiah would he be? Would Jesus continue to refuse to become the charismatic revolutionary that Peter's confession may have implied?

If so, why? If not, why not? The story unfolds in three phases that anchors it in early Hebraic understanding of the Presence of God.[5]

The Transfiguration of Jesus

Jesus ascended a high mountain with his friends, Peter, James, and John. "And he was transfigured before them, and his clothes became dazzling white, such as no one on earth could bleach them" (Mark 9:2b-3). Matthew adds, "his face shone like the sun" (17:2b). The introductory phrase, "six days later," would remind the disciples of the ascent of Moses up the mountain with Aaron, Nadab, Abihu, and the seventy elders. "The glory of the Lord settled on Mount Sinai, and the cloud covered it for six days; on the seventh day [God] called to Moses out of the cloud" (Exod 24:16). When God spoke to him, the Lord would "speak to Moses face to face, as one speaks to a friend" (Exod 33:11a). When he came down from Mount Sinai, without knowing it himself, the face of Moses shined with the glory of God (Exod 34:29), and he had to veil his face among the people. The light of Moses' visage, nevertheless, cannot be compared with the Transfiguration of Jesus. The entire person of Jesus glistened with the glory of God. The radiant form of Jesus and the shimmering white brightness of his clothing magnified the intimate nearness of the Presence of God.

The image of the Transfiguration is apocalyptic, the eschatological pressure upon time rapidly nearing the end-time. Jesus was transfigured in eschatological glory. Past, present, and future converge, uniting history and hope, the confrontation of a vulnerable messianic Presence with a Future willing to become present. The Biblical Story of covenant and call, exodus and the land, judgment and exile, promise and restoration, advent and kingdom, crucifixion and exaltation—the Story rushes to unveil the messianic secret in a messianic exodus and the transformation of

---

[5]Lehmann, *Transfiguration*, 79-94. While Lehmann has especially influenced me with his analysis of the structure and significance of the Synoptic accounts of the Transfiguration, the formulation of a politics of providence and its subsequent application in the cleansing of the Temple—a politics of confrontation in the service of a politics of compassion—remain my own perspective. This perspective provides the framework for the selection and interpretation of the three representatives of a contemporary politics of providence.

reality through the eschatological glory of God. In the Transfiguration of Jesus Christ the politics of God transfigures all the politics of humanity. Indeed, the radical interpenetration of Presence and power in the Transfiguration of Jesus promises the imminent transformation of everything in the eschatological arrival of God.

The Appearance of Elijah and Moses

The mystical Presence of the incomparable glory of God so claimed the minds of Peter, James, and John that they were drawn into and participated in the vision. The glory of God transparent in the figure of Jesus evoked the images of Elijah and Moses: "And there appeared to them Elijah with Moses, who were talking with Jesus" (Mark 9:4). The disciples saw his glory, because only Jesus had been transfigured: Moses and Elijah stood talking to him.

If the accent is on Elijah, as in Mark 9:4, the fulfillment of all things is no longer imminent but has arrived. When Peter subsequently asked if Elijah must come before the Messiah, Jesus tells him that Elijah has already come in the murdered John the Baptist, and what they did to John, they conspire to do to Jesus (Matt 17:9-13). What does it mean in Matthew to accentuate the appearance of Moses and Elijah together? Moses and Elijah witness to the righteousness of God in the Law and the prophets that now constitutes judgment against Israel and hope for a new humanity. They contextualize Israel's election and calling to participate in God's humanizing activity in the world through covenant and commitment, freely offered and freely accepted. The Law expressed the dynamic direction of the will of God and therefore the boundaries of covenantal faithfulness that nurtures genuine humanness, God's work of humanization in the world. The prophets, from Moses the Lawgiver to Elijah the Law-fulfiller, were the appointed guardians of the righteousness of God in action. Contrary to something like an ethical norm, the righteousness of God is quality of relation offered to and accepted by Israel, a relationship of fellowship and reciprocity.

The righteousness of God refers to the Presence and activity of God for the help and salvation of the chosen people, the most important affirmation about God in covenantal relationship with Israel. Correspondingly, righteousness had central significance for the relationships of all human life in Israel in covenant with God. A person is righteous who fulfills the specific claims that fellowship with God required in relationship to other persons. Since God's help and salvation are especially intended for the deliverance of the poor, the level of concern for the outcasts, the impoverished, and the oppressed constitutes the essential measure of justice in the life of a people. When Matthew identifies Moses and Elijah in conversation with Jesus on the Mount of Transfiguration, the Gospel of Matthew identifies Jesus of Nazareth as a new Moses, the one in whom authentic humanity takes form and who discloses the way of love as the fulfillment of the Law and the prophets, hence, the practice of righteousness. Thus the appearance of Moses and Elijah together means the beginning of the messianic age and the arrival of the eschatological glory of God.[6]

What kind of glory transfigured the Nazarene with a Galilean accent clothed in peasant's garb? Whereas Moses and Elijah had only glimpsed the divine glory—Moses in the cleft of a rock, Elijah in the still, small voice of silence—Jesus had become dazzling bright through the Presence of God. No one could be compared to him in the whole history of Israel, because Jesus not only fulfilled but transcended the Law and the prophets. Moses' glimpse of divine glory occurred at Mount Sinai after he had killed three thousand who had worshiped the golden calf. Likewise, Elijah's experience of the Presence of God's glory happened after he had killed hundreds of the priests of Baal in the victory at Mount Carmel. Both Elijah and Moses enacted God's judgment by killing the enemies of God in the Name of God: They had hands bloodied with the sword. Conversely, Jesus would enter the valley of the shadow of death with an awareness of the veiled Presence of God's glory in his life. God had sometimes accomplished a particular providential purpose through violence in the past, but the Presence of divine glory in the face of Jesus turned toward the cross meant that God would never again sanction or authorize violence to achieve providential goals.[7]

Is this unwarranted speculation? Only the Gospel of Luke tells us what Moses and Elijah discussed with Jesus: "They spoke of his exodus that he was to accomplish in Jerusalem" (Luke 9:31, RSV). The messianic work of Jesus can be described as Exodus in reverse: The Exodus

---

[6]Ibid., 87-88, 257-58.
[7]See E. Frank Tupper, "The Providence of God in Christological Perspective," *Review & Expositor* 82 (1985): 586.

of Jesus is an Exodus into Egypt rather than out of Egypt. The Exodus of Jesus means the giving of the first-born son instead of taking the son first born. The Exodus of Jesus into Egypt culminates in the weakness of God on the cross instead of the power of God in liberating deliverance. Jesus would not be the political Messiah of Israel for whom his people prayed, but he would incarnate the Presence of God for all people in every time and place.

The Cloud and the Voice

The memory of the theophanies of Moses and Elijah on Mount Horeb converge in a dramatic climax: a cloud, like the cloud that descended over the mountain wherein Moses met with God; and a voice, like the voice that addressed Elijah after the sound of utter silence. As a cloud overshadowed them, the Voice of God said: "This is my Son, the Beloved; listen to him" (Mark 9:7). Then with breathtaking speed it was over. Jesus stood calm and alone.

Put precisely: What makes the Transfiguration of Jesus the transfiguration of politics? The appearance of Moses and Elijah with Jesus denotes in part the political character of this event, because each had exercised decisive political leadership. Furthermore, the phrase, "six days later," correlates the Transfiguration with the Feast of the Tabernacles, an annual festive celebration in Jerusalem. Peter reinforces the point with his unreflective, anxious suggestion to build three "tabernacles" for these three prophets of God. The Feast of the Tabernacles stirred the expectation that God would once again dwell with the people in a tabernacle as God did in the wilderness wandering. In fact, "stirring" does not say enough, because a messianic fever sometimes seized the crowds of worshipers during the excitement of the feast. The culmination of the celebration on the seventh day roused hope for imminent national deliverance through the coming of the Messiah and the inauguration of the messianic age. The Zealots would be in Jerusalem recruiting the faithful to join them in their preparation to overthrow the blasphemous, oppressive Roman rule over Israel, a revolutionary bid that they would win with the people and then lose to Rome forty years later.

Now the fundamental question: Why did Jesus go up the mountain with Peter, James, and John instead of celebrating the Feast with his disciples and friends in Jerusalem? In the midst of the pain and suffering of God's people, the temptation to become a political Messiah and the deliverer of his people, the third temptation in the wilderness, still haunted him. With his immeasurable compassion, Jesus deeply desired to relieve their suffering and revitalize their faith in God. The Transfiguration lies between the temptations in the wilderness on the one side and the agony in Gethsemane on the other. Those closest to him, remembering him, knew that the Presence of God in his life occasioned a transfiguration through attending sensitivity to "a very present voice— glory in an overshadowing cloud, *power in darkness.*"[8] Jesus rejected the political messianism of the Zealots, and he registered his dissent through his refusal to go to Jerusalem to celebrate the Feast of the Tabernacles.

The question of Jesus' relationship to the Zealots requires a brief analysis, because the question of Zealotic revolution impinges on Jesus' perspective on politics, and here, the politics of violence.[9] (1) Like the Zealots, Jesus preached the nearness of the Kingdom of God. The Zealots anticipated the coming messianic kingdom through a war of liberation against Rome. Jesus rejected the option of military violence, because it would signify his lack of confidence in the eschatological action of God. (2) Jesus understood his ministry to anticipate the Kingdom of God, the participation of others through the free gift of grace. More than the Pharisees, the Zealots demonstrated a radicalized legalism of the Law *and* the land, but Jesus rejected the legalism of each in favor of the righteousness of God, a gift of grace to be received like a child and pursued as an adult. (3) Unlike the Zealots, who despised all collaborators with Rome, Jesus included tax collectors, harlots, and sinners within his circle of friends. In the midst of Roman oppression he actually celebrated the arriving Kingdom of God, "a glutton and drunkard" (Luke 7:34) his opponents tagged him, ridiculing him for his folly amid the desperate condition of his people. (4) While the Zealots opposed the social injustice and political exploitation of the poor, a situation demanding revolution, Jesus refused to summon the poor to revenge against those who

---

[8]Samuel Terrien, *The Elusive Presence: Toward a New Biblical Theology* (New York: Harper & Row Publishers, 1978) 427 (italics added).

[9]See Jürgen Moltmann, *The Crucified God* (New York: Harper & Row, Publishers, 1974) 136-45. The best account of the Zealots available is probably Martin Hengel, *The Zealots: Investigations Into the Period From Herod I Until 70 A.D.* (Edinburgh: T. & T. Clark, 1989).

oppressed them. Jesus believed the righteousness of God to be the way of peace: "Love your enemies and pray for those who persecute you" (Matt 5:44). (5) Jesus rejected the right of human beings, Romans and Zealots alike, to pass judgment and execute vengeance for the sake of their own cause, because the *Abba* God is not the righteous avenger but the coming God of forgiveness and grace. (6) Like the Zealots, Jesus challenged the status quo and those who maintained it for their own gain. He provoked considerable political unrest for all sides: To the Zealots he was a traitor and to the Romans another Jewish instigator of political discontent. The Roman governor Pilate could not distinguish between an anti-Roman Zealot leader and a non-Zealot agitator for peace. Therefore, Jesus knew, public confrontation with his adversaries would precipitate religious condemnation and the probability of political execution.

The eschatological fore-shortening of Jesus' expectation of the Kingdom of God gave him confidence in the transfiguration of politics that would transform all injustice and oppression into the justice and peace of God. "Six days later" anticipated a new Sabbath, the coming of the Shalom of God in justice and peace through love. Jesus relativized all established political systems, then and now, with his proclamation of the Kingdom of God, and the Voice from the cloud said: "Listen to him" (Mark 9:7b). The Transfiguration of Jesus contains a paradigmatic political mandate: the rejection of political messianism and the necessity of messianic politics.[10]

The Transfiguration of Jesus and the cloud overshadowing them combined to signify the power of the Most High, but the power of the Most High accomplished its deeds in darkness. The Voice from the cloud echoed the blessing of Jesus earlier at his baptism, but the proclamation of "my Son, the Beloved," within the darkness of the cloud discloses pathos in the blessing of God. As the Lucan account concludes, the disciples who had witnessed the sight and heard the voice must have grasped the ominous character of the scene: "When the voice had spoken, Jesus was found alone. *And they kept silent*" (Luke 9:36a). Previously at Caesarea-Philippi Peter had confessed Jesus to be the Christ, but Jesus had rebuked Peter for protesting the path of his suffering and death. Now God enjoined the disciples to listen and to obey Jesus. He is more than

---

[10]So Paul Lehmann, *Transfiguration*, 91-92.

the Christ: He is the Son of God. The vision of glory coincides with the voice of pathos and anticipates the tragic destiny that awaits Jesus in Jerusalem.

The Cleansing of the Temple

The entry of Jesus into Jerusalem riding a colt evoked a spontaneous outpouring of jubilation from the crowds. Many spread their garments on the road and others leafy branches cut from the fields. Those who ran in front of him and those who followed shouted words of welcome: "Hosanna! Blessed is the one who comes in the name of the Lord! Blessed is the coming kingdom of our ancestor David! Hosanna in the highest heaven!" (Mark 11:7-10). What kind of entrance into the Holy City is this one? While it is not the obvious entry of a Christ-King, the event is a messianic act, a royal entry that at least stirred messianic hope. With a commanding presence Jesus walked into the Temple and surveyed everything, an inspection to determine clearly and personally whether or not the worship in Temple fulfilled the purpose of God. It would be naive to assume that the Roman garrison paid scant attention to the sudden and prolonged excitement of crowds surrounding the entry of a striking figure riding into the city and going directly to the Temple. A city crowded with Jewish pilgrims from the world over and a royal welcome for a charismatic Nazarene of whom they had already heard would intensify their surveillance and heighten their readiness to respond to trouble in the city.

Protest in the Temple

The faithful Hebrews believed that only in the Temple at Jerusalem could they adequately worship God. Only in the Temple could they offer sacrifices according to the Law through the service of the priesthood. The importance of the Temple in Jerusalem for the worship of God can hardly be overestimated. The splendor of Herod's Temple, the massive crowds of pilgrims who gathered to celebrate the principal feast days, the devotion of the Jews in the care and defense of the sacred place—all underscored the people's veneration of the Temple. Four markets on the Mount of Olives within the Temple grounds enabled pilgrims to buy doves and other ritually pure offerings for sacrifice. Yet these markets were under the jurisdiction of the Sanhedrin instead of the High Priest. Precisely when the sale of animals began in the Court of the Gentiles remains uncertain, but the availability of the markets on the Mount of Olives meant that another market place was not necessary. Rather, it was an exceptional and shocking license that the priests, all Sadducees, initiated for monetary gain. Entering the Temple, Jesus expressed his moral outrage at the flagrant abuse of the purpose of the Temple of God. The abuse of the Court of the Gentiles put everyone involved in disobedience to God—priests, merchants, and worshipers alike. Jesus actually drove the marketers out of the Temple, an act of prophetic confrontation but not an assault of intemperate violence.

While Jesus vigorously established order in the Court of the Gentiles, he did not interrupt worship within the sanctuary. The Court of the Gentiles was a wide enclosure with a high partition wall that separated it from the inner courts of the Temple. Aside from prohibition to use the court as a thoroughfare, it generally had little sacred significance to the people. Within this forecourt the priests provided space for money changers and sellers of offerings. Since the circulating currency in the country consisted of Roman or Greek coins, which could not be used to pay the annual Temple tax, Jewish pilgrims had to exchange their money into the Tyrian or Hebrew half-shekel, at an exorbitant rate. Likewise, pigeons were sold at unfair price for the offering of the poor, the purification of women, and the cleansing of lepers. Stalls for the sale of animals and of tables loaded with wine and oil turned the Court of the Gentiles into a cattle market and an oriental bazaar.

The disregard for the sanctity of a place for Gentiles who had not become proselytes to Judaism angered Jesus. Driving out merchants, their goods, and their patrons; overturning the tables of money changers, scattering coins everywhere; unseating those who sold doves; standing guard over the courtyard to prohibit anyone from using it as a short-cut or carrying anything through it—what Jesus did to cleanse the Temple was clearly a parabolic and prophetic act, indeed, an act of eschatological judgment. The action of Jesus fulfilled the prophecy of Zechariah 14:21: "And there shall no longer be traders in the house of the Lord of hosts on that day."

Jesus provided scriptural warrants to justify his action: "Is it not written, 'My house shall be called a house of prayer for all the nations'? But you have made it a den of robbers" (Mark 11:17). Beyond the ancient characterization of the Temple as "a house of prayer," the phrase "for all nations" occurs only in Isaiah 56:7, a prophecy that speaks of the intention and purpose of the Temple of God for Israel and for all nations. The use of the Court of the Gentiles as a marketplace excluded them from the one place available in the Temple to pray to God. The second part of the protest—"But you have made it a den of robbers"—comes from Jeremiah 7:11, which sharply contrasts what the Temple had become contrary to what God intended. To whom and for what purpose does the word "robbers" apply? At least to the Sadducees who sold animals for sacrifice at extortionate prices and their money changers who made an exorbitant gain. These practices notwithstanding, the action referred essentially to the desecration of the Holy Place, which robbed the people of God monetarily and robbed the Gentiles of any place to worship whatsoever. That Jesus would insist on the availability of a place for Gentiles to worship during the Passover, the celebration of God's deliverance of the Jewish people from Egypt, would be quite significant and clear to the predominantly Gentile readers as well as the minority Jewish readers of the Gospel of Mark at Rome. Actually the two citations reinforce each other in the explanation of Jesus' protest in the Temple: the exploitation of the people, especially the poor; and the exclusivism of the Jewish leaders, their disdain for all Gentiles.

An Adversarial Response

The chief priests and the scribes listened to what Jesus said and watched what he did in the Temple. Though the multitude of pilgrims were astonished with Jesus' action and his teaching, positively and hopefully, the priests and scribes feared him. He threatened their authority as well as their extravagant way of life. Therefore, they decided to kill him and began to make plans to do so (Mark 11:19), but in a fashion that would not alienate the multitudes (Mark 14:1-2). This event is in all probability the basis of the charge against Jesus at his trial.

What kind of disclosure happened in Jesus' cleansing of the Temple? Through his confrontation of the priestly abuse of their power in the Temple, Jesus exposed the violence intrinsic in economic exploitation and privileged exclusivism, violence that surfaced in the single-minded determination of the chief priests and scribes to destroy Jesus. Likewise, the occupying Roman authorities recognized the potential threat of Jesus and his followers to their mandate to maintain order and control of this unruly but subservient state. The vested interest of the Jewish leaders and Roman rulers alike required the preservation of the status quo, for very different reasons. Restlessness and recklessness could endanger the peace of the Holy City and threaten worship in the Temple, and thereby the special life-calling and comfortable life-style of the priests. Another Jewish agitator could destabilize the Roman governing of Judah and perhaps provoke a serious rebellion, which would cost Rome troops and revenues and whatever future the already dispirited Roman governor might have. The non-violent confrontation of Jesus with the rulers of Jerusalem—direct confrontation with the Jewish leaders and indirect confrontation with the Roman authorities—would unleash the systemic violence entrenched in the ruling power that each exercised and controlled. Over against the political messianism of the Zealots, a politics of violence, Jesus pursued messianic politics, a politics of confrontation, because the politics of confrontation contains within itself the potential of a politics of compassion.

Part Two: The Politics of Compassion

The transition from the story of Jesus to stories of the followers of Jesus belongs to the history of the Christian church in its multiple expressions of life in the world. My introduction and interpretation of three contemporary life stories within the framework of a political theology presupposes the already and not yet of Jesus' proclamation of the oncoming Kingdom of God, the activity of the Holy Spirit nurturing sociopolitical change for the sake of more humane structures of existence in the variable forms of corporate life, and the critical requirement of leadership shaped through Jesus' vision of the Kingdom of God to facilitate transformation in the social, economic, and political arenas of human community. These three life stores are distinctive and unique as well as contingent and indigenous to the multifaceted context within that each one has lived. I consider Marian Wright Edelman, Oscar Romero, and Langdon Gilkey proponents of the politics of compassion, which includes a politics of confrontation.

Marian Wright Edelman:
A Prophetic Voice for Our Children

Marian Wright Edelman,[11] the leading advocate for children's rights in the United States today, founded the Children's Defense Fund in 1973. In this last decade before a new millennium CDF plainly states its essential purpose:

> The Children's Defense Fund exists to provide a strong and effective voice for the children of America who cannot vote, lobby, or speak for themselves. We pay particular attention to the needs of poor, minority, and disabled children. Our goal is to educate the nation about the needs of children and encourage preventive investment in children before they get sick, drop out of school, suffer family breakdown, or get into trouble.[12]

Although community agencies must continue to help families on the basis of case-by-case, CDF focuses on the sociopolitical process, drafting social policy to care for large numbers of children and working to establish these programs through congressional action. CDF addresses the broad issues of child health, education, and welfare; childhood development, adolescent pregnancy prevention, and youth employment. Although its main office is in Washington, D.C., the Children's Defense Fund is a national organization that provides information on key issues affecting children to communities and agencies throughout the United States. The 1990s constitute a moral struggle for America's conscience and its future: Will we accept responsibility for all children and willingly provide for them, especially the poor?

Edelman's rapid fire delivery and accumulation of facts can overwhelm an audience, but she gets the message through: In 1992 14.6 million children, about 21.9 percent of all children in the United States,

---

[11]Calvin Tomkins, "Profiles: A Sense of Urgency," *The New Yorker* (27 March 1989) 48-74, provides a brief biography of Marian Wright Edelman which includes her work with the Children's Defense Fund.

[12]Marian Wright Edelman, "A Struggle for America's Conscience and Future" (Washington D.C.: Children's Defense Fund, 1991), inside cover.

lived in poverty.[13] The largest percent are black children, but the largest single group numerically are white children. Inadequate day care programs for children of mothers who must work outside the home reinforces the tragic cycle of poverty and neglect. In 1993 a surprising 57.9 percent of mothers with children younger than six worked in the market place. One in four of today's working mothers must raise their children alone, more than one in three without child support of any kind. A productive and healthy nation cannot abandon almost 22 percent of its future to unproductive and unhealthy lives. Unless preventative investment for all children in early childhood becomes national policy, therefore, our future work force will be crippled with a disproportionate number of poor, unhealthy, untrained, and uneducated laborers.

Family Life and the Civil Rights Movement

The family of Marian Wright dramatically impacted her life, especially her father, Arthur Jerome Wright, pastor of the Shiloh Baptist Church in Bennettsville, South Carolina. Born in 1939, the youngest of five children, Marian Wright's parents taught the children the importance of getting an education and their Christian duty to help others. Since the segregated black school of Bennettsville lacked recreational facilities, Arthur Wright organized the community to build a playground behind the church. He established the Wright Home for the Aged, which her mother, Maggie Leola Bowen Wright, effectively managed. The Wrights nurtured their children with a healthy self-esteem, and they heard every prominent Negro leader who came anywhere in driving distance. When her father died, Marian was with him, and she was never the same again.

While not her first choice, Marian Wright attended Spelman College in Atlanta, a private liberal arts college for black women. Martin Luther King's sister taught at Spelman, and King occasionally spoke in chapel, compulsory chapel six days a week. With a Merrill Scholarship to do her junior year abroad, Wright spent the summer at the Sorbonne in Paris, moved to Geneva for the remainder of the academic year, and concluded

---

[13]*The State of America's Children Yearbook 1994* (Washington: Children's Defense Fund, 1994) 1-2.

her study with a Lisle Scholarship in the Soviet Union the next summer. She had decided to enter the foreign service after college.

When Marian Wright returned to Spelman College in the Fall of 1959, she became inevitably and deeply involved in the civil rights movement. Growing-up, she knew that segregation was morally wrong, that it must be vigorously fought and eventually eliminated. She says, "That whole last year of my Dad's life, when I was fourteen, he kept waiting for the Brown decision to come down from the Supreme Court. He died ten days before it came."[14] Wright joined with other students from other black colleges in Atlanta for one of the first large sit-ins at the City Hall cafeteria.

The civil rights movement turned her from preparation for the foreign service to Yale Law School to enable her to help black people. Although she really did not relish the course of study in law, Wright enjoyed good friends, and they shared a clear vision about what they wanted to do. At Yale she met Bob Moses, one of the first members of the Student Non-violent Coordinating Committee, who had traveled alone in the Deep South in 1960 to recruit blacks for one of the earliest SNCC organizational conferences in Atlanta. When Marian met him, he was a field secretary of SNCC, organizing in Mississippi, earlier considered too dangerous for civil rights workers.

In 1963 Wright went to Mississippi during the spring break of her third year at law school. Medgar Evers met her in Jackson and drove her to the SNCC office in Greenwood. Her first night somebody fired shots into the house of a local man, a frightening experience. On her last day Bob Moses took a group to the courthouse to register to vote, hazardous work. "He walked at the head of that scraggly bunch of courageous people; I was at the end of the line, behind an old man on crutches. This was the first time I'd seen police dogs in action, and I've been scared of them ever since. . . . The cops came at us with the dogs, and led them to attack us."[15] A terrifying scene, dogs charging, people running—Bob and the others were arrested, throwing Marian their car keys. After she called the Justice Department in Washington, she returned to the courthouse, but an unruly crowd of whites would not let her inside. Those arrested spent

---

[14]Tomkins, "Profiles," 60.
[15]Ibid., 61.

several weeks in jail until the SNCC could get the money for bail. That is when she *really* decided to become a lawyer.

Activist Lawyer in Mississippi

Marian Wright returned to Yale and finished her law degree that spring. The NAACP Legal Defense and Education Fund selected her as one of its first interns and trained her in New York for a year. In the Spring of 1964 she chose to go to Jackson, Mississippi to open a legal office focussing on civil-rights cases. Since the state required a year's residency before applying for the bar, she worked with the other three black lawyers in Jackson who signed the legal documents necessary for her work. The Mississippi Summer Project of 1964 brought thousands of white students from northern colleges to help register black voters throughout the state, including Michael Schwerner, Andrew Goodman, and James Chaney whom the Ku Klux Klan murdered after their release from jail in Neshoba County. Marian Wright almost never had a client leave jail who had not been beaten, one young boy actually shot and killed, but she learned to control her rage and fear. She passed the bar exam without difficulty, the first black woman admitted to the bar in Mississippi.

When the Office of Economic Opportunity initiated its Head Start project in 1963 to provide education, nutrition, and health services to preschool children of poor people, Wright led several others to put together the Child Development Group of Mississippi in April 1965, and it received a one-and-a-half-million-dollar Head Start grant. The program created twenty-five hundred new jobs, enrolled and accommodated twelve thousand children its first year, and established centers with local participation in small communities throughout the state.

The Mississippi white leadership struck back. Senator John Stennis charged CDGM had misused federal funds and used its main office at Mount Beulah outside Jackson as a center for racial agitation. Since the CDGM had operated on enthusiasm and imagination without careful bookkeeping, the accusation claimed some credibility. In the subsequent crisis Marian Wright led the organization to save the Head Start program. John Mudd, the new director, put the accounts in order, and they moved the main office to Jackson. The program secured refunding that continues to benefit innumerable preschool children in Mississippi today. Marion

Wright made a pivotal choice at this juncture, "to work inside the system," and the effectiveness of Head Start nationwide vindicates her decision.[16]

Head Start remains a fundamental component on the agenda of the Children's Defense Fund, and for good reason. Since 1965 Head Start has offered health, education, and social services to more than 12 million poor children and their families. It served more than 713,000 children in 1992, about 36 percent of those eligible.[17] The poor preschool children who attend Head Start score higher on achievement tests, and they are more likely to meet basic requirements in the transition into elementary school. In fact, they are less likely to become school dropouts, teenage parents, on welfare or in jail, more likely to become literate, employed, and enrolled in postsecondary education. Every dollar invested in high quality preschool programs eventually saves the government about six dollars in the cost of special education, welfare, and crime later on. Since more than 90 percent of Head Start families live below the poverty line, the children receive a variety of essential services: all required immunizations; medical exams and treatment; dental examination and care.

The War on Poverty and the Voting Rights Act of 1965 was a victory short-lived in Mississippi. Mechanization in the cotton industry had displaced the need for massive cheap labor in the Delta and thrown thousands of poor black people out of work. They faced starvation in hopeless unemployment. In April 1967 the Senate Subcommittee on Employment, Manpower, and Poverty held public hearings in Jackson. Senators Jacob Javits, George Murphy, Joseph Clark, and Robert Kennedy heard a lengthy denunciation of the War on Poverty from Senator Stennis. Then they listened to young Marian Wright describe the desperate plight of people facing starvation in the lush Mississippi Delta. Peter Edelman, one of Robert Kennedy's advisors, had already talked with her, and three days later Marian Wright took Senators Kennedy and Clark on a tour of the Delta. They could hardly believe it—shacks without water, heat, or light, children obviously hungry and many of them sick. She described a kind of epiphany that Robert Kennedy had in a shack near the town of Cleveland.

---

[16]Ibid., 63-64.
[17]*The State of America's Children 1994*, 29-30.

There was a baby sitting on the mud floor. The baby was filthy, and it had a swollen, bloated belly, and Bobby sat there trying to get that baby to respond, and he couldn't. It was one of the most moving things I've ever seen. You could see him get a sense of rage. He couldn't stand it.[18]

When Kennedy and Clark returned to Washington, they went directly to the Secretary of Agriculture, Orville Freeman, and told him something had to be done immediately to relieve the hunger in the Delta. Freeman investigated, and he acted quickly and decisively to change the situation.

Transitions

Since the poor children who needed Head Start had no one to speak for them in Washington, Marian Wright moved to the capital in March 1968 with a grant to study how to make laws work for the poor, a venture called the Washington Research Project. After Martin Luther King, Jr. was killed in April and Robert Kennedy in June, the civil rights movement floundered for lack of leadership. Bitterness surfaced. The Vietnam War shifted the focus of national concern and divided the nation. In the middle of it all, Baptist Marian Wright and Jewish Peter Edelman married on 14 July 1968 (and they have three sons, each celebrating his "Baptist Bar Mitzvah" with members of both families and their friends).[19]

In 1969 Marian Edelman and her small staff discovered that the 1965 Elementary and Secondary Education Act provided considerable money to educational institutions across the country, but very little of it reached poor children. Their carefully prepared report made the front page of the *Washington Post*, but nothing happened. If you tell people the truth, Edelman had thought, they will do the right thing—an illusion. When conservative congressmen decided to shift Head Start from national management to state control, she put together a broad-based coalition to protect Head Start and to extend its health and educational benefits to more preschool children. The bill went through the House and Senate virtually untouched, but Richard Nixon vetoed it. With the subtle racism of the Nixon Whitehouse and the conservative retreat on public social

---

[18]Tompkins, "Profiles," 64.

[19]Ibid., 66 and 70. See Marian Wright Edelman, *The Measure of Our Success: A Letter to My Children and Yours* (Boston: Beacon Press, 1992).

concerns, the civil rights movement and the war on poverty of the 1960s had mostly run its course.

The Children's Defense Fund

Marian Edelman founded the Children's Defense Fund in 1973, which intended from the outset to cut through racial and class barriers in order to focus on the needs of children throughout the country, especially poor children. Entirely through private funding, she put together a staff and began to publish carefully documented reports on children's health, nutrition, day care, and other needs. CDF designed its reports to capture the attention of congressional representatives to show them clearly and convincingly what they could do to help.

The Nixon Administration increased federal spending on food programs for the poor during the 1970s, but the conservative climate of the Nixon years and the fiscal conservatism of the Carter Administration limited what CDF could do. Yet Congress increased Head Start funding from $425 million to $900 million and in 1980 enacted a child welfare bill. The Reagan revolution ended this era of small gains and began to dismantle the social legislation and welfare programs of the four previous administrations. The Reaganites claimed that the social legislation of the sixties and seventies had created a welfare state that drained the economy and intensified the problems it intended to solve. In 1981 President Reagan's budget reduced programs for low-income families and children a total of $10 billion. The cuts continued; the results were brutal. In 1980, 1981, and 1982 more than a million children a year were added to the poverty rolls. By 1987 the numbers totaled twelve-and-a-half million children.[20] While Reagan weakened or repealed every federal program for children and the poor, CDF gave priority to preserving the laws that kept the programs in place rather than monetary appropriations for the programs. Things began to change in 1984 because of increased poverty and the new problem of homelessness. CDF lobbied extensively in 1984, 1986, and 1988, and it helped persuade Congress to expand Medicaid to poor children. Meanwhile, CDF expanded its concerns to investigate

---

[20]Marian Wright Edelman, *Families in Peril: An Agenda for Social Change* (Cambridge MA: Harvard University Press, 1987) 40-41.

homelessness, child abuse, child neglect (twelve million, two hundred thousand), runaway youths (more than a million a year), and "the appalling epidemic of teenage pregnancy."

In 1983, puting a book together called "Black and White Children in America," Marian Edelman suddenly realized that 55.5 percent of all black babies are born out of wedlock, many to teenage girls. "It just hit me over the head—that situation *insured* black child poverty for the next generation. I felt enormous guilt that I had missed seeing it until then."[21] Initial research showed that half-a-million babies are born each year to teenage girls of all races, costing the government a billion, four hundred million dollars annually. Though the rate of teenage pregnancy is higher among blacks than whites, many more white than black teenagers give birth each year. Poverty and the lack of training in basic skills are two common denominators for all: "Far higher poverty rates and weaker basic academic skills among Black and Latin teenagers are key reasons why their teen birth rates are much higher than those of Whites." [22]A statistical profile of a pregnant teenager is disheartening: a school drop out, unmarried, unemployed, on welfare; without prenatal care, an inadequate provider, unable to parent responsibly. The number of births to women younger than 20 is astonishing, the percentage of unmarried teenage mothers frightening. So CDF has launched a sophisticated campaign targeted for teenagers to warn them against sexual promiscuity and the consequences of sex without birth control.

The probelm of teenage pregnancy is symptomatic of a larger and more difficult developmental issue. The traditional steps to adult responsibility through education, employment, marriage, and parenthood usually breaks down with teenagers who grow up in disadvantaged circumstances. These teenagers are mostly poor, products of single-parent families and residents of neighborhoods with poor-quality schools and few community resources. Black youngsters are more than twice as likely as white youths to grow up in single-parent families. These low income families need a support system within their communities, an education with marketable

[21]Tompkins, "Profiles," 70.
[22]Edelman, *State of the American Children 1994*, 94. See *Adolescent Pregnancy: An Anatomy of a Social Problem in Search of Comprehensive Solutions* (Washington DC: Children's Defense Fund's Adolescent Pregnancy Prevention Clearinghouse, January 1987) 2-15. CDF's teen pregnancy prevention posters are dramatic and plain-spoken.

skills, appropriate health care, and community activities for their children. Working parents cannot provide these opportunities but require the extensive help of the communities. Since the best contraceptive to prevent teenage pregnancy is *hope*, new resources through governmental legislation is absolutely necessary.

The debate over the number of homeless children in the United States reflects staggering statistics: The conservative estimate of the National Academy of Sciences is at least 100,000, and they admit the problem is growing. Homeless families are usually single-parent families, young families, and rural families. Being evicted; losing furniture, toys, and books overnight; moving from shelter to shelter, a common experience of homeless families—all these factors have negative emotional impact on children such as regression, withdrawal, delayed personal development, short attention spans. Poor health, the emotional distress of extreme poverty, and unstable housing put homeless children years behind in their schooling.

The Agenda of the Children's Defense Fund

"Leave No Child Behind" names the nonpartisan campaign of CDF to put children and families at the top of the agenda of every politician. The goal is to get all national leaders to make a commitment to "a Healthy Start, Head Start, Fair Start, and Safe Start" for all children through an increasing investment in comprehensive health care, quality child care with early preschool education, and economic security for poor families with children.

Healthy Start. A healthy start in life for every child is critical now. Every child and its mother need basic health care that includes quality prenatal and maternity care, regular checkups, immunization for all preventable diseases, and special care for sick and disabled children. Through governmental programs like the Special Supplemental Food Program for Women, Infants, and Children, as well as Medicaid, the children who are our future will be healthy.

Head Start. The enrollment of all eligible children in Head Start through the expansion of programs and the appropriation of necessary funds is essential. Quality child care for children of working parents, early preschool education, and a place in Head Start for every needy child is a costly but money-saving goal: helping children get ready for elementary school, minimizing the need for expensive special education later, and promising a future to deprived children through education in school rather than on the street.

Fair Start. Poor children need the opportunity to begin life alongside rather than behind other children. The sick child, the hungry child, the homeless child—these children inevitably lag in learning, and we lose their potential for productive life. A Fair Start includes reforming the welfare system to prevent child abuse and to help families remain together.

Safe Start. The national plague of violence destroying American communities has spread to younger and younger children. The escalating violence against children and by children is the accumulation of long neglected problems, but the single most dominate is poverty and its corollary of hopelessness, a spiral of violence that begins with the breakdown of the family but coils through the layers of violence in the home, gangs in the streets, and dead-end education without jobs. Edelman's passionate plea, "Cease Fire! Stopping the War Against Children in the United States," confronts us with only a glimpse of the violence trashing the fabric of American society. [23]

The solution to most of these problems is not so puzzling or too expensive. Preventing the illness and death of thousands of children, getting these children ready for school, teaching them job skills that promises employment—all together will save millions of dollars in later illnesses, remedial education, teen pregnancy, welfare, and prison costs. Edelman says:

> There are millions of children who don't require massive government intervention and money. They need a regular check-up, not an intensive care bed; a tutor, not a guardian; a Head Start, not years in a specialized school. Their parents need decent wages, not a public job. They need intensive family preservation and support services, not foster care for the children. These are things that *can be done* to help produce a new generation of healthy, well-educated, productive citizens. [24]

---

[23]See Edelman, "Cease Fire! Stopping the Gun War Against Children in the United States," *The State of America's Children Yearbook 1994*, vii-xxix. Cf. Michael Ryan, "What *Our* Children Need Is Adults Who Care," *Parade Magazine* (9 October 1994): 4-5.

[24]Marian Wright Edelman, "Foreword," *Precious in His Sight* by Diana Garland

Edelman sees the problems, but solutions require the attention of government. Although the programs for the poor must be reformed *and* their effectiveness strengthened, will the political realignment of America in November 1994 provide help to those most needy, the 14.6 million children in poverty?

Providence in Historical Contingencies

That the providence of God is a story to be told more than a doctrine to be explored is quite vivid in the story of Marian Wright Edelman and the work of the Children's Defense Fund. One can analyze the purpose and goals, the current working agenda, the measure of success and failure in shaping legislation and policy, and other equally significant elements in an interpretation and evaluation of the Children's Defense Fund. However, the social and political significance of CDF is inadequately understood and its unique role in contemporary American life insufficiently appreciated apart from the life history of Marian Wright Edelman. Early life in the home in Bennettsville, South Carolina, especially the guidance of her father; the identification of the Christian faith with religious and social issues, doing the work of helping others; Spelman College and Yale Law School; the stark impact of racism in Mississippi, symptomatic of the larger problem of racism in America; a passionate concern for poor children; the shaping of marriage and family with Peter Edelman, the affirmation of two different legacies together—these factors and many more, some circumstantial and others decisional, mark the life of Marian Wright Edelman, the founder of the Children's Defense Fund and a creative participant in the politics of the provision of God.

Marian Wright Edelman could have chosen to invest her life elsewhere, e.g., a career in the foreign service. She might have reacted differently to the poor Southern blacks unable to appreciate what her participation in the civil rights movement demanded of her. The assassination of Martin Luther King, Jr. and Robert Kennedy as well as the fragmentation of the civil rights movement at the end of the 60s could have turned her in a different direction, as it did many others. While nothing in her heritage stands contrary to Edelman's choice to spend her

(Birmingham: New Hope, 1993) 13.

life in Washington, D.C., as a voice for poor children, nothing in her heritage required her to do so. Using providence as a frame of reference, Marian Wright Edelman has acted in concurrence with God for the benefit of the children trapped in poverty. Likewise, she decided to work in the sociopolitical system wherein God acts to guide and direct human history. When she founded the Children's Defense Fund, Edelman chose not to continue the kind of local investment that characterized her early days as an activist lawyer in Mississippi. The decision to lobby through the 1980s to keep programs in place despite the radical cuts in funding indicates astute judgment and political self-discipline. The discovery of "the epidemic of teenage pregnancy" and its dead-end street energized her to an unequaled commitment to stop it. In fact, she interprets her work in the Children's Defense Fund as a moral struggle for the soul of America. A very simple and providentially provocative question: Where would Marian Wright Edelman be today and what would she be doing if she had not gone to Greenwood, Mississippi, during her 1963 spring break in her final year at Yale Law School?

Archbishop Oscar Romero:
The Politics of Liberation

On Sunday, 23 March 1980, Archbishop Oscar Romero of San Salvador, a prophetic voice in behalf of the poor for three years, preached a homily that radio station YSAX broadcast to the entire nation of El Salvador. He concluded with a passionate appeal:

> I would like to appeal in a special way to the army's enlisted men, and in particular to the ranks of the Guardia Nacional and the police—those in the barracks. Brothers: you are a part of our own people. You kill your own campesino brothers and sisters. And before an order to kill that a man may give, God's Law must prevail that says, *Thou shalt not kill!* No soldier is obliged to obey. . . an immoral Law. . . . The church, defender of the rights of God, of the law of God, of human dignity, of the person, cannot remain silent before such abomination. We want the government to understand seriously that reforms are worth nothing if they are stained with so much blood. In the name of God, and in the name of this suffering people, whose laments rise to heaven each day

more tumultuous, I beg you, I beseech you, I order you in the name of God: *Stop the repression!*[25]

At 6:00 P.M. on Monday Romero celebrated a Mass in the little chapel of Divine Providence Hospital for the family of his friend, Jorge Pinto. Near the end of the simple mass, a shot rang out, and Archbishop Romero slumped unconscious to the floor. Blood turned his violet vestment and white alb martyr's red. Although rushed to the Policlinica Hospital, minutes later Archbishop Romero lay dead, a victim of assassination who had lived the gospel of Jesus Christ for the sake of the suffering poor of El Salvador.

El Salvador and the Roman Catholic Church

Since 1932 a military government has ruled El Salvador, but an oligarchy of fourteen families controls the political and economic life of this most densely populated country of more than five million, the smallest country in the Americas and the only Central American country without a Caribbean coast. Only two percent of the people own 60 percent of the land. The oligarchy dominates the land, property, farming, and industry in close association with transnational corporations in the United States. Cash crops are sold abroad despite widespread hunger and malnutrition at home. With peasant labor to work the land, they have reaped massive profits and accumulated inestimable wealth. Through wealth gained from the impoverishment of the dispossessed, the oligarchy controls the government, the military, and the press.[26]

As Archbishop of San Salvador for 38 years, Luis Chávez y González supported the rights of the peasants to organize for political power. He led the church to side with the poor, who had lived under ever worsening repression for over fifty years. Half the population lives on less than $10

---

[25]James R. Brockman, *Romero: A Life* (Maryknoll NY: Orbis Books, 1989) 241-242. See Placido Erdozain, *Archbishop Romero: Martyr of Salvador* (Maryknoll NY: Orbis Books, 1981); and of special importance, Jon Sobrino, *Archbishop Romero: Memories and Reflections* (Maryknoll NY: Orbis Books, 1990).

[26]See Dean Peermann, "El Salvador's Fallen Hero," *The Christian Century* (9 April 1980) 398-99; also, Theodore Buss, "El Salvador: Murder in the Chapel," *One World* (May 1980): 3-4.

a month; three-fifths of the rural and two-fifths of the urban population are unable to read or write. Readying to retire in 1977, Chavez left a legacy of the church committed to the poor according to the directions of Vatican Council II and the 1968 General Conference of Latin American Bishops at Medellín. Since the new archbishop could address social problems or ignore them, the clergy favored Arturo Rivera Damas, but the government wanted someone significantly more conservative who would not arouse the peasants and lower class with talk of justice and liberation. Rome chose Oscar Arnulfo Romero.[27]

Profile of a Conservative

Born 15 August 1917, in the remote village of Ciudad Barrios to a family of modest means, Oscar Arnulfo Romero y Galdámez began seminary studies in 1930 in San Miguel but went to Rome in 1937 to complete his theological education at the Gregorian University. Romero received his licentiate in theology in 1941 and was ordained at the minimum age of twenty-four in April 1942. After summoning Romero home to El Salvador in late 1943, the bishop subsequently made him secretary of the diocese of San Miguel, where he became an effective pastor and achieved fame as a preacher over the next twenty-three years. Although he personally pondered the reforms of Vatican II, Romero resisted major change and unhesitatingly exercised his influence as the most powerful priest in the city.

As a new monsignor in 1967, Romero moved to San Salvador as Secretary-General of the National Bishops Conference, and in 1969 he became Executive Secretary of the Central American Bishops' Secretariat. In 1970 Archbishop Chávez requested Romero be named an auxiliary bishop. Rutilio Grande and other friends worked to make the episcopal ordination a grand event, and prominent Latin church officials, numerous political dignitaries, and busloads from San Miguel celebrated the ordination under Grande's leadership in lavish style.[28]

When the editor of the archdiocesan newspaper *Orientación* published praise for the Colombian guerrilla priest Camilo Torres, Chávez replaced

[27]Brockman, *Romero*, 3-4.
[28]Ibid., 33-44. However, some thought Romero too tradition-bound and his ordination an ostentatious offense amid the dire poverty of El Salvador.

him in May 1971 with Romero, who gave social problems scant attention. In 1973 Romero attacked implementation in a Jesuit high school of the Medellin call for liberation in education as "demagogy and Marxism" and warned against the evils of "certain fashionable theologies" with "dangerous Marxist positions." Although he later published the report that exonerated the school, Romero buried it on the last page. In 1973-1974 *Central American Studies* criticized his editorship for defending the established order, concealing the roots of national problems, and hindering the transformation needed in the nation.[29]

On 15 October 1974, Rome named Romero bishop of Santiago de Maria, an action that he declared was the pope's silent approval of the ideology of *Orientación* under his editorship. The diocese stretched from Honduras to the Pacific, with a mostly rural population of 425,000, a diocese poor like most of its people. Romero witnessed the random killings of the Guardia Nacional, which he mildly protested in private. Over against the greed of the landowners who robbed the harvesters of their just wages, he made only sermonic appeal.

As one of three consultors on the Pontifical Commission for Latin America, Romero visited Rome in November 1975, and he participated in a discussion of the "Priests Political Movements in Latin America." In a confidential memorandum, he blamed the politicization of the clergy in El Salvador on the widespread influence of the Jesuits who espoused a political theology using Marxist analysis to critique the government. Romero admitted El Salvador had "a repressive military government" and "a cruel social differentiation, in which a few have everything but the majority live in destitution." The bishops' greatest pastoral concern should focus nonetheless on the transcendent hope of Christian faith.[30] Theologian Jon Sobrino knew Romero to be very conservative and an adversary of those who accepted the Medellín commitment to justice for the poor, accusing them of a false ideology and labeling them "Marxist."[31] Unsurprisingly the wealthy and the powerful all favored the choice of Romero. On 22 February 1977, Romero became Archbishop of San Salvador.

---

[29]Ibid., 47-49.
[30]Ibid., 56-58.
[31]Sobrino, *Archbishop Romero*, 4.

The Massacre in Plaza Libertad

Meanwhile, electoral officials announced on February 26 General Romero of the government party to be the newly elected president [unrelated to the Archbishop]. As the extent of another massive electoral fraud became known, people began to gather in Plaza Libertad, and the crowd swelled to more than 40,000 by Sunday. After an evening mass, most returned home. Troops with armored cars surrounded the plaza about midnight and ordered the crowd of 6,000 to disperse, but about 2,000 did not do so. The troops opened fire, killing 100 to 300. As trucks hauled off the dead and wounded, the survivors remained under seige in El Rosario Church until Archbishop Chávez, Bishop Rivera, and the Red Cross arranged a truce at 4:00 A.M.

The Salvadoran bishops met in special session on March 5 because of the violence against the church, and Romero insisted the church make a statement about the outrages happening. They drafted a statement of concern for the violence against the campesinos; for the arrests, torture, and deaths of hundreds; for the fate of the "disappeared"; for the media campaign, slander, threats, and intimidation of the church; for the expulsion of priests and the flight of opposition political leaders from the country. These abuses of human rights revealed a greater and deeper evil, the social injustice and the attendant suffering of the vast majority of the people. The church's mission, they said, is "to struggle for and to further justice, to know the truth, to achieve a political, social, and economic order conformed to God's plan." The idols of profiteering, privilege, and power must be exposed and a decent existence to those forgotten and excluded affirmed. "Therefore, even at the risk of being misunderstood or persecuted, the church must lift its voice when injustice possesses society."

> [It] cannot remain unmoved before those who have great tracts of land and those who have not even a minimum to farm for subsistence, between those who have access to culture, to recreation, to an opulent life, and those who must struggle day to day in order to survive, who live in habitual unemployment and with a hunger that debases them to the direst levels of undernourishment.[32]

---

[32]Brockman, *Romero*, 7-8, but in the context of 5-8.

With a call to stop the violation of human rights, the statement was to be read at mass in every church on Sunday, March 13. On Saturday Romero expressed second thoughts about reading the statement, and he decided to read it in the eight o'clock mass broadcast by radio from the Metropolitan Cathedral but not to read it in San José de la Montaña, the church next to the seminary and his new offices, a service many people from the wealthy Colonia Escalón would attend.

The Murder of Rutilio Grande

That same Saturday Rutilio Grande with an old man and a boy left Aguilares, where he had pastored 30,000 campesinos since 1972, to say mass at a village a few miles away. Halfway there in the middle of flat fields of tall sugar cane, an assassin with high powered bullets killed Rutilio and the two campesinos. When the news reached San Salvador, President Molina called Romero to offer condolences and assured him of a thorough investigation of the murders. On Sunday, March 13, Romero read the bishops' statement at eight o'clock in the cathedral and again at noon in San José de la Montaña. On Monday morning Romero spoke at a funeral mass in the cathedral for the three victims. Although he referred to his longtime friendship with Father Grande, Romero addressed the nation with the message contained in his death, the struggle of the third world peoples for liberation. "On Evangelization in the Modern World," Romero said, Pope Paul VI strongly affirmed liberation from temporal evil as an essential part of the church's work of evangelization. Thus the liberation that Grande preached was grounded through faith in Christ with the church, "but because it is often misunderstood, even to the point of homicide, Father Rutilio Grande died." Romero thanked Grande and his two companions, "co-workers in Christian liberation."[33]

Later in the day Romero wrote President Molina of the importance of an immediate investigation of the three murders. Romero told him that the church "is not willing to participate in any official act of the govern-

---

[33]Ibid., 9-11. Though the repression of the campesinos was not new and a number of priests had been expelled from the country, Jon Sobrino saw profound significance in the murder of Rutilio: "But for a priest to be murdered in El Salvador was unheard-of. . . . Anything could happen in the country if the powerful had dared to murder a priest" (*Archbishop Romero*, 2).

ment as long as the [government] does not put all its effort into making justice manifest in regard to this unprecedented sacrilege, which has horrified the whole church and stirred up in the country a new wave of repudiation of violence."[34] Molina replied that he had ordered "an exhaustive investigation," which never occurred, because the police were the likely murderers.

The murders had changed everything. Romero convened all the archdiocean clergy for a meeting the next day to discuss the persecution of the church and the murders of Grande and the campesinos. With strong support from the clergy, Romero issued a news bulletin that evening, March 15: He suspended classes in all Catholic schools for three days for study, reflection, and prayer on the Bible, Vatican II, and Medellín. In an act of high drama Romero announced that a single mass for the entire archdiocese would be celebrated on Sunday, March 20, at 10:00 A.M. in the Metropolitan Cathedral. On Sunday, people filled the plaza and the side streets, 100,000 strong, singing and praying, receiving communion and finding courage, the largest demonstration of Salvadoran church unity anyone could remember. Yet this single mass and the refusal of the church to participate in any official government function marked the beginning of Romero's long journey of hierarchical misunderstanding and charges of disloyalty to the church.

The Remaking of an Archbishop

Romero had been archbishop for less than a month, but he had set a clear course. Throughout his three years Romero faced the painful opposition of the Salvadoran bishops and the pettiness of the church institutional. While his country screamed in agony and priests were murdered, the church institution did not give him support but opposition. Fifty-nine years old, a new archbishop, the candidate of the conservative right— Romero changed radically on the occasion of Rutilio's murder. He would not accept the beautiful palace the wealthy offered to build him and went to live in a little room at the Divine Providence Hospital for terminally ill cancer patients. He would not only refuse to be an ecclesiastical comforter for the elite, but he would actually oppose the powerful against

---

[34]Brockman, *Romero*, 11.

the weak: the oligarchy, the government, the security forces, his brother bishops, different Vatican offices, and the United States government. Behind him stood a group of priests and nuns who had initially most regretted his appointment as archbishop and in front of him the suffering people of El Salvador, the campesinos who immediately gave him their acceptance and affection. When Romero visited their base communities, the poor rushed to him and he took them into his heart. He said later to Jon Sobrino: "With this people, it is not difficult to be a good shepherd."

Repression and persecution increased rapidly in May 1977: The arrest of a young Jesuit; the murder of Father Alfonso Navano; the military occupation of Aquilares, expelling the remaining three Jesuits, desecrating the church, ransacking houses, killing many campesinos, arresting hundreds of others, and declaring a state of emergency. Finally on June 19, Romero succeeded in his attempts to go to Aquilares to denounce the atrocities and to try to inspire the terrorized people with hope. The opening words of his homily to the 5,000 campesinos gathered for worship were unforgettable—a phrase that he would repeat in some fashion many times: "I have the job of picking up the trampled, the corpses, and all that [the] persecution of the church dumps along the road on its way through."[35]

An Archbishop of the Church

In August 1978 Romero issued a Third Pastoral Letter, addressing the relationship of the church to the peasant's unions and the question of the use of violence. The letter affirmed Christian participation in political movements in the context of a liberation that changes structures for the sake of a just society, and it rejected violence, unless all else failed. Whenever people organize to claim their rights, the question of violence inevitably surfaces. The most acute form of violence is institutional violence, systemic violence that uses people as laborers to benefit a privileged few, the day-by-day violence of economic structures. The state uses repressive violence to blunt any protest against economic injustice and to defend institutional violence. Terrorist or seditious violence mistakenly assumes revolution to be the only effective means of social

---

[35]Sobrino, *Archbishop Romero*, 25. Cf. Brockman, *Romero*, 62.

change, but it prevents the possibility of real dialogue. The only alternative to violence is the power of nonviolence. The gospel injunction to turn the other cheek has the moral strength to overcome injustice. Yet insurrection may be justified in the exceptional case of prolonged tyranny that negates human rights and destroys the common good, whether through unjust political, economic, or social structures. Governments, therefore, must strive to make insurrection unnecessary, ending institutional and repressive violence through the vigorous pursuit of social justice.[36]

Yet the persecution of the church continued. On 20 January 1979, Father Octavio Ortiz led a Friday night exercise in a retreat for about thirty teenagers and young men. Police and guardsmen attacked at 6:00 A.M., killing Ortiz and four young men, arresting all the others. They attempted a massive cover-up: El Despertar became a guerrilla training camp, its guitars weapons, its songbooks subversive literature, the result a gun battle. Over a hundred priests came to the funeral mass in the cathedral at eight o'clock the next morning, and a crowd of ten to fifteen thousand gathered outside in the square.[37]

As a consultor of the Pontifical Commission for Latin America, Romero went to to the Third General Conference of Latin American Bishops in Puebla, Mexico, in January 1979 but without the right to vote. Midway through the conference he agreed to a press interview at a hotel in downtown Puebla. When asked about his conversion through his experience with the poor, Romero acknowledged a change in the previous

---

[36]Brockman, *Romero*, 142-43.

[37]Ibid., 154-56. Unlike the murder of Father Octavio Ortiz and four young men, Father Ernesto (Neto) Barrera was apparently killed in a five-hour gun battle between security forces and four members of the Popular Liberation Forces. The government falsified facts in their report, but the FPL claimed Barrea as an active member of the guerrilla organization with the nom de guerre "Felipe." Romero presided at the funeral mass and burial of Neto as a priest of the church. He sought information about Neto's priestly work and finally concluded that Neto had been a member of the FPL, though not necessarily a combatant. Two years later he still believed Neto had been killed before the supposed shoot-out and that the security forces killed the only witness who could have provided factual information. Although Neto did not always convey a priestly message but reflected some influence of revolutionary ideals, the "fundamental ideology" of Father Neto "remains unknown" (150-53).

two years but not an actual conversion.[38] In the interview, however, he appealed to the oligarchy to resolve the tragic predicament in El Salvador, relinquishing their selfish advantage and listening to the God of the poor. In addition, Romero spoke of the mothers, wives, and sisters of political prisoners and the "disappeared" who had come to Puebla from El Salvador and Argentina, seeking help from the church.

At Puebla the bishops affirmed "the preferential option for the poor." Working quietly on the commission of evangelization and human development, Romero addressed the assembly only once with his recommendations about the final document:

---

[38]Ibid., 160. Jon Sobrino, *Archbishop Romero*, knew that "Archbishop Romero did not particularly like to hear his change referred to as a conversion" (7), but Sobrino called his change a conversion evoked by three factors. The murder of Rutilio Grande was the initial factor. The support of those who had earlier opposed him and the abandonment of his "nonpolitical" supporters would be another. The definitive factor in his conversion, "the one that kept him faithful to God's will to the end—was his people, a people of the poor," who loved him. "Before the church had made an option for the poor, the poor had made an option for the church" (9-13).

Romero's reluctance to label his developing perspective as "conversion" may have been mandatory in the light of his encounter with Cardinal Sebastino Baggio, prefect of the Sacred Congregation for the Bishops. Baggio invited Romero to Rome in June 1978 for "brotherly and friendly conversation," because, he said, letters concerning El Salvador, the archdiocese, and Romero himself came to the Congregation "with a frequency that knows no precedents and with the most contrary reports, good and bad" (Brockman, *Romero*, 125-26). Since he had already written but had not mailed a twenty-three-page letter to Cardinal Baggio reporting on events of the preceding year, Romero went to Rome as he had previously planned and met at length with Cardinal Baggio on June 20. Baggio was "severe" and Romero left the interview "dejected." Three days later Romero sent a nine-page document to Cardinal Baggio with reflections on their lengthy and private conference (127-31). Though he expected to hear "the contrary reports, both good and bad," Romero was surprised that he had only heard the negative ones which Baggio had apparently already accepted as an accurate characterization of his activities as archbishop. Baggio told Romero in their conference together that he had heard that Romero described the change in himself as a "conversion" (127). Romero denied that he had ever described the continuing evolution of his desire to be faithful to God as a conversion, but he did acknowledge a change in the expression of his ministry: "If I gave the impression before of being more 'discreet' and 'spiritual,' it was because I sincerely believed that thus I responded to the gospel, for the circumstances of my ministry had not shown themselves so demanding of a pastoral fortitude that, in truth, I believe was asked of me in the circumstances under which I became archbishop" (128).

I believe that our document will not reflect all the gospel commitment
. . . if it does not emphasize an evangelization that effectively responds
to the unjust distribution of wealth that God has created for all. . . . an
evangelization that denounces with candor arbitrary arrest, political
exile, torture, and above all the sorrowful mystery of the disappeared.
. . . if it ignored and did not evangelically encourage new phenomena
like our campesinos' efforts to organize, at times merely in order not to
die of hunger. It should note especially the heroic deaths of our priests
and pastoral workers. . . . [39]

Early in May 1979, Bishops Aparicio, Alvarez, Barrera, and Revelo
sent Rome ten closely typed pages titled, "Political-Religious Situation of
El Salvador." A vicious assault on Romero, the document portrayed him
as "imposing a politicized, Marxist idea of pastoral ministry on the
church and the country, interfering in other dioceses, led by a group of
radical priests, associated with 'Marxist' [organizations], blessing terror-
ism and defaming the government." Sympathetic with the vision of a
Marxist revolution, Romero "manipulates the Bible, adulterates the figure
of Jesus Christ our Lord, portraying him as a subversive, a revolutionary,
and a political leader." The division of the Salvadoran bishops roots in
Romero's identification with the ideology of radical leftist groups, they
claimed, and the sad events in El Salvador issue from the determination
of a few Marxists to subvert the established order and to establish a communist government. [40]

On 15 October 1979, President Romero fled El Salvador to Guatemala, for two young colonels had effectively executed a *coup d'etat*.
Archbishop Romero had hope for the future as the new government took
concrete shape, but he waited for the implementation of promised
reforms. While it faced opposition from the left, the biggest problem of
the blue ribbon junta was its own armed forces, the Guardia Nacional and
the National Police Force. By the end of December, the military had
established its control, and the new government collapsed entirely on 3
January 1980. Simultaneously, the political violence increased, over five
hundred dead and many others wounded or "disappeared." [41]

---

[39]Brockman, *Romero*, 162.
[40]Ibid., 177-84, esp. 177-80.
[41]Ibid., 200-206, 215-17, 221-24. In his private audience with Pope John Paul II, the
pope urged Romero to defend social justice and love for the poor but to avoid ideologies

In February Romero read of the intention of the United States to send military aid to El Salvador in addition to $200,000 worth of gas masks and bullet-proof vests already sent in November for crowd control. During his homily on February 17, he appealed to President Carter to recognize that this kind of aid would not favor the cause of justice but continue the oppression suffered by the people struggling for their basic human rights. The new junta had already amassed a total of dead and wounded higher than the previous government, which the Inter-American Human Rights Commission had denounced. The armed forces unscrupulously repressed the people in order to protect the interests of the Salvadoran oligarchy, and the new military equipment and American training would enable the security forces to use even greater violence against the people. Romero asked President Carter not to send any more military assistance to the Salvadoran government and to refuse to intervene directly or indirectly with the self-determination of the Salvadoran people. The next day the far right destroyed the church's radio transmitter with a bomb.[42] [Only a week after Romero's assasination President Carter repeated his support of the Salvadoran government, and the United States

---

that eventuate in dictatorships and the violation of human rights. Romero agreed. "But Holy Father, in my country it is very dangerous to speak of anticommunism, because anticommunism is what the right proclaims, not out of love for Christian sentiments but out of a selfish concern to preserve its own interests." Romero concluded with an affirmation of spiritual and Christian values and the need to defend them. He subsequently wrote in his diary of the pope's embrace and assurance of daily prayer for him: "I felt here God's confirmation and his force for my poor ministry" (224–25).

[42]Ibid., 227-29, 231. Contrariwise, Romero believed that capitalism *and* Marxism are evils to avoid. Romero titled his fourth pastoral letter, "The Mission of the Church in the Nation's Crisis," which he intended to "present officially to the archdiocese the total spirit of Puebla" (187). He addressed the question of Marxism, distinguishing between Marxism as a "scientific" analysis of the economy and society and Marxism as a "political strategy": "Many in El Salvador, as in all Latin America, use this analysis as a scientific resource that, they say does not affect at all their religious principles. The magisterium of the church, which recognizes this distinction between Marxist idealogy and scientific method, nevertheless prudently warns about the possible ideological risks" (p. 191). Since much anti-Marxism was a thinly veiled support for the status quo with its evils of profiteering capitalism, Romero cited Puebla: "The fear of Marxism keeps many from confronting the oppressive reality of liberal capitalism. Before the danger of a system clearly marked by sin, they forget to denounce and combat the reality implanted by another system equally marked by sin." Romero concluded the letter: "The best way to overcome Marxism is to take seriously the preferential option for the poor" (192).

announced $5.7 million in military aid and $50 million in economic
assistance for the junta—a misinformed decision contrary to Carter's own
commitment to human rights.[43]]

Reconciliation and Resurrection

On 16 March 1980, Romero preached one of his longest homilies on the
theme of reconciliation. He concluded his sermon with a series of
appeals: *To the oligarchy*: "You are principal protagonists in this hour of
change. On you depends in great part the end of violence. . . . If you
realize that you are possessing the land that belongs to all Salvadorans,
be reconciled with God and with human beings, yielding with pleasure
what will be for the peace of the people and the peace of your own
conscience." *To the government*: "I say [to those of good will]: Make
your power felt or confess that you cannot command, and unmask those
who are doing the country great harm under your shelter. . . . I say [to
those against reform and for repression]: Do not be obstructionists—in so
historic a moment for the nation you are performing a sad role of
betrayal." *To the Coordinating Commission*: "You are a hope if you
continue to mature by opening up and dialoguing." *To the guerrilla
groups*: "To [you] who advocate violent solutions . . . nothing violent can
be lasting. There are still prospects, even human ones, for reasonable
solutions. And above all there is God's word . . . reconciliation! God
wills it—let us be reconciled, and we shall make of El Salvador a land
of brothers and sisters, all children of one Father who awaits us with
outstretched arms."[44]

Near the end of February 1980, the Archbishop made his annual
retreat with six priests to the Passionist Sister's retreat house on the hills
above San Salvador. Romero wrote during the retreat of his fear of death:
"I find it hard to accept a violent death, which in these circumstances is
very possible." José Calderón Salazara, Guatemala correspondent of the
Mexican newspaper *Excelsior*, reported the words of Archbishop Romero
to him on the telephone about two weeks before his assassination:

[43]Buss, "Murder in the Chapel," 4.
[44]Brockman, *Romero*, 238-39.

I have often been threatened with death. I must tell you, as a Christian, I do not believe in death without resurrection. If I am killed, I shall arise in the Salvadoran people. . . .

As a shepherd, I am obliged by divine mandate to give my life for those I love—for all Salvadorans, even for those who may be going to kill me. . . .

Martyrdom is a grace of God that I do not believe I deserve. But if God accepts the sacrifice of my life, let my blood be a seed of freedom and the sign that hope will soon be reality. Let my death, if it is accepted by God, be for my people's liberation and as a witness of hope in the future.

. . . A bishop will die, but God's church, which is the people, will never perish.[45]

Archbishop Romero—Unexpected Instrument of Providence

The conversion of Oscar Romero is a study in contrasts. For over twenty years he pastored in San Miguel: the most powerful priest in the city, uncompromising and severe, but, some remember, compassionate for the needy and concerned for the whole person. He pondered the personal summons of Vatican II but sharply disapproved of reform-minded young priests. As editor of *Orientación* he ignored social and political problems. Though a witness to the random murders of the Guardia Nacional in Santiago de Maria, he protested privately and not publicly—a model of response that he recommended to other bishops. He recognized the landowners' exploitation of seasonal workers, opening the church with food and shelter for the laborers, but he made only mild sermonic appeals for fairness to the wealthy who paid unlivable wages. After describing "the repressive military government" and "a cruel social differentiation" wherein a few have everything and the vast majority live in destitution, he advocated primary attention to the transcendent hope of Christianity.

How did Rutilio Grande and Oscar Romero become such good friends at the Jesuit seminary in San Salvador from late 1967 onward in light of their very different perspectives on the gospel? Pastoring from 1972 among the 30,000 campesinos of Aguilares, Grande preached the gospel of liberation and denounced the injustice of the few who im-

---

[45]Ibid., 247-48.

poverished the many. He urged organization and Bible study among the campesinos that had already begun to open their eyes and heighten their aspirations—all of which threatened the wealthy landowners. Conversely, the wealthy considered Romero their friend who accepted the necessity of the stability they gave to Salvadoran life. What would have happened to Romero apart from his friendship with and respect for Rutilio Grande? The mystery of God's providence—at fifty-nine, conservative theologically and aligned with the establishment, Oscar Romero became an advocate of the liberation theology of Rutilio Grande and died as he died, martyred for the sake of the Gospel for the vast multitudes of the poor of El Salvador.

After Romero?

Eight months after the assassination of Archbishop Romero in March 1980, four North American church women were brutally assaulted and murdered. At least 75,000 Salvadorans suffered the same murderous fate during the decade of the 80s, another 7,000 Salvadorans "disappeared," and 1.5 million endured displacement from their homes in the terror.[46]

On 16 November 1989, the Salvadoran armed forces dragged six Jesuit priests, their cook and her daughter, from their beds in the Oscar Romero Pastoral Center at the University of Central America in San Salvador and brutally murdered them. Though living in the same community, liberation theologian Jon Sobrino survived only because he was out of the country, but one of the Jesuits was found in Sobrino's room: Juan Ramon Moreno lay in a pool of his own blood, and a Moltmann book lay fallen in his blood, *El Dios Crucificado—The Crucified God.*[47]

These martyred Jesuits, like so many others, simply told the truth of life and death in El Salvador. They dared to touch and identify the national idols, dangerous, because the survival of idols requires victims. Neither Romero nor the North American church women nor the Jesuit priests were killed defending the church's rights. Rather, Sobrino says, "They were killed for defending the rights of the poor."[48] Like Jesus, they

---

[46]Jim Wallis *et al*, "Rising from the Ashes," *Sojourners* (April 1990): 10.

[47]See Jürgen Moltmann, *Jesus Christ for Today's World* (Minneapolis: Fortress Press, 1994) 48-49.

[48]"The Greatest Love: Interview with Jon Sobrino," *Sojourners* (April 1990): 17-18.

dared to unmask the lies that disguise the idols, to seek justice through truth, and thereby to affirm their faith in God—the God of life, the God of the poor.

The twelve-year Civil War ended in El Salvador in January 1992 with a Peace Accord between the government and the revolutionaries. In the elections under the scrutiny of international observers during March and April 1994 Armando Calderon Sol of the Republican Party (ARENA) became President, but the coalition of various organizations in the leftist front (FMLN-CD-MNR) won twenty-one seats of the eighty-four-member National Assembly. Would Romero have been disappointed with the election results? I believe that Archibishop Romero would have celebrated democratic elections. However, if the new government does not move forward with land reform and other changes for the sake of justice for the poor, he would be profoundly disappointed. The story of El Salvador has not ended but remains open to the promise and threat of the future.

Our Response

What is the appropriate response of the United States government to Latin and South American countries, especially El Salvador, where the radical disparity between the rich and the poor nurtures civil discontent and repressive government policies? What is the appropriate theological response of American churches to indigenous liberation theology south of our border that *uses* Marxist analysis to judge justice and repression but does *not* call for a Marxist or communist government? As Sobrino says, they are looking for new models, because neither capitalism nor Marxism offers hope to the poor for freedom and survival in life. What action, if any, should be taken against multinational corporations that supply the American economy with goods and produce, but they do so through the exploitation of the peasants who work the land for profanely inadequate seasonal wages and the urban poor who work under inhumane conditions for little more than starvation wages?

We have to learn to distinguish revolutionary movements against oppression from Castro-style communist revolutionaries. We must be careful not to send military aid to totalitarian regimes in Latin and South America or elsewhere who will use our weaponry to repress and kill their own people. We ought to couple foreign economic aid with the requirement that the country receiving foreign aid demonstrate genuine land reform and humane industrial standards. Indeed, we must be willing to pay more for less goods for the sake of a decent living for those in Latin and South America as well as imports from other "underdeveloped" countries. Multinational corporations should be required to show an identifiable practice of adequate wages and livelihood for the workers who make possible the food and products that we import—or face stiff penalties that will offset all excessive profit gained through the exploitation of cheap labor. Can it be done? Yes, but it will be costly and difficult, yet right.

Langdon Gilkey:
Premier American Theologian

Langdon Gilkey is one of the most important American theologians for the second half of the twentieth century, but he is especially important in this essay for his work on the theme of providence, *Reaping the Whirlwind: A Christian Interpretation of History* (1976). Gilkey began his study of providence in 1960 with a Guggenheim Fellowship in Munich. Out of that study he intended to publish a doctrine of providence as a companion to his earlier work on creation, *Maker of Heaven and Earth* (1959). Beyond the lack of a useful theological method and the absence of relevant concepts, "even more," he says, "during that time my own life seemed to fall apart into meaningless pieces," certainly a liability in an endeavor to write on "providential meaning in history" with existential relevance. So he shelved the project for a decade.[49]

On the Way to Conversion

Born in 1919 into a liberal Protestant home in the lively and progressive academic environment of the University of Chicago, Gilkey grew up in an unusual family. His father was the minister of Hyde Park Baptist Church, the "University Church," later the first dean of the University

---

[49]Langdon Gilkey, *Reaping the Whirlwind: A Christian Interpretation of History* (New York: Seabury Press, 1976) vii. This is the book Gilkey intended to write more than a decade earlier, but different, of course.

Chapel (1928), and for many years head of the Chicago American Civil Liberties Union. His mother was an early feminist, a superb hostess for the university community, and a leading YWCA officer. "Together they created a potent, open, morally and socially concerned home . . . filled every week with visiting preachers and church persons, students, professors, and prominent religious and secular reformers."[50]

Theologically and politically the Gilkeys were liberal. As for so much liberal Protestantism to be religious and therefore genuinely Christian in this home meant a critical spirit and the social gospel: to be relatively relaxed about doctrines and rules, to be free of obvious moral faults and the vices of tobacco and alcohol, to be tolerant of the ideas, the habits and mores of other groups, to be vastly concerned about social and racial justice and peace—*above all peace*. With this heritage young Langdon Gilkey entered Harvard in 1936. Religion had no place in his life, and he knew nothing of and thought less about Christian doctrine. He was, if anything, an ethical humanist. He detested Hitler, but he hated war even more. Hitler's *Blitzkreig* of Europe created an impasse for the young liberal. The commitment to peace required him to avoid war at all costs, but the commitment to justice, equality, and freedom demanded active resistance to Nazism. He was as confused inside as the world outside.

One Sunday in April 1939, Hitler's armies on the move in Europe and cynicism conquering his idealism, something unexpected happened. Young Gilkey writes:

> I went to Harvard chapel to listen to an old friend of Father. [He] had repeatedly said, "You ought to go hear Reinnie preach sometime." And, knowing nothing else but that, I wandered in. Suddenly, as the torrent of insight poured from the pulpit, my world of disarray spun completely around, steadied, and then settled into a new and quite firm and intelligible structure.[51]

Reinhold Niebuhr gave young Gilkey a new "duality" of a fallen world and the transcendent God, a God always seeking to bring it back

---

[50]Langdon Gilkey, "A Retrospective Glance at My Work," in *The Whirlwind in Culture: Frontiers in Theology*, ed. Donald W. Musser and Joseph L. Price (Bloomington IN: Meyer-Stone Books, 1988) 3.

[51]Ibid., 6.

to its true self, all of us to our true selves. In *this* framework one could be realistic and morally concerned, even more, one could have confidence and hope because of the continuing relatedness of the purposeful God of love. Gilkey calls this experience "my conversion," quick and complete. He heard Niebuhr twice again that day, bought and read all of his books then in print, and at the end of two more weeks he had become a "Niebuhrian." Gilkey's ethical norms did not change. What did? Since it had been his "world," his understanding of human existence and history that had collapsed and crumbled, it was, Gilkey says, "the *theological* message of Niebuhr that gripped me, and the theological teachings of the Christian tradition that captured my interests."[52] When he graduated in June, however, he continued to be torn between two worlds, on the boundary between his bankrupt ethical humanism and his new intimations of the reality of God.

China: The Shantung Compound

In mid-August 1939 Gilkey sailed via Yokahama and Kobe to Peking with a two-year contract to teach English at Yenching University, an American-British University for Chinese students.

> This experience in the Orient—I did not return home for five years—represented without question the most significant and formative period of my life. Whenever subsequently I have asked myself: "What is real and true in human experience? Where can I go to touch *reality*?" I find myself returning to that sequence of experiences.[53]

Between September 1940 and December 1941 Gilkey experienced the dominance of the old colonial world of European superiority over everything in the Orient. The aura of innate Western superiority covered every level of cultural life. The other dominant political impression was the ruthless brutality and harsh oppression of the Japanese occupation of China. Although few remember the outrageous brutality of the Japanese stranglehold on China, Gilkey's brief contact with it convinced him that

---

[52]Ibid., 8.
[53]Ibid., 9.

evil can become so vast that armed resistance to it becomes inescapable. In principle, at least, he ceased to be a pacifist.

When the war began in December 1941, Gilkey and others became enemy nationals and were put under house arrest. He read theology and taught groups of missionaries volume one of Niebuhr's *The Nature and Destiny of Man*, which his father had sent him just before the United States entered the war. Fifteen months later, in March 1943, the enemy nationals were sent to an internment camp in Shantung province until the war ended in August 1945. The Shantung Compound moved the young pacifist far beyond Harvard Yard.

Gilkey tells the story of the internment camp in *Shantung Compound* (1966).[54] Populated by 1,500 to 2,000 civilians of men, women, and children, the internment camp became a kind of laboratory experiment in social living surrounded and contained by guards and guns. The camp had to organize politically, administer work assignments and schedules, stoke the fire and cook the food, repair buildings and equipment, discipline and entertain themselves, in short, "construct and maintain a miniature civilization." They did so with radical limitations: the lack of machinery of any kind; a minimum of equipment and supplies; overcrowded and cramped for space; a continuing and profound anxiety about the future. Despite real achievements, moments of joy, and sometimes meaningful personal relationships, life was full of frustration, hunger, and insecurity.

More and more Gilkey was impressed with the moral necessities for communal living: Without self-discipline and order they faced anarchy, but without justice they lived with the explosive threat of violence. Moral decay undermined order and justice, as dangerous to their life together as the stoppage of supplies or a serious epidemic. Nothing was more difficult in these circumstances than to share space and supplies with others or not to steal common goods. Regardless of the organization of the work force or the production of goods, the pervasive and inordinate self-concern of everyone meant a continuing "Fall" in the face of these spiritual requirements that are essential for a human community: "We refused to cooperate or share, we hoarded goods to ourselves, we stole." Consequently the camp suffered recurring and increasing crises. Beyond knowledge, communication, and technical skills, a genuine human

---

[54]Langdon Gilkey, *Shangtung Compound* (New York: Harper & Row, Publishers, 1966).

community requires moral strength: justice, equality, freedom, and self-control. Yet nothing is more difficult and elusive in corporate human existence than such moral strength. We were made for it, but we continually reject it.[55]

These two-and-a-half years of an involuntary experiment in human community validated for Gilkey his Christian understanding of the human situation. Although we live in the presence of a moral and loving God, we function with a predominant and destructive self-concern. Yet we continually encounter the new possibilities of repentance, trust, and reconciliation. The experience in the Shantung Compound convinced Gilkey more than ever of the theological perspective that characterizes Christian faith: "the relevance of the symbols of sin and estrangement, and the necessity of moral awareness and responsibility, of spiritual self-understanding and repentance, and most important, of a deep trust in God if creative personal and communal life is to be possible."[56]

When he returned home on a troop ship in November 1945—underweight; confused about his future; estranged from the militaristic, materialistic, and self-righteous spirit throughout the United States—the parallels between moral failures in Shantung Compound and the self-concern of prosperous America struck him deeply. After brief consideration of a career in diplomacy, Gilkey decided to study theology, philosophy of religion, and ethics. He had no question of where to go to study: Union Theological Seminary in New York, the teaching post of his "spiritual father," Reinhold Niebuhr. Eventually he completed his Ph.D. dissertation on the relationship of the Christian doctrine of "creation out of nothing" and the "process philosophy" of Alfred North Whitehead.

Fate and Destiny in Nashville

In 1951 Gilkey went from Union to a teaching position at Vassar College and in 1954 joined the faculty of the Divinity School at Vanderbilt University in Nashville. By 1959 everything seemed to be going well for him: happily married to a charming Virginia lady, a successful first book out, and a newly adopted baby son. But the New South began to surface.

---

[55]Gilkey, "A Retrospective Glance," 11.
[56]Ibid., 12.

Although a few black students had studied at the Vanderbilt Divinity School during his tenure on the faculty, Vanderbilt University, the city of Nashville, and the entire region of the mid-South remained in 1959 and 1960 thoroughly segregated. During the year black college students in much of the South began "sit-ins" to protest one of the most blatant racist injustices of Southern culture: Black people could shop but they could not eat at restaurants downtown. When black students from Fisk University and Tennessee A&I in Nashville started "sit-ins" at lunch counters and restaurants, refusing to leave until served, they endured verbal and physical abuse, and because of their violation of the law, arrest. Students and faculty at the Divinity School admired their protest against segregation, because nonviolent protest was an appropriate Christian response to an obvious injustice, but not to Nashville. A city of steeples and church-goers, Nashville felt humiliated at the nationally publicized nonviolent protest against its customs and afraid the situation could become bloody with violence, these "uppity" blacks the cause of it all, breaking the law and shattering the peace of "this lovely Christian city."

The arrest of a number of Fisk students led to the discovery that James Lawson, a black student at the Vanderbilt Divinity School, had been "coaching" the protesters in nonviolence. The Divinity School was proud of him, but the city was not. Though hard to believe now, the initial and irrational response of the community was anger and disbelief. How could a Christian provoke these confrontations and deliberately break the law? He must be a Communist. The one-time progressive-looking chancellor of the University, sensitive to his conservative board, expelled Lawson immediately. The faculty of the Divinity School refused to approve the expulsion and went on national radio and television as frequently as possible to make the position of the faculty and students clear to the country. As the senior member of the Divinity School faculty at forty-two, Langdon Gilkey became its spokesperson. Negotiations between the Divinity School and the University continued for three months. Finally, the Divinity School readmitted Lawson, and the faculty threatened to resign if the University failed to recognize the readmission. The administration refused, and the Divinity School faculty resigned. Then the unexpected happened: The dean and four full professors of the prestigious Vanderbilt Medical School resigned. So the chancellor reversed his decision and readmitted Lawson, over the protest of the genteel board. Meanwhile, Lawson had been admitted to Boston University and chose to remain there. Ironically the city integrated its restaurants in May before Vanderbilt capitulated in June.[57]

The twist in Gilkey's experience happened at the level of his personal life. Slowly over the years he and his wife, as a couple, had become a part of the younger Nashville social scene. The Lawson incident deeply offended most of the community, and the status of the Gilkeys among them was badly shaken. Gilkey remembers his doctor's wife remarked that he was the first Communist she had ever met. Close friends remained loyal, but things had changed, more than he knew. In April his wife left to visit her family in Virginia, and in the summer he realized that his family had now completely disintegrated, though the Lawson case was by no means the sole cause.

He says:

> We spent an uneasy and alienated fall and winter on sabbatical leave in Munich, but that spring (1961) my wife left Munich to live along with our son in New York. The following summer on my return from Germany she refused to accompany me back to Nashville, and so I agreed to seek a divorce.[58]

Although he had gone to Germany to write a book on faith in God's providence, he returned with little faith in anything, certainly not in himself as a person or theologian. He did not condemn divorce, but he had thought it inconceivable for him, a shattering experience. With great poignancy he writes:

> I had also discovered how fallible I was: how much I had been myself at fault in this broken family, and how unable I was to handle with any grace such a personal crisis. All this deemed to represent the end: I had lost (I felt) my son, and with that all hope of creative family life; I had been a failure in the most important of life's endeavors; thus I was void of any sense of worth or even cleanness. Because of all this, I felt I could hardly function any longer as a theologian, as a witness to the power either of faith or grace. Thus—so I told myself—when I

---

[57]Ibid., 16-18.
[58]Ibid., 19.

recovered a bit, I would have to see what else at forty-two I might take up.[59]

Beyond the unwanted given of fate, new beginnings are possible. Yet the transformation of fate into a creative destiny comes from a power not our own. Gilkey entered a new loving relationship, one much more creative with a superbly attractive and talented Dutch woman. Married a year and a quarter later (1963), they started a new home, and Gilkey accepted a position teaching theology at the University of Chicago. The immense productivity of his Chicago years have given him stature almost unequaled in contemporary American theology.

Gilkey the Theologian

Gilkey sees the common thread that provides continuity in the "unplanned character" of his work a "correlational" approach through the changing character of his personal existence and the shifting forms of social existence in the panorama of events within that he has lived. Gilkey's publications reflect the correlation of his life and work: *Maker of Heaven and Earth* (1959); *How the Church Can Minister to the World Without Losing Itself* (1964); *Shantung Compound* (1966); *Naming the Whirlwind: The Renewal of God-Language* (1969); *Religion and the Scientific Future* (1970); *Catholicism Confronts Modernity* (1975); *Reaping the Whirlwind: A Christian Interpretation of History* (1976); *Message and Existence: An Introduction to Christian Theology* (1979); *Society and the Sacred: Towards a Theology of Culture in Decline* (1981); *Creationism on Trial: Evolution and God at Little Rock* (1985); *Gilkey on Tillich* (1990).[60] The recurring themes in Gilkey's publications are science and religion, the significance of modernity for theology and the church, a theological critique of culture, a Christian interpretation of history, the dialogue among world religions, and self-reflection on his vocation as theologian.

---

[59]Ibid.
[60]See Musser and Price, *The Whirlwind in Culture*, 263-70.

Providence in Political and Personal Life

The issues of peace and justice come together most remarkably in the story of Langdon Gilkey. He grew up amid multiple liberal voices of Christian faith that shaped personal values and sociopolitical concerns. The almost coincidental encounter with Reinhold Niebuhr preaching in Harvard Chapel had dramatic impact on his "world." Subsequently, he experienced European Colonialism in the Orient prior to its inevitable disintegration, and his observation of the Japanese brutality over the conquered Chinese broke his non-negotiable pacifism. Reinhold Niebuhr's *Nature and Destiny of Man* gave Gilkey a theological analysis of human fallenness that addressed the pride of military power on the one side and the pervasive self-centeredness that destroys authentic human community on the other.

Although the Divinity School at Vanderbilt University did not initiate any significant effort to confront and eliminate racial segregation, they supported the black students who protested through "sit-ins" in Nashville restaurants and lunch counters. Gilkey's privileged education, life experience in the Orient, and theological vocation did not immediately awaken his conscience to action in the face of the injustice of racism in Nashville and across the nation. Through identification with the civil rights movement, however, he experienced estrangement in a different way than previously from "someone not like us." Gilkey does not rationalize his divorce on the basis of the tensions that the civil rights movement occasioned among their friends, but it was certainly a factor. He had failed "in the most important of life's endeavors." Unexpected grace transformed this fate into destiny for Gilkey, but certainly not for everyone else who has fallen into similar straits. The theological symbol of "the Fall" applied to internment in the Shantung Compound as well as to racism in Southern culture and American life, and it enabled him to interpret his life and times individually and corporately.

Gilkey's life experience stretches across continents and through decades of trouble, and he is unequaled in contemporary theology as an analyst of social and political forces that shape communal and personal life into destiny or fate. Langdon Gilkey did not begin on the underside of history like Marian Wright nor amid the inestimable disparity between the rich and poor in Latin America like Archbishop Romero. Yet he affirms the priority of working socially and politically for justice and peace through *Christian* theological reflection on the sociopolitical movement of human history.

Conclusion

A theological interpretation of history moves intrinsically toward a political theology. Precisely because Christian theology affirms the activity of God in individual and corporate life, Jesus' vision of the Kingdom of God contextualized in the interpretation of social, economic, racial, and political dimensions of human existence summons theology to corresponding responsibilities in conjunction with these multilayered aspects of societal life. The Transfiguration of Jesus is a religious event with inextricable, profound, and far-reaching sociopolitical implications, and, correspondingly, the Transfiguration of Jesus is a sociopolitical event with inextricable, profound, and far-reaching religiotheological implications. That Jesus chose not to participate in the Feast of the Tabernacles but did subsequently confront the religious and political establishment of Jerusalem with the claims of the Kingdom of God constitutes a mandate for nonviolent confrontation with the historic, systemic evils that inhere in every heritage, institution, tradition, and culture. The life stories discussed herein are not more important than other short-storied biographies accessible to us. Yet the different life stories of Marian Wright Edelman, Oscar Romero, and Langdon Gilkey together illuminate, however fragmentarily, the scope of God's activity in the vast movement of human history to turn us toward the Kingdom of God. Perhaps all the stories of humanization available to anyone of us are at best small excerpts or maybe only brief footnotes that document the activity of God in the multiple circles of every society working to establish peace and justice through truth and love. The God who works in individual and corporate human history is the God of Abraham, Isaac, and Jacob, of Sarah, Rebekah, and Rachel, the YHWH God of the covenant at Sinai, the *Abba* God of Jesus of Nazareth, the God who acts and interacts with and among us with a vulnerable compassion.

Chapter 6

Grace and Healing

ONE OF AMERICA'S RARE MEN OF LETTERS, Reynolds Price has published fiction, plays, and essays over the last thirty years. The poetry of *The Laws of Ice* is compelling, but none more significant than his auto-biographical reflections in "Days and Nights: A Journal." On 13 February 1984, he began a notebook of short poems that sketched the actual events of his days and nights, but he could not anticipate the catastrophe that announced itself on June 2, a malignancy the size of a pencil twisting down his spine that threatened his life. A month after surgery on his spinal cord—its ugly scar on his upper back boxed with a long rectangle of durable dye—Price lay awake at dawn remembering the violence of his surgery and anticipating his first radiation treatment. The remarkable entry titled "Vision" is a surprise to the reader.

Vision

I'm sleeping with Jesus and his twelve disciples
On the vacant east shore of Lake Kennereth—
The Sea of Galilee—near where he exorcised
The demon Legion. We're flat on the ground,
Cocooned in clothes. Mine are light street clothes
(Apparently modern, theirs are classic robes);
And I wake early, well before dawn—
Hour of the worm that desolates hope.
I give it long minutes to line another tunnel
With eggs that will yield the next white wave
Of ravenous heirs.
                            Then I roll to my right side
And I see in the frail dark that Jesus has somehow
Moved nearer toward me. I listen to hear
If he sleeps or wakes.

> Then we stand in the lake,
> Both bare to the waist. Light creeps out toward us
> From the hills behind; the water's warm.
> I see us both as if from a height.
> My spine is scored by a twelve-inch incision,
> Bracketed now by gentian-purple
> Ink that's the map for X-ray therapy
> Due in two days. Jesus's beard
> Is short and dry, though with both broad hands
> He lifts clear water and pours it down
> My neck and scar.
>   Then we climb toward shore.
> I get there first and wait on the stones—
> We're still the only two awake.
> Behind me he says, "Your sins are forgiven."
> I think "That's good but not why I came."
> I turn and say "Am I also cured?"
> He comes close but looks down. He says "That too,"
> Then wades strong past me and touches land.[1]

For those who are seriously ill, especially those who face the the stark probability of a terminal illness, the concern is for healing. The prayer for healing focuses on the person who is sick but includes family and friends, because they participate in the illness itself as primary caregivers. Multiple questions surface simultaneously: Will I be healed? Completely? Partly? Not at all? When? How? Why? Why not? The question of healing is not simple but complex, partially because healing, however limited, is a process that addresses numerous aspects of the life of a sick person. The outcome most dreaded is the prospect of death.

Since the ministry of Jesus included healing the sick, the question of the providence of God almost inevitably arises when a Christian faces a serious illness. The purpose of this chapter is to explore the theme of "grace and healing" with sensitivity to the opportunities and limitations in the response of God to human illness. Such sensitivity means to avoid

---

[1]Reynolds Price, *The Laws of Ice* (New York: Atheneum, 1987) 67. Price has chosen the descriptive term "Vision," because when it occurred he was entirely awake.

easy answers and to identify damaging distortion. Initial attention focuses on Jesus' cure of the boy who suffered from epilepsy, highlighting the realism of the Gospel narratives. Beyond the activity of Jesus in the Gospels, analysis shifts primarily to the stories of God's response to illness in other New Testament settings and their relevance for the life experience of Christians today.

The Healing of the Epileptic Boy

One of the most remarkable stories of Jesus' ministry of healing is his healing of the epileptic boy, a narrative of healing found in each of the Synoptic Gospels. When Jesus came down from the mountain, he saw the other disciples surrounded by a crowd and some scribes arguing with them. He asked what they were discussing:

> Someone from the crowd answered him, "Teacher, I brought you my son; he has a spirit that makes him unable to speak; and whenever it seizes him, it dashes him down; and he foams and grinds his teeth and becomes rigid; and I asked your disciples to cast it out, but they could not do so." He answered them, ". . . Bring him to me." And they brought the boy to him. When the spirit saw him, immediately it convulsed the boy, and he fell on the ground and rolled about, foaming at the mouth. Jesus asked the father, "How long has this been happening to him?" And he said, "From childhood. It has often cast him into the fire and into the water, to destroy him; but if you are able to do anything, have pity on us and help us." Jesus said to him, "If you are able!—All things can be done for the one who believes." Immediately the father of the child cried out, "I believe; help my unbelief!" . . . Jesus rebuked the unclean spirit, saying to it, "You spirit that keeps this boy from speaking and hearing, I command you, come out of him, and never enter him again!" After crying out and convulsing him terribly, it came out, and the boy was like a corpse, so that most of them said, "He is dead." But Jesus took him by the hand and lifted him up, and he was able to stand. When he had entered the house, his disciples asked him privately, "Why could we not cast it out?" He said to them, "This kind can come out only through prayer." (Mark 9:14-29)

The Synoptic Gospels together paint a graphic portrait of the illness and healing of the epileptic child, and several aspects of this narrative require attention from the perspective of contemporary theology: First, the narrative focuses on the young man who suffered from epileptic seizures, which his father attributed to an unclean spirit. Jesus healed the boy through an exorcism. The essential point is not the characterization of the source of the boy's epileptic seizures but Jesus' power to heal the young man of his illness. The question, "Can demon possession exhibit the symptoms of epilepsy?" is functionally unimportant, for the Gospel of Matthew says, "He is an epileptic" (17:15a). Moreover, the lad was an only child, and his illness had been chronic since childhood. The boy experienced seizures: convulsions, foaming at the mouth, grinding teeth, and death-like rigidity. These unpredictable seizures endangered the lad, throwing him often into fire and into water, elements essential for the routine of life at home but dangerous to his son. Thus the boy had to be watched continually for his own protection.

Second, the story concentrates on the father, but the frustration of the father echoed that of the entire family: "If you can do anything, have pity on *us* and help *us*." The desire for pity reflected the family's sense of helplessness, the continuing frustration of a history of searching for someone with healing power without finding anyone. "If you are able to do anything" translates as "Are you another dead-end street?" And the cry to "help us" charts the history of this illness: "I believe; help my unbelief!" The disciples had failed to heal his son. Would Jesus fail too? The honesty of the believing/unbelieving father indicated the long-term impact of the son's illness on his father and family of chronic stress, broken dreams, and useless trips for healing.

Third, attention shifts to the disciples, who asked Jesus privately, "Why could we not cast it out?" The difference between Matthew and Mark on this point is not unimportant. In Matthew 17:20-21 Jesus answered: "Because of your little faith. . . . if you have faith the size of a mustard seed, you will say to this mountain, 'Move from here to there,' and it will move; and nothing will be impossible to you." In Mark 9:29 Jesus said, "This kind can come out only through prayer." In Matthew Jesus' answer juxtapositioned the inadequacy of "little faith" and the power of faith as small as "a mustard seed." What is the difference? Both mustard seed and mountain are images that accentuate the possibilities of the disciples. Does Jesus literally mean that mustard-seed-faith can move mountains? Of course not! Yet Jesus does say that genuine faith, even exceedingly small, evokes the gracious power of God. Despite the choice of language, therefore, the contrast reflects the quality of faith rather than quantity, the authenticity of faith instead of its measure, a realism personified in the words of the boy's father: "I believe; help my unbelief." In Mark 9:29 Jesus explained that this kind of brokenness, a child suffering from epilepsy, can be overcome only through prayer, which is itself an exercise of faith.

The Experience of Providence: *Grace*

What is the experience of providence in the life of a person with a serious or chronic illness? The experience of providence that the New Testament discloses for persons with different kinds and in various stages of sickness is "grace." On almost every page of the Gospels Jesus performed miracles of deliverance and healing through the grace of God, but such miracles are not commonplace today. Is healing grace the potential response of God to all or almost all human disability or illness? Since Jesus himself encountered little, if any, such limitation in his works of healing, is it a mistake to assume that the miracle of healing grace is always a possibility? The inability of the disciples to heal the epileptic boy reflects the ambiguity that the church has continually experienced in its ministry of healing. Is the problem too little faith and too little prayer? Perhaps, but not necessarily. On the one side, what Jesus could do through faithful prayer lay beyond what the disciples could do and what we can do. On the other side, while a miracle is not always a possibility, the absence of faith voiced in prayer can frustrate or terminate the possiblity of healing through the transforming power of God, a measure of healing that God might otherwise cooperatively work in the life of a sick person. The situation of the church leads us through the Gospel traditions to the letters of the Apostle Paul, because he offers the most constructive insight into the experience of grace that occurs in the community of faith.

If grace is the experience of providence to those who suffer illness and disability, what does grace mean? How does grace happen? What can grace do? Grace, we must remember, is not a "something" but the Presence of God. Grace is always God's grace. Yet the integrity and the importance of the questions remain: What does God's grace mean for a child who suffers from an ongoing illness that might be self-destructive? For a child who suffers a severe illness, perhaps a life-threatening illness? What does God's grace say to a family for whom the healing agents available for a child prove inadequate? For a family living with the pressures of a broken child who can never be healed but remains permanently impaired, physically or mentally? What does God's grace connote in the aftermath of the healing of one child, perhaps surprisingly, while others with similar illnesses remain beyond healing?

What does the provision of God, summarized in the word "grace," identify in a situation of illness, affliction, or disability? Does God do more than nurture a positive, responsive attitude that aids in healing? *Does God act and interact with the sick person, making a contribution to the process of healing beyond the subjectivity of the patient that would otherwise be unavailable?* The variations of this question surface the crucial question: *What does God do?* Moving from the Gospels through the remainder of the New Testament with special attention to the letters of Paul confronts us with the variation and ambiguity in God's response to different situations of human illness. The grace of God happens in diverse and distinctive forms.

Suffering and Prayer

What should the Christian do in the midst of illness and suffering? The practical value of "The Letter of James" is well known.

> Are any among you suffering? They should pray. Are any cheerful? They should sing songs of praise. Are any among you sick? They should call for the elders of the church and have them pray over them, anointing them with oil in the name of the Lord. The prayer of faith will save the sick, and the Lord will raise them up; and anyone who has committed sins will be forgiven. Therefore confess your sins to one another, and pray for one another, so that you may be healed. The prayer of the righteous is powerful and effective. (5:13-16)

In suffering and sickness we turn to God in prayer. That the cheerful are to praise God reminds us that the word of prayer for those who suffer is not the only word to be offered to God in the community of faith. Thanksgiving for "common grace" that is ours through the gift of life should always be part of the worshiping life of the church. Sickness and suffering are not the only experiences that should turn us to God. On the contrary, illness and handicaps must be set in the larger context of the celebration of life. Gratitude for life, for family and friends, for the forgiveness and acceptance of God, for the memory of good days, the affirmation of this day, and the hope for new days—gratitude to God for the extraordinary goodness of "common grace" is a continuing and positive response of all of us in the Christian community.

The counsel of James is significant: In the midst of sickness and suffering we are to pray, seeking the help of God. Likewise, we summon the help of others who offer various kinds of assistance. No one of us is to suffer alone. Rather, the leaders of the community of faith are to come with the gift of prayer and with the anointing of oil in the name of Christ, because the Christian who suffers should experience the encouragement and assistance of brothers and sisters in Christ. Within this circle of concern the Christian who is ill confesses sin and seeks the forgiveness of God. James knows that a healthy relationship to God through the forgiveness of sin is one of the first steps toward wholeness, because it enhances the possibility of healing. Whatever happens—overcoming a disability; wellness beyond illness; coping with continued suffering; deterioration from sickness, rapidly or slowly—whatever happens, whether physical or psychical, the Christian experiences grace through the community of faith, some measure of the peace and strength of God.

The brief passage in James is not without difficulty, because it does not qualify its encouraging affirmation with a corresponding realism. In fact, James adds an example that tends to generalize inappropriately and unnecessarily from a specific, delimited historical context to the everyday life of the Christian: "Elijah was a man *like us*, and he prayed that it might not rain, and for three years and six months it did not rain on the earth. Then he prayed again, and the heaven gave rain and the earth yielded its harvest" (Jas 5:17-18). James intends to encourage his readers to practice petitionary prayer, a legitimate concern. However, while "Elijah was a man like us" in his need for faith, the text fails to declare his identity as a mighty prophet of God during the evil days of King Ahab and Jezebel (1 Kgs 16:29-34). Moreover, the drought occurred as God's judgment (17:1, 18:18) and ended according to God's Word to

Elijah (18:1, 41-46), without any reference to the activity of prayer. Unfortunately, therefore, the text is liable to misunderstanding and disappointment.

Furthermore, the phrase, "the prayer of faith," may nurture the inappropriate correlation of the amount of faith with the power of prayer, a correlation that reduces the expectation of God's grace to the single possibility of healing grace. If healing occurs, those who pray think the combination of the strength of faith and persistence in prayer constitute "the prayer of faith" that made the sick person well. If healing does not occur, those who pray believe the weakness of faith and the insufficiency of prayer are the reason the sick person remains ill, and perhaps dies. The failure to recognize the different positive expressions of the grace of God as well as the complexity of human illnesses places the naive believer in the formula of "the prayer of faith" in a tragic plight. Inappropriate guilt: "We did not pray strong enough or long enough." Or pious superstition: "Well, it must be God's will."

Since the providence of God is historically contextualized with limits and possibilities, the Christian interpretation of healing grace entails multiple factors beyond the specificity of prayer. The complexity of a serious illness or handicap and the possibility of healing defies easy generalizations, but at least four elements are identifiable: (1) What kind of illness or disability is the source of concern? Is it a problem with permanent consequences beyond cure? Is it life-threatening and potentially terminal? How rapidly does it develop, with or without definable stages and specific complications? Is it treatable? With what kind of results? Is it a recurring illness? With what frequency? (2) When did the diagnosis of the illness, the disability occur? Is the timing of the diagnosis of critical significance for the treatment of the problem? If so, did the diagnosis and treatment occur early enough to impact the progress of the illness or the extent of the handicap? Case in point: The tragic, untimely death of Jim Henson, "the gentle giant who gave us Kermit and the Muppets," happened because "he ignored the infection ravaging his body until it was too late."[2] Since the time frame may be critical in a life and death struggle with a particular illness, the question of "When did treatment begin?" can be the decisive question. (3) What resources are

---

[2]"Legacy of a Gentle Genius," Cover Story, *People Magazine* (June 18, 1990): 89-96.

available for treatment and how effective are these resources on the outcome? If resources prove to be the most significant element for wellness on the other side of an illness or functioning on the other side of a handicap, what does the category of "resources" include? Several factors are pertinent: an understanding of the history of the illness; the development of improved techniques, instruments, and procedures; the quality of the equipment available; the medical expertise of physicians on the scene; a knowledge of helpful medications and their effectiveness. Which of these resources are available for effective treatment? (4) Does the specific disposition of the patient affect the intractability of the disability or the severity of the illness? Are the questions surrounding physical condition, mental attitude, and inner resources critical for the recovery of health or for transcending the troubling impairment that endures? What can be done to maximize the positive disposition of the sufferer?

God is active in all these elements, each with its own configuration, which means God does not begin to act at the point of petitionary and intercessory prayer. Rather, God has worked in the whole history of a given illness or handicap, though the concern for God's activity is now focused through prayer for a particular person. The orientation of life is itself a form of prayer, but the act of prayer cannot finally substitute for essential medical requirements or undo inalterable physical processes. Prayer does engage God directly in response to the concern of the one who prays, a mutual participation in whatever movement is possible toward wholeness. God acts in the margin of mystery available to God, whether large or small, which lies beyond our vision but not beyond our prayers. Probably the margin of mystery wherein God works depends on the factors already identified: the character of the illness, the timing of diagnosis and treatment, and the medical and spiritual resources of the persons involved. God does not act only in the subjectivity of the suffering person, because God interacts and impacts the situation of need beyond the subjectivity of the one who suffers. God is an active agent, one agent among other agents and certainly not always the most significant agent in relation to the illness itself, who contributes something to the situation of the sick person that would otherwise be unavailable.

The affirmation of the efficacy of prayers of petition and intercession immediately raises the crucial question: What are the possibilities and limits of petitionary and intercessory prayer? Although the *Abba* experience has an ego-limiting and self-enhancing dimension within it that cleanses prayer of much pious superstition and sinful self-serving, the *Abba* experience itself does not establish in advance the limits and possibilities of petitionary prayer. The appropriate prayer, especially in the face of a bitter cup, can only be determined through praying. How should we pray focuses the issue most pointedly. Prayer is prayer to God; consequently, all our difficulties in prayers of petition issue from our understanding of God's relationship to the world, more specifically, God's relationship to us in the particular circumstances of life wherein we offer our prayers to God. If God relates to the world with the dynamic and active concern of the loving *Abba*, the cosmos must be structured to constitute a dependable environment on the one side as well as the flexibility to respond to the engaging and transforming Presence of God on the other.

How does such "engaging transformation" occur? God always does the most God can do in a situation of dramatic need with its specific historical context, which shapes the limits and possibilities available to God therein. But how? When we pray prayers of petition and intercession, we make ourselves available to God in a fashion that apart from these prayers we do not do. The interaction that occurs energizes some possibilities that remain only latent prior to our asking and thus our availability to God. Whether these possibilities through engaging transformation include healing or strengthening, comfort or assurance, relief or acceptance—what the possibilities are in the context of petitionary or intercessory prayer for someone ill cannot be determined in advance but only retrospectively. The immanent Presence of God in the world does not mean that God is equally present *in* everything, but in varying levels God is in some sense present *to* everything. The measure of God's investment in a specific situation of illness or disability depends, at least in part, on our prayers—the reciprocity of mutual investment with God in this particular moment of need. The interconnectedness of all life in the field structure energized through the Holy Spirit enables us to intercede in behalf of another,[3] likely qualified by the measure of closeness to the

---

[3]Wolfhart Pannenberg, "The Doctrine of Creation and Modern Science," in *Cosmos as Creation*, ed. Ted Peters (Nashville: Abingdon Press, 1989) 152-76, esp. 163-67, where he discusses the relationship of "field" in modern physics and "the field structure" of

other person and the shared connection that accounts for such proximity in relationship to the other. Time eventually clarifies what God does do in response to or in conjunction with our prayers for someone seriously ill or in some way disabled. The possibilities that exist within the force field of the situation become visible in the light of the ones actualized, which enables us to say how God has responded. The tangible factors in the nature of an illness or given condition, the timing of the diagnosis and treatment, the various medical resources available—God works within these and with our prayerful investment, but God is never simply a substitute for these tangible factors.

When we pray for someone ill, near and dear, God nonetheless actively participates in the living with, adjusting to, suffering in, and perhaps dying of the sick person as an agent of healing alongside other primary caregivers. In the specific historical context of a serious illness or impairment, whether physical or psychical, the God of love always does the most God can do, which includes the coherent possibilities available exclusively in the transcendence of God. Of course, God does not do for us what we can and should do ourselves, but what we do does impact what God can do. God's work is helped or stymied through our actions and attitudes, the availability or lack of necessary resources, the investment or absence of our asking in prayer. When we do all we can do in action and prayer, when we see the possibilities of hope increase or decline, whatever the outcome of the illness should eventually evoke some measure of gratitude to God in the midst of numerous other feelings about the course of an illness or the problem of impairment in a loved one's life. Such gratitude presupposes confidence in the loving activity of God doing all that can be done for the sake of one terminally ill or permanently impaired, gratitude for all that God has done and attempted to do in the life of the other. Of course, the God to whom we offer gratitude is not the do Anything, Anytime, Anywhere kind of God who inexplicably withholds the best from us, a "God" who does not exist

---

spiritual dynamics. Cf. Nancey C. Murphy, "Does Prayer Make a Difference," *Cosmos as Creation*, 235-45. She concurs with Arthur Peacock that "God is the all-encompassing 'environment' for the universe, whose plans and actions can influence all else without necessarily violating constraints placed on events by the laws of lower levels" (243). She concludes that God must be able to affect the world in different ways at each level of the hierarchy of being. See above, "Interlude."

except in theological systems and pious naivete. Rather, the God to whom we offer thanksgiving is the loving *Abba* to whom Jesus encourages us to pray, the God who gives good gifts to children known, blessed, and loved.

The Elimination of Suffering through Healing Grace

Jesus healed the sick during his ministry, and healing grace that overcomes illness happened from time to time in the churches of the New Testament. Moreover, healing grace that delivers from sickness sometimes happens today.

The Healing of Epaphroditus

In Philippians 2:25-30 Paul describes the illness and healing of Epaphroditus. Unlike the epileptic boy, we do not know the nature of Epaphroditus' illness. The church at Philippi had sent Epaphroditus to Paul to assist him in his ministry. In the meantime Epaphroditus had become seriously ill, sick over a sufficient duration of time for the congregation in Philippi to learn of his illness. Indeed, time enough had passed for the news of their concern for him to get back to Epaphroditus, a situation that greatly distressed him. Paul has sent Epaphroditus home to Philippi so they can celebrate his healthy return and Paul can be less anxious about all of it. Paul candidly acknowledged that Epaphroditus had been "so ill that he nearly died" (2:27a). Yet God had mercy on Epaphroditus in his illness and on Paul in his concern, lest he should have "one sorrow after another," restoring Epaphroditus to good health. He does not say that he had prayed for Epaphroditus, but Paul's interpretation of the experience of God's mercy reflects the asking of prayer. The affirmation of prayer, including petitionary and intercessory prayer, characterized Paul's entire ministry. So he and others prayed for Epaphroditus, sick and near to death, and he experienced healing. The recovery of Epaphroditus is a classic case of God's healing grace in response to illness in the churches of the New Testament.

A Contemporary Witness

On 9 June 1966, the day after his twenty-fourth birthday, Don Musser entered the hospital for diagnostic tests. A biopsy revealed that he had lymphoma, an inoperable but treatable cancer of the lymph system. He began chemotherapy immediately. He became nauseated and listless, and he lost weight and his hair. In fact, he felt much worse after the treatment than before. Ten days later he returned home to his wife in an apartment at The Southern Baptist Theological Seminary, where he had just completed one year of theological studies. His parents rushed to Louisville to see their only son, whom everyone thought was dying. The chemotherapy worked: The disease that "swelled his belly like a shiny balloon and his lymph glands like golf balls" went into remission.[4]

During the first years with cancer Don lived to be "cured," which meant disease-free without recurrence for five years, for 1,825 days to pass and 8 June 1971 to come. He hoped and prayed and attended to his physician's instructions, all with the goal of remission that would rid him of the fear of cancer. In 1986, two decades later, he writes: "I cannot say, 'I *had* cancer.' It is more accurate to say that for twenty years I have lived with cancer."[5] Musser says that the illness that threatened his life resulted in a transformation of his attitude, values, and Christian convictions.

As he reflected on his journey of faith during the early months of chemotherapy, Musser experienced considerable confusion. In September 1963 he felt a compelling urge to prepare for the ministry. He saved enough in two years to resign his position in chemical engineering and enroll in Southern Seminary. Like Abraham, he had left his homeland in response to God's call into a strange country. Now he felt like Isaac, the son Abraham was willing to sacrifice without clear reason. Why had this happened? Was he being punished for some grievous sin? Had he misunderstood his sense of vocation? Was this a test of his commitment? Nothing made any sense. He says, "An aching loneliness, a sense of abject abandonment gripped me."

---

[4]Donald W. Musser, "On the Edge of Uncertainty: Twenty Years with Cancer," *Second Opinion* 5 (September 1987): 120.

[5]Ibid., 121.

A reorientation of his life started to occur: Earlier he had viewed each day merely as a means to a future goal; now he began to value each day as a gift. Earlier he had been interested in ideas, now he found people and their stories interesting. Earlier he had been "a dogmatic rationalist" who filtered everything through a fundamentalist religious perspective, but now its conceptual structure of biblical questions and answers had collapsed. He says, "In my newly emerging viewpoint, the Bible became a storybook whose characters were trying to understand an ambiguous existence in the light of an Elusive Presence who had revealed to them some measure of truth and value." Earlier he had known the facts in the stories in the Bible, but now he found his own story in the stories of Abraham, Isaac, and Jacob. He continues: "I could sense the anguish of the Hebrew exiles in Babylon in the face of Jerusalem's destruction, the despair of the Psalmist who felt tragedy alone, and the forsakenness of the One who hung on the cross." Then he adds: "While allowing a fresh way of being in the world to stir within me, I was terrified when a fellow student contracted leukemia. I could hardly bear to see him on campus and avoided any conversation with him. . . . He died in a few months, and I sobbed through his memorial service. I think my grief was over my own impending death. I felt I was next."[6] The journey proved difficult, but grace sometimes happened. He experienced grace as "an inexplicable, strange, and strong presence."

In July 1968, with his Master of Divinity degree in hand, Musser became pastor of a small urban church in Pittsburgh on a bluff of the Ohio River overlooking his hometown. The decision to become a parish minister was mixed, but one reason stands out: If he were to die, he wanted to be home and buried with his own people. Life became a strange mixture of fate and destiny. Fate clouded his future with cancer, but a new destiny began to emerge, the sense of the Psalmist's affirmation: "Thou art with me." With this emerging destiny, fragile to be sure, on 22 February 1970, some 472 days shy of cure, the Mussers' welcomed into their home a five-day-old daughter. As he held her, Don was overwhelmed with a sacred terror and a trembling ecstasy.

8 June 1971—1,825 days beyond diagnosis—Don Musser was cured, at least statistically. But he was turned down for life insurance as a bad

---

[6]Ibid., 122-23.

risk; he had to continue to see his doctor, and he himself was not convinced of his cure. For a while he was in a tailspin of depression. When he came out of it, he U-hauled his family across Ohio and Indiana to the Divinity School of the University of Chicago. Don Musser's vocation and calling was alive again, as he was. Another decade passed without medication and with renewed physical vigor. Today he teaches at Stetson University in Florida, doing what he understood his call to be in 1963, but with a different perspective.

After living with cancer for twenty years, cured four times over, Musser says that he sees all present and past through the window of that experience, which hardly a day passes without thinking of some event related to it. Yet he knows that he is a different person in at least two ways. First, though teaching courses in religion and philosophy, he sees himself primarily teaching students who are more important than the contents of his courses. Second, he finds religious truth opaque and unfathomable. He says, "The ways of God are a mystery to me." Theological reflection cannot explain why he developed cancer nor why he is alive instead of dead, leaving him with "an impenetrable surd." He confesses, "I have learned that I must believe *in spite of* rather than *because of*, if I am to believe at all."[7] Faith is a faltering trust in God, primarily relational rather than conceptual, receiving each new day as a gift. How do you celebrate twenty years with cancer? You recognize its profound impact on your life. You contemplate how it has changed you. "Without a flush of triumph or a pulse of pride," Musser says, "but with humble gratitude to the One who has graced you with life, you embrace your wife and daughter and puppy dog and invite a few friends in to share a moment of *l'chaim*."[8] Then you meditate on a text like Isaiah 38:17-19a, with great gratitude.

The Inappropriateness of Generalization

Jesus cured the epileptic boy with the miracle of healing grace, and he connected the power for healing with prayer. Likewise, the Apostle Paul

---

[7]Ibid., 126.
[8]Ibid., 127.

interpreted the healing of Epaphroditus in terms of the mercy of God. Again, Don Musser's cure of cancer is eloquent testimony to God's healing grace. We cannot generalize, however, from the stories of healing in the biblical traditions and contemporary experience to all, or even most situations of disability and illness. That some miracles of healing cannot be done apart from prayer does not mean that every illness can be cured through prayer. When illness occurs, the sufferer must reject the guilt inherent in the question: "Why is God punishing me?" Similarly, when healing does not occur, the participants in the situation of illness and disability must reject the guilt intrinsic in the lament: "Did we pray long enough and believe sincerely enough to warrant the gift of healing?" The miracle of healing grace is not always possible, regardless of the continuing and faithful prayers of God's people. Remember Musser's fellow seminary student who died of leukemia?

More than fifteen years ago Don Harbuck described the callous insensitivity and destructive character of the simplistic correlation of the prayer of faith with the promise of healing. He says:

> Shortly after finishing college, . . . I came down with polio. The disease left me severely crippled, especially in my arms. Most activities I had enjoyed as an athlete and sportsman I would never do again. . . . From my earliest remembrance I had lived in a Christian home. Both of my parents were active and devoted Christians. During my illness, they did everything in their power physically and spiritually, emotionally and materially to get me well. So you can imagine how stunned I was many years later when a woman confronted my mother with this accusation: "Don is not healed today because you never prayed for him in faith."[9]

Where did such a harsh remark originate? Was the woman who spoke those words cruel and unfeeling, coarse and indifferent to another's deep hurt? Of course not! Harbuck describes her as a pleasant and capable woman to whom his mother had been kind over the years, teaching her the ways of Christ in Sunday School and caring for her children when she was sick. Faith-healing theology, however, had twisted and turned her into "a haughty and arrogant bigot."

---

[9]Don Harbuck, "Providence, Prayer, and Healing," First Baptist Church, El Dorado, Arkansas, August 28, 1977.

What are the possibilities of grace when healing does not, indeed, cannot occur? Is the Presence of God, the grace in God's Presence, inaccessible and unavailable?

The Confrontation of Suffering through Sustaining Grace

Sometimes God's grace takes the form of "sustaining grace," a particular rendering of grace that defined Paul's own experience in 2 Corinthians 12:1-10. The word of grace to Paul and countless others with stabbing pain in the history of the church has often been difficult to hear: "My grace is sufficient for you" (12:9a).

Paul's Thorn in the Flesh

Paul endured what he called "a thorn in the flesh," in all probability a physical affliction, piercing bodily pain. It was undoubtedly of lengthy duration, because he set it in the context of a spiritual autobiography of fourteen years. Over against the mystical experiences and raptured revelations through his life in Christ, Paul said: "Therefore, to keep me from being too elated, a thorn was given me in the flesh, a messenger of Satan, to torment me, to keep me from being too elated" (12:7). Paul prayed specifically for healing grace three times, but the grace of God in healing did not occur. Why did he continue to pray three times? Did God not answer his prayer until the third plea from Paul? When you pray single-mindedly for healing grace and restoration does not occur, you hear nothing from God and feel as if you have received nothing of grace whatsoever. Only after healing grace did not occur and plainly would not occur did Paul really listen, which enabled him to *hear* God's word: "My grace is sufficient for you, for my power is made perfect in weakness."

Sometimes the Christian feels himself or herself against a wall, a wall of frustrating pain that drags life down and saps the strength of living, a wall that may mean inexplicably and unbelievably the sentence of death. What does the Christian do? The Christian prays for a door of deliverance through the wall to life beyond it, because only the exercise of meditation and prayer enables us to determine the possibilities and limitations in a situation of great need. Occasionally something unexpected happens. Faith discerns a door to deliverance that the eyes of unfaith cannot see, and faith opens that door to healthy and productive life on the other side. The reactions of spectators and diagnosticians range from utter astonishment to only mild surprise, depending on the size and thickness of the wall. However, while faith can open a door to deliverance that the eyes of unfaith simply cannot see, *even faith cannot create a door where the possibility of a door does not exist*, beyond even God's possibility. Yet the absence of a door of healing grace indicates the availability of a window of "sustaining grace," potentially a very great gift of God. Yet the experience of a window of sustaining grace, its recognition and its appropriation, requires the realism of the Apostle Paul. What God can do and will do for us becomes far more important than what God does not and cannot do.

What makes "sustaining grace" *grace*? The continuation of the situation of need can add to rather than subtract from the meaning and purpose of life. The transformation of suffering through "grace sufficient" can occasion a particular kind of relationship with God, a blessed vantage point for understanding and experiencing the depths of meaning in life. The Lord said to Paul, "My grace is sufficient for you, for my power is made perfect in weakness" (12:9a). And Paul can boast: "Therefore, I am content with weaknesses, insults, hardships, persecutions, and calamities for the sake of Christ; for whenever I am weak, then I am strong" (12:10). Paul's experience of "grace sufficient" embraced much more than his "thorn in the flesh," which was his initial and specific concern: Paul accepted weakness, insults, hardships, persecutions and calamities. Sustaining grace—"grace sufficient"—can equal and sometimes transcend the stabbing wound in one's own life, *and much more*. That is Paul's testimony in 2 Corinthians 12. Sustaining grace can be a blessed vantage point for addressing the multiple needs and diverse circumstances of responsible Christian existence.

A Contemporary Witness

Reynolds Price, noted American author and James B. Duke Professor of English at Duke University in Durham, North Carolina, tells the extraordinary story of his confrontation with cancer in *A Whole New Life: An*

Illness and A Healing (1994).[10] On Monday, 4 June 1984, Price under-
went surgery at Duke Hospital to address the significant swelling in the
upper ten inches of his spinal cord. Late Monday evening his brother Bill
fed him crushed ice and told him of the malignancy discovered through
surgery. On Tuesday morning his neurosurgeon, Allan Friedman,
described precisely what he had found. "The tumor was pencil-thick and
gray-colored, ten inches long from [his] neckhair downward and too
intricately braided in the core of [his] spinal cord" to permit Friedman to
do more than remove about ten percent of it.[11] In addition, he had
chiseled off considerable bone in seven vertebra in his upper spine to
relax crowding in the area.

Once the incision had healed—about a month away—Friedman
recommended radiation therapy, which turned out to be the maximum
dosage then applied to the spinal cord, a total of four thousand rads in
increments of five days a week for five weeks. Preparation included
molding a plaster cast to hold him motionless while lying on his chest as
well as small reference points tattooed on his back and boxed in a long
rectangle of gentian-purple dye to ensure the exact focus of an overhead
X-ray on the scar-covered tumor. Such a massive dose of radiation
involved a five percent risk of losing the use of both his legs.[12]

As Price lay in bed at home about dawn on July 3, he had the
remarkable "Vision" introducing this chapter on "Grace and Healing."
Unlike the poetic rendering of his vision in *The Laws of Ice*, Reynolds
Price recounts his experience in vivid narrative style in *A Whole New
Life*, the most unusual experience of his entire life. Suddenly he lay fully
dressed in modern street clothes among Jesus' twelve disciples clothed in
the garb of first-century Palestine, sleeping beside the big lake of
Kennereth, the Sea of Galilee. Jesus woke and came toward him; he bent
and beckoned Price to follow. Price says:

---

[10]Reynolds Price, *A Whole New Life: An Illness and A Healing* (New York:
Atheneum, 1994). Cf. Reynolds Price, "A Writer at his Best," An Interview by Michael
Puhlman, *New York Times Magazine* (September 20, 1987): section 6, 60-61, 131-35.

[11]Price, *A Whole New Life*, 28.

[12]Ibid., 41-42. Price remembers thinking: *"Don't tell me that; driven as I've always
been to stand in the winner's circle, I'll surely land in the crippled five percent"* (41-42).

> We waded out into cool lake water twenty feet from shore til we stood waist-deep.
>
> I was in my body but was also watching my body from slightly upward and behind. I could see the purple dye on my back, the long rectangle that boxed my thriving tumor.
>
> Jesus silently took up handfulls of water and poured them over my head and back til water ran down my puckered scar. Then he spoke once—"Your sins are forgiven"—and turned to the shore again, done with me.
>
> I came on behind him, thinking in standard greedy fashion, *Its not my sins I'm worried about.* So to Jesus' receding back, I had the gall to say "Am I also cured?"
>
> He turned to face me, no sign of a smile, and finally said two words—"That too." Then he climbed from the water, not looking round, really done with me.[13]

Price followed Jesus onto shore, and without any break he was home again in his own bed. On his calendar for 1984 at the top of the space for July 3, Price has drawn a star and written:

> 6 A.M.—By Kennereth, the bath, "Your sins are forgiven"—"Am I cured?"—"That too."[14]

From time to time Reynolds Price has doubted the integrity of his vision, unlike anything he had ever experienced before or since. Yet through all the assaults he mounted against the assurance of his vision,

---

[13]Ibid., 42-43. Readers will note a difference between the concluding verse of the poem "Vision" and the end of Price's narration of his vision. In the poem, he says: "Then we climb toward shore. I get there first and wait on the stones. . . . I turn and say 'Am I also cured?' . . . He comes close. . . . Then wades strong past me and touches land" (*Laws of Ice*, 67). In his narrative account, Price writes: "I came on behind him. . . . I had the gall to say 'Am I also cured?' He turned to face me. . . . Then he climbed from the water . . . really done with me. I followed him out" (*A Whole New Life*, 43). It is a minor discrepancy, but puzzling.

[14]Ibid., 44.

he could never quite destroy for two consecutive days "the unassailably physical core of that morning—the credible acts that I've watched, felt, and heard in what was an actual place on Earth, a place I've visited and photographed. That hard integrity clung to the memory" and promised eventual healing.[15] Indeed, Price locates his surprising experience in the context of an unchurchly Christianity nurtured in childhood, months of translating the Gospel of Mark in the 1970s, a second visit to the Sea of Galilee in the north of Israel the previous October, and the conviction of the unique relationship of Jesus to the Creator, who apparently takes closer note of some creatures much more than others.

Although Price received assuring messages from friends outside his immediate circle that he would not die—eight in number, mostly from women—fear flooded him with increasing frequency toward the end of radiation therapy, a depth of fear that he could not tell his doctors. Three weeks later, when Price hesitatingly asked, his cousin Marcia accepted responsibility to care for him, coming to stay with him in Durham on August 27 and moving him to Goldsboro with her and her husband Paul on September 13. Paul soon left for a month's work at a medical mission in Bangladesh; meanwhile, Marcia and Reynolds read Scripture together, reflecting on their different interpretations in conversation. Eventually he told her of his vision, and she suggested that he illustrate it with sketches—drawings that became meditative sketches of the face of Christ that extended over the next two years. Neither guilt nor judgment but a sense of the core of Jesus' meaning to him formed the character of these faces. *"All is forgiven where forgiveness is sought: all but the failure to trust that forgiveness."*[16]

While under his cousin's care, Price experienced the increasing severity of pain and faced the truth of losing the use of his legs. During the first few days of confronting this fate, Reynolds Price had his second uncanny experience. "In that black trough" he looked up beyond the ceiling to God, asking: "How much more do I take?" He heard one voiced word: "More."[17] Early the next day Marcia called her Methodist minister with his request for the sacrament of communion. On a clear hot morning the minister came to his bedroom and read Jesus' words of

---

[15]Ibid., 46.
[16]Ibid., 75-77.
[17]Ibid., 80.

institution and memory from the Last Supper, feeding him communion, which had meant the real presence of Jesus to him from childhood. As he partook of bread and wine, Price says:

> I experienced again the almost overwhelming force that has always felt to me like God's presence. Whether the force would confirm my healing or go on devastating me, for the moment I barely cared. No prior taste in my old life had meant as much as this new chance at a washed and clarified view of my fate—and that from the hands of a strange young minister in a room that didn't belong to me. In many calmer hours to come, I'd know that my answer to the one word *More* was three words anyhow—*Bring it on.*[18]

On October 8 Price returned to Durham with his friend and onetime student Dan Voll.

In November 1984 Price accepted the commission to write a play for Hendrix College in Arkansas, and he began to write again in self-confinement within the safety of his home. With his physical health continuing to decline, however, he finally entered a rehabilitation program in July 1985. In rehab for four weeks, Price was trained in washing and dressing himself. He learned to manage his "compromised" bladder, catheterizing himself several times daily. He accepted the necessity of the rubber-gloved removal of his feces from the lower intestines. Yet intimate day-and-night contact with others in a similar or worse condition than he proved to be the most important gain. At this point in the story Price refers to himself for the first time as a "gimp."[19] Yet the summer also marked his consciousness of unbearable pain, and it drove him to the Pain Clinic of Duke Hospital, where he learned that he had "central pain" from massive damage to his central nervous system. Thus began the fruitless treadmill of a narcotized life.

In early October, Price traveled to Hendrix College to begin rehearsals of *August Snow* and to make on-site revisions. On the third day back home from Arkansas, October 23, he began a sequel to *August Snow*: With surprising and unprecedented speed he completed the first draft of *Night Dance* in one week. The safe spell ran into Christmas

---

[18]Ibid., 81-82.
[19]Ibid., 100-108, esp. 103, 104.

1985, a peaceful dream before a new nightmare swept him into a long stretch of dark tunneling.

Price returned to teaching his annual semester at Duke in January 1986, and a graduate student moved into his house to assist him. On February 8 Price leaned too far back in his wheelchair, and it rolled over. Within a week he noted back stiffness and intense pain. Less than two weeks after the accident, he could not sit up to slide out of bed, the pain so ferocious and frightening that he had to be fed through a straw. Price knew, *"This cancer is alive again and racing to take me."*[20] With intensified pain he returned to Duke Hospital by ambulance on February 27 for tests. Although the tumor was surely moving again upward toward the base of his brain, Price vetoed Friedman's recommended surgery. Despite pain constantly rising, causing "nausea and mental malaise," he was determined to complete one term of teaching.

On April 28 Reynolds Price had his second major surgery. Friedman found three large cysts and a considerable tumor in the spinal cord above the hairline of the neck. After he drained and permanently shunted the cysts, he removed the visible tumor for some inches downward with a newly developed ultrasonic laser scalpel. The results proved so positive that Friedman became really hopeful, proposing a six month pause and then removing the remainder of the tumor. This rescue could not have occurred a few months earlier but only through "the uncanny timing" of the availability of the new scalpel for "the hairbreath transactions of neural surgery."[21] On October 3 Friedman removed most all the tumor left.

Into 1987 Reynolds Price returned to a relatively normal routine, but the pain continued to roar with heightening intensity. On June 6, after two excruciating days of pain, Price telephoned Friedman who told him the problem was dead nerves, and he suggested amitriptyline again. Though skeptical, Price experienced dramatic and unprecedented psychic relief within twenty-four hours. As he sought to stabilize the gain, he met on July 17 with Patrick Logue in the Duke Department of Psychiatry who used hypnosis to free him of the pain. Through weekly sessions with Logue during July and August, as well as a helpful tape of his guiding

---

[20]Ibid., 130.

[21]Ibid., 137, but in the context of 133-37. Note also 174 for Price's confidence regarding the elimination of the malignancy.

monologue, Price learned to separate himself from the notice of the pain, locating it on the far horizon of his consciousness and turning it off. The pain remains, but he does not allow it to intrude into his daily life and work. "I must *feel* it as *real* but not suffer from it"[22] Now Price is conscious of pain about fifteen minutes scattered here and there in a sixteen-hour day. *"The harm is done. It cannot be repaired; pain signified nothing. Begin to ignore it."*[23]

How does Reynolds Price understand this new life four years on the other side of his catastrophe? If he had to compare his present life with his past, 1933-1984, he says that these recent years beyond the disaster have gone better: "They've brought more in and sent more out—more love and care, more knowledge and patience, more work in less time."[24] Yet the gain requires a radically new perspective, because the kindest act anyone could have done for him after surgery and radiation would have been to say to him: " 'Reynolds Price is dead. Who will you be now? Who *can* you be and how can you get there, double-time?'. . . *Come back to life, whoever you'll be. Only you can do it."*[25]

Beyond the necessary care of family and friends, nurses and doctors,[26]

---

[22]Ibid., 158, but in the context of 151-58.

[23]Ibid., 159. Price describes the intensity of his pain graphically: "If however you're presently free of chronic pain, and I could instantly transfer mine to you in all its savagery from neck to toe, I think I'm realistic in saying that you'd lay yourself flat instantly and beg to be taken to a hospital, fast." He continues: "Even now, especially in the night, I'll awake to a level of pain in my back that's like nothing so much as my wound reopened and barbed-wire laces tearing at the inmost quick of the flesh and sending great licks of fire down my legs" (157-58).

[24]Ibid., 179.

[25]Ibid., 184, but in the context of 180-84.

[26]Ibid., Price's reliance on his brother Bill and, on occasion, Dan Voll comes to mind. However, alongside his deep appreciation for doctors and nurses, especially Dr. Allan Friedman, Price expresses disappointment in Dr. X and especially Dr. Z. On 22 July 1985, he spent two-and-a-half hours in a magnetic resonance imager (MRI) for detailed pictures of his spinal cord, and the result was delivered to him "deadpan a week later by [his] neurologist on his usual very brief visit with a huddle of interns, all working hard to look glum as ashes." Price noted that "Dr. X said my scan shows 'no change' during the past thirteen months" (114).

Price saves his sharpest words for his radiation oncologist, Dr. Z. Before his treatment began in July 1984, Price had his first encounter with the presiding radiation oncologist, who told him "with all the visible concern of a steel cheese-grater, that [his] tumor was of a size that was likely unprecedented in the annals of Duke Hosptial—some

Price acknowledges the crucial significance of his religious experience in his recovery—prayer, a vision, and the *More*. If the Creator does consult you unexpectedly, he counsels, it probably means that you have already invested in the effort to know God, but the Creator will "almost surely lurk beyond you in heavy drapery with his face concealed."[27] In any case, the answer to most prayers remains *No*.

Reynolds Price claims this new life is better for him. In the twenty-two years of professional life before the tumor's discovery he published twelve books, whereas in the ten years afterward he has published thirteen, authentic energy flowing from one life into another with profound consoling gains, especially patience and watchfulness. He lives and works with remarkable and increased vitality, a full and happy life, but everything has changed, even the appearance of his handwriting: "Cranky as it is, it's taller, more legible, with more air and stride. It comes down the arm of a grateful man."[28]

---

fifty years of annals." Price wondered: *"Does he want me to cheer with personal pride?"* (40-41). Three weeks after all the spinal radiation Price could get in a lifetime, Dr. Z was discouraged by his continuing loss of strength and motor power. "He had nothing more to offer by way of human exchange than the patent fact that I'd have to wait now and see what resulted." Price heard the instructions to return for an examination in six weeks "with harsh precision, as the arrangement of one more opportunity for a research scientist to update his files on one more failed experiment." In response to his inquiry for suggestions in the interim—diet or exercise or medication—Dr. Z gave him the "blankest look, shrugged and said, 'Write the Great American Novel.' " Cousin Marcia Bennett, "the wife of a tirelessly human family physician," stared "the oncologist dead in his eye and said, 'He's already written that' " (66-67). The last encounter occurred two years later: "Dr. Z walked in, with no buffer troops. No smile, no handshake, no expressed pleasure in the surgical outcome. He wanted only to say that these surgeries, in spring and fall, had shown that indeed [Price's] five weeks of radiation had slowed the tumor considerably." Price thanked him, and he left (144).

Reynolds Price has concluded that doctors ought to cultivate people skills: "Those are merely the skills of human sympathy, the skills for letting another creature know that his or her concern is honored and valued and that, whether a cure is likely or not, all possible efforts will be expended to achieve that aim or ease incurable agony toward its welcome end." A doctor unable or unwilling to develop such essential skills, whatever the reason, is "a flawed practitioner" who ought to display a warning on his office door or his starched lab coat—*"Expert technician. Expect no more. The quality of your life and death are your concern"* (145-46).

[27]Ibid., 185.
[28]Ibid., 193.

When I finished reading the powerful witness of Reynolds Price, I found his astonishing "cure" from cancer and his remarkable transformation of life comparable at several points to the experience of Paul with his "thorn in the flesh" in 2 Corinthians 12:2-10. He has endured a savage and violent assault on his entire personhood, but he is more than a survivor, because everything has changed. This man is another Reynolds Price, a self-described gimp devoid of self-pity who has learned to cope with immeasurable pain and innumberable difficulties of daily existence, doing so with extraordinary wisdom and unprecedented productivity. Even in a wheelchair Reynolds Price has been graced with a blessed vantage point to experience "a whole new life" full of wonder, joy, and gratitude.

Sustaining Grace: A Continuum

As the story of Reynolds Price indicates, the understanding of sustaining grace as a blessed vantage point for experiencing the depths of meaning in life does not encompass the whole of "grace sufficient." A better understanding recognizes that sustaining grace constitutes a broad continuum rather than a single kind of experience. On the one end, sustaining grace transforms weakness into strength, like Paul's thorn in the flesh; and on the other end, sustaining grace enables a capacity for coping with the afflictions and adversities, the difficulties and frustrations that drain life of energy and purpose, productivity and satisfaction. The capacity for coping may refer to a recurring physical problem, an ongoing disability or bouts of depression, but effective coping will inevitably include some of the inner resources necessary to maintain a sense of balance in life. Yet the gift of grace sufficient that only nurtures coping is quite different from and much less than a blessed vantage point for experiencing the depths of meaning in life. Rather, life may move forward more slowly, the grace for the day may prove more fragile, and personal accomplishments may become more restricted. On one end of the continuum *transformation* characterizes grace sufficient, but on the other end *coping* defines the sustaining grace of God.

Romans 5:3-5 might very well describe the transformation of suffering into blessing, of weakness into strength through sustaining grace:

> We boast in our sufferings, knowing that *suffering* produces endurance, and *endurance* produces character, and *character* produces hope, and *hope* does not disappoint us, because *God's love* has been poured into our hearts through the Holy Spirit that has been given to us.

The transformation of suffering through sustaining grace into a blessed vantage point, whatever the process might be, must reflect on Paul's experience with his "thorn in the flesh." Several crucial elements informed his experience: (1) He understood his own spiritual autobiography as a Christian and an apostle. (2) He could identify his thorn in the flesh and its continuing negative impact on his life and ministry. (3) He prayed fervently for God to remove it, but he had the capacity to shift his focus in prayer to enable him to discern God's answer to his prayers. (4) He had the physical capability and mature receptivity to integrate this experience into his own journey of faith, which proved essential for his continuation in ministry.

Beyond his description of the process of the transforming power of sustaining grace in Romans 5, Paul describes the coping power of sustaining grace in the midst of the complexities and difficulties of his life in 2 Corinthians 4:8-10:

> We are afflicted in every way, but not crushed; perplexed, but not driven to despair; persecuted, but not forsaken; struck down, but not destroyed; always carrying in the body the death of Jesus, so that the life of Jesus may also be made visible in our bodies.

Paul offered a litany of praise for the coping capability in sustaining grace: "but not crushed," "but not driven to despair," "but not forsaken," "but not destroyed." All these instances of "but not" refer to the coping power of sustaining grace at various points on the continuum of ongoing human need. In the extremity of a particular human situation, however, the capacity for coping may blur with an overwhelming helplessness, and coping may be so tenuous that the graced person hangs on with her fingernails.

Sustaining grace is genuinely sustaining: sufficient to transform weakness into strength as well as to empower a capacity for coping. The Divine Word, "My grace is sufficient for you, for my power is made perfect in weakness," is therefore eminently positive: On one end of the continuum, sustaining grace adds to life, the continuing transformation of

weakness into strength, of pain into joy. On the other end of the continuum, sustaining grace provides or endeavors to provide the capacity to
cope with some measure of effectiveness amid the destructive adversities
of life, the continuing experience of help and gratitude for life in the light
of Jesus Christ crucified.

Another Contemporary Witness

Flannery O'Connor (1925–1964) of Milledgeville, Georgia, is America's
greatest post-World War II short-story writer, and she left a small but
arresting miscellanea of writings.[29] O'Connor identified herself as "a
Catholic peculiarly possessed of the modern consciousness."[30] In or out
of the church today, nihilism is the gas you breathe. Likewise, she wrote
in fidelity to the South, "certainly Christ-haunted" but "hardly Christ-
centered,"[31] because it believes that all of us have fallen and are only per-
fectible by God's grace, not by our own unaided efforts. In 1945
Flannery O'Connor escaped from her home in Milledgeville, Georgia, to
pursue a literary career in the North within the stimulating company of
the literary elite, which included more than a year and a half with the
family of poet Robert Fitzgerald near Ridgefield, Connecticut
(1949–1950).

When Flannery traveled home to Milledgeville in December 1950 to
spend Christmas with her mother, Regina, she suffered a sever attack of
lupus erythematosus that almost killed her. Through blood transfusions
and injections of the experimental drug ACTH, she survived, but at
twenty-five she had a serious case of the same disease that had killed her

---

[29]Flannery O'Conner's published works include: two novels, *Wise Blood* (1952) and
The Violent Bear It Away (1960); two collections of short stories, *A Good Man Is Hard
To Find* (1955) and *Everything That Rises Must Converge* (1965); a posthumous
collection of speeches and essays, *Mystery and Manners* (1969); of letters, *The Habit of
Being* (1979); of book reviews, *Flannery O'Connor: Her Life, Library and Book Reviews*
(1980).
[30]Flannery O'Connor, *The Habit of Being: The Letters of Flannery O'Connor*, ed.
Sally Fitzgerald (New York: Vintage Books, 1980) 90. I use O'Connor's *Letters* rather
like a diary, because she expresses her feelings about the impact of her illness on her life
with striking candor—a remarkable woman and a devout Christian.
[31]Flannery O'Connor, *Mystery and Manners*, ed. Sally and Robert Fitzgerald (New
York: The Noonday Press, 1969) 44.

father in three years. Flannery left the Atlanta hospital in late spring for a severely restricted life under the constant care of Regina and her Uncle Louis in permanent residence at Andalusia, a large dairy farm near Milledgeville.[32] She felt her literary career had ended. She later wrote to Maryat Lee:

> This is a Return I have faced and when I faced it I was roped and tied and resigned the way it is necessary to be resigned to death, and largely because I thought it would be the end of any creation, any writing, any WORK from me (9 June 57).[33]

Although she regained her health slowly with periodic stays in the hospital, during the first full year of her illness O'Connor completed the revision of her novel, *Wise Blood*. She bought a pair of peacocks for amusement and began to write stories for a collection. Three years later she had completed nine stunning short stories. Under the pressure of her illness and circumstances she acquired power and an extraordinary finish in her writing. While she had thought that she could be a writer only outside the South, she confessed to a friend: "I would certainly have persisted in that delusion had I not got very ill and had to come home. The best of my writing has been done here" (16 July 57).[34]

The cortisone treatment developed after her father's death improved O'Connor's prospects for a longer and productive life. Yet her physical ordeal continued, because the steroid medication keeping her alive gave her necrosis, deterioration of the bones, beginning in the hips and forcing her to use crutches to walk. She accepted both lupus and ACTH, however, and established a routine that would enable her to write two or three hours a day.

Since her audience did not hold her beliefs, O'Connor the author made her vision apparent through shock—to the hard of hearing she

---

[32]O'Connor, *Letters*, 3-4, 11-12, 21-22. See Lorine M. Getz, *Flannery O'Connor: Her Life, Library and Book Reviews* (New York: The Edwin Mellen Press, 1980) 14-29; Harold Fickett and Douglas R. Gilbert, *Flannery O'Connor: Images of Grace* (Grand Rapids MI: Eerdmans Publishing Co., 1986) 24-34. Cf. Sally Fitzgerald, "Introduction," *Three by Flannery O'Connor* (New York: Nal-Viking, 1986) xvi.

[33]O'Connor, *Letters*, 224.

[34]Ibid., 230.

would shout and for the almost-blind draw large and startling figures.[35]
She wrote her new friend "A":

> One of the awful things about writing when you are a Christian is that
> for you the ultimate reality is the Incarnation . . . and nobody believes
> in the Incarnation; that is nobody in your audience. My audiences are
> the people who think God is dead (2 August 55).[36]

O'Connor believed "a shock of grace" happens "when the good
intrudes upon evil," an atypical perspective. She wrote in another letter
to "A": "The force of habit and weight of possessions" makes it difficult
to open up lives to grace. "You accept grace the quickest when you have
the least" (21 September 57).[37] Beyond the shock of grace in conversion,
she believed in the deepening of conversion:

> I don't think of conversion as being once for all and that's that. I think
> once the process is begun and continues that you are continually turning
> inward toward God and away from your own egocentricity and that you
> have to see this selfish side of yourself in order to turn away from it (4
> February 61).[38]

Occasionally O'Connor traveled to visit friends, give a lecture, or
participate in a conference. In 1955 the daily injection of ACTH was
replaced with Merticorten, a medication she could take orally. Off her
salt-free diet, she became more comfortable with her illness. In 1958 her
cousin Katie paid for a trip for Flannery and Regina to go to Lourdes and
then to Rome for an audience with the Pope, a trip that Flannery initially
resisted but finally consented to take. At Lourdes Sally Fitzgerald

---

[35]Getz, *Flannery O'Connor*, 42. In her stories O'Connor uses the "grotesque"—the
deliberate distortion of what appears normal; irony, violence, and caricature; comic yet
terrifying actions, exaggerated situations, and abnormal characters. She employed the
grotesque not so much as a literary device as a description of reality. Grotesque images
portray ordinary people as the freaks they are, the alienation, displacement, and fallenness
of everyone; furthermore, they accentuate the futility of human action to remedy the
human condition. So O'Connor's characters, steeped in pride and egoism, usually
experience some violence that forces them to see their sinfulness.

[36]O'Connor, *Letters*, 92.

[37]Ibid., 241.

[38]Ibid., 430.

convinced Flannery to bathe and drink the water from the shrine's spring, and Flannery liked to associate the subsequent but temporary recalcification of her hipbones with her visit to Lourdes. However, she had actually prayed for the grace to finish her novel, *The Violent Bear It Away*, and she received this grace, a miracle in itself.[39]

Whenever she could, O'Connor nurtured her faith through going to mass and saying daily prayers out of the missal. Moreover, she read widely and knowledgeably in the history of Catholic spirituality as well as in Roman Catholic theology, from Augustine and Thomas Aquinas to Baron von Hugel and Teilhard de Chardin, with an occasional Protestant excursion. She knew her own faith to be a gift of grace and said with sardonic humor: "I distrust pious phrases, particularly when they issue from my mouth" (2 August 55).[40] She candidly acknowledged her own struggle of faith:

> I think there is no suffering greater than what is caused by the doubts of those who want to believe. *I know what torment this is, but I can only see it, in myself anyway, as the process by which faith is deepened.* A faith that just accepts is a child's faith and all right for children, but eventually you have to grow religiously as every other way, though some never do. . . . *It is much harder to believe than not to believe* (1959).[41]

She affirmed faith to be a gift, but she accentuated the role of the will. With the tutelage of experience she wrote a young poet at Emory University: "If you want your faith, you have to work for it. It is a gift, but for very few is it a gift given without any demand for equal time devoted to its cultivation" (30 May 62).[42]

Glimpses of O'Connor's struggle to cope with the loneliness and boredom of her sharply curtailed life surface occasionally in her letters, but her most revealing comment is unexpected and poignant, a profound disappointment: "Needing people badly and not getting them may turn you in a creative direction. . . . [My father] needed the people I guess and

[39]Fickett and Gilbert, *Images*, 68.
[40]O'Connor, *Letters*, 92-93.
[41]Ibid., 353-54 [italics added].
[42]Ibid., 477.

got them. Or rather, wanted them, and got them. I wanted them and didn't." She added, "We are all rather blessed in our deprivations if we let ourselves be, *I suppose*" (11 August 56).[43]

The fourteen-year battle with lupus gave Flannery O'Connor a certain perspective on suffering and death. She accepted her illness, and said:

> I have never been anywhere but sick. In a sense sickness is a place, more instructive than a long trip to Europe, and it's always a place where there's no company, where nobody can follow. Sickness before death is a very appropriate thing and I think those who don't have it miss one of God's mercies. (28 June 56)[44]

Although written 28 June 1956, eight years before her death, O'Connor's attitude did not change but attained a deepening discernment:

> The creative action of the Christian's life is to prepare his death in Christ. It is a continuous action in which this world's goods are utilized to the fullest, both positive gifts and what Pere [*sic*] Teilhard de Chardin calls "passive diminishments" (1961).[45]

She appropriated "passive diminishment" and defined it in terms of her own illness: Teilhard means that "the patient is passive in relation to the disease—he's done all he can to get rid of it and can't so he's passive and accepts it" (31 March 63).[46]

Although the end was near, Flannery managed to finish *Everything That Rises Must Converge*, which included a rewriting of her first story, "The Geranium," into a completely new story, "Judgement Day." She had brought everything full circle. At home in Milledgeville on June 24, 1964, she wrote a friend of the severity of her illness, four blood

---

[43]O'Connor, *Letters*, 169 (italics added). The relationship of Flannery and her mother was one of closeness and mutual respect, though they were of a different temperament from one another. See Ralph C. Wood, "Talent Increased and Returned to God: The Spiritual Legacy of Flannery O'Connor's Letters," *Anglican Theological Review* 62 (1980): 160-61.

[44]Ibid. 163.

[45]Flannery O'Connor, "Introduction," *A Memoir of Mary Ann*, in *Mystery and Manners*, 223.

[46]O'Connor, *Letters*, 512.

transfusions in the previous month: "They expect me to improve, or so they say. I expect anything that happens."[47] Resignation? She recognized the end to be near and wrote Janet McKane: "Yesterday the priest brought me Communion. . . . I also had him give me the now-called Sacrament of the Sick. Once known as Extreme Unction" (8 July 64).[48] Flannery O'Connor died August 3, 1964.

Through her letters Flannery O'Connor tells us of her experience of grace, "sustaining grace," a gift to her and her witness to grace one of her gifts to the church. Seldom, if ever, all the way over to an unqualified blessed vantage point, she moved back and forth on the continuum of sustaining grace with considerable variation in her coping. She knew the difference between grace and healing, and with fierce honesty accepted whatever measure of grace she had for "today."

The Inappropriateness of Generalization

"Healing grace" is not always a possibility, but "sustaining grace" can offer a genuine sense of fulfillment or the possibility of some measure of coping. The difference in the stories of Reynolds Price and Flannery O'Connor illuminates the variation in sustaining grace and accentuates the complexity of grace itself. Nevertheless, a fundamental question endures: Is sustaining grace always available? Always available and sufficient for our need? When the sufferer does not experience "sustaining grace," is the needy person somehow at fault? Like the miracle of healing grace, the confrontation of suffering through sustaining grace, whatever form it takes, is not always a possibility.

Some interpret 1 Corinthians 10:13 (NRSV) to mean that sustaining grace is always available and always equal to the needs of the Christian.[49]

No testing has overtaken you that is not common to everyone. God is faithful, and he will not let you be tested beyond your strength, but with

---

[47]Ibid., 587.
[48]Ibid., 591.
[49]See Wayne Oates, *Temptation: A Biblical and Psychological Approach* (Louisville: Westminster Press, 1991) 22-24. However, Oates would allow for "uncommon" testing, which may prove beyond endurance.

the testing he will also provide the way out so that you may be able to endure it.

While Paul's affirmation and insight confirms the understanding of sustaining grace as the capacity for coping with some measure of effectiveness, the text, I would argue, refers to testing that is common to human existence. What happens to the Christian who is overtaken and overwhelmed with *uncommon* adversity? When life takes a turn into "the valley of the shadow of death" but does not move "through" it, what then? When fatigue wears life down and drains life of all energy, with responsibilities left undone and relationships strained too thin, what then? When all available resources cannot bear the weight of obligations and the constant push of pressure, when life suffers a breakdown, what then?

Here pastoral theology sometimes reinforces rather than relieves a broken person's confusion and guilt. They counsel: The problem is attitudinal or perspectival: "Is the glass of water half empty or half full?" The assumption is devastating: If the sufferer does not experience the relief and perhaps joy of sustaining grace, the fault and the guilt must be the responsibility of the sufferer. The assumption is damning but false. The glass is sometimes really empty, the halfway mark only an illusory stain of earlier days—conceptually, perhaps only an abstraction. In the routine of suffering and death, a worn down or medically naive pastoral theology has no place for Gethsemane on its horizon.

In Romans 8 Paul moves beyond Romans 5:

> I consider that the sufferings of this present time are not worth comparing with the glory about to be revealed to us. (8:18)

> Likewise, the Spirit helps us in our weakness . . . that very Spirit intercedes for us with sighs too deep for words. (8:26)

We are never simply done with suffering. The transformation of suffering through sustaining grace is inevitably part-way and part-time. Sustaining grace, like healing grace, is not always available.

Sustaining grace? On the edge of the abyss of Nothingness in the darkness of night, the believer is self-consciously empty, without even a flickering candle to touch the dark. Attentive to the noise of silence, the Christian hears a lament, a parody of Romans 5:

We tremble in our suffering, because suffering breeds exhaustion, and exhaustion rouses helplessness, and helplessness wakens despair, and despair threatens us with *dread*, the accusation that life itself is without intrinsic meaning and value, WITHOUT ANY GOD.

Sustaining grace? The Divine Word, "My grace is sufficient for you, for my power is made perfect in weakness," is not always operational or applicable. Like the miracle of healing grace, the gift of sustaining grace is not always a possibility.[50]

John was admitted through the emergency room to intensive care on a brilliant autumn afternoon.[51] He had run in a cross-country track meet on Tuesday afternoon, but that night he had awakened with a fever and headache. When his physician saw him on Wednesday afternoon, already seriously ill, he immediately referred him to intensive care. John's case was special, because an infectious illness is almost always controllable with antibiotics and time, and a life-threatening illness usually develops at a pace that allows time for treatment. John, however, had run a 5-km race one day and was near death the next. Those treating him were unprepared for the ferocity of his illness or the speed of his deterioration. John was dying of something that physicians could normally manage, but it had raced beyond their control and threatened to destroy a strong, healthy adolescent youngster.

Since the ordinary sense of control is our parental buffer against chaos, the unexpected randomness of the assault of this infection on John and the awareness of the vulnerability of everyone made it even more

---

[50]See H. Wheeler Robinson, *Suffering: Human and Divine* (New York: The MacMillan Company, 1939) 124. Wheeler Robinson, himself no stranger to suffering, recounted four instances of futile and meaningless suffering, the most vivid the suffering of a married couple whom he had known from childhood: "They were both devoted Christians, giving time and energy and what they could afford out of a very small income to all manner of good works. Besides this, they impoverished themselves in the support of parents who lived to a great age. As the time of the compulsory retirement of the husband from the post drew near, financial anxiety so told upon him that he lost his reason. A few months after, his wife, who had looked after him herself with the utmost self-sacrifice so long as it was possible, lost her own reason, and had to follow her husband to the asylum where they both died."

[51]Paula S. Butterfield, "The I of the Storm," *Journal of the American Medical Association* 264 (July 25, 1990): 462.

menacing. Without reference to any irresponsible behavior John lay deathly ill. It had just happened, and at a frightening speed. John's case triggered the chilling fear of how quickly any parents can lose a child. Who has not been through a child's high fever in the night and trusted a quick telephone conversation the next morning with the pediatrician who said to call back in two or three days if the symptoms persist. How can anyone accept that counsel now? When should parents sound the alarm? What can revitalize the earlier assumption of predictability about the minimum danger of a sudden rash or a high fever?

The sense of tragedy intensified when people learned that John's father had been killed in an accident a short time before. People felt deep sympathy for John's mother. How does a person put life back together after such an assault? "One tragedy can be ascribed to random occurrence. But two?"[52] Then came welcome relief: John went from near death on Wednesday night to seeing visitors on Friday. Through the resilience of an adolescent, the wonders of modern medicine, and the mystery of the immune system, the sixteen-year old kid was going to make it. However, he deteriorated over the weekend.

On Saturday John passed through what one attending physician called "the eye of the storm," and on Sunday his organ systems began to fail. After disheartening news on Monday, John died on Tuesday, and everyone mourned. Only God knows how much his fatherless and sonless family mourned. Several months later the illness and death of John continued to evoke anxious feelings for the hospital staff. Paula Butterfield concludes: "[John's] story exposed how illusory our sense of control is, how fragile our seemingly tenacious grip on life, and, perhaps most bothersome, how willingly we can be led to trust the cumulative experience of uneventful days."[53] Grace?

---

[52]Ibid. Hershey G., an oncologist in Arkansas, sent me the story, a continuing conversation between us about the activity of God in relationship to recovery from an illness. He noted: "Frank, this had a certain ring of familiarity to it." He had circled words and phrases: "chaos"; "It just happened"; "random occurrence"; "But two?" The circled phrases rolled together intensified the question: "One tragedy can be ascribed to random occurrence. But two?" Hershey answered with just one word: "Absolutely." Contrary to the usual prognosis that John's illness should have been manageable, he died. You can plot the anatomy of an illness only retrospectively, medically and theologically.

[53]Ibid.

Despite the textbook prognosis that John should have lived, he died. The expectation of healing, of healing grace, in this instance completely normal, proved illusory in "The I of the Storm." Sustaining grace never applied to John's illness, though it might have been crucial for his grief in the death of his father, a story in his story but a story unavailable. If sustaining grace did constitute a viable possibility, it would be for John's mother. A relevant but unanswerable question waits to be asked: If John's mother did not receive enough sustaining grace to cope with two deaths from random occurrence, wherein lies the fault? With the sonless widow? With God? With neither, because life can be so hard that a breakdown is normal, perhaps inevitable! When life does fall apart, the victim of multiple random occurrences of chaos may be unable to cope effectively, because sustaining grace has in fact proven to be too little in the face of so much; nevertheless, the hope of faith beyond a breakdown is for a new measure of sustaining grace that will nurture the ability to cope in a functional recovery in the future.

When healing grace proves unavailable, when sustaining grace is not operational, the hope for grace is the prayer for the survivor whose world has been shattered through chaos. Hope . . . for grace. . . .

The Risk in Suffering for Promissory Grace

Is there any reason for hope, for us to hope beyond suffering for grace, for God? Yes. The Christian risks hope in the midst of suffering for the promise of grace yet to be: promissory grace, risky grace.

The Inevitability of Death

Beyond healing grace and sustaining grace, the grace of God takes the form of promissory grace. Grace becomes sheer promise. Where in Paul's experience did promissory grace take form? The selection of any text is venturesome, but 2 Corinthians 1:3-11 might do. Paul praised God for God's mercies and comfort, and he declared that we share in Christ's suffering and through him we share God's comfort, too. Then Paul described deliverance from an affliction, itself unidentified, that he experienced in Asia.

> [W]e were so utterly, unbearably crushed that we *despaired* of life itself. Indeed, we felt that we had received the sentence of death. (1:8b-9a)

What Paul noted but did not name was probably the most negative experience of his entire life. The words are graphic: "unbearably crushed," i.e., completely overwhelmed; "despaired of life," i.e., hopeless on the edge of dread; "felt . . . the sentence of death," i.e., a searing encounter that permanently marked him with death's inevitability. What happened to Paul? In all probability he had a severe illness that threatened his life, so serious to seem to be completely beyond recovery.[54] A critical physical illness and the dark shadow of death broke Paul down. He despaired of life, which is the edge of dread. The experience became purposeful to Paul, however, because he appropriated the affliction as an occasion not to rely on himself,

> but on God who raises the dead. He who rescued us from so deadly a peril will continue to rescue us; on him we have set our hope. (1:10)

The severity of Paul's illness or situation moved him to recognize the frailty of human existence and the utter limitation, indeed, the deception of human self-confidence. Death is the last frontier of human existence. Thus a devastating illness that drains the life out of the afflicted person can become so forceful and so memorable that the only hope lies in resurrection. The God who raised the crucified Christ from the dead is the only One in whom Paul dared risk his hope. Though God might deliver him from the sentence of death again, always now temporarily, Paul realized that only the God who raises the dead is Light on the boundary

---

[54]C. K. Barrett, *The Second Epistle to the Corinthians* (New York: Harper and Row Publishers, 1973) 63-64, 66. Cf. Ralph P. Martin, "2 Corinthians," *Word Biblical Commentary* 40 (Waco: Word Books, 1986) 16. "The clause, 'that we should no longer trust in ourselves,' suggests a set of circumstances where Paul might have extricated himself by personal effort but chose not to do so." Martin is unconvincing. If anything, the refusal to trust himself reflects Paul's inability to change his circumstances. C. K. Barrett has the better explanation, "seriously ill" (64).

of absolute Darkness. In the "now" after his surprising recovery the inevitability of death remained unforgettable and henceforth unavoidable. Paul rested his hope in the promise of God who comes to us in Jesus Christ. Yet Paul was grateful for prayers on his behalf, because God chooses to work in conjunction with the prayers of God's people, prayers that reach toward grace. Sooner or later, however, when we feel the cold breath and icy stare of death upon us, we see the limits and weakness of our hope. In the face of this Darkness, Paul trusted in the promissory grace of God.

The Ambiguity of Grace

A narrative of grace—a grace of sheer promise—needs a text, some text, even a risky text. A narrative of promissory grace must know the ambiguity of grace in the vicissitudes of life. Only promissory grace hears the lament of "not enough"—not enough time, not enough resources, not enough opportunity. And the lament is personal: not enough of the-needed-thing at the-now-time in the-my-place. We need a text that knows the incongruity of *grace* and *not enough*. We find one in an obscure biographical footnote among Paul's last writings, a fragment to be sure, and maybe even a bit flimsy, 2 Timothy 4:20: "Trophimus I left ill in Miletus"—grace but not enough. The contrast is more vivid when coupled with the preceding sentence: "Erastus remained at Corinth; Trophimus I left ill in Miletus."[55]

The contradiction is graphic. "Erastus remained," "Trophimus I left." Apparently Erastus had a choice, to continue with Paul or to stay at Corinth. Why did he choose to stay? To rest or minister, for the sake of opportunities or relationships, because of doubt or fear? Paul did not say. Yet Erastus made the decision, for whatever reason, to remain at Corinth. Conversely, Pauls said, "Trophimus I left in Miletus." Grace, but not enough. Ill, not healed. Ill, perhaps sustained? Ill, and left. Left sick, left behind, left out, left to somebody else, left to himself. Left, not healed. Left, not blessed. Left, not coping? Paul left Trophimus sick at Miletus: Abandoned? Abandoned broken? Abandoned bereft? Abandoned to

---

[55]Paul does not explain the contrast, but the assumption that Erastus did not continue with Paul because of a loss of faith is unwarranted.

whomever and whatever and whenever? We do not know. 2 Timothy 4:20 is only a fragment, a story untold, a story no one knows. "Erastus remained," "Trophimus I left ill." It is a story, no, two stories of providence that we would like to know. We, too, are fragments in the correspondence of others. And perhaps our story belongs to one of these three, either Erastus or Trophimus or Paul.

The God of grace promises hope that nudges trust on. The graced person faiths: "God has not overlooked me or forgotten me." We hope for grace when everything has fallen apart, grace when just barely hanging on. Hopeful grace, graceful hope—but there is nothing here in the Darkness to warrant hope or grace. Yet we remember when we had hope. We remember Someone with whom we shared hope. We remember Someone who died *in hope*, but *without grace, Godforsaken*, hung-up and hanging-on to hope for grace. At the cross of Christ our helplessness meets God's helplessness. The cross of Christ becomes the one place for some relief, for some assurance, for some Presence. The absence of God in the Godforsaken death of Jesus becomes the place of the Presence of God for godless humanity: The absence of God in the suffering of Jesus dying mediates the Presence of God through the crucified Jesus nailed dead. Yet the promise is risky. *Surrounded with Darkness, the sufferer finds shelter from the Darkness of Nothingness in the Darkness of Christ's cross*: When we stare into nothing, when we see only Darkness, we hope in the grace of the crucified Christ. Is this only rhetoric? No, because it is a dimension of Christian experience: The Presence of God in the Crucified One who hung dead in the Darkness is its content: God is present as the One who is absent. The dead Jesus mediates a particular form of the Presence of God.

Yet security here is risky, holding to a promise one cannot see in the Darkness, an indistinguishable blanket of Darkness without any taste of Light. We cannot distinguish the assault of the Darkness of Nothingness in front of Christ's cross from the grace of the Mystery of Darkness behind it. Blind to everything but Darkness, we faith hope for grace: THE RISKY MYSTERY OF GOD. We cling to the sheer promise of grace, which stretches beyond death to hope for eternal life in God.

A Contemporary Witness

"Look, I'm an atheist. I don't believe a goddamn thing. They tell me I have five to eight months to live, and I want you to help me die."[56] So began the conversation of Will Campbell with a young woman he hardly knew just out of exploratory surgery in a Nashville hospital. The lung cancer had metastasized throughout her entire body and far beyond the help of surgery. The bad news brought Will to her bedside. Since she had made her confession, penance was supposed to follow, but Will thought penance contrary to the gospel of unconditional grace. So he ignored the necessity of penance, struck his most professional pose, and asked: "Would you like to talk about this God who has damned what you don't believe?"

"Don't give me any of your counseling [stuff], Reverend!" she said. "I just chased that [blankety-blank] nurse out of here when she said, 'And how do you feel about what has happened to you, Millie?' Thirty-five years old and just figured out what I'm doing in this world and they tell me in six months I'll be [blankety-blank] gone from it."[57] She began to cry, and Will was glad, glad she could get some of the hurt and anger out, glad for the time it gave him to do penance. He had been more offended by her profanity than concerned with her condition.

"I embraced her," Will said, "forgetting the incision running from her right scapula to the bottom of the rib cage." Crying with her, she didn't seem to care about the pain. With the pastoral façade gone, their conversation began. Campbell's description of their time together is graphic.

> We spent long hours and many days together after that. Her anger was so furious I thought it beyond abatement. Sometimes the railing was directed at me. At other times at doctors, nurses, a mother who abandoned her at three, the great aunt who raised her, the father who drank around, slept around and died young, two marriages that ended in disaster. But most often it was aimed solidly at God. After each

---

[56]Will D. Campbell, *Forty Acres and a Goat* (Atlanta: Peachtree Publishers, LTD., 1986) 154.

[57]Ibid., 155.

harsh spasm she would catch her breath, laugh, and say, "How can I hate the son-of-a-bitch so much when he doesn't exist?"[58]

Millie wanted to hear every detail of Will's out-of-town trips. She especially liked his stories of a western journey to a one-time dude ranch turned into a lavish retreat center. Part of the retreat Will attended was to be spent in silence from ten at night until noon the following day. At a sumptuous breakfast the next morning with participants trying to communicate with ridiculous gestures, Will broke the silence with an earthy shout and a slammed fist on the table. He protested the entire charade of such a retreat in a world struggling in hunger, of desperate parents and starving children. Millie thought the story wonderful. She told Will that she might join his church! Will protested that he did not have a church. If he did, he would name it and put it on a bumper sticker, and "then you can bet your life I'd run it," which would ruin it. "Bet your life"—the wrong words, he knew.

> There was another long pause. She could no longer swallow solid foods, so she liked to sit beside the Pool of Siloam and throw bits of bread to the goldfish. The symbolism of sitting there was overwhelming. But I was trying to be professional, to be *strong*. She threw the last of the crumbs into the pool and took my hand. I thought she was going to scold me. Instead, her voice was soft and kind. "I guess somebody 'bet my life.' And according to yesterday's x-rays, the [so-and-so] is about to collect."[59]

Since they had drained the pool and filled it with clean, clear water a few days earlier, all the goldfish were visible to the very bottom. They swarmed around the spot where Millie had dropped the last bread crumbs, looking for more. She loved the goldfish. After a long time, Millie spoke gently again, "Will, do you think he'll parlay his winnings?" Will recognized the cue. He had frequently told her that he did not believe that death meant the end of life. She wanted Will to tell her again. Instead, he told another story about his western trip, how he baptized a young schoolteacher who had grown up in a Christian family but had never been

---

[58]Ibid., 156.
[59]Ibid., 157.

rightly baptized. For theological reasons the retreat center director would not allow them to use the swimming pool as a baptistry. So at sunrise the next morning they ignored the "No Trespassing" sign, climbed the fence surrounding a Corps of Engineers lake, and "in violation of both the steeples and Mr. Caesar," Will baptized her in illegal water, buried from the old life and raised to the new. Will Campbell the Anabaptist felt great.

Millie loved the story and tried to dance around the pool. "I guess the next thing you know *I'll* be asking you to baptize *me*." Will assured her that he didn't push, but that "the pool is ready when you are."[60]

Earlier Millie told Will that she had joined the Hemlock Society, a euthanasia group in England, and that she had started storing up the heavy drugs to enable her to end her life. However, she tenaciously held to the last shred of it. She agreed to experimental treatment and finally to a last-ditch feeding tube that carried food directly to her stomach. Millie and Will sat alone in the small public housing apartment that one of his friends had helped Millie get after all her money was gone. Will described the moment.

> She had been nauseous all day, and I sat beside her bed with the kidney basin half-filled with the cloudy stomach fluid. She could still talk, though the esophagus was completely blocked. However, she made no verbal request, gave no oral orders. Just kept gazing at the viscid liquid, occasionally raising her eyes upward. She repeated the same movements several times. I dipped my fingertips into the basin and held them there. Her eyes accepted the offering. I slowly crossed her forehead three times, saying no words. She closed her eyes as I did. In her own way, perhaps because fate had been so cruel, she was a woman of great inner strength. It seemed proper that the sacramental came from deep inside her own body.[61]

Baptism? Extreme unction? The Hospice nurse called Will at five o'clock the next morning.

Though I have read the story of Millie many times over the last half dozen years, I missed her confession of faith until recently. She had asked

---

[60]Ibid., 158.
[61]Ibid., 159.

Will with a surprising gentle voice: "Will, do you think he'll parlay his winnings?" Grace.

Conclusion

Some would argue that Millie had not been cured but she had been healed. Death constituted her healing. This perspective is helpful, but the distinction is spurious if left unqualified. The inappropriateness of generalization applies to the story of Millie's illness and dying. In fact, she may be the exception instead of the rule. Of course, everybody dies. Sooner or later in some form or another the story of an illness culminates in death. Unquestionably death is the great equalizer. . . . Or is it? Since each one of us within our relatively small circles of personal relationships must die, should we not simply affirm that death inevitably happens, that the timing lacks intrinsic significance for the deceased, that all who suffer briefly or lengthily experience healing through death into the eternal life of God? Those of us who grieve can talk about premature death, the dying of a child or teenager or young parent, but for the deceased death does not occur prematurely. The category of premature applies only to survivors, and those left grieve appropriately but almost entirely for themselves.

The witness of the New Testament, however, stands contrary to such an unqualified positive attitude toward the inevitability of death regardless of its particular circumstances. Whether or not a person lives a full and healthy life is of considerable importance in conjunction with the purpose of God in creation. While every human death includes tragic elements, certainly not every person's death is a tragedy, but some are. The healing miracles of Jesus would not constitute the defeat of chaos and validate the significance of ongoing life, if healing were inconsequential for the larger meaning of life. Furthermore, the experiences of the Apostle Paul—from the healing of Epaphroditus to Paul's own deliverance from a deadly illness, with the breakthrough of sustaining grace for his thorn in the flesh in-between—these experiences could not be affirmed as unique expressions of the grace of God in overcoming illness, if the time and the place of the end of life's journey did not matter. Although the gathering of an untimely death into the joy of the eternal life of God poses problems of conceptualization,[62] the search for healing for those sick and suffering is fundamental to the biblical perspective on the value of life. Healthy living is an issue of Christian stewardship, and gratitude for life is a source of Christ-like compassion. While grace and healing are not the same, they are complementary in Christian experience. At the end of life's journey, when the Christian pilgrim faces the inevitability of death, the graced person hopes byond death in the promise of God for the gift of healing yet to come—the grace of eternal life.

---

[62]The problems in conceptualization of an untimely or premature death in relationship to eternal life take the form of awkward questions: Is it contradictory to believe that God has gathered some who died prematurely into eternal life whom God attempted to bless with a full and complete life but was not able to do so? Can a person's transformation beyond an untimely death into the bliss of eternal life include the element of disappointment for a life unfulfilled? Does God grieve with the grieving and share the disappointment of the dying in the midst of a joy not yet full in the glad river of life beyond death in the eternity of God?

Chapter 7

The Pathos of Providence

THE TRIUMPHANT ENTRY INTO THE HOLY CITY with unmistakable messianic drama has become a distant memory to Jesus. Cleansing the Temple of God, "my Father's house," teaching the crowds daily the Kingdom's way, confronting the guardians of the Law and the priests of the Temple with his claims about the Kingdom of God—these events in a final Jerusalem Passover have ended for him. The Last Supper behind him and the cross before him, Jesus entered the Garden of Gethsemane. Most of the disciples stopped near the gate, but Jesus took Peter, James, and John into the Garden with him. In this hour, dread upon him not unlike death itself, grievously shaken and utterly distraught, he asked his three closest friends to watch with him. A stone's throw away, almost alone, Jesus prayed so that he would not be alone: "*Abba*, Father, for you all things are possible; remove this cup from me" . . . SILENCE . . . "yet not what I want, but what you want" (Mark 14:36). With the lingering taste of bread and wine, broken bread and empty cup, Jesus stared into the depths of the cup before him, the cup filled to the brim with suffering and death, even more, dereliction and abandonment.

Agony filled Gethsemane.

When the ground crumbled beneath him, when the desperation screamed inside him, when the darkness blanketed around him, Jesus stumbled with tortured sound. Laborious sweat dripped off his brow. Blinding tears streaked from his eyes. The weight of his fate shuddered him violently to the ground. He did not kneel reverentially with his face aglow and serenely contemplate the numinous Presence of God. No, Jesus was thrown down, face down, hands grabbing Gethsemane's ground —shivering in this revulsion, throbbing on this impalement, striving against this fate. The disciples curled quietly in somnolent isolation, and God waited silently in suffering anticipation. Ravaged with silence he was already dying. To pray the prayer that Jesus prayed is to pray the prayer that kills you. Some of us think we have prayed it, but we are only dreaming. Those who actually pray it with him go through a dying with him, him and him only. In too many places and for too many hours he has done it alone, a stone's throw from where we lay sleeping.

The purpose of this chapter is to ponder the meaning of Jesus' experience in Gethsemane. Reflection on the ordeal of Jesus at this critical moment of the last night in his life is inexplicably limited,[1] but for an essay on providence absolutely necessary. The agony of Gethsemane poses a reluctant question: Why did Jesus break down in the darkness of Gethsemane? This chapter will explore the specificity of Jesus' anguish in the face of his death, the limits and possibilities of prayer, and the identity of God disclosed therein. The chapter concludes with a meditation on "Suffering in Christian Experience," a correlation of Mark 14 with Romans 8 initially through the prayerful address to God, "*Abba.*"

The Experience of Providence: *The Silence of God*

After the celebration of the Passover, a farewell meal for his disciples, Jesus led them to Gethsemane. Most of them waited at the entrance, but Peter, James, and John accompanied him farther. Jesus needed their companionship in this hour of travail and sorrow, both of these circles of friendship. The providence of God took a sharp turn at this point: Jesus experienced apparently for the first time in his life "the silence of God," a deafening Divine Silence.

Can anything else be said? Yes, Jesus experienced the silence of God in the company and companionship of his closest friends. Did they fail him? Yes, perhaps here more than anytime earlier in his ministry, but

---

[1]See Alistair Kee, *From Bad Faith to Good News: Reflections on Good Friday and Easter* (Philadelphia: Trinity Press International, 1991) 50, who says: "The Agony is seldom discussed in New Testament studies, or even in theology. Its implications are too alarming." The recent publication of Louis A. Ruprecht, Jr., *Tragic Posture and Tragic Vision* (New York: Continuum, 1994), however, constitutes a major exception, a unique comparative analysis of the accounts of Gethsemane in the Gospels (181-229), of great value regardless of one's judgment of the book's central thesis.

they did not fail him completely, at least not yet. They were with him—awake or asleep, aware or preoccupied, understanding or confused. These friends had remained with him. He was alone, but he was not entirely alone. The form of providence that characterized the experience of Jesus in Gethsemane was "the silence of God in the company of friends."

Jesus had selected each one of the Twelve. They had walked with him from town to town with the good news of the Kingdom of God. They had heard him teach, learning from him and putting questions to him. They had seen his mighty works. They had witnessed his confrontation with various authorities. They had enjoyed his parables, some they had heard several times. Yet sometimes they mirrored the expectation of the crowds. At other times they argued over who was most important among them, or who should be. They did not really believe him when he warned them of the turn of the crowd and of his rejection in death, but they had stayed with him. They were with him now, anxious and worried, tired and sleepy. They did love him, whatever their failures, that he knew. So the silence of God struck him within the company of the silent sleeping of these friends.

The Agony of Gethsemane

In Gethsemane Jesus experienced the most dreadful hour of his life. He asked Peter, James, and John to watch with him and to pray strength for him in the face of this terrible crisis. He needed their companionship in this hour.

> [He] began to be distressed and agitated. And he said to them, "I am deeply grieved, even to death; remain here, and keep awake." (Mark 14:33b-34)

Jesus himself went a little farther, and he fell face down on the ground in prayer. Mark describes the private agony in great detail, the prayers in Gethsemane quite different from anything that we would have anticipated thus far. Why was the Gethsemane experience such agony for Jesus? The fear of death? The anticipation of the excruciating ordeal of crucifixion? The unimaginable damnation of Godforsakenness?

A Dreadful Sorrow

The Gospels can only stammer the intensity of the grieving that sent Jesus reeling. Translation can scarcely express the graphic change that overcame him. Jesus agonized in almost unbearable sorrow, a sense of trepidation as devastating as the pain of death. He exhibited a "shocking dismay" and "distressing anguish" (Mark 14:33b), caught "in the grip of a shuddering horror in the face of the dreadful prospect before him."[2] Dread seized him like death itself. The burden that threatened to overwhelm Jesus concerned the cup of his suffering. Precisely what the "cup" meant to him is difficult to fathom, but some aspects of his fate are identifiable though immeasurable: the untimely end of his life and the apparent failure of his mission; the flight of all his disciples, the betrayal of one and the repudiation of another; the rejection of the people, who wanted the "Messiah" in him to become someone other than he could ever be; the utter brutality of his execution with the sanction of the Law of God and under the mandate of the peace of Rome. The cup included all this and more, but the "more" was so deep within Jesus that only he knew or could say. Death would rip his life from top to bottom, shredding any and all patterns of beauty in his living. The Gospel of Mark feels the contradiction of this hour, of this cup, of this fate. *Affirmation*: "*Abba*, Father, for you all things are possible" (14:36a). *Petition*: "Remove this cup from me" (14:36b). Jesus intended to do the will of God, but the contradiction of this fate threatened to overwhelm him.

Jesus felt with unqualified realism the unbearable contradiction between the *Abba* experience that he had lived and breathed with ever expanding consciousness throughout his life and the bitter cup of his impending death that would terminate and invalidate his vocation in behalf of the Kingdom of God. He would suffer a death of public humiliation and private damnation. The Gospels can describe the one but only glimpse the other. We cannot comprehend the inner quality of his life or the inward desolation of his death.

The depth of his sorrow pushed Jesus to pray the very same prayer three agonizing times: "My Father, if it is possible, let this cup pass from

---

[2]C. E. B. Cranfield, *The Gospel According to Saint Mark* (Cambridge: University Press, 1959) 431.

me; . . . yet . . . not what I want but what you want" (Matt 26:39b). After groaning his travail to God for seemingly hours without end, he turned to Peter, James, and John and found them sleeping. He asked them:

> So, could you not stay awake with me one hour? Stay awake and pray that you may not come into temptation; the spirit indeed is willing, but the flesh is weak. (Matt 26:40-41)

What do the words of Jesus mean? He needed them to pray with him, helping him to bear the burden that had crushed him to the ground. He knew that they faced temptation, because he himself did. Had temptation, always skewed with persistent self-deception, almost persuaded him that *this* cup was not his cup, or if so . . . ? Jesus knew that "the spirit is willing, but the flesh is weak," because he himself agonized with his own unflinching devotion to God and his own human weakness. Had exhaustion suggested, the cup is mine, but *now* is not the time?

An Overwhelming Anguish

Why was the agony of Jesus so intense? Why would this cup be so bitter? Why did he plead with God to spare him? Several answers are forthcoming, none mutually exclusive: Obviously the temporal distance from the fate of rejection and death that he had anticipated and affirmed had ended, and now his fate loomed before him with shocking clarity. With the Last Supper behind him Jesus faced the awareness of his fate that had increasingly confronted him but always heretofore with a temporal buffer between its anticipation and its arrival. In Gethsemane, however, the temporal distance completely disappeared: "What will happen" had become "What is happening."

Yet the now included a waiting. Kim Malthe-Bruun, a twenty-one-year-old Danish sailor who belonged to a resistance group in World War II, suffered torture during four months of imprisonment before his execution by the Gestapo on 6 April 1945. He reflected again and again on the figure of Jesus, and he answered the question "Why?" with "waiting":

> The time of waiting, this is the ordeal. I will warrant that the suffering endured in having a few nails driven through one's hands, in being crucified, is purely mechanical that lifts the soul into an ecstasy

comparable with nothing else. But the waiting in the garden—that hour drips red with blood.³

Though seemingly valid, at least in part, Malthe-Bruun remains unequivocally wrong. The mechanics of crucifixion did not lift Jesus into ecstasy but Godforsakenness. Because he correlated the experience of Jesus onesidedly with his own ordeal, Malthe-Bruun reduced the agony of Jesus to his own torture and death; moreover, he illegitimately abstracted Jesus' suffering and death from his *Abba* experience and proclamation of the Kingdom of God, the most distinctive characterization of Jesus' life.

Beyond the waiting, another word must be said. Jesus recognized that all his disciples would abandon him because the end of his mission meant the termination of the possibility of discipleship. Yet the other word that must be said is more odious in the shared journey of life than he was alone in Gethsemane's dark night. It is the serpent's hiss in loyalty's kiss —betrayal. As Jesus well knew, an acquaintance can offend you, an enemy can strike and kill you, but only a friend can betray you. Betrayal does not occur on impulse: It is deliberate and calculated. Arrogance lies at the heart of betrayal, the repudiation of the worth and integrity of the betrayed. The arrogance of Judas lay in his rejection of Jesus' messianic path for the sake of his own messianic vision for Jesus—the deliverance of the people of God from the subjugation and oppression of Rome. The temptation that Jesus resolutely resisted Judas determined to impose on him. The arrogance hid under the pretense of love. Betrayal—whatever reason seems worthy, however the treachery takes form, whoever conspires in the killing, wherever the deed gets done—only a friend can betray you. Betrayal followed Jesus into Gethsemane and would meet him coming out in the kiss of a friend. The pathos of providence includes bitter irony.

---

³Helmut Gollwitzer, Kaethe Kuhn, and Reinhold Schneider (ed.), *Dying We Live: The Final Messages and Records of the Resistance*, trans. Reinhard C. Huhn (New York: Pantheon Books, 1956) 79-80. Dorothée Sölle, *Suffering*, trans. Everett R. Kalin (Philadelphia: Fortress Press, 1975) 81-86, uses this story, among others, to refute the claim of "the suffering and death of Jesus as unique," that "Jesus suffered more than and differently from other martyrs because he saw himself as cast out and cursed, as God was inaccessible to him as he suffered" (81). The time of waiting might be the ordeal; however, Mark's portrayal of the agony in Gethsemane begins to anticipate but does not really compare, much less surpass, Jesus' experience of the Godforsakenness of the cross.

Furthermore, the harsh contradiction of his living with his dying confronted Jesus, its impact stunning him. Everything began to unravel, for the end was about to begin. Jesus anticipated his arrest and the flight of his disciples, the charges of blasphemy and sedition during his trials through the night, the failure of his mission in his condemnation to death, the brutality of crucifixion and the abandonment of God. Understandably, therefore, Jesus was afraid. He feared death, the antithesis of life, and worse, Godforsakenness. The cup that he did not want to drink was "the cup of staggering" (Isa 51:16, 22), the overwhelming fear of nothing less than the death of God, separation from the *Abba* God whose Presence had sustained him all his days and nights, the withdrawal of his God already beginning in the darkness of a Passover already ending. The fear that paralyzed him and lacerated him inside out issued from the appalling silence of God that provided a hint of the depth of emptiness that stretched out before him. The silence of God threatened him, a fearful threat that he sought to alleviate by calling to God, "*Abba*," and through the watchful company of Peter, James, and John.[4]

What else did this agony of Jesus in Gethsemane contain? It included the fear of the unknown, an experience quite different from judgment and death, because death as the end is the death already known. The agony was in part the inescapable terror of the unknown. What, if anything, might be on the other side of death? The waiting in Gethsemane happened in the context of hope for the coming Kingdom of God: waiting for death, but hoping for . . . God? Did the promise [!] of resurrection in the eschatological future of God shrivel almost empty and hollow, practically meaningless and irrelevant in the darkness of Gethsemane?

Another line of inquiry—indeed, insight—takes form: Jesus knew for the first time in his life a conflict of his will with the will of his *Abba* God: "not what I want," which is for you to remove this cup from me; "but what you want," which is for me to drink it, all of it, regardless of its consequences, and without waiting, now. Although Jesus submitted to the will of God, trust had to be disciplined with obedience at a level that

---

[4]Cf. Jürgen Moltmann, *The Trinity and the Kingdom*, trans. Margaret Kohl (San Francisco: Harper & Row Publishers, 1981) 76, who writes: "But in Gethsemane for the first time he does not want to be alone with his God. He is evidently afraid of him. That is why he seeks the protection of his friends." Jesus feared separation from his Father, "horror in the face of 'the death of God.' "

he had never endured before. At this point the question can be put more precisely: Why did he hesitate and momentarily stumble? Why this pause and this trembling? Karl Barth has the most perceptive analysis and the most convincing insight, a depth of insight almost lost in the small print and thousands of pages of the *Church Dogmatics*. Jesus had resisted the Tempter all of his life, and he had lived purposefully to do the will of God. Now the will of God coincided with the way of evil. This was the deeper darkness that enveloped him in Gethsemane. Barth says:

> The riddle confronts Him with all the horror that it evokes: that of the impending *unity* between *the will of God* on the one hand, that will which He had hitherto obeyed, and which He willed to obey in all circumstances and whatever it was, that will which He was quite ready should be done—and, on the other hand, *the power of evil* which He had withstood, and which He willed to withstand in all circumstances and in whatever form He might encounter it, which He could not allow to be done.[5]

The terrible thing that shook him was the concealment of the lordship of God under the condemnation of blasphemy against God. He cried to God alone in Gethsemane that this future should not become present. When "if it be possible" faded into impossibility, Jesus remained in ongoing trust in and obedience to his *Abba* God: "Your will be done" (Matt 26:42b).

Was Jesus afraid in Gethsemane? Earlier in his ministry he had spent nights alone in prayer with God, but he did so during days of joy in the celebration of the arriving Kingdom of God. Those festive days and nights lay far behind him, because he encountered nothing in Gethsemane but the silence of God. So the Gethsemane experience meant something very different for Jesus. He had prayed for the removal of "this cup," a prayer answered negatively with dead silence. Jesus broke the silence nevertheless with the cry, "*Abba*," affirming his relationship to God and framing the silence of God with hope rooted in his deep faith in the coming Kingdom of God. Since abandonment by God was the cup he did dread, Gethsemane marked the beginning of his agony of Godforsakenness. Was Jesus afraid? Yes, but he overcame his fear for the sake

---

[5]Karl Barth, *CD* IV/1: 269 [Italics added].

of the will and purpose of God. Was Jesus afraid of *God*? No, that would say too much. Precisely where the multiple streaks of fear originated in Gethsemane cannot be neatly identified—the tragic end of his ministry, the horrible loneliness of this hour, the inevitable destination of this dark path? He was afraid, but he was not overcome with fear. The discriminating awareness that the will of God coincided with the judgment of his adversaries finally enabled Jesus to embrace "this hour" (John 12:27). He could have left Gethsemane for some safe retreat, but he would not. On the contrary, he seized the initiative, telling the disciples: "Get up, let us be going" (Mark 14:42a).

Prayer and Providence

Through his agony in Gethsemane Jesus experienced the pathos of God for the tragic in all human life, but especially for his own singular life. Jesus' *Abba* experience presupposed a powerful and profound sense of communion with God. Indeed, he never knew himself apart from the energizing Presence and guidance of his *Abba* God. Jesus had always sought to discern God's will with insight mediated through the experience of prayer, but he had never prayed in Gethsemane before. Unlike energizing communion with God, the pathos of God expressed itself in this tragic situation through the silence of God.

The Meaning of Prayer

The anguish of Jesus in Gethsemane requires a re-examination of the meaning and significance of prayer, namely, petitionary and intercessory prayer. Yet two concerns surface here. First, and most important, who is the God to whom Jesus prayed? Matthew, Mark, and Luke all specify the identity of God in his prayer: "Father." Only Mark uses the Aramaic, "*Abba*, Father." The God to whom Jesus prayed and before whom he pleaded was the *Abba* God whose Presence he had lived and breathed all his life. Second, the prayer he voiced to God was simultaneously a petition and a commitment.

> *Abba*, Father, for you all things are possible; remove this cup from me; yet, not what I want, but what you want. (Mark 14:36)

Jesus did not simply petition God for the strength to do God's will. He struggled with precisely what God's will meant in these circumstances. The prayer is not the simple petition: "Give me the strength to drink this cup." Rather, he prayed: "Remove this cup from me." Nevertheless, Jesus continued to surrender *his will* to *God's will*. Through the night he wrestled with the declaration of the silence of God. Although the point can be overstated, Jesus' instructions to Peter, James, and John indicate his concern for their help: "Remain here, and stay awake with me" (Matt 26:38b). The request was not to stay awake to watch for his adversaries but to stay awake with him, supporting him in this hour of sorrow. The text hints at intercessory and petitionary prayer, the disciples praying for Jesus as well as for themselves.

The Limitations of God

Why raise the theological question of the meaning and purpose of prayer in conjunction with Jesus in Gethsemane? What can be learned about prayer in Gethsemane that cannot be learned elsewhere? Is the question not too abstract for the anguish of Gethsemane? Here more than any other place we have no choice but to face "the limitations of God" and the "efficacy of prayer." What are the possibilities and limits of petitionary and intercessory prayer? What are the limits and possibilities of God to whom we pray? These are not different concerns but aspects of a single concern.

Of course, God sees multiple options in the movement of history and the variables in the journey of each person's life. The envisioning of these multiple possibilities constitutes the opportunities for the actualization of God's purpose and the fulfillment of human life. Yet the alternatives with regard to a specific historical progression decrease in number and scope as possibilities are actualized—even for God. And God was in Gethsemane, though silent, because Jesus called out, *"Abba."*

The development of a particular series of events in the life of an individual can reach a point that dramatically focuses on a single decision, a Yes or No that determines everything. This happened to Jesus at the Last Supper and drove him to Gethsemane. Everything had come down to this single point and this single decision, a decision that meant inevitably and irrevocably the sentence of death, of death and only death. Jesus had only one option, one choice in his Gethsemane, whether or not to drink the bitter cup of rejection and condemnation, humiliation and death. All other options that had been his earlier had lapsed, just as he had anticipated they would. Indeed, that was part of the great tragedy of Gethsemane—this bitter cup, his and none other, now and not later, this choice and this choice alone. The words that screamed out inside Jesus during his ordeal in Gethsemane were not just a petition for God's help to do God's will. His petition was first and foremost: Has it come down to this—this hour, this place, this cup? And, of course, it had.

Throughout this essay I have reiterated a single proposal about the providence of God in the tragic moments of human life: *In every critical situation with its multiple contextual variables God always does the most God can do.* The essential rationale for this argument in the midst of tragedy is to be found in the darkness of Gethsemane. The eternal God could not—would not and could not—deliver Jesus from his cross. Even God could not—would not and could not—define the identity of God *beyond* the good news of the Kingdom of God through some event other than the cross of its Christ. In Gethsemane Jesus learned with utmost clarity the limitations within the commitments of the identity of God, the limits that inhere in the freedom of God's love.

The death of Jesus was and is unique, as singular as his proclamation of the Kingdom of God. Now the Kingdom of God arriving with Jesus collided with the limitation of God in the dying of Jesus. The cross of rejection proved inevitable for the incarnation of the Kingdom. So God could not save Jesus from the cross and be who the *Abba* God is.

The application is plain: Sometimes we stand in the aftermath of an irrevocable tragedy already done and at other times in the wake of an inevitable tragedy still ahead. Gethsemane addresses all the tragic events in life. Before and after a great sorrow the affirmation endures: *In the givens of a specific historical situation of desperate human need—with the particular limits and transforming possibliites intrinsic within it as well as the transcendent possibilities available only to God beyond it— God always does the most God can do.*[6] The problem in much Christian spirituality and Christian theology is the notable absence of a place for

---

[6]This affirmation that I continually use to refer to a tragic inevitability, whether before or afterward, has its theological foundation in the experience of Jesus in Gethsemane. It is not speculative, theological opinion. See chapter 1, 45.

the agony of Gethsemane in the life of the Christian and in the theological reflection of the church.

The Problem of Limitations

Gethsemane marked the beginning of the end of Jesus' days and nights, and he accepted the cross not simply as his fate but his destiny—through prayer. Yet the severity of his circumstances at the conclusion of his life does not undercut the importance of petitionary and intercessory prayer earlier in his ministry. On the contrary, Jesus prayed in Gethsemane for the discernment of God's will just as he had sought and followed God's will at other critical moments throughout his life. The Nazarene's journey of faith had included limits and possibilities for him and his recognition of the limits and possibilities in others. Jesus knew that possibilities in human existence always entail limitations.

The question of the possibilities and limits of petitionary prayer is most severe in Gethsemane, but it cannot be restricted to "this hour" and "this cup." Why not? "This hour" marked the culmination of the mission of Jesus, which occurred after a significant public ministry in Galilee and which brought him to confrontation with the religious and political authorities in Jerusalem. He had always recognized various possibilities and the particular limits of each possibility, actualizing those most appropriate for his mission. Similarly, "this cup" involved the definition of his destiny, which presupposed a unique vocation undertaken and fulfilled, almost. He had made choices about his vocation early on, and those choices informed the destiny that led him to Jerusalem. A history of opportunities and limitations, personal decisions and their attendant consequences, preceded Jesus' ordeal in Gethsemane.

The Origin of Divine Limitations

Where do the limits that we encounter in life and experience in petitionary prayer originate? Do the limits emanate from the inscrutable will of God? Do the limits root in the absence or inadequacy of human faith? Or beyond the inscrutability of the will of God, who is always the *Abba* God, beyond the measure of our faith, whether weak or strong, does creation in the movement of history place certain limitations on God's activity?

The question of the origin of the limitation of God that we experience in prayer concentrates on two alternative but not unrelated options. *Option 1*: The self-limitation of God coincides with the act of creation and the movement of history, a self-limitation that God the Creator has established for the sake of some measure of independence of the world as well as the possibility of genuine human freedom in the world. The central reference point is the continuing self-limitation of God.[7] *Option 2*: The limitations of God belong within the good structures of creation in the dynamics of history begun and sustained through God's faithfulness, because God established in creation the processes necessary for the relative autonomy of the existence of the world and humanity within it. The central reference point is God's continuing affirmation of the structures of creation in historical passage.[8] These two options are invariably interrelated but with a certain difference in orientation.

The Limits of Petitionary Prayer

The appropriateness of petitionary prayer requires the praying person to recognize the possibilities and limitations that originate in the nature and purpose of God within the context of creation and history. The Christian who continues to experience the transforming Presence of Christ in life will often gain the insight of love for what things he or she ought to pray. Most Christian people do instinctively recognize certain limits to their prayers, and they have always done so. Those who participate regularly in public worship know that the prayers of petition and intercession

---

[7]The category of the self-limitation of God has a firm place in contemporary theology: See Georgia Harkness, *The Providence of God* (Nashville: Abingdon Press, 1960) 104-107; H. Wheeler Robinson *Suffering-Human and Divine* (New York: The Macmillan Company, 1939) 39; Jürgen Moltmann, *The Trinity and the Kingdom*, 108-111.

[8]Although Pannenberg does not like the use of the term "self-limitation" with reference to God the Creator, he understands creation to mean "an existence of their own is granted to the creatures. Since this is a logical requirement inherent in the idea of creation, it applies to all conceivable ontological models of God's relation to a world of God's creation" (Wolfhart Pannenberg, "Providence, God, and Eschatology," in *The Whirlwind in Culture: Frontiers in Theology*, "In Honor of Langdon Gilkey," ed. Donald W. Musser and Joseph L. Price [Bloomington IN: Meyer-Stone Books, 1988] 179).

within the life of the church in behalf of others frequently end with a slight echo of Gethsemane: "If it be your will."

One of the most important aspects of Christian spirituality is to learn to distinguish appropriate petitions from inappropriate ones, prayers that include the worshiping life of a Christian community and the devotional life of the Christian believer. Apart from the cultivation of some substantive style of Christian spirituality, prayers of petition and intercession will sound strained and probably superficial, without sensitivity to the possibilities and limitations of God. Some of the limits to prayer may reflect God's purpose of shaping the life of the Christian in trust and love; nevertheless, the circumstances that evoke the prayer for relief to God are not difficulties that God has directly laid on us but troubles that occur in the givenness of life. God's response will be some form of grace, the form and measure of grace itself delimited by the circumstances. Although sensitive Christians draw the limits of prayer in different places, the decision not to pray or not to continue to pray for a particular matter is actually the negative side of the positive intention to accept the limits of the possibilities available even to God.[9]

Some limits inhere in the dynamic structures of creation that are not rigid but flexible, which are not closed by the past but open to the future. Therein God works through envisioning and engaging the possibilities in the givens of creation through the contingencies of human history. What God can and cannot do in a specific situation must often be determined through meditation and prayer, a reflective discernment of the identifiable objective and subjective factors that actually shape the scope of our specific prayers to God.

---

[9]The similarity of my choice of words with H. H. Farmer's words is deliberate: "Nor is it of great concern that different Christians will draw the limits in different places, provided only that in every case the decision not to pray for this, that, or the other thing is only the negative side of a positive endeavour to grasp *every situation* in love, and to share, both in heart's desire and active deed, *whatsoever they can understand of God's austere purpose of love within it*" (*God and the World*, 268 [italics added]).

Does God have "an austere purpose of love within" "every situation"? Or does God act in a situation within which a purpose of love does not already exist to establish some "austere purpose of love" in relationship to it? I would argue: An austere purpose of love does not always exist in a tragic situation but must be brought to it.

A Conceptual Difficulty

Where do the limitations to petitionary and intercessory prayer originate? Earlier I worked with the options of "the self-limitation of God" or "the limitations in the structures of creation," concluding: "With some ambivalence I opt essentially for the limitations in the structures of creation, because the concept of the self-limitation of God ultimately concedes too much and promises too little."[10] However, the ambivalence left me dissatisfied.

The disadvantage of the limitations in the structures of creation in the dynamics of history is its lack of an immediate and direct reference to God, a problem that the self-limitation of God does not have. Limitations in the structures of creation in the dynamics of history say more precisely where the limits actually occur, but the investment of God in the structures of creation within the contingencies of history remains unclear. Again, the disadvantage of the self-limitation of God stems from the characterization of God as limited, that is, without an explanation of how or when, if ever, God transcends the self-limitation that God has chosen in the act of creation. Actually both concepts are useful. The concept of limitations in the structures of creation within the contingencies of history does accentuate what God does and does not do, limits that are intrinsic to the givens of creation and the gift of freedom. Similarly, the concept of the self-limitation of God accentuates that these limitations are the consequence of God's own choosing. Are these two perspectives the primary options for understanding the limitations of God that we experience in daily life as well as in personal prayer? I think not. Rather, these two apparent alternatives are really different aspects of the same option for describing God's relationship to the world: Self-limitation characterizes the posture that God takes in the decision to create, and the limitations in the structures of creation within the dynamics of history concentrate on the world that God has already created and sustains. The two perspectives are not different options but complementary sides of the same option.

---

[10]E. Frank Tupper, "The Providence of God in Christological Perspective," *Review & Expositor* 82 (1985): 589 [adapted].

The Self-Giving of God

Is there a normative perspective that can account for self-limitation of God concretized in the limitations in creation and provide greater clarity at the same time? The inquiry moves behind these alternatives in search of a perspective that would account for these two vantage points as the source and origin of each. Since Jesus Christ is the paradigm for God's relationship to the world, the overarching perspective to characterize the relationship of God to the world is nothing less than self-giving. The Christian story affirms, "God is love," an affirmation that understands the identity of God on the basis of the story of Jesus. The God who is love is always self-giving, and the Self who is giving is always love. God is the self-giving God of love. Of course, any formulation of a normative perspective, however helpful, is an abstraction, because God is *the living God* who *is* the self-giving God of love. Both the concept of the self-limitation of God and the limitations in the structures of creation within the contingencies of history must remain subordinate to this characterization of God. Within this framework, which understands God to be the God of self-giving love, the difference between the limitations in the structures of creation in the dynamic movement of history and the self-limitation of God in the history of creation becomes almost inconsequential. The priority of the concept of the self-giving of God reorders these categories to a subordinate status but retains their instrumental value, and therein the concept of the self-limitation of God may prove to be most useful. What appears to be the self-limitation of God in the history of creation is in fact the expression of the self-giving of God. The essential mark of God's divinity is the act of self-giving love. Indeed, this staggering dynamism of the total and mutual self-giving, the dynamism of giving and receiving, characterizes not only God's relationship to the world but also the mutuality of the relationships of love within the life of God. Accordingly, the essential characterization of the God whom Jesus called *Abba*, to Jesus, who lived out the good news in the world, is not self-limitation but self-giving.

What is God like in relationship to people? The self-giving God exercises God's power in relation to humanity through self-giving love. God has a specific nature, a particular kind of power that characterizes the essence of God: the power of self-giving love. Thus God cannot act contrary to this mode of power anymore than God can reject the constitutive reality that defines God's life. Instead of dominating power, the power of God is donative power.[11] That is, the power of the self-giving God of love is the power of "a vulnerable compassion," the scandal of the strength of weakness.

God's Relationship to the World

Limitations are real. Otherwise, the struggle of living would not be so difficult nor the realities of life so tragic. The movement of creation in historical passage does place limits on God's activity: the existence (and brokenness) of this world; the dynamics (and distortion) of personal relationships, the experience (and abuse) of human freedom, the possibility (and pervasiveness) of radical evil. These ever present limits of creaturely existence in our world make the concept of the self-limitation of God more than attractive. Indeed, the conceptions of the self-giving of God and the self-limitation of God are not mutually exclusive. On the contrary, the characterization of God as the self-giving God of love might best find expression in conjunction with the self-limitation of God, but such self-limitation must remain a subordinate concept with functional value rather than a definitive concept with normative status. Why is this pattern of correlation of the self-giving of God with the self-limitation of God essential and necessary? It conforms to the revelatory history of God with creation that culminates in the coming of Jesus the Christ.

The Paradigm of Jesus Christ

The essential paradigm for understanding God's relationship to the world is Jesus Christ. Or better: The Story of Jesus is the paradigmatic Story of God. In the light of the self-revelation of God in Christ, the overarching perspective to characterize God's mode of being toward the world is self-giving. Although creation precedes Incarnation, the God who creates is the God who comes in Incarnation. Why did God create the world and humanity within it? God did not create out of necessity but out of

---

[11]Arthur C. McGill, *Suffering: A Test of Theological Method* (Philadelphia: The Westminster Press, 1982; 1968) 75-76.

freedom, the overflowing joy in the life of God. Creation is the expression of the self-giving of God, the creativity of love in the sharing of life! Yet creation inevitably entails a risk for God and includes a self-limitation of God in the preservation of nature within the contingent movement of history, the preservation of a fallen creation warped through human sin, afflicted with chaos, and continually threatened by Nothingness. Accordingly, the dynamic history of creation stretches toward a pattern of providence with an impelling pathos. The limitations of the structures of creation within the contingencies of history mean that whatever pattern providence takes will be a pattern inscribed with a wrenching, painful pathos. Nevertheless, the God whose identity is essentially the act of self-giving love retains the power to move history, often painfully and slowly, to the completion of its goal.

God has a covenantal relationship with creation and humanity within it, a covenant that originates in the freedom of God. What is the nature of the covenant of God with creation? with humanity in creation? When an observer looks at a marriage from outside the marital relationship, the vows between the man and woman appear to be the mutual and voluntary limitation of the one to the other for the rest of life. From the outside the basic pattern of the relationship seems to be self-limitation. From inside the marriage covenant, however, it is not self-limitation but self-giving that the covenant provides. What appears to be normative to an observer outside the covenant of marriage is self-limitation, but what proves normative to those inside the covenant of marriage is self-giving. The limitations are the consequence of the self-giving. The self-giving is primary; the self-limitation is secondary. The self-giving is the definitive reality; the self-limitation is the dependent reality. Better said, the self-giving includes a self-limitation for the sake of the self-giving. So a healthy marriage is not characterized by preoccupation with what lies outside the limits of this marital covenant. Rather, a good marriage is characterized by the measure of fulfillment and freedom, of self-actualization and self-realization, of intimacy and communication that heretofore did not exist, but now, in covenant relationship, does exist— with the continuing possibility of an adventure in togetherness.

The prophets used the concept of covenant in marriage to characterize God's covenant with Israel, and the apostles employed marriage as an analogy for the covenant of God through Jesus Christ with the church. Within this convenantal relationship, God has purposed for us the experience of ongoing wholeness and surprising enrichment, meaningful life and community belonging, the joy of God's Presence and the hope of God's future. The accent is not on the limitations of our creaturely existence in God's covenant but on the mutuality of giving and receiving for the fulfillment of all life within the blessing of creation. Within the covenant of God with creation, therefore, self-giving has priority over self-limitation. The concept of self-limitation remains useful, but only with functional value on the basis of the normative concept of the self-giving of God. God is never a not-giving God. To put it another way, God is love, never unlove, not not-love.

A careful interpretation of the category of "love" is necessary here. The self-giving of God is always the self-giving of the God who is love. It is not enough to say, "God has love," because, "God is love." We humans give and receive love, we have love, but only God *is* love. Yet the meaning of the affirmation, "*God* is love," can only be defined through the history of the self-disclosure of God, ultimately through the self-definition of God in Jesus Christ. What "love" means with reference to God will have, nevertheless, a certain consistency with the human experience of love, but with a difference. . . . However, if "love" means one thing to us but does not really apply to God, how do we know that the declaration, "God is love," is not a disguise for an "unloving" tyrant?[12] If the self-giving of God is anything other than or different from the actual *giving* of *Godself,* we have reason to be afraid that the identity of God, who is love, does not really correspond to what we understand "love" to be. Rather, any statement about God's love that is contrary to our experience of love can be justified on the basis of the mystery "behind" or "within" the God-kind of love. If the self-giving of God is really self-giving, and if the Self who is giving is love, whatever the self-giving God does will be stamped with a recognizable love, recognizable because this love will reflect significant features of the story of Jesus and the most positive dimensions of human relationships. While the love of God must be defined from the side of God through the self-disclosure of God, what we would not call love in human experience, because of its in-congruence with the meaning of love in genuine personal relationships, should not be identified as love because of its apparent association with

---

[12]See Ludwig Feuerbach, *The Essence of Christianity* (New York: Harper & Bros., 1957) 52.

God. The advent of the God of love in Jesus Christ discloses a mystery of love that is more than rather than contrary to the human experience of love.

Lest the point be missed, this is at least part of our difficulty with Gethsemane. What does "love" mean in Gethsemane? Had everything come down to this single point and this single decision, a decision that meant inevitably and irrevocably the sentence of death, of death and only death? . . . Had it come down to this—this hour, this place, this cup? And, of course, it had. God is love, and the self-giving God who is love embraced suffering and death. Although these words may seem innocuous, they pose a daring statement that contains a compelling mystery.

Abstract Possibilities versus Real Possibilities

Jesus' ordeal in Gethsemane locates the terrible pathos of the providence of God in the essential self-giving of God, because the limits of God that Jesus encountered in the struggle of prayer issued from the particular purpose of God for him at this decisive point in his life. Whereas Mark 14:36 words Jesus' prayer, "*Abba*, Father, for you all things are possible," Matthew voices Jesus' prayer, "My Father, if it is possible, let this cup pass from me" (26:39). A fundamental difference separates Mark and Matthew with respect to this prayer. The tension between the statements of the prayer is most significant. "All things are possible" implies that God can do Anything, Anytime, Anywhere. God is limited only by the faith of the one who prays on the one side or the mystery of the inscrutable will of God on the other: "Well, if you have enough faith." Or, "We are not able to understand." "All things," however, represents abstract possibilities removed from the concreteness of this situation in the life of Jesus. Only one real possibility existed for Jesus in lively trust and obedience to the God whom he knew to be *Abba*. Accordingly, Matthew's version of Jesus' prayer in Gethsemane is more theologically precise. In addition, and not without considerable importance, Matthew hears Jesus reject the abstract possibility of a unilateral rescue by "twelve legions of angels" (26:53).

"All things are possible" has been used to affirm that God is a do Anything, Anytime, Anywhere kind of God. If it pleases God to do it, God will. If we do enough to please God (always it seems, a little more),

God will. The do Anything, Anytime, Anywhere kind of God is precisely the kind of God that the story of Jesus unmasks and dethrones, but not without difficulty. The do Anything, Anytime, Anywhere God has his advocates. Yes, they say, God appears to have chosen to limit himself most of the time, but God is not committed to the range of possibilities in structures of creation nor to the risk of contingencies in the configuration of human history. On the contrary, God is God, a do Anything, Anytime, Anywhere kind of God who can *arbitrarily* and *unilaterally* intervene to do whatever, whenever, for whomever he chooses! Yet this God is not the God of self-giving love who wills a self-limitation to preserve creation with the risk of human freedom. This God of unilateral intervention is preeminently the God of omnipotent power, more accurately phrased, the God of unlimited force. "God is love," all seem to agree, but this God of love can be arrogantly coercive and blatantly arbitrary, answerable to no one, not even to the revelation of himself, because the ways of God are beyond human understanding. The do Anything, Anytime, Anywhere kind of God remains under the appearance of self-limitation until he decides to do otherwise. Any less, his proponents claim, denies the sovereign majesty of Almighty God.

This God, this do Anything, Anytime, Anywhere kind of God, this God cannot be found in the dreadful darkness and agonizing contradiction of Gethsemane.

Suffering in Christian Experience
Romans 8:15b–39

"When we cry, '*Abba*! Father!' " a cry from deep within the self that expresses the deepest concern of the self, the Apostle Paul declares "it is [the] Spirit [of God] bearing witness with our spirit that we are children of God" (8:15b-16). We pray *Abba* as Jesus did. The Presence of the *Abba* God, the Motherly Father, stamps Christian experience. We know that we are children of God and fellow heirs with Christ, "if, in fact," Paul adds, "we suffer with him so that we may also be glorified with him" (8:17). What characterizes Christian identity? We are children of God, we are joint heirs with Jesus Christ, we suffer with Christ, and we will be glorified with Christ. Paul's understanding of Christian identity inevitably includes suffering.

An Eschatological Tension

Yet Paul affirms an eschatological tension within the experience of the Christian: "I consider that the sufferings of this present time are not worth comparing with the glory about to be revealed to us" (8:18). *Abba,* suffering, hope—the passion narratives in the Gospels preview the journey of the Christian, at least a fundamental part of it. Yet our suffering as the children of God is not at all comparable to the glory that awaits us. On the contrary, Paul contends that the suffering of the present pales in the light of the future Kingdom of God!

The whole of creation groans with the labor pains of birthing, straining for its completion in the future of God. Likewise, we ourselves groan inwardly for the healing of life and the fulfillment of our destiny as the children of God. We feel the eschatological tension, indeed, the frustrating contradiction, between what God has already begun in us and what God will yet do with us. The not-yetness of the experience of salvation stretches faith into hope, hope that remains *hope.* Christian hope faces the horizon of the future, awaiting the salvation of God, yet unseen but patiently[!] anticipated (8:24-25). Although Paul does not say so, the hope for what we do not see intensifies the eschatological tension between "the sufferings of this present time" and "the glory about to be revealed to us." Did Paul see the hope of glory too clearly for it to remain *hope*? Or does hope precisely as hope require the embrace of faith to envision the future salvation of God with images and contents that stretch our imagination and language?

Part of the suffering that we experience within a flawed and unfinished creation is the judgment of God against sin, but not entirely so. Some of the suffering that we must bear belongs to human finitude.[13]

---

[13]See J. Christiaan Beker, "The Relationship between Sin and Death in Romans," *Studies in Paul and John,* ed. Robert T. Fortna and Beverly R. Gaventa (Nashville: Abingdon Press, 1990) 55-61. Beker argues: "Because of the causal relation of sin and death, there is to be sure harsh suffering in the world, but there is no meaningless or tragic suffering" (58). Conversely, in 1 Corinthians, Paul offered a different perspective on suffering: "Since the signature of the creation itself—because of its inherently mortal-

This entangling of suffering as the consequence of sin with suffering as the condition of finitude frustrates us and confuses us. We really do not know how to pray amid the groaning of creation that echoes the groaning in us. The pain of suffering, the pain itself, renders us wordless. The tragedy of senseless suffering turns us inward where words cannot be found. The single word "Why?" negates all words. The confident explanation that correlates human fallenness with the futility of creation is a naive oversimplification. Yet the languishing of creation in unfinished futility does reflect a measure of the meaninglessness in the stillborn fate of so much human existence (8:20-21). So "the Spirit helps us in our weakness, for we do not know how to pray as we ought" (8:26a). Words unavailable, we groan without clarity—inarticulate, frustrated, embarrassed. Speechless and wordless in the midst of suffering but not entirely without sound or sensibility, "that very Spirit intercedes for us with sighs too deep for words" (8:26b).

Some around me live in the pain and shame of suffering. I do not know how to pray, what prayer can actually do, or why my prayer needs to be offered for brothers and sisters who suffer. That is part of the difficulty, but only part, because others around me celebrate life! The rush of their song in glad celebration rings without effort in the joy of life. So Paul counsels: "Rejoice with those who rejoice, weep with those who weep" (Rom 12:15). It is easier nonetheless to rejoice with those who rejoice than to weep with those who weep, because sharing the pain of those who suffer is existentially more demanding and personally more costly.

The Classic Statement of Providence

---

transient nature—[suffering] is a necessary ingredient of life in this world" (60). Beker considers the references in Romans 8:18, 20, 21 to be references to suffering in creation as the consequence of human sin. There may be a different emphasis in Romans over against 1 Corinthians, but "the whole creation has been groaning in labor pains till now" (Rom 8:22) does denote a measure of suffering in conjunction with the finitude of creation—not just "subjected to futility" because of human sin. Romans 8 cannot be so exclusively categorized or sharply juxtapositioned with 1 Corinthians.

Romans 8:28 is the classic statement of the providence of God in the entire New Testament. *Abba,* suffering, hope—the passion of Christ informs Paul's most eloquent affirmation of the providence of God. This great affirmation of faith presupposes the Christian experience of suffering within the travail of all creation, and it addresses the need to know what God is doing now in the midst of human suffering. Translation is not unimportant: "We know that all things work together for good for those who love God, who are called according to his purpose" (Rom 8:28, NRSV). The translation is viable, but the theology is not. Do "all things work together for good for those who love God"? No. Evil remains evil. Pain remains pain. Death remains death. Another translation is required: "We know that *in everything* God works for good with those who love God, who are called according to his purpose" (8:28, RSV). Still these words are not easy words but difficult words. At least we know what these words do not mean: Paul does not mean that God predetermines everything that happens. Not everything that occurs is the design and intention of God. Likewise, Paul does not mean that everything that happens is in some sense good. He speaks instead of "the sufferings of this present time" (8:18a), "the whole creation has been groaning in labor pains until now" (8:22).

Whatever our vantage point we cannot look at the sunrise and sunset of each day and simply say, "That's good." The sun rises east of Eden, where life means thrownness, where brother hates brother, where the destructive forces of nature flood human excess and continual violence, where pride divides the tribes of humanity from one another. The sun sets on the western horizon, and in the twilight we say simultaneously: "That's good." "That's not good." We rejoice with those who rejoice, and we weep with those who weep.

Yet the declaration of the Apostle Paul remains: In everything that does happen, God does work, bringing order out of chaos, good out of evil, triumph out of tragedy—some out of the other, but seldom, if ever, equal to the other. Still a fundamental question nags at us: "How?" How does God work in everything for good? Some suggest unilateral intervention. As Jesus moved from agonizing prayer in Gethsemane to the bloody cross on Golgotha, he eliminated unilateral intervention with "twelve legions of angels" (Matt 26:53) as the means to accomplish the will and purpose of God. The story of Jesus defines God's action in the world in terms of personal engagement and transforming Presence. The words of Paul suggest "engaging transformation."

God does not assault the structures of nature under "its bondage of decay" (Rom 8:21) but works directly and persuasively through the unfinished structures of creation, whatever the limitations might be. God does not abrogate human freedom or predetermine the particular configuration of each moment of history. God engages human decision-making creatively and encouragingly. Limits do exist, but God works within the measure of mystery open to God, working the divine purpose in a fashion consistent with the identity of God disclosed in the story of Jesus. Indeed, God intends for the follower of Jesus to respond to life on the pattern of the story of Jesus, becoming more Christlike through the multiple experiences that shape us, including the pain of suffering. Christ is the image of God, and we are transformed into the likeness of God's Son, becoming his brothers and sisters within a large and growing family (8:29).

A Gethsemane for Us?

If God works for good in everything that occurs in the individual and communal life of the Christian, what description appropriately characterizes "the sufferings of this present time"? *Abba*, suffering, hope—does the path of Jesus through Gethsemane mean that his disciples may follow him through a Gethsemane of his or her own? Is suffering ever so singular, so intense, so bereft of consolation that we can speak of the Christian in Gethsemane? Yes, it seems so. Yet it is always less for us, whether it seems less or not. My pain might remind me of his pain, my agony of his agony, my fear of his fear, my urgent plea of his urgent plea. A fundamental difference remains, however. None of us experiences the *correspondence* of the positive purpose of God with the negative destruction of evil. For us the will of God never *coincides* with the randomness of chaos or the deception of the demonic. We are vulnerable to the unexpected destructiveness of chaos. We are vulnerable to the deliberate, calculated death-strike of Nothingness. The *Abba* God nonetheless does not intend for any of us to be victims of chaos or Nothingness.

We do experience darkness, and we pray in the darkness for the light. We groan in the darkness for the removal of a bitter cup. I say again: In every historical situation of dire human need with its innumerable and indeterminate shadows, God always does the most God can do. Night descends, and God has not removed it. Then, perhaps only then, we know that God cannot remove it. The bitter cup is there to drink.

What happens when we pray in these circumstances? The will of God and the will of Nothingness do not correspond. We could not bear the burden of such sorrow nor the bitterness of such a cup any more than the three disciples who accompanied Jesus into Gethsemane.

What happens to us in the darkness that feels like Gethsemane? The limits of God encounter the devastation of chaos—in and around us. The limits of God encounter the utter desolation of Nothingness—in and around us. God does not remove the cup, but God does not *intend* for any of us to bear the destructive assault of chaos. God does not *will* for any of us to experience the desolation of Nothingness.

So we take refuge with Jesus in Gethsemane, because we know that the tragedy that we must endure is not the hidden purpose nor the concealed intention of God. God subjects God alone, God and God only, to this unqualified burden of sorrow and the acid bitterness of this cup.

The pressure we feel—and we do feel pressure—is the pressure of the limits of God on the one side against the destructive force of chaos, of Nothingness, on the other. Between the limits of God that stretch to sustain us and hostile devastation that strains to destroy us, in between these two countervailing powers, there is nothing so thin or precise to differentiate them.

We feel the double pressure as unbearingly singular and constantly encircling. Experience asks: Why has God allowed this to happen to us? Why is God doing this to me? The deep certainty, right or wrong, is the sense of the judgment of God, the bitter cup the consequence of God's condemnation. Or experience asks: Why has God abandoned us to this annihilating Nothingness that suffocates us? Why has God forsaken me to this death of damnation? The deep feeling, right or wrong, is the sense of the abandonment of God, the bitter cup extending God's increasing distance.

Whichever experiential interpretation one chooses, it is wrong. Neither explanation reflects the discriminating awareness of the limitations of God in the extremities of the human situation nor the weakness of God in the malaise of subtle deterioration. The silence of God in Gethsemane cannot be reduced to the single alternative of judgment or abandonment.

The line between the limits of God against the force of destruction is paper thin, even less, welded and glued into something seemingly singular. Yet the line is there.

Pressure around us and within us, the line distinguishing the limits of God from the foreclosure of death is as slight as a hairline fracture. Yet the fracture is there.

The pressure itself squeezes another streak of confusion and pain, limits now indistinguishable, a pale infinitesimal streak that blurs living and dying. Yet the streak is there.

Gethsemane does not lack complexity.

The Provision of God

Is there any assurance for the Christian within the sound of the silence of God? *Abba*, suffering, hope—the Christian never experiences the Silence of God alone. The path of the sufferings of this present time is painful and lonely. At some point in the journey of suffering most friends stop at the gate of sorrow, unwilling, no, unable to go any farther. A few, perhaps three or four, continue into the land of sorrow, watching from barely inside its boundaries. Yet the one who suffers a great sorrow eventually finds himself or herself alone—always a stone's throw beyond the most intimate and loyal friends. Can anything else be said? A word, a promise, a promising word?

The promise takes the form of a question: What can separate any one of us "from the love of Christ?" (8:35). Can *hardship*, the draining of all strength and meaning from life that hounds us with hopelessness and dread? Can *distress*, the multiple situations of near desperation, trapped, without any way out? Can *persecution*, the assault of indifference on the relevance of faith and the scorn of realists for those pitiful weaklings who need faith? Can *famine*, the gnawing emptiness from deep inside for the nourishment of "bread," without anything from anyone to help? Can *nakedness*, the exposure of brokenness and inadequacy, past and present, which makes us vulnerable to ridicule and shame? Can *peril*, the daily threat to life in an urban, hi-tech, chemicaled society because of accidents, breakdowns, illnesses, and countless other risks unknown? Can *the sword*, sudden death from unexpected violence, legal or illegal, intentional or happenstance, victims all the same? No, whatever others have done to us or whatever we have done to ourselves, whatever happens, we

rest in the outstretched arms of Jesus who loved us (8:35-37), who laid
down his life for his friends (John 15:13).

Though a stone's throw removed from the dearest of friends, God
stone silent, the Christian in Gethsemane has the companionship of one
Friend who has been there before. In the silence of God in the valley of
a deep sorrow, Jesus stands with his brother and sister, arms circled
round, tears running down, sharing common ground. The Christian learns
in his Gethsemane, in her Gethsemane, that he or she is not alone. We
experience the silence of God in the silent companionship of the Friend
of tax collectors and sinners. Our Friend knows experientially the time
and place, the isolation and loneliness of the Gethsemane of the heart.
Nothing "in all creation will be able to separate us from the love of God
in Christ Jesus our Lord" (Rom 8:38-39), who is always "our Friend."

Jesus has already gone through Gethsemane, a Gethsemane that we
cannot really understand, and he stands with us in ours. That is a great
gift, but at times it seems hardly enough, not enough at all. Yet the silent
company of Jesus in the midst of the silence of God will have to do.
Sometimes it is all anyone of us has.

Concluding Questions

The portrait of Jesus with his disciples in Gethsemane is a graphic
paradigm of the painful pathos of the providence of God for all humanity.
One who resisted the invasion of Nothingness into his life is nonetheless
threatened by the overwhelming devastation of demonic powers, princi-
palities, and powers housed in religious and political movements. Those
who are not threatened seem unaware and uninvolved. Does such apathy
hinder or limit the providential activity of God in behalf of those distressed and troubled? Yes, because the providence of God is vulnerable to
the attitude and response of human agents. Does the vulnerability of the
providence of God to the action or inaction of human agents really
account for the pathos of providence? *Is humanity really that responsible?* The terror of this unspoken thought jeopardizes trust in the
providence of God, because it questions at least indirectly the affirmation
of the unqualified goodness of God.

Is God partly responsible, perhaps even mostly responsible for the
wrenching pathos of whatever providence means in the joy and tragedy

of the human story? So the question of the providence of God turns on the question of the character of God. How does God love the world that has turned against God and that, therefore, God has abandoned to the sinful consequences of suffering and Death? The providence of God happens in the midst of the wrenching pathos of human history, which accentuates an almost unbearable problem, the problem of the unqualified affirmation of the love of God. The problem is appallingly real. The existence of God is not the question in Gethsemane, all the Gethsemanes of life. Rather, it is the power of God, the essence of God, the identity of God. Jesus' life story says, "*God is love*." Jesus believed that so deeply that he left Gethsemane and embraced his cross. For him the cross was not essentially his fate but ultimately his destiny.

Chapter 8

The Mystery of the Death of God

FLOSSENBÜRG CONCENTRATION CAMP, 9 APRIL 1945: The prisoners were all conspirator, Dietrich Bonhöffer among them. Brought to the Flossenbürg camp late Sunday evening, Bonhöffer was taken to a cell in a wooden hut and ordered to change into prison clothes. Just before midnight two uniformed guards escorted him to a summary court-martial. SS Judge Dr. Otto Thorbeck convened the trial on instructions from Berlin, and SS Section Leader Walter Huppenkothen acted as prosecutor. The court examined each prisoner individually and confronted them with one another: Admiral Canaris, General Oster, Dr. Theodor Strunck, Captain Gehre, Judge Sack, and Dietrich Bonhöffer.

The interrogation of Bonhöffer focused on his associations with the Abwehr and his participation in the plot to assassinate the Führer on 20 July 1944. As the presiding judge of the court-martial, Dr. Thorback led the examination of Bonhöffer, who made no attempt to deny anything. He knew that the proceedings changed nothing. Back in his cell Bonhöffer prayed fervently on his knees through the remainder of the night.

Shortly before 6:00 A.M. Bonhöffer and the others were taken from their cells to hear the verdicts of their court-martial read to them. They were guilty of high treason and condemned to death. Ordered to strip in the chill of the dawn, they walked naked down stone steps through the trees to the silent scaffold. After Bonhöffer knelt a few moments to pray, he mounted the steps to the gaunt gallows above, brave and composed. A guard bound his hands behind him and carefully removed his glasses before settling the noose around his neck. With the trap creak and the sudden wrench of the rope, Dietrich Bonhöffer hung

*dead. The guards took down his lifeless body and burned it along
with his suitcase and papers.*[1]

Young Dietrich Bonhöffer became increasingly active in the resistance to Adolf Hitler in the 1930s but especially from 1940 onward. Because of his participation in the conspiracy to replace Hitler with another government, a conservative German one, Bonhöffer was arrested and imprisoned in Nazi Germany on 5 April 1943, more than a year before the abortive attempt to assassinate Hitler on 20 July 1944. He was kept alive for questioning almost a year after the plot had failed. On this April morning of 1945, three weeks before Hitler's suicide, the war almost over, Bonhöffer was hanged as an enemy of the state.

During his two year imprisonment Bonhöffer offered fragments of theological thought collected under the heading, *Letters and Papers From Prison*, meditations and reflections that continue to stimulate the life of the church. In an astonishing poem sent to Eberhard Bethge on 8 July 1944, Bonhöffer addressed the theme of the suffering of God.[2]

Christians and Pagans

People go to God when they are sore bestead,
Pray to him for succour, for his peace, for bread,
For mercy for them sick, sinning, or dead;
We all do so, Christian and unbelieving.

People go to God when he is sore bestead,
Find him poor and scorned, without shelter or bread,
Whelmed under weight of the wicked, the weak, the dead;
Christians stand by God in his suffering and grieving.

---

[1]See Donald Goddard, *The Last Days of Dietrich Bonhöffer* (New York: Harper & Row, Publishers, 1975) 243-44. Behind Goddard's dramatic presentation, see Eberhard Bethge, *Dietrich Bonhöffer: Man of Vision, Man of Courage*, trans. Eric Mosbacher, Peter and Betty Ross, Frank Clark, and William Glen-Dopel (New York: Harper and Row, 1970) 808, 830-31.

[2]Dietrich Bonhöffer, *Letters and Papers from Prison*, Enlarged Edition (New York: The Macmillan Company, 1971) 348-49 [adapted]. Cf. Dietrich Bonhöffer, *Widerstand und Ergebung* (München: Christian Kaiser Verlag, 1990;1952) 188 esp. line 11: [Gott] "stirbt für Christen und Heiden den Kreuzestod."

God goeth to every one when sore bestead,
Feedeth body and spirit with his bread;
For Christians, pagans alike, God dies cross-dead,
And both alike forgiving.

The story of God in the poem of Bonhöffer reverberates with the passion of Christ and reminds us of the death cry of Jesus: "My God, my God, why have you forsaken me?" In fact, Bonhöffer's line—"For Christians, pagans alike, God dies cross-dead"—confronts us with the mystery of the death of God.

This chapter explores the question of the suffering of God with specific reference to Jesus' cry of Godforsakenness in the Gospel of Mark. As an inescapable dimension of the understanding of the providence of God, the issue of the mode of the power of God in the world confronts us again. The uniqueness of the death of Christ is a central concern, and a brief analysis of other perspectives informs my proposal of "God on the cross." This descriptive presentation of the death of Jesus on the cross provides the historical framework for engaging the difficult and provocative theme of "the mystery of the death of God." [3]

The Experience of Providence:
Solidarity with the Crucified Christ

The death of Jesus in the Gospel of Mark is a tragic portrait of humanity's rejection of God and fallenness into a godless, godforsaking, and Godforsaken world. The death cry of Jesus—"My God, my God, why have you abandoned me?"—is the cry of fallen humanity, of suffering and dying humanity. Many different places signal vividly that the absence

---

[3]The theme of "the mystery of the death of God" has a firm place in the history of Protestant theology from Martin Luther to the present. The historic theme of the death of God must not be confused with the American death of God theology of the mid-1960s in the works of Thomas J. J. Altizer, *The Gospel of Christian Atheism* (Philadelphia: Westminster Press, 1966); William Hamilton, *The New Essence of Christainity* (New York: Association Press, 1966); and to a lesser extent, Paul van Buren, *The Secular Meaning of the Gospel* (New York: Macmillan Company, 1963).

of God is the death cry of fallen humanity. Lebanon, the Israeli-occupied territories, Northern Ireland, Rwanda, India, onetime Yugoslavia, Ethiopia and elsewhere—all are pockets of shattered existence throughout our world where the sound of Godforsakenness echoes through the night. Whenever massive areas of the world are singled out because of the suffering, pain, and death that mark them, the tendency is to see Godforsakenness only in the most desperate circumstances without the recognition of the threat of Godforsakenness for anyone and everyone alike. A great temptation of the church is to ignore the potential Godforsakenness that confronts every person in the world, those who live in impoverished places or war-torn nations as well as those who live in comfortable spaces or secure situations. Almost everywhere Godforsakenness occurs, some of those who bear the brunt of Godforsakenness participate in the life and worship of the church.

What is the experience of the providence of God in the suffering and death of Jesus the Christ? Abandonment. Godforsakenness. Absence. Crucified on Golgotha, Jesus suffered the abandonment of God for himself and with all humanity, the absence of the God who cares for everyone created in the image of God. Sometimes the only experience of God available in the midst of Godforsakenness is the stretched out embrace of the crucified Christ. Indeed, oneness with the crucified Christ is the form of the providence of God for the Christian in death. The provision of God through communion with Christ crucified is hope for the Presence of God on the other side of Godforsakenness. Such hope, nevertheless, does not negate Godforsakenness. On the contrary, the experience of the abandonment of God can be so stark that hope must become hope against hope, a flickering glimmer in the night through the promise of the death of the Death of life.

The Godforsakenness of death addresses every person directly or indirectly. Some die in Godforsakenness, whether they are able to name their plight Godforsakenness or not. Do those who die with an awareness of Presence escape the pain of Godforsakenness? This question probes the form of providence for the Christian who dies in Christ. Solidarity with the crucified Christ is the form of providence for the Christian, but it occurs in two variations of Christian experience. First, some die in solidarity with the crucified Christ and experience *communion with God* through Christ on the other side of the encounter with Godforsakenness. Yet Godforsakenness remains an essential element of their death that communion with God through the crucified Christ contains. While they die on the other side of the absence of God, they do so with the memory of Godforsakenness in their living and with empathy for all those who endure Godforsakenness in their dying. Second, others die in solidarity with the crucified One and suffer the absence of God in *communion with the Godforsaken Christ.* The tragic Godforsakenness of suffering and dying humanity is not an element of but central to their sense of death. They endure death with a profound awareness of the Godforsakenness that staggers the living and numbers the dead. Communion with God occurs only through the crucified One abandoned to death. Though these two experiences of Godforsakenness differ, Christians in solidarity with the crucified Christ feel deep sensitivity and compassion for the God-forsaken beyond the circle of communion with Christ.

Is Godforsakenness in one of these two patterns of solidarity with the crucified Christ the mark of Christian identity at death? Does the follower of Jesus have the option of dying with the Presence of God apart from the pain of Godforsakenness? The Christian who does not take Godfor-sakenness seriously because of the knowledge of the Presence of God lives superficially and experiences God minimally. Sharp words, but perhaps they are not sharp enough. Those who know God through Jesus Christ but who do not empathize with the Godforsaken live and die in an easy Presence, a sense of Presence that lacks identification with the crucified Christ who discloses the suffering of God. "Superficially" is an understatement.

Can the Godward person move through the passion narratives of Luke and John without criss-crossing the passion narratives of Matthew and Mark? The question seems transparent, but it is far from it. The alienation of humanity from God is the presupposition of the Lucan word from the cross: "Father, forgive them, for they do not know what they are doing" (23:34a). Likewise, the estrangement of humankind from God is the presupposition of the Johannine shout: "It is finished" (19:30a). That is, "The Lamb of God [has taken] away the sin of the world" (1:29b). Solidarity with the crucified Christ is the form of providence for us at death, and some elements of the Godforsakenness of his death for us cannot be legitimately avoided in our living toward dying.

The Case against God: The Suffering of God's World

The problem of inestimable suffering calls into question today the very reality of God. Indeed, the case against God in our time is a case more often than not built upon the enormity of evil and suffering. The suffering and death of Jesus radically questioned and dramatically undercut the truth of his message about his *Abba* God and the merciful rule of love. Similarly, the magnitude and immensity of evil and suffering counts even more in contemporary life against the reality of this kind of God, the *Abba* of Jesus. The randomness of chaos in creation and the irony of history in its deadly twists and demonic turns stand in sharp contrast to the vision of God concerned for human life like a resourceful and loving father or mother. The earthquakes, volcanoes, tornadoes, floods, hurricanes, tidal waves, drought, famine, plague; starvation, cancer, AIDS, smallpox, birth defects, retarded children, infant mortality; the Trail of Tears, Jim Crow, Buchenwald, Auschwitz, the Gulag, Hiroshima, South Africa, El Salvador—all the calamities of nature and ironies of history stand in contradiction to the affirmation of the God of love who acts with gracious providence in human history. Among the various forms of atheism, the atheism of evil and suffering is the most significant problem for a critically informed pastoral theology today. Just as the execution of Jesus called into question the existence of his God, the atheism of evil and suffering continues the debate about the existence of the God of love in a world shrouded in suffering and death. The cumulative case against the God of love who guides and provides providentially for life in our world rests upon the magnitude of evil and suffering in all human history but particularly in the modern world.

Precisely at this point the affirmation of the impassibility of God has become increasingly problematic for twentieth century theology.[4] The

---

[4]See J. K. Mozley, *The Impassibility of God* (Cambridge: Cambridge University Press, 1926). Mozley provides a historical survey of the issue of impassibility that included the current state of the debate in 1926. He conlcudes with six questions essential to a continuation of an informed discussion: (1) "What do you imply by the term 'God'?" (2) "What is the true doctrine of God's relationship to the world, and especially, with reference to creation?" (3) "Can the life of God be essentially blessed and happy, as being that eternal life that cannot, as such, be in any way affected by the time-series and its contents, and yet also a life in which suffering finds a place, in so far as the life of God

enormity and visibility of evil and suffering in modern times has reopened the question of the impassibility of God. The persistent question is: "Does God suffer?" Numerous positive responses to this question are easily identified. Dietrich Bonhöffer wrote in the crumbling fall of the Third Reich: "Only the suffering God can help."[5] Is Bonhöffer's affirmation with the question and answer that it presupposes more than pious rhetoric? Is his martyred response to the question of the suffering of God only a rhetorical flurry without theological substance? While countless theologians have rushed to affirm "the suffering of God" in the tragic twilight and demonic darkness that have threatened most of this century,[6]

---

enters into the time-series and works within it?" (4) "How is feeling in God related to feeling in men? And is there a particular kind of feeling properly describable as suffering, and experienced as suffering by God?" (5) "Is a real religious value secured in the thought of the passibility of God?" (6) "What is the relationship of the Cross as the historic means of God's redemption of the world to that eternal background of God's love out of which the Cross is given?" (177-83).

[5] Bonhöffer, *Letters*, 361. Paul S. Fiddes, *The Creative Suffering of God* (New York: Oxford University Press, 1988), provides the single-most important book on the theme of the suffering of God in contemporary theology. The range of research should not obscure the author's own contribution that centers on the multifaceted significance of the death of Jesus for understanding the reality of God.

[6] Cf. Kazoh Kitamori, *Theology of the Pain of God* (Richmond: John Knox Press, 1958). Kitamori spoke of the pain of God in Japan in the late 1930s prior to the incoming horrors of World War II, and he identified the pain of God with God's wrath over against human sin. One of his theses is: "God in his pain is the God who resolves our human pain in his own. Jesus Christ is the Lord who heals our human wounds with his own (1 Peter 2:24)" [20]. In the United States almost two decades later, Roger Hazelton, *God's Way with Men* (Nashville: Abingdon Press, 1956), said it differently: "[T]he passion of the Son is the disclosure of the compassion of the Father, and that therefore the Father suffers with the Son and not simply in the Son" (130). Daniel Day Williams, an American process theologian, explicitly rejected the notion of divine impassibility in favor of divine sensitivity. See *The Spirit and the Forms of Love* (New York: Harper & Row, Publishers, 1968), where Williams says: "As Jesus suffers in his love with and for sinners, he discloses the suffering love of God" (166). Already in *What Present-Day Theologians Are Thinking* (New York: Harper & Row, Publishers, 1959), Williams saw differing aspects of a "structural shift in the Christian mind" about the "suffering" of God (14). The brief but dense little book of Arthur C. McGill, *Suffering: A Test of Theological Method* (Philadelphia: The Westminster Press, 1968; 1982), is an implicit but powerful argument for a theopaschite understanding of God.

In 1986 Ronald Goetz noted the remarkable revolution of the ascendancy of a theopaschite theology which has occurred with little public debate: "The doctrine of the

at least since 1914, the easy and generalized affirmation of "the suffering of God" in contemporary theology often sounds empty and hollow. Hence the retort: What difference does it make whether God suffers or not? A practical question: How does God's suffering help suffering persons? More reflectively: What does the term "suffering" mean with reference to God? The question of whether God suffers logically precedes the question of the meaning of God's suffering, but the questions of the reality and significance of God's suffering are inseparable and must be addressed together.

As early as 1925 after World War I but prior to the great depression and the savagery of World War II, H. Wheeler Robinson, Old Testament scholar and principal of Regents Park College of Oxford University, wrote eloquently on the theme of the Cross in the Old Testament: "The Cross of Job," "The Cross of the Servant," "The Cross of Jeremiah." In 1925 Robinson concluded his essay on Jeremiah with words of depth and remarkable clarity: "*[W]ithin* God, the irrationality of sin is transformed into the mystery of the eternal Cross, the Cross within the very heart of

---

suffering of God is so fundamental to the very soul of modern Christianity that it has emerged with very few theological shots ever having to be fired" ("The Suffering God: The Rise of a New Orthodoxy," *The Christian Century* 103 (16 April 1986): 385. However, Goetz overlooked Edward Schillebeeckx, *Jesus—An Experiment in Christology*, trans. Hubert Hoskins (London: Collins, 1979), who locates the suffering of Jesus "outside God . . . without contaminating God himself by his suffering" (651). More recently, Wolfhart Pannenberg, *Systematic Theology*, 2 vols., trans. Geoffrey W. Bromiley (Grand Rapids: William B. Eerdmans Publishing Co., 1991), refuses to speak of the suffering of God. With delicate precision Pannenberg says that we cannot speak of the death of God because only the Son of God was crucified, dead, and buried: "To be dogmatically correct, indeed, we have to say that the Son of God, though he suffered and died himself, did so *according to his human nature*. Even to speak directly of the death of God in the Son is a reverse monophysitism." Nevertheless, he continues: "[The] Father [cannot] be thought of as unaffected by the passion of his Son if it is true that God is love. The cross throws doubt not merely on the divine power of Jesus but also on the deity of the Father as Jesus proclaimed him. *To this extent we may speak of the Father's sharing the suffering of the Son, his sym-pathy with the passion*" (1:314, italics added). Yet Pannenberg footnotes this statement with Jürgen Moltmann, *The Crucified God: The Cross as the Foundation and Criticism of Christian Theology* (New York: Harper & Row, Publishers, 1974); and Eberhard Jüngel, "Von Tod des lebendigen Gottes," *Unterwegs zur Sache* (München: Chr. Kaiser Verlag, 1988) 105-25. Pannenberg's use of "sym-pathy" instead of "suffering" is not accidental nor stylistic but deliberate and intentional, despite his affirmation of the death of Jesus in Godforsakenness.

God." The sin of humanity is taken up into the life of God and transformed into divine suffering. Very cautiously, Robinson wrote:

> We cannot lift the veil that hides [*God's*] inner life from us; we can but reverently look when His own hand lifts it for a moment in the temptation in the wilderness, in the prayer of Gethsemane, in the cry of the Cross, "My God, my God, why has thou forsaken me?"[7]

With the cry of dereliction we move from rhetoric to reality.

The Death Cry of Jesus—Godforsakenness

The cry of Godforsakenness is the only word of Jesus from the cross that did not already constitute a dimension of his life and ministry. It is a stark, solitary death cry that confronts us with the mystery of the death of the Son of God.

The Uniqueness of the Death Cry of Jesus

As the cry of Godforsakenness graphically magnifies (Mark 15:34), Jesus did not die a beautiful death like that of Socrates but a death of abandonment. He did not die the heroic death of a champion or a martyr's death for a cause. He died trembling with shouts and tears. Jesus died because his *Abba*, the living God, the God from whom the gift of life continually comes, abandoned him to death. Since he had claimed the authority of God to forgive sins and to offer the salvation of God as the gift of grace, the crucifixion of Jesus could not be construed as a misunderstanding but as the rejection of the God whom he had called "My Father." The death of Jesus, death-in-utter-rejection, this death, constituted in itself the plight of Godforsakenness.

The characterization of the cry of Godforsakenness as the definitive word from the cross has provoked considerable conversation and debate. The argument for the primacy of the death cry of Jesus in the Gospel of

---

[7]H. Wheeler Robinson, *The Cross in the Old Testament* (London: SCM Press, 1925) 192.

Mark stands partly on the grounds of form criticism: The most difficult of all the sayings of Jesus from the cross has the strongest claim to veracity. The cry of Godforsakenness is the most troublesome not only for us but also for the primitive church. The death cry of Jesus—"My God, my God, why have you abandoned me?"—stands in sharp contrast with the unbroken communion that characterized Jesus' relationship to God in his living and undergirds its authenticity in the description of his dying.

Unlike the cry of Godforsakenness, every other word from the cross can be correlated with Jesus' messianic mission: The word of forgiveness: "Father, forgive them; for they do not know what they are doing" (Luke 23:34). The word of promise: "Today you will be with me in paradise" (Luke 23:43). The word of trust: "Father, into your hands I commend my spirit" (Luke 23:46). The word of family concern: "Woman, here is your son. . . . Here is your mother" (John 19:26-27). The word of human need: "I am thirsty" (John 19:28). Even the climatic word of triumph: "It is finished" (John 19:30). All these sayings from the cross in Luke and John have corollaries in the life of Jesus. The cry of Godforsakenness is unique and authentic, but it does not have canonical singularity that excludes the other sayings of Jesus from the cross in Luke and John.

Yet the cry of Godforsakenness does have claim to canonical primacy, to canonical priority: *The cry of Godforsakenness is the only word of Jesus from the cross that did not already constitute a dimension of his life and ministry.* Godforsakenness is the primal word of the cross in the light of which all other sayings from the cross must be understood. The cry of Godforsakenness is not just one interpretation of the death of Jesus among others, but the essential description of how he died. Jesus experienced the death of Godforsakenness, and he cried out to his God, "My God, my God, why have you abandoned me?" The other words from the cross are not sayings to be eliminated, but rather these additional words from the cross must be understood in the light of the lonely death cry of Jesus in Mark, a death cry problematic for all the other Gospels. When Matthew picks up the Godforsaken death cry of Jesus, he immediately softens its impact with an explanatory word of what will happen on the third day (Matt 27:52-53). Luke and John move in different directions entirely, for the sake of their respective understandings of the death of Christ and the salvation of humanity.

Interpretations of the Death Cry of Jesus

The endeavors to understand the death cry of Jesus in Matthew and Mark follow two identifiable patterns of interpretation. Almost all interpreters affirm the probability of the experiential dimension of felt forsakenness in Mark's account. The death cry of Jesus describes the travail and desolation of his dying. Did Jesus only feel forsaken but was not in fact forsaken? Interpretation turns on the appropriate context for understanding his death cry: The lament of Psalm 22:1 turns into the praise of God in the conclusion of the Psalm in gratitude for God's faithful deliverance. *OR*: The lament of Psalm 22:1 acquires a new context in the Gospel of Mark framed on the basis of the particularity of Jesus' unique mission in anticipation of the arriving Kingdom of God. The issue is much larger than the interpretation of Psalm 22:1 in "the Story of Mark." Beyond all literary analysis and narrative criticism, the fundamental concern is the historicity of Mark's recounting of the death of Jesus.

Many commentators affirm the sense of mystery surrounding the death of Christ in Mark 15:34, but they argue that the recitation of the first verse of Psalm 22 is the affirmation of the Psalm in its entirety. Though it begins with an individual's suffering, Psalm 22 concludes with praise for God's deliverance of all. The Psalm shows one forsaken and beleaguered, but he has unshakable confidence in the goodness of God and God's ultimate dominion over all the nations. Thus Psalm 22 from beginning to end is the affirmation of faith of the crucified Christ and the appropriate pattern for understanding his dying. Contrary to Godforsakenness, this pattern of interpretation magnifies the obedience of Jesus to the will of God and the confidence of Jesus in the future of God.

Some interpreters of Mark 15:34 affirm this perspective but offer a more nuanced interpretation. The difficulty in believing that God would ever abandon Jesus strengthens the authenticity of his lonely cry. The death cry from Psalms 22:1 may mean that Jesus did not have the strength to die with the triumphant faith with which Psalm 22 concludes, an indication therefore of the desolation of his death on the cross. Why this death cry? Jesus identified so completely with sinful humanity that he abandoned himself to the ominous consequences of the disregard for God and the hardness of heart so characteristic of human existence in the world. He did feel that God had abandoned him to this tragic fate. Neither Mark nor his readers, however, would have thought that God had really abandoned Jesus, because he was doing God's will. The Marcan death cry indicates felt abandonment through Jesus' self-abandonment to the whirlwind of devastation intrinsic in human sin, but not actual God-forsakenness. The essential context for understanding the death cry of Jesus remains Psalm 22 in its entirety.

Through multiple and sometime interesting variations in this line of interpretation, such commentators reject the serious consideration of Jesus' abandonment at the cross, because, they say, the quotation of the beginning of Psalm 22 implied its positive ending: Godforsakenness? Absolutely not! The interpretation of these impatient scholars turns the death cry of Jesus into an affirmation of faith. What they offer, however, has little to do with the agony in Gethsemane, trials through the night, the scourge of the whip, the taste of a bitter cup, or the end of a Kingdom's dawn. The interpretation of the cry of Godforsakenness exclusively and/or essentially in terms of Psalm 22 threatens to empty Jesus' death cry of its tragic contradiction and to neutralize it with abiding confidence in God. The death cry of Godforsakenness becomes an anticipatory affirmation of the joy of Easter morning.

An alternative pattern of interpretation *shifts* the primary context for understanding Jesus' death cry in Mark 15:34 *from* Psalm 22 *to* the Gospel of Mark itself. The Gospel provides the essential context that defines the cry of dereliction: the stark affirmation of God's abandonment of Jesus to suffering and death. The prayer of Jesus in Gethsemane (14:36) before the crucifixion remains the only place where Mark uses the Aramaic *Abba* that characteristically expressed Jesus' personal communion with God. Therefore, "My God" on the lips of the crucified Jesus (15:34) referred to none other than his *Abba* to whom he had called earlier in Gethsemane, the God whom Jesus addressed with the tenderness of a child and the respect of a son, the God from whom Jesus continually received his life and to whom Jesus constantly surrendered his life. The unique relationship of Jesus with God, a filial relationship of the "Son" with the *Abba*, "Father," constituted the context of Jesus' death cry in the Gospel of Mark.

Thus the death cry of Jesus, "My God, my God, why have you abandoned me?" acquired a new context beyond Psalm 22, another context that requires a distinctive interpretation framed in the perspective of the Gospel of Mark: "The beginning of the good news of Jesus Christ, *the Son of God*" (1:1), introduces the story. The drama opens with the baptism of *"my Son,* the Beloved" (1:11-12). The demons recognize him: "You are *the Son of God"* (3:11; 5:7). Beyond the messianic confession of Simon Peter at Caesarea Philippi, the story turns toward Jerusalem with the transfiguration of *"my Son,* the Beloved" (9:7). "The parable of the Wicked Tenants" who murder the *son* of the owner of the vineyard has a key place in the plot (12:1-12). It moves steadily to the dramatic question of the high priest, "Are you the Messiah, *the Son* of the Blessed One" (14:61b). Jesus voiced self-awareness, *"I am"* (14:62a), a stunning response that condemns him to blasphemous death. The story culminates with the crucifixion of Jesus, and it attains its climactic word in the confession of the Roman centurion, "Truly this man was *God's Son!"* (15:39).

Although the death cry of *this* Jesus was a quotation of Psalm 22:1, the cry on the lips of Jesus the Son cannot be restricted to the cry of faithfulness from the pious Jew to the covenant God, YHWH, which Psalm 22 presupposes.[8] On the contrary, the "My God" of Jesus does more than refer contextually to YHWH, the covenant God of Israel, because the "My God" of Jesus referred to *"Abba,"* "My Father." Further-more, the "I" abandoned was not essentially the covenant partner who lived with fidelity to the Law of God and with reverence toward the Temple of God. On the contrary, the "I" abandoned was the "Son" who without precedent and without credentials proclaimed the nearness of the *Abba* God, a merciful nearness that he claimed to mediate apart from the Law and outside the Temple of God. The repudiation and execution of Jesus on the basis of the sacred Law and in the name of the covenant God of Israel, when he had proclaimed his *Abba* God gracious and near, called the existence of his *Abba* YHWH into question. Jesus named YHWH as *Abba* and proclaimed this God near, but he was condemned in the name of YHWH, the covenantal name of God with the chosen people. Precisely because the rejection and abandonment of Jesus on the cross negated the experience of God as the near and loving *Abba,* Jesus' death cry ultimately means: "My God, my God, dear *Abba,* dear *Abba,* why have you abandoned Yourself?" The narrative depiction of the

---

[8]Cf. Moltmann, *The Crucified God.* More than anyone else in contemporary theology Moltmann has explored the significance of Jesus' death cry of Godforsakenness. Despite criticism of aspects of his theological proposal, Moltmann initiated a complete rethinking of the death of Jesus Christ in current theology.

Gospel of Mark and the historicity of the death of Jesus coincide at the critical point of Jesus' death.

So Jesus cried to God for the sake of God, for the sake of the *Abba* God whom he had proclaimed and whose Presence he had lived and breathed all his life. The "My God," the very identity of God as *Abba*, went down to the grave with Jesus, because he had named God the *Abba*-come-near and claimed God salvifically available through his ministry. So the death cry of Jesus was not simply for himself abandoned to death but for the sake of the God whose Presence he had proclaimed, the *Abba* whose Kingdom comes, the Motherly Father of the beloved Son. This particular death of Jesus, the alleged Son of God, made it impossible to continue to speak of God as *Abba* in any normative fashion, because the one who authorized this name for God and who had brought[!] God uniquely present and mercifully near was executed a blasphemer against God. The rejection of Jesus in the name of YHWH historically falsified and irrevocably nullified the very existence of his purported *Abba* God. So Jesus called to God against the verdict of his execution: the rejection of his identity as Son and the repudiation of his *Abba* as God. Whether Jesus endured Godforsakenness in his crucifixion ceases to be the critical theological issue in this context. Why so? This particular death of the blasphemous, presumptuous Nazarene on a Roman cross outside Jerusalem constituted in itself abandonment: Jesus was executed in the name of God because he usurped the authority of God over the Law and he claimed to displace the Presence of God in the Temple. At this point the crucial theological question is no longer the question of the God-forsakenness of the Crucified but the question of God's identity: WHO IS GOD? WHAT IS GOD? WHERE IS GOD?

The Weakness of God

A major theological issue underlies and occasionally surfaces in the endeavor to understand the Godforsaken death of Jesus. The elusive but critical issue is the definition of "power." More precisely (and precision is desperately needed here), the definition of the power of God in conjunction with as well as in distinction from the ordinary meaning of "power." In a letter to Eberhard Bethge on 16 July 1944, Bonhöffer proffered intimations of the Presence of God in the world of human experience with remarkable sensitivity to the interpenetrating themes of Presence and power.

> The God who is with us is the God who forsakes us (Mark 15:34). The God who lets us live in the world without the working hypothesis of God is the God before whom we stand continually. Before God and with God we live without God. God lets himself be pushed out of the world on to the cross. He is weak and powerless in the world and that is precisely the way, the only way, in which he is with us and helps us. Matthew 8:17 makes it quite clear that Christ helps us, not by virtue of his omnipotence, but by virtue of his weakness and suffering.[9]

Bonhöffer's assessment of the non-necessity of God for the existence of the world is eloquent. God cannot be thought without the world, but the world can be thought without God. What are the theological grounds for this assertation? "God lets himself be pushed out of the world on to the cross." The God who exists in the crucified Christ is the crucified God. God is weak and powerless in the world, and that is the only way that God stands with us and helps us. Jesus does not help us through the exercise of overwhelming power but, conversely, in the weakness of his suffering and death.

Bonhöffer rejected an understanding of God's activity in the world in terms of supernatural intervention. The God of religiosity to whom people turn in distress for escape from the problems of life is an idol, a false conception of God. Over against the "rescue" God of unilateral intervention with supernatural power, Bonhöffer said: "The Bible directs man to God's powerlessness and suffering; only the suffering God can help." The God of the Bible is the God "who wins power and space in the world by his weakness." Bonhöffer offered a striking sense of weakness as the power of God. So the affirmation of the suffering of God is not an affirmation of the impotency of God: The weakness of God over against the powers of this world does not mean that God lacks power. Rather, Bonhöffer recognized the necessity for a redefinition of the Presence and the power of God in the world, but he regretted "putting it all so terribly clumsily and badly."

---

[9]Bonhöffer, *Letters and Papers*, 360.

If judged on the basis of the powers of this world, the power of God seems to be only weakness and not power at all. In a letter to Eberhard Bethge on 18 July 1944, Bonhöffer referred specifically to the poem "Christians and Pagans."

> "Christians stand by God in his [suffering and] grieving"; that is what distinguishes Christians from pagans. Jesus asked in Gethsemane, "Could you not watch with me one hour?" That is the reversal of what the religious man expects from God. Man is summoned to share in God's suffering at the hands of a godless world.[10]

Bonhöffer presented a series of polarities that juxaposes God and the world: "The God who is *with* us" is "the God who *forsakes* us." "[We live] *before* God and *with* God," but "we live *without* God." "God lets himself be pushed *out of* the world on to the cross," yet "[God] wins power and space *in* the world by his weakness." When Bonhöffer speaks hypothetically of the nonbeing of God, "as though God did not exist," he describes the contemporary historical experience of life in the world and the self-disclosure of God in the death of the cross. Since God permits humanity to expel God from the world through death on the cross, the concept of weakness belongs to the concept of God and, its ultimate corollary, the concept of death. That "God lets himself be pushed out of the world on to the cross" occasions a dramatic reinterpretation of God's relationship to the world: We must learn to rethink "the omnipotence of God as the *withdrawal* of his omnipresence" and, correspondingly, to rethink "the presence of God as the *withdrawal* of his omnipotence."[11] The revelation of God in the death of Jesus Christ discloses the weakness of God in the world. [12] God is not impotent, but the mode of God's

---

[10]Ibid., 361.

[11]Eberhard Jüngel, *God as the Mystery of the World* (Grand Rapids MI: Eerdmans Publishing Co., 1983) 103.

[12]Cf. Langdon Gilkey, *Reaping the Whirlwind: A Christian Interpretation of History* (New York: The Seabury Press, 1976) 269. Within a very different frame of reference the sense of the weakness of God stamps Langdon Gilkey's understanding of the story of Jesus, especially his death on the cross: "In embodying the powerlessness rather that power; in identifying with the outcast, the oppressed, and the guilty against the creative, the significant and the distinguished; in identifying himself with suffering and death rather than the power that contends against suffering and death, Jesus revealed the alienation of

power in contradistinction to the corrupted powers of this world is "the power of weakness," the vulnerability of compassion. The strength of weakness in the foolishness of the cross is the scandal of the Gospel.

The Uniqueness of the Death of Jesus

The understanding of the crucifixion of Jesus in terms of the suffering of God has its advocates and opponents in contemporary theology. The differences are not simply variations in the interpretation of the story of the passion of Christ but different depictions of the story itself. The fundamental question that requires narrative exploration focuses on the path of the execution of Jesus and the corresponding interpretation of his death. Is a theopaschite rendering of the story of the death of Jesus Christ a compelling and viable theological proposal?

The Silence of God

With an extensive analysis of the various dimensions of the "good news" of Jesus Christ in the multiple Gospel traditions, Edward Schillebeeckx considers Jesus' *Abba* experience the secret of his life and the eschatological prophet the crux of his identity.[13] Jesus proclaimed the cheerful good news of the oncoming Kingdom of God with the accent on the present rule of God. The failure of his mission in Galilee and his probable death in Jerusalem required Jesus to integrate the increasing certainty of his own violent death with the will of God and to reconcile this fate with his message of the oncoming Kingdom of God. Beyond the simple acceptance of his death, therefore, Jesus actively integrated it into his total mission and understood his death as his final service to the cause of God as the cause of humanity.

At the Last Supper Jesus carefully prepared his disciples for the shock of his death so that afterwards they would not fall into complete

---

even the creative world from its true self, from the kingdom he preached. . . .*In a world of corrupted power, the divine must appear as powerlessness*" (italics added).

[13]Edward Schillebeeckx, *Jesus—An Experiment in Christology*, 256-59 and 475-80 respectively.

despair. So during the Supper he passed the cup to his friends and suggested to them that "fellowship with Jesus is stronger than death." Since he already understood his death as an essential part of his mission, even prior to Easter Jesus could communicate to the disciples the prospect of renewed fellowship with him in the Kingdom of God after his death. Though not without ambiguity, the self-understanding of Jesus created the possibility and laid the foundation for their subsequent Easter conversion.

The Temple police arrested Jesus at the Garden of Gethsemane, and they took him to the high priest, which eventuated in a trial before the Sanhedrin. Since he understood himself to be sent directly from God to summon Israel to faith in the rule of God, Jesus refused to submit his mission to the doctrinal authority of the Jewish court. This contempt for Israel's highest authority constituted the Jewish legal ground for Jesus' condemnation, despite some doubts about the condemnation of him to death on the basis of Deuteronomy 17:12. The Sanhedrin handed Jesus over to the Romans who executed him for apparent political reasons. [14]

Schillebeeckx concedes that Jesus' anticipation of his death subjected him to an inner conflict between his mission in behalf of the Kingdom of God and the utter silence of God whom he called Father. The struggle of Jesus in Gethsemane and his loud death cry from the cross are the only historical certainties in the description of the last hours of his life. Yet Schillebeeckx flatly rejects the possibility that Jesus died abandoned by God. Whatever its historical origin, the Marcan quotation of Psalm 22:1—"My God, my God, why have you forsaken me?"—evoked in Jewish spirituality the entirety of Psalm 22. In situations where God's support cannot actually be experienced, in circumstances without any glimmer of hope, Psalm 22 expresses the conviction of salvation through God's nearness in the dark night of faith. While hidden, God remained constantly near to Jesus until the very moment of the dereliction of his death on the cross, the moment of "the silence of God." Therefore, the argument that God abandoned Jesus to death lacks any basis in Scripture.

The salvation from God "in the non-identity" of Jesus' suffering and death located the calamity of his suffering outside God and inside the mundane arena of the human condition. Over against Jesus, God remained sovereignly free. In the radical alienation of his innocent suf-

[14]Ibid., 306-12, esp. 310-11.

fering and death, which is by definition "non-divine," Jesus endured and preserved his identification with the coming rule of God without contaminating God with his suffering. At the cross Jesus overcame the "anti-divine" in human history, faithful to God in an "anti-godly" situation for the sake of human salvation. Thus the definitive revelation of God occurred in a silent but intimate nearness of God to the suffering and death of Jesus.[15]

Despite instances of significant insight Schillebeeckx's construction of a post-critical narrative rendering of the story of Jesus proves fundamentally flawed. Over against his stated intention, he thoroughly mitigates the pathos of Jesus' passion and resolves entirely in advance through the self-understanding of Jesus the irreconcilable elements in the contradiction of his death. The comprehensive understanding that Schillebeeckx attributes to Jesus in the shadow of his cross enabled Jesus to prepare his disciples for their Easter conversion[!] after the shock of his death—an imaginative but ill-founded proposal. Apart from and prior to his dense traditions-history analysis, he has already eliminated the possibility of a theopaschite interpretation of Jesus' death, a perspective buttressed with the theological dictim that even the innocent suffering of Jesus would "contaminate" God. Schillebeeckx's presuppositions inappropriately control his historical and theological conclusions.

God on the Gallows

The meaning of the death of Jesus Christ in contemporary theology requires a detour, a sharp detour through Auschwitz. The prophetic voice of Elie Wiesel identifies the Nazi murder of six million Jews with "the Holocaust." A survivor of the death camps, liberated from Buchenwald, Wiesel vowed that he would not even begin to speak of his experience for ten years. Rather, living in France, he studied at the Sorbonne and reported from Paris for the Israeli newspaper, *Yediot Achronot. Night*

---

[15]Ibid., 643, 651-52. Cf. Edward Schillebeeckx, *Christ: The Experience of Jesus as Lord*, trans. John Bowden (New York: Seabury Press, 1980) 824-25.

was born when Wiesel was assigned to interview Francois Mauriac, a Nobel laureate and a devout Christian.

> He was talking about Christ, Wiesel recalls, and I simply said to him, "Ten years ago I knew hundreds of Jewish children who suffered more than Christ did and no one talks about it." And he wept. He said, "You know, you should talk about it." And that moved me more than anything.[16]

Wiesel broke his silence about the kingdom of Night with an 800-page handwritten memoir published in Yiddish in Buenos Aires in 1956 under the title, *And the World Remained Silent.* Two years later he hewed it down to the 127-page French autobiographical novelete, *Night.* "It had to be something so austere, so sober," he says. "Pure as a police report." With a preface by Francois Mauriac, *Night* attracted some acclaim in Europe. However, dozens of American publishers turned it down. The rejection letter from Scribner's was typical: "We have certain misgivings as to the size of the American market for what remains, despite Mauriac's brilliant introduction, *a document.*" Hill & Wang published *Night* in 1960, but it stirred little interest. Eventually "the document" cracked indifference and roused a reluctant world.

One of the central questions in the depths of Wiesel's autobiographical novelette concerns the inactivity of God: How could the God of Israel allow the Holocaust to happen? Wiesel poses this question in a graphic portrait of absurdity that he paints in a key episode of *Night.*[17] As the story begins, the electric power station at Buna had just been blown up, and the Gestapo suspected sabotage. They followed a trail that eventually implicated four prisoners: the giant nicknamed the "Dutchman," the *Oberkapo* of seven hundred prisoners whom he never mistreated and who loved him like a brother; two other men caught with arms; and the *pipel* of the Dutchman, a beloved young boy who served him, a child with a

---

[16]Samuel G. Freedman, "Bearing Witness: The Life and Work of Elie Wiesel," *The New York Times Magazine*, October 23, 1983, Section 6, 66; but see the entire article, 32-36, 40, 65-69. Cf. Robert McAfee Brown, *Elie Wiesel: Messenger to All Humanity* (Notre Dame IN: University of Notre Dame Press, 1983); also, Graham B. Walker, *Elie Wiesel, A Challenge to Theology* (Jefferson NC: McFarland & Company, Inc., 1988).

[17]Elie Wiesel, *Night*, trans. Stella Rodway (New York: Bantam, 1960) 60-62.

beautiful face, "the face of a sad angel." Though tortured for a period of weeks, the Dutchman would not give a single name. He was sent to Auschwitz. The little servant endured torture too, but he would not speak. The SS sentenced him and the other two prisoners to death.

When the inmates of the camp returned from work one day, they saw three gallows standing in the assembly place, "three black crows." The traditional ceremony: roll call; the SS all around with machine guns trained; three victims in chains, one "the sad-eyed angel." The SS were more restless than usual, because hanging a young boy in front of thousands of prisoners was no little matter. As the head of the camp read the verdict, everyone stared at the child—"lividly pale, almost calm, biting his lips," the gallows throwing its shadow over him. When the Jewish *Lagerkapo* refused to act as executioner, three SS replaced him. The three victims mounted chairs together, and their three necks were placed in the nooses at the same time. A moment just before the hanging, the two men shouted, "Long live liberty!" The child said nothing.

"Where is God? Where is He?" someone behind Wiesel asked. The SS tipped the chairs over. Silence spread throughout the camp, the sun setting on its horizon. "Bare your heads," the head of the camp yelled. Although their dried-up bodies had long forgotten the bitter taste of tears, they were all weeping. "Cover your heads." Then the march past the gallows began. The two men died immediately, tongues swollen and blue. The child, so lightweight, dangled for more than half an hour, struggling between life and death, dying in slow agony. All the prisoners had to look him in the face. When Wiesel passed in front of the boy, he was alive, tongue still red and eyes not yet glazed.

Behind him, Wiesel heard the same man ask again: "Where is God now?"

Deep within himself Wiesel heard a voice answer: "Where is He? Here He is—He is hanging here on this gallows. . . ."

The suffering of this child dangling between life and death is a portrait of the silence of God and the death of all Wiesel had previously imagined of God. This metaphor of God signifies the vulnerability and impotence of God experienced in the death camps. Some Christian theologians find in Wiesel's story of "God on the gallows" an affirmation of the suffering presence of God in the midst of evil. The story might suggest "a shattering expression" of a theology of the cross,[18] but such usage is completely contrary to Wiesel's intention. The story is more a parody of Christ's crucifixion.

The similarities are obvious, too obvious and quite limited: three nooses, three Jewish victims; an execution with religious and political dimensions; attention concentrated on one innocent face; the question, "Where is God?"

The differences are radical: (1) Jesus died as a consequence of his vocation, which he had vigorously and publicly pursued: The beautiful child died before he had an opportunity for vocational pursuit. (2) Jesus was crucified between two criminals, but because of the suffering he had already endured, he died first, while the two brigands had to have their legs broken so they would die before the sabbath began: The two freedom-loving adults bore witness to liberty, and they died almost immediately, while the sad-eyed angel said nothing and died in slow agony before everyone. (3) Against Pilate's hesitancy to condemn Jesus, the very Jewish Jesus, the Gospels of the mostly Gentile church accentuate Jewish responsibility in the crucifixion of Jesus: "His blood be on us and on our children" (Matt 27:25), making all future generations of Jews "Christ-killers" and sanctioning pogroms wherever the cross has been found: The Jewish *Lagerkapo* refused to act as executioner in the hanging of the beloved young boy, and three German SS replaced him, three Gentile Christians became the executioners. (4) The execution of Jesus contained elements of betrayal, denial, cowardice, and fear: Neither the Dutch *Oberkapo* nor his little servant, though tortured, would betray any others. (5) Jesus established a ritual for remembering him with the Bread and Cup of his Passover: The sad-eyed angel, the child, the little servant—he died nameless and forgotten.

What can theological reflection on the providence of God in the story of Jesus learn from Elie Wiesel? First, Wiesel confronts the church past and present with its hands blood red because of pogroms against the brothers and sisters of Jesus of Nazareth, the anti-Semitism barely beneath the surface of the traditions of the church that has "authorized" persecution and deadly pogroms against the Jews as "Christ-killers" for centuries. Wiesel sees only one choice: Will the church identify with the

---

[18]See Moltmann, *Crucified God*, 273; and Burton Cooper, *Why, God?* (Atlanta: John Knox Press, 1988) 106-108.

victims or the executioners? Second, the characterization of the suffering and death of Jesus Christ should not be quantified as "more than" anyone else has ever suffered, a quantification that Wiesel appropriately rejects. Rather, the categories for understanding the death of Jesus must locate his suffering in the context of suffering humanity as well as his unique vocation and destiny. Third, if a theopaschite understanding of God proves viable, the suffering of God must not be restricted to the suffering and death of Jesus Christ. The uniqueness of God's participation in the crucifixion of Jesus must not obscure the participation of God in the suffering and death of all humanity made in the image of God, Jew and Gentile alike.

God on the Cross

Although the suffering of Jesus Christ must be set in the context of the suffering of all humanity, the death of Jesus of Nazareth is both similar to and different from the death and dying of others. The appropriate characterization of this difference is the issue that concerns us, because the uniqueness of the death of Jesus must cohere with the distinctiveness of his identity. It would not be an exaggeration to say that Jesus demonstrated in the reformulation of his heritage profound insight into human life and human relationships, the ultimate meaning of human existence in the creation of God, indeed, what the word "God" means for humanity in the contingent movement of creation through history.

The secret of Jesus' life was his *Abba* experience, a consciousness that reflects a very early and formative stage of his life. The mysterious impression of the Other who continually engaged him in pervasive relationship conveyed the strength and warmth of a good *Abba*, a Motherly Father. He experienced everlasting arms that encircle and embrace, Another within himself yet beyond himself, an enveloping Presence who continually invited trust through the ever heightening demonstration of trustworthiness, the Other, the ever transcending Presence of his *Abba* God. Jesus lived and breathed the *Abba* Presence from his earliest memory onward.

Although any statement about the relationship of Jesus to God prior to his baptism remains mostly speculative, the spiritual formation of the Nazarene had been nourished and cultivated from early on in the depths of his being, a spirituality anchored in his flourishing communion with

God and expressed in his expanding relationship to others. The knowledge of God evermore intimately and participation in socialization evermore extensively occurred concurrently through continuing self-integration in this man's life. Thus the distinctiveness of the public life of the man Jesus indicates a corresponding uniqueness in each of the multiple stages of his personal development. As an expression of this extraordinary life emerging in otherwise ordinary circumstances, the Gospel of Luke tells the story of the twelve-year-old Jesus in the Temple (s:41-52), which unites his heightening awareness of the Presence of God and his deepening commitment to his mission from God (2:46-49). The narrative concludes with an eminently positive characterization of growth in all aspects of the life of the young prodigy from Nazareth in Galilee. This continuing development of Jesus beyond the infancy narrative to his baptism reflects the dynamic interrelationship of his communion with God— his *Abba* experience—and his vision of the coming Kingdom of God—his vocation. The years of silence shaped and grounded the scandalous Nazarene who enacted the Word of God through the proclamation of *his gospel* to all those who would listen.

When he began his public ministry without any indication of sin within himself, Jesus forgave the sins of others. Certainly without collaboration and comparatively without conscious intention, the different narratives of the canonical Gospels present strikingly similar portraits of Jesus, one who did not experience estrangement in himself but was greatly concerned about the estrangement of others. He did not in word or deed reflect any sense of alienation—alienation within himself, alienation toward others, alienation from God. He lived throughout his life with a properly centered wholeness: an expanding consciousness of God as *Abba*, an emerging vision of the Kingdom of God, and a certainty of his own vocation in the arrival of that Kingdom.

A breakthrough in terms of communal experience occurred with his baptism by John the Baptist. Driven into the wilderness to ponder his mission and the means to accomplish it, Jesus emerged in continuous, unbroken communion with his *Abba* God. The ordeal of temptation in his solitude did not occasion the bleak forsakenness that occurs in sin. Earlier he had left John the Baptist standing in the Jordan River with the bad news of sin. After John's arrest Jesus began to preach the good news of the Kingdom of God, celebrating the invigorating and fascinating enjoyment of the Presence of the near *Abba*. The consciousness of God as

Abba so pervaded the depths of his own being that he offered the forgiveness of God to those who had no reason to expect it. He set aside the regulations of the Law as the criteria of salvation. He spoke confidently to his opponents. He broke the barriers separating men and women, the sick and the healthy, the good and the bad. He lived with an awareness of oneness with the ground of Being and his unity with the environment of all Being, oneness with God, with YHWH, with *Abba*.

On the basis of the enjoyment of the *Abba* God come near, despite the difficulties and suffering that he saw all around him, Jesus and his disciples did not fast but celebrated the dawning Kingdom of God. He set aside the requirements of the Law, because he knew that salvation does not come through human achievement. Jesus embodied the power of love that anticipates and fulfills the Law, the fulfillment of the intention of the Law through the way of love that redefines the Law. And he accepted the consequences of the conflict within the Law that he precipitated.[19]

The self-actualization of God in the history of Jesus the Christ constitutes the ultimate self-revelation of God. Through Jesus, God reveals *WHO GOD IS*: Beyond YHWH, the covenantal God of the Exodus, God is the *Abba* God, who forgives those whom the Law condemns. Through Jesus, God reveals *WHAT GOD IS*: Beyond God loves the elect of Israel, a particularized verb, to, God is love, an all-inclusive noun. Through Jesus, God reveals *WHERE GOD IS*: Beyond every Holy Place, God comes near to those in the circle around Jesus, through whom they participate in the arriving Kingdom of God. These affirmations sound as though the story has ended, but we know that the journey continued and took a deadly turn.

The trip to Jerusalem, the confrontation at the Temple, the agony in Gethsemane, the desolation of crucifixion—it happened so quickly. What happened to Jesus as he hung between life and death on the cross? He

---

[19]See Wolfhart Pannenberg, *Jesus—God and Man* (Philadelphia: The Westminster Press, 1968) 251-58. "The rejection of Jesus was inevitable for the Jew . . . not prepared to distinguish between the authority of the law and the authority of Israel's God" (253). The Jewish-Christians could claim that "Jesus never turned against the law in general, but merely interpreted it with free authority." Furthermore, Pannenberg sees an obvious concentration of the law in the commandment of love: "The commandment of love as the center of Jesus' interpretation of the law indicates the sense in which a continuity between Jesus' message and the traditional law remained" (257). Cf. Jüngel, *God as the Mystery*, 359-60.

experienced for the first time in his life the life-giving Presence of God slipping away. He felt himself losing the awareness that had constituted the foundation of his whole life from the beginning, his *Abba* experience. As he had feared in Gethsemane, the fading of *Abba* nearness from his consciousness meant the invading Darkness of the abyss of Nothingness. That Jesus saw himself falling into the abyss of Nothingness, of death, was certainly not in and of itself unique. Others have experienced death this way. Yet the radical contrast of his life with his death was indescribably unique and its terror simply beyond description. Jesus had always lived in the exhilarating Presence of *Abba*, joyful Godbelovedness. He had lived and breathed God's very Presence. He had aggressively sought to share this Presence with everyone who would listen. He had devoted himself to the will and way of this Presence toward the coming Kingdom. He willingly gave himself for the sake of the Presence of the merciful *Abba* to anyone and to everyone. Now Jesus felt the withdrawal of the Presence of God, the lifelong consciousness of his *Abba* dwindling and diminishing. He saw himself plunging into the whirlpool of Nothingness.

Jesus had never experienced the alienation of Nothingness. He had known a measure of brokenness, the disappointments and neediness that belong to human finitude, but he had never experienced separation from God. Jesus had heretofore lived his whole life without any sense of self-contradiction. Now he anticipated death, which meant the loss of life and the absence of God. He saw his death for what it was. He viewed his abandonment to death-on-the-cross with an unimaginable clarity, because of its unspeakable contrast with the living Presence of God that he had always known, the contradiction of emptiness, isolation, and death—the Death of Nothingness.

Every person experiences estrangement from God and the alienation of self early on, because of sin. Our forsaking God contains in itself the judgment of Godforsakenness. In the journey of his life, however, Jesus had never known separation from God and its corollary of self-contradiction. He was never God forsaking, but now he experienced God-forsakenness. He alone, Jesus and only Jesus, was actually abandoned by God. Now he had to face estrangement in ever enlarging circles and ever penetrating depths within himself as he suffered and died. He fell into Nothingness with a death cry of utter abandonment. He did not just die. Jesus had lived the *Abba* Presence, and he died Presenceless. Godforsaken, he lost simultaneously the Presence of life and the life of Presence: Jesus died graceless but hopeful, an impossible contradiction. He died hopeful: "My God, my God. . . ." But graceless: "Why have you abandoned me?" Graceless but hopeful, Jesus died with the loud and lonely death cry of Godforsakenness.

The Mystery of the Death of God

What does "the mystery of the death of God" mean? God is the living God, eternally so. Can the word "death" ever be used with reference to God? Whatever "the death of God" might mean, God remains the living God who gives life to all creaturely existence. The phrase, "the mystery of," indicates the density and complexity of this theme, and the expression, "the death of God," must be understood in the context of the mystery of God. Two issues require exploration: Godforsakenness and Nothingness. Does Godforsakenness require the alienation of Jesus from God through the repudiation of Jesus by God? What does the death of Jesus into Nothingness mean to God? Theological reflection focuses on these two themes to probe the depths of meaning in "the mystery of the death of God" with specific reference to the Godforsaken death of Jesus.

Godforsakenness

That Jesus experienced Godforsakenness at his death means that he died with the awareness that God had abandoned him to this death of Godforsakenness. The argument that a person near to death can suffer dying but not experience death[20] ignores the unique human capacity to anticipate

---

[20]Contra Moltmann, *The Crucified God*, 243ff. Moltmann argues that a person can suffer dying but not suffer death itself. Thereby he distinguishes the suffering of the Son from the grief of the Father. While a distinction between the Father and the Son in the death of the cross is inevitable and necessary, the distinction which Moltmann employs is too sharply drawn. A person can in fact suffer "ceasing to be." Though not exclusively nor necessarily so, a person who lives under the sentence of death, an experience of utter aloneness, can anticipate the reality of "ceasing to be." The line between the one who suffers dying overagainst the one who suffers the death of the other in these instances is significantly blurred with respect to *the event of death itself.*

death in the observation of the deaths of others and especially so in the context of the sheer immediacy of the dying person's own impending end. Though not necessarily so, a person who suffers a long illness, which in its reflective depths is an experience of utter solitude, can genuinely experience through sometime agonizing anticipation the event of death itself, the reality of "ceasing to be." Of course, a dying person cannot suffer the unendingness of death but only its immediacy within a specific and definable context, a perspective nonetheless that coheres with the passion narratives generally and Jesus' agony in Gethsemane particularly.

Since Jesus increasingly reckoned on the inevitability of rejection and violent death, the Nazarene anticipated his death on the cross, an expectation that bore ever more deeply into the inaccessible depths of his being. Yet the intensity of Godforsakenness that Jesus consciously endured in his death occurred in striking contrast to his eminently positive experience of Godbelovedness that he had known throughout his life. The utter contradiction of his life and death, of his living and dying, is beyond comprehension, but some descriptive endeavor is necessary. Any attempt to conceptualize this contradiction in the death of Jesus must affirm simultaneously the stark Godforsakenness of his crucifixion and his tenacious trust in God in his death. Jesus died graceless, abandoned by God to the death of Godforsakenness, but hopeful, trust turned entirely toward the future of God.

What happened to God, or can we say? Dare we say anything at all? *God had never seen life the way God saw life through the eyes of Jesus.* For the first time in human history God saw life lived in continuing communion with God, because Jesus is the only person to fulfill the intention of God in creation as well as the call of God to vocation. *Correspondingly, God had never seen death the way God saw death through the eyes of the dying Jesus.* The execution of this Nazarene as a blasphemer and renegade terminated the heretofore unbroken communion of the *Abba* God with the beloved Son: Death in Godforsakenness, Abandonment, Nothingness.

What happened to God? Since the relation of God with Jesus ended temporally with Jesus' death on the cross, *God encountered in the termination of this relationship something of what it means "not to be."* The identity of God established through the reciprocity of the personal union of the *Abba* God with Jesus of Nazareth, this unique relationship of mutuality and the revelatory identity of God disclosed therein, ended with the death cry of the Crucified. God endured something profoundly new, the negation of this relationship of lifelong unity and indescribable intimacy with God's Beloved Child, a negation, a death in negation ultimately incomprehensible.

Theological proposals that affirm the dereliction of the Son of God in his death of Godforsakenness invariably separate the Father, who must judge sin, from the Son, who has been condemned for sin, a radical separation from one another in some form or the other. It can be put sharply: On the basis of the uncompromising righteousness of the Holy God, the crucified though innocent Jesus bore the obligatory judgment of the wrath of God against sin, which subjected him to the death of damnation in the place of sinful humanity. Or less sharply: On the basis of the righteousness of the Holy God, the crucified but innocent Jesus entered the arena of God's judgment against sin and endured the death of alienation from God for the sake of sinful humanity. The advocacy and criticisms of such proposals are well-known and need not be repeated here. In the context of Godforsakenness expounded in this essay a different proposal warrants consideration: Contrary to the abyssal separation of the alienated Son from the Father of inviolate righteousness the Godforsakenness of Jesus Christ in his suffering and death corresponded to the Godforsakenness of God from God, an event that the Godforsakenness of the Son discloses. The Godforsakenness of Jesus happened within the continuity of the Godforsakenness of God from God. Jesus suffered the abandonment of God, *his* God, the *Abba* God, in his dying: He experienced the desolation of Godforsakenness, the terror of Godlessness! What Jesus could not envision in the particularity of his death was the Godforsakenness of God from God, an event that occurred beyond his consciousness but in the unity of his death with God.

Unlike the traditional interpretations of Godforsakenness, whether affirmed or denied, the death of Jesus does not position the forsaking *Abba* in opposition to the abandoned Son. Rather, the Godforsaken death of Jesus happens in the continuity of the life of God. The Godforsakenness of God from God, *of* God *through* God *into* God, constitutes the Self-Abandonment of God. God abandoned Godself to death, the death of the *identity* of God. Since the Godforsakenness of the death of Jesus occurred in the Godforsakenness of God from God, the death of Jesus did not separate him from God but united him preeminently through his death with God. The Godforsakenness of God from God in the self-sacrifice of Jesus discloses the unity of the *Abba* God with the Samaritan Son in the arena of creation, Godforsakenness encompassing the Holy Spirit, because creation turned toward chaos amid the metaphorical rumblings of apocalyptic catastrophe: Darkness draped the land from noon til midafternoon, a violent earthquake shook Jerusalem (Matt 27:45, 51), and the curtain of the Temple ripped from top to bottom (Mark 14:38).

The judgment and execution of Jesus Christ requires us to speak of Godforsakenness, but this event of Godforsakenness cannot be restricted to the death of the Crucified. On the contrary, God, God in self-differentiation and self-differentiated unity, this God endured the radical contradiction of Godforsakenness. God abandoned God to Godforsakenness through the unity of the living God with the dying Jesus in the Spirit indwelling creation. The Presence of the *Abba* God who arrived with the enlivening Creativity of the Kingdom of God could not survive but died the Godforsaken death of the Nazarene. God abandoned the identity of God that Jesus had disclosed and vacated the life-giving vision of the Kingdom that Jesus had allegedly brought near. So the Godforsakenness of the crucified Christ reveals the Godforsakenness of God from God: Who God Is, What God Is, Where God Is. The Godforsakenness of God from God through the crucifixion of Jesus displaced and absented the reality of *his* God from the domain of creation. Whoever God is, the rejection of the Cross divulges, that God is not the God whom Jesus of Nazareth named and proclaimed. The death of God in Godforsakenness describes the Self-Abandonment of God in the death of Jesus Christ, the death of the identity of God. God suffered Self-Abandonment in the Godforsakenness of the death of the cross. That is, God identified with Jesus in his death as intensely as God had identified with Jesus in his life. Despite the limitation of language, therefore, we are compelled to speak of the death of God in the Godforsakenness of God from God, because the identity of God encompasses the existence and essence of God simultaneously.

What happened? Godforsakenness. Abandonment. Death. What happened to God? The Godforsakenness of God from God, *of* God *through* God *into* God. The *Abba* God withdrew all relational Presence from the dying Son, and the creative Spirit defected from the dawning Kingdom embodied heretofore through the activity of the crucified Jesus. The death of the Son through the withdrawal of the life-giving Spirit, who had always mediated the Presence of the *Abba* God to the beloved Son and the corresponding dedication of the Son to the near *Abba*, simultaneously included the withdrawal of the Spirit from the *Abba* of Jesus, the God for whose Kingdom he had lived. The withdrawal of the interpenetrating Presence of God in the death of Jesus Christ located the Godforsakenness of the suffering and death of the cross within the life of God.

The eternal God abandoned the Son to death and, consequently, the identity of God as the gracious *Abba*, whose unique divine Name Jesus had lived to proclaim and whose Otherness had already arrived in his captivating message and unprecedented ministry. The Spirit of God, through whom Jesus had come to be and who actualized through him the arrival of the messianic age, now hovered still in the lifelessness of the death of the Christ, the end of the beginning of the messianic Kingdom of God. The Godforsakenness of God from God, *of* God *through* God *into* God, requires theological elaboration: the withdrawal of the living God from the dying Jesus for blasphemy and lawlessness—*of* God; the withdrawal of the life-giving Spirit who mediated the Presence of God to Jesus and the continuing trust of Jesus in his *Abba* God—*through* God; the withdrawal of the eschatological nearness of God accomplished in Jesus for all creation waiting transformation in the power of the Spirit—*into* God. This Godforsakenness of God from God, *of* God *through* God *into* God, constituted the Self-Abandonment of God to death on the cross. The Godforsakenness of God from God means nothing less than the death of the living God who had arrived in the *Abba*-loving, Spirit-filled, Kingdom-coming Jesus of Nazareth, the one whom some had thought to be the Christ.

The withdrawal *of* God *through* God *into* God from a Godforsaken world forged an intense unity of Divine Self-Abandonment in the Godforsakenness of the death of the cross. The density of the unity of God in the event of Godforsakenness is comparable to the intensity of the unity of God in the act of creation. Ever how brief, whatever the form, or how else measured, the end of the *Abba* Presence in the world through the death of Jesus Christ constituted the Presencelessness, the Godforsakenness of God from God, *of* God *through* God *into* God. Self-Abandonment marked the eclipse of God as God for the whole of creation. Yet the Self-Abandonment of God occurred in the depths of the Self-Relatedness of God. The Self-Abandonment of God describes the Godforsakenness of God from God, *of* God *through* God *into* God in the death of the cross. The Self-Relatedness of God encompassed the God-forsakenness of God from God, *through* God *into* God *within* God, a Self-Relatedness enveloping the Self-Abandonment within the depths of the transcending Otherness of God. Godforsakenness happened to God, God and God only, the crucified God, God on the cross, but God-belovedness embraced and contained Godforsakenness that otherwise could not happen and without that the world could not survive.

God abandoned Godself to the death of the cross, the death of the identity of God in the world. Yet the Self-Abandonment of God in the death of the cross transpired through the depths of love within the Self-Relatedness of God: The Self-Relatedness of God encompassed the Self-Abandonment of God. This perspective of God on the cross informs the definition of God, *through* God *into* God *within* God, who God is within Godself, the withinness of a dynamic Godbelovedness that transcends Godforsakenness: *through* God, a withinness that transforms the Godfor-sakenness of humanity-forsaking-God into the suffering of God; *into* God, a withinness that preserves in resolute faithfulness the relationship of God to a wayward creation exclusively from the side of God; *within* God, a withinness of an immeasurable Godbelovedness wherein God chooses in the freedom of love to bestow on humanity the grace of life beyond death. Indeed, through the death of Jesus Christ on the cross, the love of God for humanity takes the form of self-sacrifice. The God of love endures the sacrifice of Godself: Who the self-giving God is. Therefore, Self-Abandonment does not occasion the disintegration of God but the definition of God, the disclosure of the transcending self-definition of God: "God is love."

Nothingness

Though the theme of Godforsakenness overlaps the theme of Nothingness, the two are not identical and must not be confused. Godfor-sakenness describes the death of Jesus and discloses an event within the life of God. Conversely, Nothingness is the adversary of God: the hostile, menacing, destructive force that threatens creation and assaults God through the plunder of creation. Nothingness is not the equal but the inimical, implacable enemy of God. Nothingness exists through the distortion of creation generally and the waywardness of humanity specifically. That is, Nothingness exists within the perishability of creation. In the act of creation God accepted the cost of the freedom of love in calling creation into being: *chaos* and *Nothingness*. God established boundaries for chaos and Nothingness in creation, but these boundaries do not protect creation from entangling distortion and immeasurable destruction. On the contrary, the devastation and death from chaos and Nothingness are abhorrent and incalculable, of such proportions to cast the goodness of creation in doubt and to render the act of creation itself a sometime questionable enterprise.

The advent of God in Jesus of Nazareth means that God, the God who is, has entered into perishability and therefore the menacing arena of the threat of Nothingness. [21] Death confronts us with the reality of Nothingness in the journey of life, and perishing confronts us with the tendency toward Nothingness inherent in our finitude. We experience perishability as a struggle, the struggle between being and nonbeing, between the possibility of meaningful existence and the bent toward nihilating Nothingness. The advent of God in Jesus Christ dramatically revealed the historic struggle of God with Nothingness, and God decisively engaged Nothingness in the event of the cross of Christ, enduring the dereliction and desolation of death in Nothingness. Through the suffering and death of Jesus Christ, therefore, God bears the annihilation of Nothingness within the life of God.

Though beyond our view, God has vanquished Nothingness, or better, God has judged Nothingness, and in principle God has overcome it. Moreover, God has already begun to prevail over it. Since God has historically judged and will assuredly triumph over Nothingness, a victory now underway, the revelation of God has happened at the cross. God and God alone can suffer in the very being of God the annihilating power of Nothingness, the negation of death that inheres in Nothingness and threatens the whole of creation, and God can do so and remain the living God. The God on the cross could endure death without suffering the annihilation of Nothingness, but, on the contrary, destroy the intention of death in all forms of Nothingness, because this God is weak and powerless *in the world*, but the eternal God of self-giving love is *not* weak and powerless *within Godself.*

---

[21]See Jüngel, *God as the Mystery*, 210-18.

In the suffering and death of Jesus Christ the power of Nothingness assaulted and penetrated the life of God. How? The draining, driving destruction of death cannot be restricted to the crucified Christ, because God identified so closely with him that God encountered suffering and death through him. God identified with Jesus now repudiated, abandoned, and dead as intensely as God had identified with him in the celebration of the Kingdom's coming. God remained one with Jesus in life *and* in death. This unique Presence of God in the crucified Christ requires us to speak of God on the cross, of the mystery of the death of God. The living God, however, can go through death without ceasing to be, overcoming Nothingness and the Death intrinsic in it. Nothingness belongs to the perishability of creation, but God does not. God is the living God who can choose this death on the cross as the expression of the life and identity of God. Therefore, the relationship that God has with creation and humanity within it is not terminated by death but preserved in God through death and beyond.

God embraced the annihilating power of Nothingness within the life of God for the sake of humanity, but the overcoming of Nothingness in the life of God reveals the unfathomable depths of the mystery of God. On the cross of Jesus Christ in the face of the deadly assault of Nothingness, God defines who God is in the endurance of and triumph over Nothingness. God suffers for humanity, because God has chosen in the freedom of love to come to humanity lost and ruined in "a far country," those threatened with the Death of Nothingness on the one side as well as those aligned with the deadly Force of Nothingness on the other. The God who comes to us in the confrontation with Nothingness is the God who endures death for the sake of life. Whose life? The life of humanity-forsaking-God condemns itself to Godforsakenness in its wretched waywardness of sin. That God has chosen to identify with and suffer for humanity in the dereliction of God's Beloved Child nailed dead on a cross, indeed, murdered and disappeared in the Darkness of Nothingness —this choice reveals the depths of the identity of God. The revelation of God in the death of Jesus discloses and defines who God is: "God is love."

Yet God continues to suffer for humanity under the threat and assault of Nothingness in the arena of creation. Nothingness has been judged and Death in Nothingness already overcome, but Nothingness retains incalculable power in creation and history. Nothingness and death in

Nothingness cannot escape the judgment of God, judgment already and irreversibly established in the cross of Jesus Christ. Nothingness continues to live off of and out of creation, for Nothingness does not have being in itself. Since God has willed for creation and humanity to live, because, "the Word has become flesh and lived among us," Nothingness cannot outlive humanity created in the image of God. Precisely because God went through death without ceasing to be, God has overcome death. The temporality of the triumph of God over death, over Nothingness that turns death into Death, required nonetheless a "waiting." When did God establish anew the vitality of a relationship with Jesus "crucified, dead, and buried"? A brief moment? On the third day? Sometime in between? In conjunction with the appearance to the disciples? Independent of the encounter with the disciples? The specific duration as well as the precise definition of "waiting" is itself a mystery of the advent of God in Jesus of Nazareth.

In the meantime the power of Nothingness becomes ever more menacing, ever more terrifying, ever more vicious, ever more deadly. Nothingness has not been vanquished to the past and subjected to the specific control of God. The power of Nothingness has not been destroyed in the life of God through the death of Christ that already negates its power of negation in creation, but Nothingness has been unmasked and its fate sealed. In the cross of Jesus Christ God has staked out in the life-giving power of love the irrevocable divine judgment against Nothingness—already judged but not yet destroyed. The judgment of God against Nothingness enlivens the promises of God and nurtures the hope of humanity still on pilgrimage. When will the judgment of God against Nothingness destroy it and whatever power it retains over creation and humanity within creation? The precise answer waits on the horizon of the future.

Therefore, "the death of God" does not mean that the eternal God ever ceases to be. That God goes through death without ceasing to be discloses that the living God transcends all the limits encountered in death. Not even death can terminate our relationship to God. When personal relationships end at death, God acts to renew these relationships and to create new relationships beyond the grasp of death through the creative power of love. The dramatic encounter of the God of love with the death of Nothingness promises new life with new relationships that transcend the limits of death. The declaration of "the mystery of the death of God" means that God has gone through death in the cross of Jesus Christ without ceasing to be, but, conversely, revealing what it means *for this God to be*. The Godforsakenness of God from God in the death of Jesus Christ, the moment therefore of the Self-Abandonment of God, coincides with the death of Jesus Christ into the abyss of Nothingness, the moment therefore of the death of God. Thus God has chosen through the Godforsakenness of God from God to confront Nothingness, even the death of Nothingness, in the death of Jesus Christ. God has chosen to make his death—the death of the Son of God on the cross—the unique place of the Presence of God. The mystery of the death of the living God discloses the unfathomable depths of the mystery of God: "God is love."

The Tragic History of Suffering Humanity

What does "the mystery of the death of God" mean for the tragic history of suffering humanity? That God suffers the Godforsakenness of God from God in the Self-Abandonment of God reveals the passionate will of God to stand by and suffer for humanity-forsaking-God. That God endures the assault of Nothingness, even the Death of Nothingness on the cross, and remains the living God offers hope for dying humanity. Can anything else be said? Yes, questions continue. How does God's suffering help suffering humanity? Does the active Presence of God blunt the nihilating force of Nothingness? Does the actual suffering of God mitigate the destructive power of chaos and Nothingness? While these questions and provisional answers have informed this essay from the outset, the questions continue to confront us and trouble us.

That God is "the fellow sufferer who understands"[22] offers brief relief, but no more. The suggestion that God exercises control over chaos and Nothingness, that God permits evil and suffering to bring us to maturity on the journey of life, must blind itself to the universal and disproportionate measure of real evil, real suffering and real death, the real-s that do not develop but destroy humanity. What does God do now in the midst of the arrogant waywardness of the human species, the

---

[22]Alfred North Whitehead, *Process and Reality*, Corrected Edition, ed. David Ray Griffin and Donald W. Sherburne (New York: The Free Press, 1978) 351.

immeasurable range of human suffering, and the devastating threat of chaos and Nothingness?

Answers are available, though their value is not unassailable. Perhaps, some say, the death of the Christ of God is in part the atonement of God to humanity for the indescribable evil that afflicts humankind.[23] A daring proposal—only if God accepts responsibility for evil, making atonement to us, do we have reason to trust God to save us from the annihilation of radical evil. If the death of the Christ of God is in part the atonement of God to humanity for evil and suffering, God is culpable to the extent that the atonement requires. Likewise, we must forgive God for what God has done to us or failed to do for us, directly or indirectly, amid the evil and suffering of this world. *OR*: Perhaps, some would say, the death of the beloved Child of God is God's acceptance of responsibility for the sinful waywardness and attendant suffering of fallen humanity: God is

---

[23]See Goetz, "The Suffering God," 144. Goetz affirms the self-limitation of God in the Incarnation: "God's love is supremely revealed in his self-humbling. God is a fellow sufferer who understands not because God cannot be otherwise, but because God wills to share our lot."

". . . God does not require of us a suffering that he himself will not endure. However, if this comfort is to be any more than a psychological prop, it must show how God's suffering mitigates evil. This explanation has been, to date, curiously lacking in the theodicy of divine self-limitation."

"To anyone who feels compelled to affirm divine suffering, the fact that God is deeply involved in the anguish and the blood of humanity forces a drastic theological crisis of thought vis-á-vis the question of evil. The mere fact of God's suffering doesn't solve the question; it exacerbates it. For there can no longer be a retreat into the hidden sense of the eternal, all-wise, changeless and unaffected God. The suffering God is with us in the here and now. God must answer in the here and now before one can make any sense of the by and by. God, the fellow sufferer, is inexcusable if all that he can do is suffer. But if God is ultimately redeemer, *how dare he hold out on redemption here and now in the face of real evil?*"

"*My own view is that the death of God's Christ is in part God's atonement to his creatures for evil.* Only on the basis of God's terrible willingness to accept responsibility for evil do we have grounds to trust God's promise to redeem evil. Only in God's daring willingness to risk all in the death of his own son can we have confidence that God finally has the power to redeem his promise. Others may not agree with this radical rethinking of the atonement, but it seems apparent that comprehensively to affirm the almighty sovereignty of the self-humbled God requires a drastic rethinking of traditional doctrine" (Italics added).

responsible because God is involved, but *not* because God is culpable.[24] That God accepts responsibility for the tragic self-centeredness and destructive egocentricity that stains every aspect of the life of sinful humanity does not actually imply God's guilt but may mysteriously reveal God's grace. Despite all disclaimers, however, this perspective does suggest some measure of culpability within God's responsibility.

This question, THIS AWESOME QUESTION, defies all answers before the question, the question itself, is really heard: Is the death of the Christ of God in part God's atonement to us for the continuing assault against us of the savagery of chaos and the life-obliterating nullity of Nothingness? Must we accept God's atonement and forgive God for the tragic and often demonic condition of our world? Can any one of us, creaturely beings that we are, dare to forgive the Creator? A tentative "Yes." If we are allowed to forgive God, however, it cannot be done as human prerogative or creaturely presumption. It can be done only with an awareness that this too, the forgiving of God, is itself a gift of God's grace. So our acceptance of the atonement of God must be received as a gift from God.

"What is the difference between 'forgiving God' and 'accepting God'?" the Wise Owl asked me. In principle, everybody can accept God. However, only victims can forgive God. Only one who is a victim can forgive those responsible for his or her victimization. So again I distinguish between chaos and Nothingness. The victims of chaos suffer from the randomness that is riddled through all the structures of creation. The

---

[24]Burton Cooper, *Why, God?*, 61-62. With the death of two of his children in the background, Burton Cooper describes an illuminating conversation concerning God's responsibility for evil: "We were discussing these matters when one of the ministers, a director of a clinical-pastoral education program, asked whether God is involved with and responsible for evil. I thought these were two separate issues, so I responded with the question, 'Are you asking whether God is involved with evil or whether God is responsible for evil?' He paused for a moment and answered, 'Is God responsible because God is involved?' "

"That was it, of course. That was the answer to [my] distressing question. . . . God is responsible because God is involved. These are not two issues but one. . . . a startling insight into biblical texts once we shift our basic imagery from the monarchial God to the vulnerable God. . . . As parents have a share of the responsibility in the actions of their children because they are so deeply involved with them, so the God of biblical faith, who is heavily involved in the life of a people, has a share of responsibility."

victims of the demonic suffer because of that twisted alliance between sin and Nothingness, the victims who had little or no opportunity to enjoy life, much less God. Only the victims have the right to exercise the gift of God to forgive God. Yet the victims have been silenced. So those who are made sensitive to human need—for the helpless and those beyond help—must speak the word of forgiveness to God for all those victimized in the long, short history of bloody humanity defaced in the image of God.

So the awareness of the atonement of God to humanity for evil in the world and the genuine possibility of forgiving God is an insight that originates in the grace of God. Yet something completely unexpected happens when the Christian accepts God's atonement and offers forgiveness to God, the *Abba* God of Jesus. The Christian, the Christian who is victim, the Christian who has internalized in some slight fashion the victimization of the victims, the Christian cannot complete the prayer of offering forgiveness to the atoning God, *because everything so intended shockingly changes*. Such daring but inviting prayer slips unexpectedly into the terrible suffering of God at its deepest level, namely, the unimaginable grieving of the God of grace: In an unbearable instance, a moment, nothing more, the Christian has a blurred, almost blind glimpse of the cumulative grief of God that stretches from the beginning of humankind through the whole history of human time.

Now the question must be asked again: Is the death of the Christ of God in part God's atonement to us for the continuing assault against us of the savagery of chaos and the life-obliterating nullity of Nothingness? Must we accept God's atonement and forgive God for the tragic and often demonic condition of our world? Can anyone of us, creative beings that we are, dare to forgive the Creator? The tentative "Yes" recoils into an absolute "No"! God grieves in disappointment and pain for the cruelty and devastation of the history of humanity, for each and every victim made in the image of God. The awareness of the magnitude of the grieving of God for all the victims in creation and history discloses that God participates in the victimization of the creature. So the moment of grace that seems to allow us to accept the atonement of God for the evil that permeates and perverts creation is only a transitional moment, *an instance of extraordinary and absolute reversal*. Something radically different occurs, a completely unexpected moment entirely, a moment of access into the depths of the mystery of the painful love of God, the point of entry into the mystery of the grieving of God in the vastness of grace with depths utterly unfathomable, Holy Silence the response to the glimpse of the ineffable. *God does not make atonement for evil, and God cannot be forgiven for the victims chaos and Nothingness in the history of creation, because God is THE VICTIM.*

Though God accepts responsibility for sin to redeem us from it, God who is THE VICTIM, who participates in the victimization of every victim, cannot make atonement to us and cannot be forgiven by us. God may accept our misguided endeavors in prayer, but God does not need our forgiveness. God is the Motherly Father of love, the One who grieves every time anyone made in the image of God dies a victim of oppression, the God who suffers in the midst of all sin and brokenness, the God who endures chaos in creation, the God who is vulnerable to Nothingness. Irrevocably judged already, Nothingness continues its brutal assaults on creation in the meantime. So God is The Victim who embraces all the victims of chaos and Nothingness and takes them gently into the healing of God's eternal life and love.

What can this mean? God has identified with the victims instead of the executioners. God has endured the chaos in creation, and God has owned the goodness of Godself. Creation continues to reflect the goodness of God. More so, God has endured the Nothingness that assaults creation and viciously butchers targeted humanity. The great God always labors to vanquish the deadliness of Nothingness for the sake of humanity made in the image of God, constantly working in every instance to deny Nothingness the last word. Indeed, God has already judged Nothingness in the cross of Jesus Christ, judgment sometimes seemingly in doubt. So the Creator God who creates out of nothing and preserves the work of creation suffers with all who suffer and participates in the victimization of all victims. The God of suffering love is none other than the Creator who has suffered with creation from the first moment it went awry. And the death of Jesus Christ in Godforsakenness, the Godforsakenness of God from God, discloses the identity of God as THE VICTIM who bears all the victimization of humanity within the depths of a great suffering love, so great a sorrow and suffering that only the love of God can contain it. The love of God, however, is an eminently active love that creatively transforms suffering into healing, death into life. *Precisely as Victim, therefore, God is Victor.*

Yet an essential problem remains in the concept of God as The Victim: A victim does not choose to be a victim. A martyr may choose martyrdom, faithful to the death for a cause. A hero may choose a courageous action for some admirable purpose and die heroically. However, a fundamental characteristic of a victim is that the victim is subjected to victimization. Even in resistance the victim remains victimized without any choice of its fate. The victim does not choose to be a victim, a lack of choice that often expresses itself through the element of passivity, the inability to act decisively as the consequence of helplessness. We dare not miss the clue in the transition from the agony of Jesus in Gethsemane to his arrest, trials, and execution, the transition between what went before and what happened afterward.

Prior to Gethsemane Jesus actualized his intention and purpose through the strength of his personal decision-making. After the agony of Gethsemane a transition occurred in his confrontation with his adversaries, a transition from strength and power to weakness and powerlessness, from the authority of free agency to his acceptance of events already underway, from the decisiveness of action to a posture of passivity. Did he not act with the mark of passivity, of powerlessness in passivity, as he was dragged through trials in the night and driven with nails from this world into the Godforsakenness of death? Here I must affirm in situations of victimization the inevitability of identification. God has always chosen to identify with the victims, because one must either identify with the victims or the executioners: And *not* to identify with the victims *is* to identify with the executioners. The problem nonetheless is not restricted to the activity of God. "Neutrality" in the light of the righteousness of God is an impossibility. The disclosure of God's identification with the victims in the life and death of Jesus constitutes an act of identification that the followers of Jesus cannot ignore.

Berlin, 10 November 1938, *Kristallnacht*: The windows of elegant Jewish stores were broken, and well-dressed people took fashionable merchandise. Synagogues were burned to the ground, and holy books were destroyed. Jewish men disappeared to concentration camps. Father Bernhard Lichtenberg of the *Hedwigskirche* walked the streets of Berlin and saw the destruction of Jewish property and sacred places. He did just one thing. He returned to his church and prayed publicly "on behalf of the Jews and the poor concentration camp prisoners." He prayed in public rather than private. At great risk for nearly three years, Father Lichtenberg prayed for Jews *in public* and *by name* until his arrest on 23 October 1941. In prison Lichtenberg decided after his release to join the Berlin Jews who had been deported to the Lodz Ghetto, where he could give pastoral care, becoming a *Judenseelsorger*. When his bishop visited him in prison, Lichtenberg told him what he intended to do, wondering what the Holy Father in Rome would think of it.

Finally brought to trial on 22 May 1942, Lichtenberg was found guilty and denied clemency because he had shown no repentance during his six-month imprisonment. Father Lichtenberg asked for permission to speak:

> Mr. Prosecutor, . . . the last point you made . . . to the effect that I have not changed and would speak and act exactly as before, that . . . is completely accurate.

When the presiding judge asked how he could pray for the Jews, Lichtenberg replied:

> This question I can answer quite precisely. It happened in November 1938, when store windows were smashed and the synagogues burned. . . . When I saw this destruction, with the police looking on doing nothing, I was scandalized by all this vandalism and asked myself what, if such things were possible in an ordered state, could still bring help.

Emphasizing every word, he concluded:

> Then I told myself that only one thing could still help, namely, prayer. That night I prayed for the first time as follows: "Now let us pray for the persecuted 'non-Aryan' Christians and Jews."[25]

Soon afterward, Lichtenberg died on the way to the concentration camp at Dachau.

Father Bernhard Lichtenberg was weak and powerless in his world, but he was not impotent. He publicly identified with the victims of his church and beyond it, as Christ himself had identified with the victims

---

[25]Emil L. Fackenheim, *To Mend the World* (New York: Schocken Books, 1982) 289-90.

(Matt 25:34-45). He prayed for Christians and Jewish victims by name, but they would never hear his prayers. He prayed to the listening God, believing God would hear the voice of the voiceless. Father Lichtenberg did not die a hero or a martyr but a victim, between the world of the innocent dead and the world of the listening God.

WHO IS GOD? WHAT IS GOD? WHERE IS GOD? God is the Godforsaken God on the cross. God is THE VICTIM who suffers with all the victims of Nothingness. First, God identifies with the victim and will not abandon him or her, whether the sufferer senses God's Presence or not. God knows and loves each victim in the particularity of his or her personhood. Second, the God who suffers death for the sake of life participates in the victimization of the victim—the rejection, abuse, oppression, pain, and powerlessness, whatever its form. Contrary to various forms of traditional Christian theism and the scourge of a sub-Christian piety cloaked with a feigned humility, God does not withhold power that would alleviate the anguished plight of the sufferer. Third, the crucified God binds the victim to Godself in the solidarity of Godforsakenness and promises new relationships on the other side of death through the creative Spirit of life. Victims are not victimized eternally through mere registration in the labyrinth of the memory of God. Fourth, the creative power of God whereby God participates in the intricacies of human suffering is the selfsame power whereby God envisions and purposes a new possibility beyond it. God unites the victims of innocent death with the hope for eternal life, the promise of the transformation of victimization into humanization in the coming Home-Coming of God.

What else, can anything else be said? To conclude with God THE VICTOR precisely as God THE VICTIM? If this is gospel, good news, it is a scandal, because this God, THIS GOD ON THE CROSS, is very unGodlike.

"God Lay Dead on the Sabbath"

The death and burial of Jesus does not just mean: "The Son of God lay dead on the Sabbath." The death of Jesus the Son split the limitless horizon of the very life of God. With specific reference to the narrative of God in the story of Jesus, on the basis of the self-differentiation of the Vision of God who Energized the life of Jesus, another word must be said: "*God lay dead on the Sabbath.*" The Son of God lay silent in the tomb of the dead. The *Abba* whom he had brought near went down to the grave with him, as distant from life as death from birth. The Spirit of creative love languished in utter lifelessness. The declaration—"The Son of God lay dead on the Sabbath"—is an announcement detached from God. Rather: "God lay dead on the Sabbath."

The word that God lay dead on the Sabbath corresponds to the mystery that Nothingness penetrated the very life of God in the particularity of the Godforsaken death of Jesus Christ, and in the inexhaustible plenitude of the life of God, Nothingness, indeed, the Death of Nothingness, exhausted itself: into nothing, nothing at all, a not something—*with reference to God and God only*. That God has overcome Nothingness in Godself constitutes the irrevocable judgment of God over Nothingness. Yet Nothingness continues its savage rampage through creation and toward all human beings. The judgment of God has sealed its fate, but God has not eliminated its destructive brutality in creation and with creaturely humanity in the contingency of history. The destruction of Nothingness is the sure promise of God and the faltering hope of humanity. Through the Godforsaken death of the One whom God has sent into the world with the good news of the Kingdom's coming, God becomes a nameless, faceless father of a nameless, faceless son. God is Victim. God has endured the assault of Nothingness on the Creator through creation, always Presence to victims as THE VICTIM, whether the victims sensed a suffering Presence or not.

The death of Jesus of Nazareth, the Son of God, confronts us with "the mystery of the death of God," the night of the Light who is God. Is such talk nonsense? On the contrary, whatever the limits of language such talk is necessary. Jesus surrendered his identity as the Son for the sake of the will of his *Abba* God: the will of self-communicating love. The God of Jesus surrendered God's *Abba* identity as the Motherly Father for the sake of the way of the Son: the way of self-sacrificial love. The Spirit surrendered her identity as Spirit for the sake of the work of the *Abba* through the Son: the work of reconciling love. Though the death of God does not mean that God ceases to be, such radical self-giving within the living God coalesces through the Godforsaken death of Jesus on the cross into "the mystery of the death of God," the revelation of God's self-identification with the victims of chaos and Nothingness from the beginning of humankind till the end of human time. An unfathomable mystery—God lay dead on the Sabbath: without Identity, Presence, Creativity. The overwhelming legacy of the tragic history of the suffering of humanity curtains and conceals this dark night of "the death of God."

Chapter 9

The Vision of Providence

THE RESURRECTION OF THE CRUCIFIED JESUS SEEMED HARDLY BELIEVABLE. The two disciples on the road to Emmaus certainly did not ponder its reality, or they would have waited in Jerusalem. Restless in a bewildering confusion of disappointment and grief, they left the city of Jerusalem for the village of Emmaus. Why did they leave the others for an out-of-town excursion? Emmaus is where you go when you lack anywhere else to go, because going Somewhere offers more than staying Nowhere, and getting there eventually means coming back. Only time seems to stand still. So the two friends walked together from Jerusalem to Emmaus, alone and preoccupied.

The risen Jesus joined the two travelers incognito and asked them what they were discussing. These onetime disciples stopped in their tracks, their faces a mixture of sadness and surprise, a deep sorrow momentarily visible in the pools of their eyes. Cleopas caught his breath and answered the stranger with a shock-struck question: "Are you the only person in Jerusalem who does not know what has happened during the last few days?"

"Tell me, what things?" the Intruder asked.

"About Jesus of Nazareth," the two answered with one voice.

Continuing their journey with the Stranger, they recounted the story of Jesus. First one disciple and then the other, back and forth, they reached into their memories of Jesus' ministry in Galilee, speaking with sudden enthusiasm and occasionally flashing quick smiles almost on the edge of laughter. Their mood changed dramatically, however, as the stories shifted from Galilee to Jerusalem.

"Jesus was a great prophet from God with powerful words and extraordinary deeds that everybody recognized—except his enemies in Jerusalem. The chief priests and leaders of our people rejected his proclamation of the Kingdom of God, because Jesus challenged their authority and claimed his authority came directly from God. They arrested him and condemned him to death."

" . . . They turned Jesus over to the Romans who did exactly what you would expect them to do. The Romans condemned him as another Galilean revolutionary and crucified him. The sign on his cross read, 'King of the Jews.' "

They walked together in silence.

"We had hoped that he was the Messiah who would deliver Israel."

Although the Nazarene remained a prophet, murdered like the prophets before him, Jesus' death on a cross disqualified him as the Christ of God.

"All this happened three days ago. Some of the women who followed Jesus told us an incredible story just before we left. They went to the tomb early this morning, but the body of Jesus was not there. They came back and told us they had seen a vision of angels who said, 'Jesus is alive.' Some of the men went to the tomb, but they did not see anybody or any angels! . . . An idle tale . . . It is ridiculous what women will believe when they want to believe it."

Then the Stranger sharply reprimanded both of them: "You are so quick with your skepticism. How reluctant you are to believe what the prophets boldly anticipated. Was it not necessary for the Messiah to suffer these things before entering into God's glory?" Thereupon Jesus incognito interpreted everything about himself in the Scriptures, from Moses through all the prophets.

As they neared Emmaus, the Stranger walked ahead of them, apparently to continue his journey, but the two disciples urged him: "Stay with us. It is almost evening, and the day is nearly gone." So the Stranger remained with them. When he joined them at the table, he took bread, blessed and broke it, and gave it to them. In the familiarity and clarity of this mealtime moment, they recognized Jesus . . . and he vanished.

The two disciples remembered what Jesus had said along the way, how he stirred their hearts and captured their minds with stunning insight into the Scriptures. They returned immediately to Jerusalem and found the Eleven together with the other disciples. Before they could say anything, however, the others told them, "Jesus is alive! He is risen, and he has appeared to Peter!" The two disciples rushed through their story of meeting a Stranger enroute to Emmaus and recognizing Jesus in the breaking of bread.

Suddenly Jesus appeared among them and said, "Peace be with you." Despite everything some had seen and all had heard—the angelic vision of the women at the empty tomb, the appearance of the risen Jesus to Peter, the two disciples' encounter with Jesus incognito on the way to Emmaus—despite all these witnesses they were startled and terrified. They thought they were seeing some kind of ghost.

The risen Jesus said to them: "Why are you doubting and frightened? Look at my hands and feet. Touch me and see that it is I." Then he showed them his once crucified hands and feet, but in their joy they remained disbelieving and unconvinced. So Jesus ate a piece of fish to substantiate his resurrection life. (Luke 24:13-42)

The believability of the resurrection of Jesus Christ crucified is an issue in all four canonical Gospels, and appropriately so. The assertion of the resurrection of the Crucified from the dead is the recurring scandal of the gospel in antiquity and the pervasive scandal of the gospel in the relativism, empiricism, and pluralism of the contemporary world. The story of Jesus, however, attains its dramatic climax in the declaration of the resurrection of the Christ crucified. The event of the resurrection of Jesus Christ from the dead retroactively reframes the entire story of Jesus and mandates the theological investigation of its significance for envisioning the destiny of humanity. Critical historical consciousness and a modern scientific conception of the universe notwithstanding, contemporary theological reflection on the providence of God cannot avoid but must grapple with the issue of death and resurrection, the question of the resurrection of Jesus Christ and the viability of a Christian eschatology in its light.

Eschatological hope must listen to Holy Scripture today with life face-to-face with death, death face-to-face with life. The arena for testing eschatological hope is the valley of the shadow of death, the edge of the abyss of Nothingness, the empty horizon of Godforsakenness. The most dramatic symbol of death in all the todays of yesterday and tomorrow is *The Holocaust*, the kingdom of Night. The Holocaust has twin reference points, one in the past and the other in the future: *Auschwitz*, the who-would-have-ever-thought-it-possible extermination of six million Jews in Nazi Germany, almost half the Jewish population in the world; *Nuclear Winter*, "the day after" nuclear war, which threatens the very possibility of life on planet Earth. The threat of the cold of winter is not new, but the possibility of the cold night of a nuclear winter is unquestionably so. Death remains the testing ground of eschatology, of hope against hope, but now the testing ground encompasses the whole Earth simultaneously. The situation is different but strangely the same. The possibility of a nuclear Holocaust intensifies the issue of eschatology, but the problem remains preeminently personal in the contemplation of "ceasing to be."

Conflicting Interpretations of Jesus' Resurrection

Two fundamentally different interpretations of the resurrection of Jesus Christ from the dead generally stamp Christian theology today, a mythical interpretation and a historical interpretation. Each constitutes a distinct paradigm with multiple variations among the proposals of its respective advocates. The following brief summary of the two views of Jesus' resurrection moves from a mythical characterization to a historical under-standing of the resurrection of the crucified Jesus.

The interpretation of the resurrection of Jesus as a *mythical event* that refers to the rise of the disciples' Easter faith has a powerful attraction in the modern world.[1] The pre-scientific context of the New Testament

---

[1]See Rudolf Bultmann, "New Testament and Mythology," *Kerygma and Myth*, 2 vols., ed. Hans Werner Bartsch, trans. Reginald H. Fuller (London: S.P.C.K., 1964) 1:38-44. Bultmann remains the most influential proponent of the mythical interpretation of the

church stands in opposition to the scientific perspective on reality that stamps contemporary life: The creative inventions of modern science have given the industrial world a life-style of automated convenience heretofore unavailable except in dreams. The technological revolution in communication and commerce has reduced the size of the Earth to a neighborhood with constant contact and extensive exchange between one-time distant places. The marvel of modern medicine promises not only longer life but also an enhanced quality of living. These advances in the explosion of human knowledge have effectively negated the pre-scientific world-view of the Gospel traditions—ancient traditions of miracles and exorcisms, the resurrection of the dead, the apocalyptic coming of the Kingdom of God. Therefore, the church must demythologize its Scriptures for the sake of the intelligibility and applicability of the gospel to the modern and/or post-modern world.

In addition, the church must find the courage today to accept the hard truth of human mortality and revise its historic teaching concerning human destiny. Those who die return to the dust of the earth either rapidly through cremation or slowly through decay in the grave. The affirmation of the event of the resurrection of Jesus belongs to a precritical historiography. When taken literally, the resurrection of Jesus inevitably refers in some fashion to a mythical event like the resuscitation of a corpse. The debates about the historicity of Jesus' resurrection, the actuality of the appearances, and the eschatological character of the category of resurrection—these disputes indicate how flimsy the claim of resurrection really is.

---

resurrection of Jesus in the twentieth century. In "New Testament and Mythology" (1941) he characterizes the proclamation of the resurrection of Christ crucified and the expectation of the parousia during the lifetime of his disciples as "a mythical eschatology." The historical claim of the resurrection of Jesus from the dead is utterly inconceivable. "Indeed," he explains, "*faith in the resurrection is really the same things as faith in the saving efficacy of the cross*, faith in the cross as the cross of Christ" (41).

Moreover, he writes: "If the event of Easter Day is in any sense an historical event additional to the cross, it is nothing else than the rise of faith in the risen Lord, since it was this faith which lead to the apostolic preaching. The resurrection itself is not an event of past history. . . . For the historical event of the rise of the Easter faith means for us what it meant for the first disciples—namely, the self-attestation of the risen Lord, the act of God in which the redemptive event of the cross is completed" (42).

Finally, the resurrection narratives of the New Testament are an indispensable element in the life and faith of the church. The stories of the risen Jesus confront us with the unique identity and universal vision of the crucified Nazarene. He is the Son of God who mediates the Presence of God and discloses authentic existence under God. This Christ invites us to meaningful life and community vitality; moreover, he calls us to the work of peace and justice, the liberation and humanization of life for everyone in the world. The crucified Nazarene summons us to a vision of reconciliation in relationships that not only benefits others but nurtures fulfillment among those who accept the message of God's love. The proclamation of the crucified Christ was and remains eloquent testimony to the depth of his identity and the height of his vision. The critical issue is not the problem of an Easter event that points to an alleged future but the integrity of Easter faith in the crucified Christ, which confronts every present.

Conversely, *a historical understanding* of the resurrection of Jesus affirms everything positive in the mythical interpretation but maintains much more. That the resurrection does not belong to a pre-scientific world view but to *a historic Christian world view* is the fundamental difference. This Christian worldview transcends the revolution in world pictures form a pre-scientific to a scientific era as well as the changing world pictures that occur in continuing scientific research.[2] The

---

[2]See Karl Barth, *CD* IV/1: 351-52. Throughout his writing on the theme of *The Doctrine of Reconciliation*, IV/1, Barth says that he found himself "in an intense, although for the most part, quiet debate with Rudolf Bultmann" (ix). Contrary to the dissolution of the Easter event into the rise of Easter faith of the disciples, Barth argues for the objectivity of the resurrection of Jesus as the beginning of the parousia whereby the living Christ stands over against us and addresses us with the Yes of God beyond the No of death. In this Yes and No the living Jesus liberates us from judgment and death for fellowship and peace with God as God's children.

Over against Bultmann's collapse of the resurrection of Christ into the subjectivity of his disciples, Barth she necessary objectivity of the event of the resurrection of the Crucified. "If Jesus Christ is not risen—bodily, visibly, audibly, perceptibly, in the same concrete sense in which he died, as the texts have it—if he is not also risen, then our preaching and our faith are vain and futile; we are still in our sins. . . . If [the apostles] were true witnesses of [Christ's] resurrection, they were witnesses of an event which was like that of the cross in its concrete objectivity" (352). Through the reliability of the apostolic message that the crucified Jesus lives, we are energized with hope for an eschatological future through the promise of God. Barth's protest against Bultmann rests

affirmation of the resurrection of Jesus Christ crucified is not a statement about the disciples' faith but an event that happened to the dead Jesus. God raised this Jesus from the dead. Whether directly available to the historian or not, the resurrection was an eschatological event: Jesus has been transformed into another kind of life, the eternal life of God. Resurrection does not involve a resuscitated corpse, a caricature of the confession of faith in the primitive church. Rather, the possibility of this kind of life presupposes the reality of the living God. If the conception of eternal life belongs to a pre-scientific worldview, the question of the eternity of God becomes as problematic to Christian theology as the question of the resurrection of Jesus. The destiny of Jesus does not require a return to the supernaturalism of a pre-scientific world-view any more than faith in the living God, but a contemporary reformulation of the reality of resurrection must inform the church's understanding of human destiny.

Furthermore, the resurrection of Jesus cannot be abstracted from his execution. The death of Jesus in Godforsakenness negated the vision of God that he had proclaimed, it terminated the dawning of the Kingdom of God, it canceled the offer of eschatological salvation to those who had accepted his message, and it nullified Jesus' claim to authority directly from God. The issue is not a pre-scientific worldview versus a modern scientific worldview but the integrity of the gospel. *If God did not raise the crucified Jesus from the dead*, the verdict of the cross stands: The Nazarene was another Jew who suffered from delusions of grandeur and died therefrom. An appeal to the creativity of the devastated disciples cannot account for the witness of the single resurrection, because neither the content of their heritage nor the teaching of Jesus prepared them for the single resurrection of a crucified Messiah in the ongoing of history. Rather, the rise of the disciples' Easter faith presupposed the foundation of the Easter event, the resurrection of the dead Jesus who subsequently appeared to them.

If Jesus Christ is not risen, an event in *his* history on the other side of the cross, the apostles misrepresented the action of God in their preaching. The earliest proclamation of the apostolic church affirmed nothing less than the resurrection of the crucified Christ from the dead,

on a prior conviction of the happenedness of Jesus' resurrection, a judgment which continues in various forms of theology today.

an actual event sequential to the death and the burial of Jesus. So the church must find the courage in the midst of modernity's skepticism to affirm the hard truth of the resurrection of Jesus and the hope of humanity's destiny in God. That the crucified Jesus is risen, that he in fact does live, constitutes the foundation of the gospel and the faith of the church. Precisely in this hope of the transformation of Jesus from death into life, the church invests itself in the tasks of justice and peace, liberation and humanization, for the transformation of our world in the light of the coming Kingdom of God.

A subjective view versus an objective view, a mythical interpretation over against a historical interpretation—these very different understandings of the resurrection of the crucified Jesus divide the church today. Wherever the conflict and confrontation of these two perspectives on the resurrection of the Christ crucified occur, whatever the exact theological posture of the opposing protagonists, the content of the gospel itself is at stake that inevitably scandalizes the gospel anew. The scandal is unavoidable, because warrants count for and against each view of the resurrection of Christ and the form of hope contained therein.

The purpose of this chapter is to clarify the experience of providence that the vision of resurrection into the Kingdom of God involves. While mindful of the values of the mythical interpretation of the resurrection of Christ, the line of argument that I employ affirms the historical understanding of the resurrection of the crucified Jesus and the eschatological vision that it sustains. For doing eschatology in the context of this essay, an examination of a single resurrection narrative in the Gospel of Matthew is a significant starting point. Though not unaware of other theological perspectives on Christ's resurrection, I offer my own proposal for affirming the resurrection of the crucified Nazarene. After examining arguments and counterarguments for hope of "an eschatological tomorrow," the chapter concludes with the stories of three contemporary witnesses.

The Experience of Providence: *Eternal Life*

What is the experience of providence in the resurrection of Jesus Christ— crucified, dead, and buried? The answer, though fraught with difficulty, is plain: the hope of the resurrection of the dead, the eschatological arrival of the Kingdom of God through Jesus Christ, and the destiny of individual and corporate humanity into the eternal tomorrow of God. The experience of creative newness through the Spirit of life here and now in the suffering and joy of this broken world is an indispensable feature of Christian hope, but the hope for resurrection into eternal life in the Kingdom of God is the ultimate hope of the gospel of Christ. Although the hope for the resurrection of the dead in the eschatological Kingdom of God must be remythologized in the light of the ever expanding scientific knowledge of the universe, the eschatological symbols of the New Testament remain opaque but not without content: the incorporation of the people of God into the life of God through Jesus Christ; individual personhood in ongoing consciousness and communal relationships; the continuing experience of joy in the exercise of authentic freedom, freedom for God.

While the remythologizing of the New Testament symbols of eschatological hope with meaningful metaphors is a profoundly difficult task that theologians have hardly attempted, the Christian vision of an eschatological tomorrow is not ancillary or irrelevant for faith in the God of love revealed in Jesus Christ. Sin, chaos, and Nothingness—does radical evil have the final word beyond the Word of God? Is the Word of God relevant only for life in the face of death? Shrouded in immeasurable suffering and staggering grief, sometimes death without life but sooner or later life with death, will Project Earth end for many, perhaps most as an absurd experiment in failure?

Thousands suddenly dead in a gigantic earthquake; volcanic destruction of a city without escape; islands leveled in a typhoon; a continent decimated by plague: For the stillborn, innumerable victims of infant mortality; for the retarded, life a confusing maze; for the deranged, life a constant nightmare; for the blind, without sight of a smile or sunset; for the deaf, neither music nor laughter ever heard; for the mute, voiceless without words; for the lame, lagging behind and left out; for the sick, never without pain—is this their unfortunate fate? Within the vast process of the evolution of the universe are the victims of chaos a tragic but acceptable loss?

The helpless and hopeless; the self-despising; those who lived only to hate; the stunted, through malnutrition or ignorance; the suicides; the lynchings; the "disappeared"; death row, some innocent but executed; the marginalized in ghettos; the alienated, always outside; the unloved, who know so: For herds of slaves, sometimes encaged in sinking ships; for the hungry masses, for whom food meant everything; for the peasants, the work force of injustice with muzzled shrieks and silent cries; for the crippled and dead in holes of coal; for preventable accidents, the unnecessary dead; for young soldiers killed in wars; for the innocent ones sacrificed to the gods; for the butchered and bloodied in entertainment and sport; for all trapped in killing raids of lust and greed; for the raped, ravaged, and destroyed; for slaughtered children and weeping parents; for helpless babies abandoned to die; for small children dying in ghastly pain; for the millions and millions of the oppressed, destroyed beyond number on the underside of history—is this their bitter fate? Through the ongoing movement of the history of humanity does Nothingness in all its murderous forms sound the Alpha and Omega of the participants[!] in the human story? Does chaos enable the survival of the fittest? Does Nothingness mock those fit to survive?

"In the beginning God created the heavens and the earth. . . . God saw everything that he had made, and indeed, it was very good" (Gen 1:2, 31a). *IT WAS?* . . . The experience of providence for billions of human beings from the beginning of humankind to the end of Earthly time is hope, hope recognized or unrecognized, known or unknown, hope for the *Abba* God of Jesus, hope for resurrection in the coming Home-Coming of God—hope in the Holy Other who creates out of nothing, the Holy Other who gives life to the dead, the Holy Other who is self-giving love.

An Unusual Resurrection Narrative

The Gospel of Matthew tells us that Mary Magdalene and the other Mary watched the hurried burial of Jesus in the tomb of Joseph of Arimathea before the Sabbath began. When they returned to the tomb of Jesus in the dawn of Sunday morning to complete burial preparations left undone, the stone had been rolled back from the door of the tomb and an angel of God said to the women:

> Do not be afraid; I know that you are looking for Jesus who was crucified. He is not here; for he has been raised, as he said. Come, see

the place where he lay. Then go quickly and tell his disciples, "He has been raised from the dead, and indeed, he is going ahead of you to Galilee; there you will see him." This is my message for you (28:5-7).

The women ran in fear and joy to tell the disciples, but the risen Jesus met them and said, "Do not be afraid; go and tell my brothers to go to Galilee; there they will see me" (28:10).

When the women told the disciples what they had seen and what the disciples should do, the eleven disciples went to Galilee to the mountain where Jesus had sent them (28:16). What follows is one of the most surprising scenes in the entire New Testament: "When they saw him, they worshiped him; but some doubted" (28:17). What do they doubt? And why? The obvious answer is "the reality of Jesus' resurrection." That is too obvious, for there is a prior question. The initial murmurings began long before the plunge of doubt into despair during Passover with Jesus' execution in Jerusalem. Could the Christ of God be crucified? Could the Savior of his people not save himself? Could the dawning Kingdom of God have been an illusion? The first doubt, the initial stumbling block, was the execution of the Nazarene for blasphemy and insurrection on a cursed Roman cross. The Jesus movement began in the sunshine in Galilee but ended in the darkness of Golgotha. From that point onward, the disciples could only say, "We had thought, . . ." nothing else. This Jesus, this crucified Christ, has been raised from the dead? The assertion is incredulous! Whether Enlightenment or post-Enlightenment, modern or post-modern, the idea itself remains dubious. The resurrection of a Godforsaken "King of the Jews"? The cross is always a scandal, at least the cross of Jesus of Nazareth through whom the Kingdom of God came near. And the resurrection of the scandalous Preacher of good news cannot be abstracted from the cross of the Godforsaken Christ.

Matthew narrates the story of the resurrection of the crucified Jesus from the point of his death forward. Immediately after Jesus' death cry, Matthew affirms the resurrection of Jesus from the dead. . . . In an astonishing theologomenon Matthew connects Jesus' resurrection from the dead with the future resurrection of the dead . . . . Matthew reports the observation of the two Marys beyond the cross to Jesus' entombment by Joseph of Arimathea. . . . Matthew describes the women's return to the tomb on the first day of the week, an empty tomb interpreted for them through an angelic vision. . . . As they carried the word of resurrection

to the disciples, Matthew recounts the sudden appearance of the risen
Jesus to them. . . . Matthew knows the women's faithfulness in carrying
the instructions of Jesus to his disciples. . . . Matthew relates the positive
response of the disciples in going to the mountain in Galilee where Jesus
had directed them. . . . "When they saw him, they worshiped
him . . . but . . . some doubted[!]" After all these events in Matthew's
resurrection narrative, why does Matthew include the phrase, "some
doubted"? That "some doubted" in the worship of the risen Jesus simply
does not fit. It suggests ambivalence. It communicates an element of
uncertainty. It lacks the sound of unquestionable "good news."[3]

---

[3]The way the risen Jesus responded in doubt or the hesitancy of faith in Matthew on
the one side and Luke and John on the other is quite different. In Luke 24 Jesus suddenly
appears to the disciples in Jerusalem, and "They were startled and terrified, and thought
they were seeing a ghost" (24:37), despite the testimony of the women at the empty tomb,
an appearance to Peter, and the conversation of the two disciples on the way to Emmaus
with Jesus incognito. . . . Touch me and see; for a ghost does not have flesh and bones
as you see I have" (24:39). Though still disbelieving, Jesus asked if they had anything to
eat: "They gave him a piece of broiled fish, and he took it and ate it in their presence"
(24:42-43). Only after direct response to their doubt did Jesus teach them from the
Scriptures about himself. The anti-Gnostic polemic in Luke's narrative accentuates the
continuity of the historical Jesus with the crucified but risen Jesus, evidenced in the
reference to his "flesh and bones" and eating "a piece of broiled fish." Conversely, Paul's
anti-Gnostic polemic in 1 Corinthians 15:35-37 accentuates the discontinuity of one's
physical body with one's spiritual body (15:44): "flesh and blood cannot inherit the
Kingdom of God, nor does the perishable inherit the imperishable" (15:50b). "For this
perishable body must put on imperishability, and this mortal body must put on
immortality" (50:53). The common point of reference for Luke and Paul is the continuity
of personal identity.
    In John 20:19b-20 Jesus came to the fearful disciples in hiding and said: "Peace be
with you." Subsequently he showed them his hands and side, and "they rejoiced when
they saw the Lord." However, Thomas was not with them, did not believe them, and said:
"Unless I see the mark of the nails in his hands, and put my finger in the mark of the
nails and my hand in his side, I will not believe" (20:25). The next Sunday Jesus came
to them with the same greeting of peace. Since Thomas had specified what he would have
to do before he could believe, Jesus said to him: "Put your finger here and see my hands.
Reach out your hand and put it in my side. Do not doubt but believe" (20:27). Thomas
responded with the most exalted confession of faith in the New Testament: "My Lord and
my God!" (20:28).
    In Matthew 28 the situation is different, because "some doubted" does not mean
unbelief but nonetheless genuine and honest hesitancy, that is, doubting. The risen Jesus
makes neither direct nor indirect response to their doubting. "They worshiped him, but

The Eleven heard the instruction of the risen Jesus from the women. They went to the mountain in Galilee, faithful and obedient. The risen Christ appeared to them, just as he had promised. But "some doubted"? How could they be faithful to the instruction of Jesus, experience the faithfulness of Christ Jesus to them, and still doubt? Matthew says: "When they saw him, *they* worshiped him, but *some* doubted." Does Matthew mean: "*Some* worshiped him, and *others* doubted"? No. Does he mean: "*They* worshiped him, but *they all* doubted *some*"? No. Does Matthew mean: "*They* worshiped him, but *some* did not worship because *they* doubted"? No. Since they had followed the instruction of "the women" to meet the risen Christ in Galilee and Christ did indeed meet them, how could it happen: "They worshiped him, but some doubted"?

The truth is surprising and startling. Authentic faith does not exclude honest doubt. Though doubt in and of itself is not a virtue, certainly not "a badge of courage," doubt can have an eminently positive dimension. Doubt does not mean unbelief but belief with hesitancy, the hesitancy of uncertainty, the hesitancy of questions, troublesome and perhaps profound questions. Doubt can identify the places where valid questions dwell. There is a stewardship of doubt: Faith translates doubt into intelligible questions, and the questions housed in doubt can be crucial for the integrity of faith. Those who hear the Great Commission of the living Christ must be sensitive to the questions of people outside and inside the church, questions among others *and* within themselves. Doubt can reflect the questions that trouble people who worship and doubt as well as the questions of those who do not worship because of their inability to get beyond the questions housed in doubt, doubt so pervasive to make the worship of God unconscionable or simply irrelevant. Doubt is not unbelief, but the severity of doubt can verge on the inability to believe.

What are the critical questions housed in shadows of doubt that make the affirmation of Christ's resurrection from the dead haunt us today? The questions are multiple and interrelated, yet singular and independent.

Does God exist?

---

some doubted" remains unaddressed. Why? The Great Commission from Christ and the Presence of Christ with those on mission does not require the answer to all questions and the elimination of corresponding doubt. Unlike Luke and John, Matthew leaves the question mark in the text. Narrative exegesis requires us to do the same.

Is God as good as Jesus said God is?
Does God know my name and intend joy for my life?
Does God help? How?
Does God suffer with us?
Does the arc of the universe bend toward justice?
Is there life after death?
Do I matter?

And the contextual question that stimulates, aggravates, and perpetuates all these questions, and more: Why suffering?

These questions are admittedly questions of modernity, but they are not simply superimposed on the biblical text but converge with questions within the gospel traditions. The most obvious intersection is the question of life after death, which converges with the debate between the Pharisees and the Sadducees concerning the resurrection of the dead, a debate wherein Jesus confirmed the perspective of the Pharisees (Matt 22:23-32). Significant connections between all these questions and queries in the Gospel traditions are embedded in the teaching of Jesus. These questions endure because we are summoned to trust in God in the face of incalculable suffering and senseless death, under the threat of mundane existence and often a fearful loneliness. We live in a world of sometime remarkable beauty and bright sunshine, but simultaneously a world shrouded in the gray shadows of suffering and death. Before and after worship, sometimes in the midst of worship, the questions assert themselves and require acknowledgement. These are the questions, at least some of them, with which we live, and they trouble us enough to require some ongoing response.

Are the questions larger than the answers? The recurring question is the unrelenting question, "Why?" Why radical evil? Why do the righteous suffer? Why do little children die? Why do marriages fail? Why do families fester in pain? Why do the aged sometimes hang in between life and death? Why does God do so little, so little or nothing? Why are there so many of these "Whys?" Are these questions quickly answered through reference to the Scriptures in the life of the church? Or do these questions leave us frustrated and discontent, because our best answers from the Scripture and church tradition contain elements that are elusive and ambiguous? Are the answers distant, but the questions near? Put differently, are the questions larger than the answers? At one time I would have answered, "Yes." Now I understand the relationship of questions and answers differently. The questions are not larger than our answers, but our answers are more fragile. The questions and answers are marked with mystery, but the answers are drenched with a mystery of a different kind. Hope. Resurrection. God.

The story of the resurrection of Jesus nurtures a vision of providence for all the people of God in an eternal tomorrow. The New Testament continually connects the resurrection of the crucified Christ with the life of the people of God in the future of the Kingdom of God. The Gospels provide energy and testimony for us to gain confidence in life today and to hope in the promise of God's eschatological tomorrow. The goal of providence is the future action of God in resurrection and new creation, wherein the God of Jesus Christ crucified will transform the present structures of creation into the everlasting Kingdom of God. As we journey in faith, the ongoing experience of the guidance and watchcare of God, whether slight or bright, nudges and nurtures the vitality of this hope and the integrity of this vision—not only for ourselves, for the moment survivors, but also for those for whom we mourn, victims known and unknown, almost everyone gone and forgotten. With gratitude to God for the gift of life, providence ultimately takes the form of hope, of eschatological hope for the future of God. Yes, they did see him on this side of the other side of death, and they did worship him . . . BUT . . . "some doubted," the hesitancy of legitimate but not unanswerable questions.

Through this final scene, the Gospel of Matthew incorporates its readers into the story. On the one side, the Eleven went to the mountain in Galilee where Jesus had directed them. "When they saw him, they worshiped him; but some doubted" (28:17). On the other side, the risen Jesus came to them and said, "All authority in heaven and on earth has been given to me. Go therefore and make disciples of all nations baptizing them . . . and teaching them. . . . And remember, I am with you always . . ." (28: 18-20). The juxtaposition of the doubting disciples with the promise of Jesus' Presence creates narrative space for all of us, faithing and doubting, believing and questioning; and the God who has come to us in the crucified but risen Jesus assures us of the provision of Presence in the joy and sometime uncertainty of the journey of discipleship.

The Convictions of a Theologian

The arrest, condemnation, and execution of Jesus devastated the Eleven. They could not continue to follow Jesus as his disciples. On the contrary, he had been condemned to death in the Name of YHWH, and subsequently executed as a blasphemer against God and a renegade from Galilee. Who could have anticipated the mockery of the title on his cross: "The King of the Jews." The former disciples fled to Galilee in the desolation of disappointment and in fear for their lives, with nothing in their memory or hope to sustain them in what might have been.[4] They did

---

[4]The devastation of the disciples is fundamental to Wolfhart Pannenberg, *Jesus-God and Man* (Philadelphia: The Westminster Press, 1968) 92-97, but esp. 96: The death of Jesus exposed "his disciples to the most severe stress. One could hardly expect the production of confirmatory experiences from the faith of the disciples that stood under such a burden." Because Jesus anticipated the imminent end of the world and the arrival of the Kingdom of God (fulfilled *in principle* in his singular resurrection from the dead), "the faith of the disciples could not have survived the crisis of Jesus' death." He says: "The Easter appearances are not to be explained from the Easter faith of the disciples; rather, conversely, the Easter faith of the disciples is to be explained from the appearances."

Cf. Jürgen Moltmann, *The Way of Jesus Christ: Christology in Messianic Dimensions* (New York: HarperCollins, 1990) 215-45, esp. 217. Moltmann argues that the disciples fled Jerusalem for Galilee out of immeasurable disappointment and in fear for their lives. They returned home, "giving up discipleship." They are subsequently called back to Jerusalem after the unexpected appearances of Jesus. Moltmann concludes: "The verdict of the disciples about Jesus' resurrection is not a reflective verdict of their faith. It is a reality judgment about Jesus' fate: he has in very truth been raised" (235).

Conversely, Edward Schillebeeckx, *Jesus—An Experiment in Christology* (London: Collins, 1979) 310-11, thinks that Jesus prepared his disciples for a renewal of their faith after the initial shock of his death through the cup of fellowship at the Last Supper, because he intended for them to know that "fellowship with Jesus is stronger than death." Elsewhere he adds that the disciples' conversion experiences happened prior to any appearances and the story of the empty tomb. The disciples had failed, but they had not lost their faith, only thrown off balance. Since Jesus renewed for them the offer of salvation after his death—indeed, he had provided a foundation for them to do so—they experienced the forgiveness of Jesus, which means Jesus must be alive: "A dead man does not proffer forgiveness" of their sins[!] (391, in the context of 380-97). All expressions of their conversion experience, e.g. the appearances, are the faith-motivated experiences of the disciples (644-52 are especially important, because Schillebeeckx wants to distance himself from Rudolf Bultmann and Willi Marxsen, who equate resurrection with the rise of Easter faith). Nevertheless, Schillebeeckx does sound very similar to the

not experience a temporary lapse of faith. The faith of these onetime disciples was as dead as the crucified Jesus, and the resources to think and do otherwise were completely unavailable to them.

The Risen Jesus Appeared

In Galilee Jesus appeared to his disciples. Were they frightened? Did their voices ring with laughter? Could they believe what they were seeing? Jesus, the very same Jesus who had been rejected by God and killed by men, now appeared to them—once dead, but not now, he lived. He was who he had been, but he was more than ever before. Jesus had been raised from the dead. He is risen. Jesus himself is alive in the glory of God.

Did they stammer among themselves in the Presence of the Crucified? Did each see and hear what each other saw and heard? Did they understand what his appearing and commissioning meant—for him, for who he is now; for them, for who they are now? Only one word could describe the coming of Jesus to them from the dead: "resurrection." Only one explanation could capture the identity of this Jesus coming to them from the dead: "Lord and Christ." The identity of Jesus communicated through his Presence, the Presence of Jesus mediated through his identity, these are two aspects of a single reality: The crucified, dead, and buried Nazarene now confronted them as the living One, the dead Jesus but a Jesus not dead, the risen Jesus, the Christ of God, the Lord Jesus Christ.

They could never think of him the same way again, because they would never be the same again. The Kingdom of God would no longer be essentially a hope they shared with him, and without him no hope at all, because now they could see: They glimpsed unforgettably the Kingdom of God in him and through him, now and forever. Jesus had embodied the Kingdom of God yet to come, and the resurrection of Jesus from the dead established the fulfillment in advance of his proclamation of the imminence of the Kingdom of God. The resurrection of Jesus is the *prolepsis* of the eschaton, a proleptic eschatological event that

---

post-Bultmannians, especially with his explanation of all Easter "events" as faith-motivated experiences.

discloses the ultimate goal of history and its fulfillment in the future of God.[5]

The characterization of the destiny of Jesus with the word "resurrection" constituted a radical revision of the disciples' heritage that their experience required them to make, theologically unsophisticated though they might be. The tradition and the hope of the *resurrection of the dead* at the *end* of history in the apocalypse of God had to be reconceived in the light of the *resurrection of Jesus from the dead* in the *ongoing* of history. What had already happened in and to Jesus demanded a reconceptualization of what would happen in the definition of the future of God.

The implications of the resurrection of the Christ crucified proved staggering. The vision of God and the Name for God that Jesus had taught them included and transcended the history of God with Israel: God is God, the *Abba* God, YHWH coming *Abba* near, *Abba*/YHWH, the God of all. God had reversed the judgment of the judges against the judged. Jesus had been executed innocent instead of guilty and lives anew[!] with compassion instead of condemnation. The compassion of God embraced not only the sympathizers but also the adversaries of Jesus, some who had opposed him as a matter of conscience, others as a threat to their position and power. They included simultaneously the high priest and rulers of the people as well as Pilate and the legions of Rome. Whatever might happen in the immediate future, the God of the Lord Jesus Christ is the future of the world.

Unimaginable? As unimaginable as a Nazarene from Galilee of the Gentiles doing and redoing the hope of his people for the coming of the Messiah. As unimaginable as lepers and demoniacs, harlots and tax collectors, the Somebodies and the Nobodies feeling cleansed clear through, a heart warming Presence of wholeness never to be forgotten. As unimaginable as the *Abba* God naming any and all wayward ones, "My Beloved Child," available to each one individually and to everyone

---

[5]The prolepsis of the eschaton in the proclamation and singular resurrection of Jesus has been central to the theologizing of Wolfhart Pannenberg, e.g., "Dogmatic Theses on the Doctrine of Revelation," *Revelation as History* (New York: The Macmillan Company, 1968; German, 1961) 125-58. Note also *Basic Questions in Theology: Collected Essays* (Philadelphia: Fortress Press, 1970– 1971; German, 1967), but the essays date from 1959.

simultaneously. The resurrection of the crucified Jesus is as unimaginable as the naivete of a childhood song, "God is love. . . ."

The coming One has come, who mediates the Presence of the eternal One, who comes to dwell with us through the Other One, and the One always on the horizon of the future, the One who will come, this One meets us going into the Darkness before the daybreak of morning Light. *Darkness*: In the midst of radical evil and ghastly suffering in this world, Darkness identifies the continuing threat of meaninglessness, despair, and dread on the one side, the sociopolitical oppression and violent repression of the impoverished masses on the other. The resurrection of Jesus is more than the reversal of the verdict of condemnation in his execution on the cross. Rather, the cross of Christ continues to qualify the resurrection of Christ in the darkness and death of a world-forsaking-God, transforming the future coming of eschatological fulfillment into an arriving present of new life through love. Although the Presence of God in the world cannot be reduced to the singular mode of "suffering Presence," the suffering of God in the death of Christ is the form of the Kingdom of God in the alienation and desolation of the world, and the crucified Nazarene incarnates the living Word of God in the midst of suffering humanity.[6]

The Tradition of the Appearances

The Apostle Paul addressed the death, burial, and resurrection of Christ in 1 Corinthians 15:3-8. Since Jesus died a public death, indisputably so, the liturgical tradition of the Jerusalem church that Paul used does not refer to any witnesses to his execution and burial, though these events are integral to the tradition. Rather, the early litany on the way to tradition concentrates on those persons to whom the risen Jesus appeared. Paul does not specify when or where the appearances occurred, because the tradition focuses only on those to whom Jesus manifested himself. Thus Paul transmitted to the church at Corinth an already existing tradition of the appearances, which he received from the church in Jerusalem about six years after Jesus' death and some three years after the appearance to

---

[6]Jürgen Moltmann, *The Crucified God* (New York: Harper and Row, 1974) 185.

Paul himself, more than a decade before his letters to the Corinthian church.[7]

Beyond a specific time frame within which the appearance took place—the symbol of "the forty days" before the Day of Pentecost after the death and resurrection of Jesus—the Jerusalem church formulated a litany of appearances into recognizable elements of tradition. The litany informed the liturgical celebration of the worshiping life of the church long before Paul's conversion. "Last of all, as to one untimely born, he appeared also to me" (1 Cor 15:8). Though the tradition is quite early, the geography of the appearances goes unaddressed, whether Galilee (Matthew and Mark) or Jerusalem (Luke and John). Sequence is not a decisive issue, but the appearances to Peter and the Twelve (1 Cor 15:5) are likely the first, and the appearance to Paul unquestionably the last, far beyond the time frame of the other appearances. Furthermore, Paul did not mention the empty tomb, though he almost certainly knew of it before his conversion, because the tradition of the empty tomb would be presupposed in the Jerusalem church giving witness to a crucified Christ, dead and buried, but now allegedly alive. The authorities in Jerusalem did not contest the claim of an empty tomb but the explanation for it: "The disciples stole the body of Jesus."[8]

---

[7]Raymond Brown, *The Virginal Conception and Bodily Resurrection of Jesus* (New York: Paulist Press, 1973) 81-96, offers an excellent summary of scholarly opinion on the formulation of the tradition but expresses his preference for a pre-Pauline tradition, 81-83, esp. n. 141. See especially Reginald H. Fuller, *The Formation of the Resurrection Narratives* (New York: The Macmillan Co., 1971).

[8]That the tomb was empty is seldom disputed, but whether or not it indicated the resurrection of Jesus prior to the disciples return from Galilee—on the basis of the appearances—is an issue of debate. Are the angelic witnesses a literary solution of the problem for the authors of the Synoptic Gospels? Or, are "the women" recipients of appearances apart from the Eleven a better solution for the Synoptics and John? See Moltmann, *The Way of Jesus Christ*, 217, 219. However, Schillebeeckx, *Jesus*, interprets the story of the empty tomb as a negative symbol of the mystery of Jesus' resurrection in the cultic celebration of the Jerusalem church, but: Is it the tradition of an "empty tomb" or "the holy tomb"? (334-37, and 703, n. 32).

From a different angle entirely, Eduard Schweizer, *The Good News According to Matthew*, trans. David E. Green (Atlanta: John Knox Press, 1975) 515-16, 519-36, affirms the empty tomb but criticizes its significance in the Matthean community: Because "the resurrection cannot be proved or disproved" (526), the response of the Christian community of Matthew to the untenable charge that the disciples had stolen the body was

The appearances of the risen Jesus did not occur through the new insight, the transformed memory, or the grace of forgiveness of the disciples. They lacked any resources within themselves for the stimulation of such experiences. The hope of yesterday for the dream of tomorrow hung dead. Then Jesus appeared to them, that is, the appearances of the risen Jesus happened to them. The initiative of the appearances could not and did not originate with these devastated disciples. Jesus appeared to them, a revelatory "seeing" of the resurrected Christ within the glory of God, hence, anticipatory eschatological visions wherein Christ called them to mission—"a revelatory seeing," "within the glory of God," "anticipatory visions." But . . . they *recognized* him, once crucified, marked forever with his trust in and obedience to God, the God who went through death for the sake of life, the life of humanity-forsaking-God.

Perhaps the major surprise in the litany of appearances is the name of James (15:7a), the brother of the Lord (Gal 1:19). Nothing is said of James in any of the Gospels. Though much earlier than the appearance to Paul, James experienced an appearance and turned into a post-resurrection convert. Did the appearances of the risen Jesus make it impossible for the recipients not to believe? No, because an-appearance-mandated-belief would be coercion. Either the appearances happened only to those who were open in some significant fashion to believe, or the initiative toward appearances happened to some who did not believe and whose aborted experience remained hapless and unavailable.[9]

"arrogant"—"its self-righteousness in assuming that the resurrection was an obvious historical fact, which only the malevolent could deny—its assumption in other words, that unbelief was merely willful refusal to accept what was secretly believed to be true. . . . Nonetheless, we can also see that through [the community's] words there speaks an unshakable faith, for which the resurrection of Jesus is so clearly the basis of all joy, of all life and death, that it can no longer even imagine harboring doubts." Schweizer concludes: "Perhaps this shows that *a faith* that is too unshakable, unfamiliar with any sense of doubt, is in particular danger of giving *false explanations*, thus *losing those* who are closest to having faith (25:31-46!)" (527).

[9]Note Jürgen Moltmann, *The Way of Jesus Christ*, 226, where he says: "The people to whom Christ 'appeared' were so overwhelmed that they apparently had no choice."[!] Again, "Whereas the seeing of Christ allowed those involved no freedom of choice, the word of proclamation brings men and women face to face with the decision of faith. Faith of this kind . . . is possible only when Christ's appearances cease." Earlier Moltmann says of the "inner" experience of Paul (Gal 1:15f.): "He experienced this manifestation contrary to all expectation and *against his will*" (216) [italics added].

The narrative realism of Acts 9 in recounting Paul's experience is astonishing but not coercive: an appearance of blinding light, the self-identification of Jesus, the charge of wrongheaded persecution, instructions to wait in the city. Paul could have thought himself seriously ill, and for good reason—blinding light, falling down, hearing voices. He had vigorously persecuted those on the Way, he could not forget their faces, and he remembered their testimonies. He had been too relentless in persecution, too tired to continue, too close to it all, thus, an understandable breakdown. Paul's question nonetheless indicated his awareness of and openness to Someone else, a personal encounter prompting the question: "Who are you, Lord?" (Acts 9:5a).

The Logic of Tradition

The tradition of the appearances in 1 Corinthians 15 presupposed the resurrection of Jesus, who had been killed but whom God had raised from the dead. The New Testament excludes any witness to the event of the resurrection itself: WHO or WHAT could be available to the act of creation?[10] All those in the litany of appearances knew Jesus of Nazareth to be dead, but now in these manifestations they knew him to be alive. All those to whom Christ appeared could know only through an inference that God had raised the Crucified from the dead. The integrity of every appearance rested on an inference, an inevitable transition on the basis of the acceptance of the immediate givenness of the Other. Indeed, such openness to another is necessary for any authentic personal encounter. Can we move behind the witnesses to the appearances of Jesus, executed but now exalted? Only to the extent that the witnesses themselves permit. An enduring feature of all the appearances, those named without description and those described with stammering, is the recognition of Jesus—except Paul to whom Jesus identified himself. The question behind the question is in some sense unavoidable: Is the resurrection an historical event?

The claim of the facticity of the event of the resurrection of Jesus confronts us as an historical assertion: Either the resurrection happened,

---

[10]It is infantile to think a human witness or some kind of recording device could have "seen" the resurrection of Jesus. Neither could have survived such an eschatological act of creation.

or it did not happen. Yet the acceptance as well as the rejection of the claim of the resurrection of the Crucified is ultimately historical and eschatological. Whether positive or negative, *any response* to the claim of Jesus' resurrection includes a network of beliefs within which the Yes or No occurs: the existence of the kind of God that the New Testament discloses; the integral relationship of the hope for the resurrection of the dead with the coming of the Kingdom of God; the unique significance of human beings to God, a theological rather than an anthropological valuation; the intelligibility of the concept of resurrection in reflection and imagination, conversation, and debate. Other factors pertain, but these are enough to clarify the historical/eschatological character of the Yes or No to the assertion of the historicity, the eventness, the happenedness of the resurrection of Jesus.[11]

---

[11]Pannenberg's characterization of the resurrection of Jesus in a very precise sense to be an historical event is well known, and I readily concede to him that it does take the form of an historical claim. Panneberg argues: The Apostle Paul traced the emergence of primitive Christianity back to the appearances of the resurrected Jesus in 1 Corinthians 15:1-8, which presupposed the event of the resurrection of the crucified Jesus. If the most rigorous examination of the tradition proves intelligible only in the light of the eschatological hope of the resurrection of the dead, the instance so designated—the resurrection of the dead Jesus—constitutes a historical event regardless of our lack of additional knowledge about it. "Then an event that is expressible only in the language of eschatological expectation is to be asserted as a historical occurrence" (*Jesus—God and Man*, 98).

   Pannenberg's affirmation of the historicity of Jesus' resurrection has generated considerable debate, which includes many who dispute Pannenberg claim but who believe the resurrection of Jesus actually happened. Does he claim too much? Bultmann's rejoinder to Barth illuminates the specific context within which Pannenberg makes his point: "The Problem of Hermeneutics," *New Testament and Mythology*, trans. Schubert M. Ogden (Philadelphia: Fortress Press, 1984). Bultmann says: "[Barth] grants my claim that the resurrection of Jesus is not a historical fact that could be established as such by means of the science of history," but he does not think that the inaccessibility of the resurrection to the historian mean "that the resurrection did not occur." Barth asks: "Is it true that an event alleged to have happened in time can be accepted as historical only if it can be proved to be a 'historical fact' in Bultmann's sense," i.e., open to the verification of the methods and presuppositions of modern historical scholarship? The resurrection of Jesus and his appearances belong to a history that happened, but Barth insists: "We may well accept as history that which good taste prevents us from calling 'historical fact,' and which the modern historian will call 'saga' or 'legend' on the ground that it is beyond the reach of his methods, to say nothing of his avowed assumptions"

The claim of Jesus' resurrection does qualify as a historical claim: *who*, Jesus of Nazareth; *where*, outside Jerusalem; *when*, ca. 30 C.E.; *what*, the enlivening of the crucified Jesus who appeared to his disciples in eschatological glory. The response to the claim of the resurrection of the dead Jesus is historical and eschatological, historical insofar as it encompasses the appearances of the living Jesus to his disciples and the women's discovery of the empty tomb. Yet the historical character of the knowledge of the resurrection of Jesus depends upon the credibility of these witnesses to the appearances of the risen Jesus in the context of the intelligibility of the history of tradition within which they lived.

Of course, the rejection of the claim of Jesus' resurrection can sound very much like a negative historical judgment, because the other factors can be "historically" neutralized through the demythologization of the kerygma of the primitive church. A program of demythologizing provides a supplementary explanation within historical causation without recourse to the transcendent action of God with reference to Jesus himself. The essential presupposition is: There must be some other explanation for the claim of resurrection, because someone who actually dies remains dead, ceasing to be.

Another line of inquiry attempts to shift the argument away from an historical inquiry to the use of a scriptural formula: Does 1 Corinthians 15:4, "that Christ was raised on the third day in accordance with the Scriptures, and that he appeared," move us beyond the historical question to a theological affirmation that has existential roots in a scriptural formula? The tradition of a three-day pattern, that is, "after three days" or "on the third day," seems to be an established Old Testament formula that occurs in the passion predictions and in the resurrection narratives of the Gospels. One could argue that the Jewish perspective is critical here, because the third day is the decisive day. Since suffering and death

---

(*CD* III/2, 446). Bultmann asks what Barth understands by "history" "happened"? "What kind of event is it of which one can say that 'it far more certainly really happened in time than all things that the historians as such can establish'?" (*New Testament and Mythodology*, 89 [*CD* III/2, 446, ET]). Bultmann accuses Barth of a *sacrificium intelletus* and "arbitrary assertions." Barth's conclusion is representative of his life-long perspective: "There are good grounds for supposing that the history of the resurrection of Jesus is a pre-eminent instance of such an event" [beyond historical verification] (446). Over against Bultmann but unlike Barth, Pannenberg poses a *historical answer* to the *historical question* about the resurrection of Jesus.

through the forces of evil cannot be sustained indefinitely, the scriptural formula of "the third day" marks the limit of the powers of evil and the triumph of the power of God (Hos 6:2). The combination of "the third day" and "in accordance with the Scriptures" signals the unique significance of the resurrection of Christ as the definitive eschatological event of salvation, "the great turning-point of all times, in accordance with God's plan of salvation ('according to the Scriptures')."[12]

Although this line of reasoning is appealing, the structure of Paul's argument does not turn on use of the scriptural formula but on the truthfulness of the tradition of the appearances, the "witnesses" to whom the crucified Jesus appeared. The scriptural formula is an interpretive device with reference to the meaning of Jesus' execution and his resurrection, yet neither the event of the cross nor the reality of the resurrection depend on a scriptural formula for their concrete actuality but for their interpretive significance in the context of the history of tradition. Paul appealed, therefore, to the witnesses of the appearances of the murdered but risen Jesus. Indeed, the reference to "the third day" may have originated with the discovery of the empty tomb. The scriptural formula of "the third day," therefore, "fits" the sequence of events and subsequently served the theological concerns of the Jerusalem church.

---

[12]Schillebeeckx, *Jesus*, 531. The scriptural formula is critical to Schillebeeckx's interpretation of the resurrection of Christ (526-32), because it shifts the issue from a historical framework to a literary frame of reference: "The third day" is always in God's hands." Actually he acknowledges his interpretation of the appearances in 1 Corinthians 15 "constitutes a break with a centuries-old hermeneutical tradition" (710, n. 119). However, he charges: "Only we suffer from the crude and naive realism of what 'appearances of Jesus' came to be in the later tradition, through unfamiliarity with the distinctive character of the Jewish-biblical way of speaking" (346). But his charge is unfounded. Essentially he thinks that our knowledge of Jesus' resurrection is not very different for us than it was for the initial disciples. Since he is convinced that all expressions of Jesus' resurrection originate in a faith-motivated experience—especially the appearances of the risen Jesus—Schillebeeckx can conclude: "So for all Christians the affirmation of their belief that God has raised Jesus from the dead may fairly describe an immediate experience of reality, and not a secondary interpretation . . ." (647). Is "a secondary interpretation" really the issue? For a more extensive analysis and critique, see E. Frank Tupper, "Theology, Christology, and Eschatology," *Perspectives on Scripture and Tradition: Essays in Honor of Dale Moody*, ed. Robert L. Perkins (Macon: Mercer University Press, 1987) 114-23.

To whom did Paul address his exposition of the resurrection of Christ from the dead? Corinthian Christians who did not affirm the actual resurrection of the crucified Christ. On the one side, some substituted contemporary ecstatic experiences for any kind of future promise of resurrection. On the other side, some considered the resurrection of the dead unintelligible, posing questions about bodily resurrection over against the immortality of the soul, questions they thought unanswerable. Against the "charismatics" who equated the ecstasy of glossolalia with resurrection life, Paul argued for the facticity of the resurrection of Christ to be essential for the very possibility of an experience with God, from the forgiveness of sin to the gifts of the Spirit. Against the "rationalists" who denigrated the resurrection of the "body," Paul argued for the appropriate bodily form for all the different kinds of life God had created, an argument that undergirds the promise of God for the transformation of this perishable body into an imperishable body: As the resurrection of the dead Jesus disclosed, the living God can preserve the identity of a person beyond the dissolution of death through resurrection into eternal life. These Corinthian distortions required Paul to clarify Christian eschatological hope on the basis of the reality of the resurrection of the crucified Jesus, all scriptural formulas notwithstanding.

The reference to the Scriptures in the history of traditions would hardly have the same significance for the church at Corinth as for the church in Jerusalem, where Paul learned the tradition that he preached in Corinth and of which he reminded them now. The Jerusalem church would have had the elements of a litany of resurrection appearances within a year[!] after Jesus' death, but probably much less. Yet the accounts of the appearances would be even older and undoubtedly carefully screened. Since the community of faith in Jerusalem confessed a crucified Nazarene to be the Messiah from God, the testimony of these witnesses interpreted through the Scriptures had to shoulder the weight of the church's claim in Jerusalem. The threat to the church's proclamation of the resurrection of the crucified Jesus required vivid testimony that would be subjected to the most intense scrutiny and interrogation. So Paul made his case to the Corinthian church almost entirely on the historical witness of those to whom the risen Christ appeared.

1 Corinthians 15 and the Gospels

Why did Paul not mention any women in 1 Corinthians 15 among the persons to whom the risen Jesus appeared? The question seems simple enough, but it is not. The question is all the more difficult because the tradition that Paul had transmitted was a tradition that he had received much earlier from the Jerusalem church. One response to the question focuses on the initial independence of the earliest tradition of appearances, 1 Corinthians 15:3-8, from the earliest tradition of the empty tomb, Mark 16:1-8. The subsequent integration of these two traditions in the narrative endings of the Gospels proves so diffuse and legendary that they lack credibility in the endeavor to affirm the historicity of the resurrection of Jesus. The Eleven experienced appearances in Galilee, and the women in Jerusalem discovered the empty tomb.[13] Contrary to its intention, however, this approach does not necessarily strengthen the truth claim of 1 Corinthians 15 and Mark 16 but can heighten skepticism

---

[13]See Pannenberg, *Jesus*, 88-106. Since the Gospel of Mark ends with the discovery of the empty tomb but without any resurrection appearances, some scholars suggest that the narrative ending of the Gospel has been lost. Donald H. Juel, *A Master of Surprise: Mark Interpreted* (Minneapolis: Fortress Press, 1994) 107-21, presents a significant but subtle argument for the integrity of Mark's concluding narrative. The women who returned to the tomb to complete the anointing of Jesus' body for burial experienced a great surprise. The stone-door of the tomb had been rolled back, and a messenger of God made a declaration and promise. *Declaration*: "You are looking for Jesus of Nazareth who was crucified. He has been raised; he is not here. Look, there is the place they laid him" (16:6). *Promise*: "But go, tell his disciples and Peter that he is going ahead of you to Galilee; there you will see him, just *as he told you*" (16:8). The woman fled in amazement and terror, "and they said nothing to anyone, for they were afraid" (16:8). The story of Jesus in Mark qualifies as good news, because the readers can believe what Jesus "told you." Someone does tell the story, though the women fail in the task of testimony. The key is the open tomb, the stone rolled away. Beyond his critique of the interpretation of Frank Kermode, Donald H. Juel is eloquent: "*Jesus is out, on the loose, on the same side of the door as the women and the readers.*" The words of the angel move the reader beyond the confines of the narrative: "There you will see him, as he told you." The future contains great promise. "The doors in Mark's Gospel are emphatically open: The curtain of the Temple is rent asunder. . . . and the stone is rolled back from the tomb. There is surely disappointment as the women flee. . . . But Jesus is out of the tomb; God is no longer safely behind the curtain" (120, italics added). We do not hear Handel's "Halleulia Chorus," but we do hear the music of a resurrection song.

regarding all resurrection narratives in the Gospels and all references to the appearances of the living Jesus elsewhere in the New Testament.

The difficulties must be faced: A pattern of correlation between 1 Corinthians 15 and the resurrection narratives in Matthew, Luke, and John is unavailable and will remain so. Although the Synoptic Gospels stand together with numerous parallels, all the Gospels are different and unique throughout, each with its own trajectory distinct from the others. Likeness and contrast, approximations and conflict, similarities and disagreements, even exactness and contradictions—all these polarities characterize the canonical Gospels in relation to each other from beginning to end. Each Gospel faithfully narrates the story of Jesus with sensitivity and appropriateness to the cultural, geographical, sociohistorical factors of the community of faith within which each Gospel was treasured. Yet the tensions between the Gospels probably prove more vivid in their respective resurrection narratives than anywhere else. The sharp disparity between the resurrection narratives of the canonical Gospels resists, even defies harmonization, but the Gospels express through their individual and collective witness the news of the resurrection of the crucified Jesus—the One shrouded in mystery without need for grave clothes on the other side of death.

The resurrection narratives of the canonical Gospels cannot simply be dismissed as legendary and nonhistorical. Although the reality of the resurrection of Jesus Christ does not depend upon any one of these very diverse resurrection narratives, the reality of resurrection shines through them. In fact, Matthew, Luke, and John did something that Paul and the Gospel of Mark did not attempt to do: They accepted the impossibility and the necessity to conclude their Gospels with stories of the Easter Jesus in continuity and discontinuity with the stories of the pre-Easter Jesus.

The initial and enduring connection of the discovery of the empty tomb with the appearances to the apostles in these Gospel narratives occurs through faithful disciples of Jesus who were women. Their experiences in Jerusalem—none of the Gospels differ on this point—were initially independent of the appearances of Jesus to the apostles, in fact, entirely so until the final scenes in Luke. *Within the Gospels* these *women* testified to the empty tomb and its explanation of Jesus' resurrection prior to the narration of the appearances of the risen Jesus to the Eleven. Why did the traditions-history of 1 Corinthians 15 that Paul received from the

Jerusalem church not include the involvement of any women at all? Women could not provide valid testimony in a court of law, because the testimony of women could be dismissed anywhere as "an idle tale" (Luke 24:11), could and would! Yet these same unreliable women remain the initial witnesses in the Gospels to the resurrection of the crucified Jesus in Jerusalem.

"Why did Paul leave them out?" poses another question, "Why did the Gospels leave them in?" Why are women given such unique opportunity and unparalleled responsibility in a patriarchal society where legally they had no credibility at all? Jesus called the Twelve, men like the twelve sons of Jacob, to reconstitute the new Israel of God, because only men had access to places of privilege and power in Jewish society. Since patriarchy could be dismantled only from the inside, Jesus relativized the places of religious and political authority through his message and ministry in the name of his *Abba* God. Now the death and resurrection of Jesus permanently fractured all the structures of hier-archical control summarized in the current interpretation of the Law.

At this critical juncture in the story of Jesus, *only women* are called to carry the good news to the Eleven and the other disciples. They are enlightened, commissioned, and sent to tell the glad news to the others. In the Gospels wherein Jesus had called the Twelve, Jesus commissioned these women as apostles to the apostles. Jesus had exposed the inequity and injustice in the structures of patriarchy through his unprecedented affirmation and scandalous behavior toward women during his ministry. Now the risen Jesus in the canonical Gospels authorized the essential leadership role to the women among his disciples—women who had followed him from Galilee past the cross and to his grave—with the responsibility to tell the news and instruct the Eleven on the resurrection side of the cross. In all the Gospels everything begins to become new.

The Stories in the Story

The event of the resurrection of Jesus remained a story untold in the Gospels, a story told exclusively through the stories of the disciples. Accordingly, Luke 24 tells the story of Jesus' resurrection through multiple but interrelated stories. *Story 1*: The women discovered the empty tomb, and two messengers of God explained, "Jesus has risen." These women returned to the other disciples and told them what had happened, but they thought the story "an idle tale." *Story 2*: Jesus incognito joined the two disciples walking from Jerusalem to Emmaus, and they told the inquiring Stranger of the rejection and death of Jesus of Nazareth. In Emmaus, when the Stranger joined them at the table, blessing and breaking bread, they recognized Jesus, and he vanished. *Story 3*: The two disciples returned immediately to Jerusalem to all the others, hearing instantly another story: The Lord has risen and appeared to Peter! They told their story of the Stranger and their recognition of Jesus in breaking bread. *Story 4*: Unexpectedly Jesus appeared among them, terrifying them, but Jesus showed them his wounds and proved his resurrection identity through eating a piece of fish. Commissioning them to proclaim the good news throughout the world in the power of the Holy Spirit, Jesus blessed them and ascended to heaven.

Luke 24 continues the story of Jesus beyond the cross with stories of the risen Jesus appearing to his disciples. The cross did *not* conclude the *story of Jesus*, because Jesus crucified, dead, and buried had been raised from the dead in the power of God, and this risen Jesus appeared to his disciples. Only these stories can complete the story of Jesus, without which the story lacks the ending that the resurrection of the crucified Jesus required. Likewise, Luke 24 summarizes the story of the pre-Easter Jesus in the Gospel and anticipates the story of the church in Acts, a purpose fundamental to the structure of Luke-Acts. That Jesus is the surprising fulfillment of Old Testament prophecies on the one side and that he summons his disciples to preach the gospel to all nations in the power of the Holy Spirit on the other constitutes the essential bridge between the Gospel of Jesus Christ and the Acts of the early church.[14]

---

[14]In *The Identity of Jesus Christ* (Philadelphia: Fortress Press, 1975) Hans Frei sketches a Christology on the basis of the narrative identity of Jesus Christ in the Synoptic Gospels. Utilizing his well-known characterization of the Gospel traditions as *more* history-like than historical, Frei affirms Jesus' identity through an intention-action description which moves from the crucial moment of obedience in the Garden of Gethsemane to its climactic conclusion in the crucifixion and resurrection: "Jesus was what he did and suffered, the one whose identity was enacted in his passion and death" (115). The manifestation of Jesus' unsubstitutable individual identity comes into focus most clearly in the narrative of the resurrection of the crucified Jesus. Throughout the passion narrative but especially in the climax of Jesus' resurrection, "fictional description, providing direct knowledge of his identity in, with, and through the circumstances [like the central character of a novel], merges with factual claim, whether justified or not. The

Could the story of Jesus in the Gospels end without stories of the revelatory appearances of the crucified but risen Jesus? The tradition of the appearances in 1 Corinthians 15:3-8, which identifies those to whom Jesus appeared without any description whatsoever, and the tradition of the empty tomb in Mark 16:1-8, which announces the resurrection without any appearances of Jesus to his disciples—these two independent and unrelated traditions could not historically conclude the story of Jesus in the Gospels nor effectively bridge the story of Jesus with the story of

---

narration is at once intensely serious and historical in intent and fictional in form, the common strand between them being the identification of the individual in his circumstances" (145). To know *who* Jesus is in conjunction with what happened is to know *that* he is, the resurrection the climax of the story and his claim. The narrative says that "the being and identity of Jesus in the resurrection are such that his nonresurrection becomes inconceivable. . . . [H]owever impossible it may be to grasp the nature of the resurrection, it remains inconceivable that it should not have taken place" (145). Frei states his argument in a very Anselmian fashion quite unlike the Gospels: "[T]o grasp what this identity, Jesus of Nazareth (which has been made directly accessible to us), is is to believe that he has been, *in fact*, raised from the dead." Can one suppose that the most perfectly depicted character and the most nearly lifelike fictional identity would always have lived a factual historical life? This argument remains cogent "only in this one and absolutely unique case, where the described entity (who or what he is, i.e., Jesus Christ, the presence of God) is totally identical with his factual existence" (146). The factuality of the resurrection of Jesus inheres in the narrative, because the claim belongs to the identity of Jesus enacted and manifest in the narration of the Gospel story. That Jesus is and who Jesus is are one and the same. Thus this Jesus cannot *not* live, and to think of him as not living misunderstands who he is (149). Yet all endeavors to establish the truth of the resurrection of Jesus lack conclusive support. If true, the resurrection is unique, but if false, it is neither true nor unique. Frei says: "Until such evidence comes along, however, it seems proper to say that there is a kind of logic in the Christian's faith that forces him to say that disbelief in the resurrection of Jesus is rationally impossible." Then Frei adds: "But whether one actually *believes* the resurrection is, of course, a wholly different matter"[!] (151). Belief in the resurrection is a matter of faith. Frei concludes: "Why some believe and others do not is impossible for the Christian to explain. Like many a pilgrim, he may find himself strangely on both sides at the same time. All he can do then is to recall the that the logic of his faith makes it rationally impossible for him not to believe" (162). Unsurprisingly, Frei makes no appeal beyond the Gospel narratives and the logic of faith to anchor his proposal. What is surprising is his substitution of the summing up of history in the providence of God for the Christian hope of resurrection into eternal life in God. Frei argues: "Not even the event of Jesus Christ can be such an absolute clue" to the future; otherwise, the future would not be genuinely open (163). The eschatological dissonance in his argument is puzzling—at least.

the early church. Resurrection narratives could do so, however, and they do so quite effectively in Matthew, Luke, and John.

The Recollection of the Passion Predictions

The passion predictions, which in fact occurred, included two different but related declarations: the violent execution of Jesus on the one side and the expectation of God's vindication of him on the other. The passion predictions themselves, however, contained details that describe precisely what happened, an after-the-fact specification that accounts in part for the striking similarity between them in the Synoptic Gospels. Likewise, the singular resurrection of Jesus interpreted with reference to the discovery of the empty tomb "on the third day" constituted an after-the-fact description of the way God had vindicated him, a vindication that Jesus anticipated despite the agony in Gethsemane.

The three passion predictions in each of the Synoptic Gospels stand parallel together: The first passion prediction identifies the *elders*, *chief priests*, and *scribes* as the ones who will kill Jesus (Mark 8:31; Matt 16:21; Luke 9:21-22). The second passion prediction specifies *betrayal* into human hands, *death*, and *vindication* (Mark 9:30-31; Matt 17:22-23; Luke 9:44). The third passion prediction refers to Jesus' condemnation by the chief priests and scribes, but, even more explicitly, the *Romans* will *humiliate* him, *beat* him, and *kill* him (Mark 10:33-34; Matt 20:17-19; Luke 18:31-34). The retrospective explication of the passion predictions, "after-the-fact details," corresponds to the agony of Jesus in Gethsemane committed to do the will of his *Abba* God as well as the shock and devastation of the disciples at his arrest and condemnation. They could only flee to Galilee, without any faith or hope within them that would enable them to continue as disciples of a crucified Messiah, an incontrovertible contradiction in terms: blasphemer, revolutionary, God-forsaken—a Galilean dead on a Roman cross "outside the gate."

When Jesus appeared to them, the path of the pre-Easter Jesus could become understandable to them for the first time. The scriptural formula, "on the third day" God raised Jesus from the dead, enunciated the verdict of God on the death of the Son, the retrospective definition of the mode of eschatological validation. Luke 9:44 might well be the most original form of the passion predictions in the Synoptic Gospels: "Let these words sink into your ears: The Son of Man is going to be betrayed into human hands." Like the Christians in the churches of the New Testament, which included those who framed the four narratives of Jesus that we call Gospels, we know the end of the story from its beginning. That is, we read the Gospels forwards and backwards simultaneously: Jesus is risen, the crucified Christ, the good news of Jesus Christ, Godforsaken, the Son of God, Jesus' proclamation of the dawning Kingdom of God, the resurrection of the Crucified, the friend of tax collectors and sinners, good news, Jesus is risen.

An Eschatological Tomorrow?
Arguments and Counterarguments

The questions central to the formulation of eschatological statements cannot be answered simply through biblical exegesis. The cogency of different patterns of New Testament interpretation, while subject to critique and evaluation, resist ready-made translation into contemporary theological proposals. The reluctance of theologians to do constructive doctrines of eschatology roots partly in the diversity and complexity of the biblical traditions and corresponding theological interpretations, but only partly. Theological reticence stems also from underlying problems of the importance, the truthfulness, or the intelligibility of eschatological proposals. In fact, several major arguments against "an eschatological tomorrow" restrain ventures into eschatology, which sometimes conceal a basic skepticism or fundamental rejection of eschatological fulfillment in the coming Home-Coming of God.

Although these arguments cannot be glibly dismissed for lack of substance, they are certainly not unassailable. Each argument can be met with a strong counterargument that contains a critique of and a constructive proposal beyond the argument itself. The counterarguments nurture Christian hope for future life in God. These arguments and counterarguments are shaped through research, but they are well-worn through continual confrontation and interaction day after day.

Argument 1: The essential anthropomorphic character of Christian eschatological hope graphically overestimates the place and importance of human life on planet Earth. Of the millions of galaxies, each containing billions of stars, the Earth is in orbit around a second-rate star on the edge of its own galaxy—hardly noticeable in this galaxy, much less the universe. The handful of people who authored the biblical traditions could articulate their positive valuation of human life from God through various eschatological projections, because they lived in an apparent geocentric universe centered on this very human world. Yet the obscurity of planet Earth in the vastness of the universe enables us to recognize and affirm the abiding purpose of these eschatological proposals, namely, the good gift of life on this Earth. The supposition that these projections actually entail the destiny of individuated human beings on the almost invisible speck of dust called Earth in the vastness of the universe is nowadays hopelessly naive.

Counterargument 1: The obscurity of the Earth in the vastness of the universe and the accompanying insignificance of humanity is not in the first instance an argument against the feasibility of eternal life, because it negates the affirmation of God's care and concern for human life at all. The startling affirmation of the Gospel is that God knows us and loves us, precisely in our obscurity and apparent insignificance. The foolishness of the good news begins here: God is "for humanity," "for us," "for each of us." That God created humanity in God's own image, that God chooses to be in relationship with humankind, that God really does love us individually and collectively—that is the starting point. The issue is not initially eschatology but primarily theology, namely, the identity of God, the God to whom humanity matters. Apart from the affirmation that God genuinely cares for humanity, all other affirmations of Christian faith become irrelevant. And it is precisely this affirmation that is at stake in the anthropocentric character of the biblical statements of faith. God chooses to be in relationship to humanity, and this choice constitutes the foundation for all the experiences of human relatedness to God. The anthropocentric character of any and every affirmation of faith originates in the human experience of the love of God. The foundation of the Christian hope for eternal life is the identity of God who has come to us in the insignificance[!] of the man Jesus of Nazareth with good news: God loves us.

Argument 2: Beyond an understandable pre-scientific naivete, the anthropological character of eschatological hope conceals another fundamental problem: the persistence and creativity of human egocentricity. The Christian hope for eternal life "on the other side of death" is ultimately a thinly disguised exercise in egocentricity, to be more than creature, to become "like God." The refusal to accept one's own creatureliness under the masquerade of hope in the promises of God is an act of self-assertion in the form of self-preservation that is nothing less than idolatry.

Counterargument 2: While some expressions of hope for eternal life root in human egocentricity, Christian hope for the fulfillment of life on the other side of death is essentially a vision of salvation. Of all life-forms on Earth, only humans created in the image of God have the capacity for self-transcendence. We humans know, and we know that we know. Each of us can look back retrospectively at the past; each can look forward imaginatively into the future; each can look reflectively on his or her particular present. We humans die, and we can anticipate and contemplate death. Through the remarkable capability of self-transcendence each of us can ponder the meaning of life and the mystery of death. Accordingly, we humans know death self-reflectively. We are able to see the unmendable brokenness and unhealable estrangement of life precisely because of our capacity for the reflective anticipation of death. Human need for wholeness in the face of death coheres with the promise of eternal life, but eternal life remains the gift of God. Indeed, the Christian sense of the gift of life itself nurtures the hope for God's gift of eternal life. The story of Jesus simultaneously affirms the surprising gift of new life in God and of eternal life with God. Christian eschatology acknowledges both dimensions of the story of Jesus in its vision of the Kingdom of God. The hope for eternal life does not collapse the distinction between Creator and creature nor the creature's utter dependency on the Creator; on the contrary, the hope for eternal life is the creature's radical trust in God in the face of death, a trust nurtured through the Presence of Christ in living and in dying. Such trust is the opposite of egocentricity, because it is not self-centeredness but the self that centers itself in the Presence and promise of God.

Argument 3: Biblical faith does not require an eschatological confirmation for its validity or its vitality. Like the historic faith of Israel in its covenant with God, the experience of Jesus Christ in the memory of the church has proven significant and sustaining in the ordinary and sometimes heroic lives of countless Christians across the centuries — obviously without eschatological consummation! An implicit or explicit demythologization of the eschatological symbols of the biblical traditions is necessary now more than ever for accepting the responsibilities of life and the limitations of faith. Hope in this world rather than hope beyond the world is the gift of faith to the promise of love: Life is meaningful and good in itself without the necessity for compensation of another life in a different world.

Counterargument 3: New Testament faith loses the substance of its vitality if the horizon of eschatological hope is itself an empty horizon—a limit instead of a promise, a limit that defines creaturely perishability instead of a promise that defines the purpose of God. The Biblical Story becomes a story "without an ending." The prophets had already turned toward the future before Jesus appeared, and the Gospels narrate Jesus' proclamation of the coming Kingdom of God with an "already" but "not yet" of its arrival. The Christian community across the centuries has anticipated hearing the "Welcome" of God in new life on the other side of death, and this *expectation* has proven "significant and sustaining in ordinary and sometimes heroic lives of countless Christians" in service for others amid the suffering of this world. The completion of life in God does not mean the necessary compensation for the fragmentation of life in this world; nevertheless, the goodness of life is certainly not an unqualified affirmation. The Gospels address those who are oppressed and hard-pressed, people who know pain, who experience misery, who flee dread. So hope for the future in the Kingdom of God does not negate responsibility for life in this world. On the contrary, the vision of the oncoming Kingdom of God has nurtured an energizing investment in this everyday world through the light of Christian hope for the tomorrow of God. Eschatological hope in Jesus' proclamation of the Kingdom of God confronts the historical present with the demands of the eschatological future. The Biblical Story does envision an ending: the transformation of all reality into the Kingdom of God through Jesus Christ in the power of the Holy Spirit.

Argument 4: The enormity of evil and suffering in the world make faith in God all the more important and all the more difficult. God does help humanity bear the pain, injustice, and meaninglessness of life in the risky process of history: God inspires joy in the midst of pain, the good against evil, purpose in the face of meaninglessness. If God can do more, however—as eschatology promises—why does God not do so? The difference between God's fulfilling power eschatologically and God's limited power historically constitutes a nearly intolerable contradiction. Christian eschatology adds the problem of "a waiting God" to the ever aggressive, almost unbearable problem of evil and suffering. The empty promise of a waiting God on the horizon of the future threatens the very availability of a caring God in the struggles of the present.

Counterargument 4: The problem of evil and suffering that threaten the integrity of Christian faith does make faith in God all the more difficult and all the more important. Accordingly, the so-called "free will argument" that makes the human abuse of freedom the essential source of evil and suffering proves dismally inadequate, cursory at best. Similarly, the Irenean theodicy that considers the pain of life an essential means to growth in character and faith is an appalling oversimplification, disproportionate at least. Neither the abuse of human freedom nor the instrumental value of human suffering corresponds to the measure of radical evil that stalks every step of human history. On the contrary, these explanations mask the terrifying mystery of evil and obscure the immeasurable depth of human suffering.

Beyond the free will defense and an instrumental view of suffering, two counter points demand attention. First, the creativity of God must not be reduced to the *givens* that inhere in creation nor the power of God to the *limits* within the present structures of creation. Rather, the creativity of God should be measured by the surprising story of Jesus and the power of God by the resurrection of Christ crucified. Second, evil, suffering, and death are not the first word or the last word to humanity in history. On the eighth day of creation, God has spoken the first word of creativity anew, the first word of *light through the darkness* in the ever surprising story of Jesus, the Alpha and Omega of God. Likewise, God has spoken the last word of purposefulness done, the last word of *life beyond death* on the first day of the week in the ever surprising compassion of God. The first Word and the last Word of God say the same: God is love.

Furthermore, the distinction between a coming God on the horizon of the future and a caring God in the struggles of the present constitutes different expressions of the *self-giving* of God to us, a temporal transition rather than a conceptual contradiction. As the appearances in the resurrection narratives of the Gospels portray, only the resurrection of Jesus located him outside the limitations of space and time in the eternal mystery of God. These transcending features of the appearance stories in the Gospels wherein the sequenced movement of the living Jesus lies completely beyond our view confront us with a life lived in the mystery of the eternity of God and apart from the definitive character of the creaturely norms of space and time. The self-giving of the God who is love takes the form of self-limitation in relation to creation and our creaturely existence within it, but the self-giving of the God who creates out of nothing takes a different form on the other side of death: God gives new life in the Kingdom of God wherein the restrictive dimensions of space and time as we know them are not applicable. Thus resurrection is the gift of God to humanity in its creatureliness, a creatureliness born in space and time that remains, an essential dependency on God the Creator that endures, a humanness healed through the overflowing love of God that continues. The apparent contradiction between the brokenness of life lived under the providence of God and the wholeness of life anticipated through the promise of God is not an essential contradiction but *a temporal transition*. The God of historical Presence and the God of eschatological hope, the compassionate God in the struggles of the present and the coming God on the horizon of the future, is one and the same God: God is the self-giving God of love: God is love.

Argument 5: The vision of an eschatological tomorrow on the other side of death is literally incomprehensible and finally inconceivable. Eschatology cannot answer its own questions: How would it happen? What would it look like? Who would "you" or millions of others be in it? An eschatological vision with a specifiable, describable state of affairs is actually indefinable and unintelligible. Eschatological proposals are perhaps interesting, but they remain unreal.

Counterargument 5: The vision of an eschatological tomorrow on the other side of death stretches the imagination to the limits and beyond, leaving the reflection of the mind in glimmering disarray. The imagination can only glimpse and thought can only stammer the mystery of the morning after death. Yet the language of eschatological hope is not unlike all language about God: God-talk is odd-talk. So eschatological dreaming breaks the boundaries of human language, it defies the reach of the loftiest conceptualization, and it exceeds the vistas of the most extraordinary imagination. The vision of the Kingdom of God is a vision of hope, hope against hope, hope beyond hope. The God-talk of hope and the hope-talk of God is odd-talk, finally the stuttering of faith in the future of God who is love.

Underpinnings of hope nonetheless do venture words: The hope for the fulfillment of life is probably as ancient as faith in God, fulfillment increasingly projected beyond the contradictions and estrangement of every future become present and every present become past. Christian hope for the future in the eternal God goes beyond the transitions of finite futures that become concretely present and subsequently constitute an irreversible past. Between Jesus' proclamation of the Kingdom of God, God's future becoming historically present, and the church's proclamation of the story of Jesus, the historical future becoming God's present— between Jesus' vision of the arrival of the Kingdom of God and the church's vision of the future of Jesus Christ—in between, in between the future of its past and the present of its future, in between, in between the church dreams in behalf of all humanity for the messianic banquet of God in the indescribable coming Home-Coming of God on the morning after death.

The unobtrusive and uncalculated rendering of the sinlessness of Jesus in the Gospels acquires striking but seldom seen eschatological significance for us. The sinlessness of Jesus in a sinful world anticipates life where freedom and destiny are not in contradiction but in unity: Jesus embodied the Kingdom of God in a broken, sinful world. We hope for the Kingdom of Jesus in an unbroken, sinless "world," a world of wholeness, harmony, peace. Eschatology takes a daring risk: Since Jesus lived out God's life in a fragmented and hostile world, the promise that Jesus has given us for another life in God beyond the brokenness and alienation of this world is certainly conceivable, actually possible, real-ly hope-able.

The Weakness of God

The *content* of the promise of resurrection is one of *power*, the power of the self-giving God who is love, who creates life, who raises the dead. However, the *form* of the promise of resurrection is one of *weakness*. Strong warrants count against it. So the promise of God in the resurrection of Jesus Christ participates in the weakness of God that characterizes the cross of Jesus of Nazareth. The fragile hope of love for resurrection into the Kingdom of God is as scandalous as faith in a crucified Christ. The story of the Nazarene Preacher says: God is love. When the awesome depths of God's love revealed in the death of the crucified Jesus truly grasps us, the stunning creativity of God in the sheer wonder of the resurrection of the dead Jesus irrepressibly continues to captivate us. Thereafter we live believing and faltering in the joyful foolishness of eschatological dreaming—Jesus of Nazareth, Son of God and Brother to us all, the story of Jesus encircling and encompassing us in the glad Welcome of the coming Home-Coming of God. The cross of Christ Jesus, a Godforsaken "King of the Jews," reveals the weakness of God among the powers of this world. Correspondingly, the resurrection of Jesus Christ from the dead constitutes the promise of God for eternal life beyond this world, an eschatological hope that God continues to sustain in the strength of weakness, a hope scandalously vulnerable to ridicule within the conventional wisdom of this world. The resurrection of the crucified Presence of God remains therefore a *theologia crucis*. A scandal, all of it, cross and resurrection alike, a scandalous providence that refuses to be silenced on this side of the Darkness in the hope for morning Light.

Contemporary Witnesses

The strength of weakness took personal form in the churches of the New Testament through the multiple witnesses to the resurrection of the crucified Jesus in 1 Corinthians and the resurrection narratives in the canonical Gospels. The testimony of these earliest witnesses constitutes a chorus of voices joined together in the song of the resurrection of Jesus. As their voices ring above all others, so their stories precede all others. A pastoral theology that listens to the story of Jesus in the New Testament will nonetheless listen to other stories that echo the promise of resurrection in the contemporary church.

The Journey of a Pilgrim

The story of Carlyle Marney provides an illuminating, theological pilgrimage. Marney worked most of his life as a pastor-theologian, primarily as pastor of the First Baptist Church in Austin, Texas (1948–1958) and Myers Park Church in Charlotte, North Carolina (1958–1967). He lived with a perceptive awareness of the ambiguities and contradictions of human life. Marney knew the silence of God, but he spoke eloquently of the Incarnation and the Cross throughout his ministry, the Christ event the basic key in "the recovery of the person." Yet Marney had little place for the resurrection. What could the resurrection add to the Gospel of becoming truly personal, coming to authentic personhood? He did not consider the resurrection a necessary theme, usually more confusing than helpful. During most of his Austin and Charlotte days Marney simply did not believe in the historicity of the resurrection of Jesus. On the contrary, he considered the resurrection a contemporary personal experience rather than a past historical event, a confession of what happen*s* to the believer instead of what happen*ed* to Jesus. Marney believed resurrection to be a symbol of renewal that is possible in every person's life. While employing personalist language, therefore, when he did speak of resurrection, Marney did so much like Bultmann.[15]

Marney suffered a heart-attack in 1966 and subsequently resigned as senior minister of the Myers Park Church. In 1967 he founded "Interpreter's House" at Lake Junaluska, North Carolina, a place for those bruised or broken by the ministry, "a house for the relief of Pilgrims."[16] The change in landscape signaled a change in Marney's theology. As his theological vision turned toward a more pronounced Christian humanism, Marney simultaneously rethought the Christian hope of resurrection. John Carey, Marney's biographer, says that a radical change occurred in his understanding of resurrection from his earlier days.

> Was it through his own brushes with death through his illness? Was it the process of aging, which itself brings different perspectives and priorities? Or was it a new theological insight, growing out of his exegesis of Paul?[17]

Perhaps through all of these, Marney came to affirm the Pauline vision of resurrection on the other side of death, the grace of the continuing gift of life from God. As early as 1970 Marney voiced his change of mind in *The Coming Faith*:

---

[15]John J. Carey, *Carlyle Marney: A Pilgrim's Progress* (Macon GA: Mercer University Press, 1980) 79-80.

[16]Ibid., 50.

[17]Ibid., 106.

Let us trust our future as well as our origins. Let us buy the whole package. I believe in the Resurrection of the dead! I believe in the Resurrection from among the bodily dead![18]

An important factor in Marney's radical shift on the resurrection happened at a famous exchange with Albert Outler at Southern Methodist University. Outler criticized Marney for his failure to take the resurrection of Jesus with appropriate seriousness, and he told Marney that one day he would. At the Furman Pastors School in June 1971 Marney recalled the conversation.

> Indeed, I remember closing a lectureship at SMU by saying: "If I had a better notion of resurrection, I could say more here; but somedays I don't believe it at all."
> Albert Outler grabbed me by the arm and said: "You shouldn't have said that."
> I said: "You're so smart, what should I have said?"
> And Outler said: "Whoever told you [that] you had to believe it everyday?"
> And I said: "You're so smart, when do I have to believe it?"
> And he said: "The day you die or the day you die with somebody, you believe in the resurrection of the dead."[19]

Did Marney misremember or misquote Outler's statement? "The day you die or *the day you die with somebody.* . . ." Did Marney mean to say: "The day you die or *the day you are with somebody who dies* . . ."? The grammar is not unimportant, because the quotation as it stands contains a depth of meaning that "the day you are with somebody who dies" simply does not have. Whatever the answer, Outler's words haunted Marney, says Carey: "It is singular that during the last decade of his life, when his health failed and several times he was on the brink of death, he changed his mind about the meaning of resurrection."[20] Beyond John Carey's attention to Marney's encounters with death, I would emphasize precisely what he said at the Furman Pastors School, whether Marney

---

[18]Carlyle Marney, *The Coming Faith* (Nashville: Abingdon Press, 1970) 134.

[19]Carlyle Marney, "The Return of the Presence," Tape 1. Furman Pastors School, 1971 (Atlanta: Protestant Radio and Television Center, 1971). Cf. Carey, *Marney*, 81.

[20]Carey, *Marney*, 81.

only intuited or consciously intended it: "The day you die or *the day you die with somebody, you believe in the resurrection of the dead.*"

Always the pilgrim, Marney believed.

The Grief of a Father

Earlier I referred to the accidental death of Carole Johnson on 21 December 1962, the day after her twenty-third birthday. L. D. Johnson reflected on the impact of his daughter's dying in the poignant little book, *The Morning After Death.* Near Oxford, North Carolina, a collision with a tractor-trailer truck collapsed her little compact into junk. "She died in minutes," he writes. "Somebody told me later the only thing she said was, 'It hurts so much.' (It still does, Carole, after all these years)."[21]

L. D. Johnson penned thoughts about his grief for Carole some fifteen years later, but he was a man who had known grief for much of his life. His father died the month he turned two, and his mother just a year later. Consciously he remembers neither. His seventy-year-old grandfather and sixty-five-year-old grandmother took the three boys to raise—two, four, and five years old. At twelve his grandfather died, and at seventeen his grandmother. A year later his brother, just older than he, was killed in an automobile accident, which almost killed his oldest brother too. Yet the deepest grief for L. D. Johnson came with losing two children: Problem-ridden Richard died at four-and-a-half, and Carole at twenty-three. In March 1975, he stared straight at death himself with the discovery of cancer. Treatment gave him hope for his future, but L. D. Johnson knew grief.

With this catalogue of continuing grief Johnson addressed his grief for Carole. He had read those analysts who say that grief is usually not for the person who has died but for one's own sense of loss. L. D. Johnson knew that he grieved partly for himself, but he identified his grief primarily for Carole.

> I grieve for her—for what there was of unfulfilled promise and unrealized potential in her young and joyous existence. I grieve because she was in love, full of expectation, gifted, open to life, eager and able

---

[21]L. D. Johnson, *The Morning After Death* (Nashville: Broadman Press, 1978; Macon GA: Smyth & Helwys, 1995) 17.

to share what she knew and felt, and that all of this perished. . . . I grieve for what Carole missed, and for what others who loved her, or would have loved her, missed. She was not fulfilled; her unripe grape fell from the vine; her blossom shed before the olive formed. (Job 15:33)[22]

From Job through the Gospels to Paul, Old Testament sage and New Testament minister, L. D. Johnson affirmed the mystery of suffering and death within the larger mystery of God. Ultimately he found comfort and confidence in the promise of resurrection, a Christian understanding of death founded on the resurrection of Jesus Christ. He knew the arguments against resurrection, but he stood in the Gospel testimony that God raised Jesus from the dead.

To palm off some lame expectation that the disciples sensed his spirit among them after his death or that they felt his continuing influence but never intended to suggest a real resurrection is to do manifest violence to their reports in the New Testament. We may refuse to credit the story, but we should not demythologize it into something not meant to be taken quite seriously.[23]

Like other Christians, L. D. Johnson experienced the Presence of Christ in his life but not in the same way that the witnesses of the New Testament did. The resurrection of Jesus does promise life on the other side of death, and he concluded: "I believe that Carole is alive and well." Did it matter that she did not live out her days and experience the fullness of life before her? Of course it mattered.

L. D. Johnson nonetheless faithed: "But Carole is alive, the person she was being the person she is, made more beautiful and holy by her presence with God."[24] L. D. Johnson entrusted Carol to another Father, a Motherly Father, more alive, more loving, more trustworthy, than even he.

---

[22]Ibid., 88.
[23]Ibid., 133.
[24]Ibid., 134.

The Dying of a Mother

Dying is a deeply personal experience, and the relationship of the one dying to the one who will remain living can occasion a natural moving apart in a slow separation or an appropriate coming together in a deeper intimacy. Betty chose intimacy, which made her dying less lonely and fearful for her but all the more difficult for me. Whatever the level of intimacy, however, there are moments that reflect not so much the intimacy of a shared dying but the assault of death on the relationship of the one to the other.

Early April 1983. I came home from work exhausted, and I simply plopped down beside her. The fatigue of the past—day after day, week after week, month after month—the fatigue had collapsed into "recurrence." The anticipatory grief of a year and a half had become an ever present inevitability. This word "recurrence," this word contained an unmanageable and suffocating intensity, overwhelming, though less than three months had passed. How do you measure the heavy weight and slow progression of time in the unending twilight of dying? This grief old and new had worn me out and drained me dry. I spoke matter-of-factly, without forethought, simply descriptively: "*I'll be glad when this is over.*"

Betty leaped up to leave the room, no, to leave me. At the doorway she turned and spoke to me sharply, quickly, and angrily: "*When this is over, I'll be dead.*"

In that moment I realized in visual slow motion that part of me had denied the truth to lessen the pain. Part of me needed desperately not to see the truth. That part of me had thought: "*When this ordeal is over, we will become a family again.*" I knew, but I refused to know that in a matter of months, certainly not a year [?], she would die. Nothing would ever be normal again. Nothing.

May 1983. We sat in the family room together, Easter long gone. Fatigue and depression left me silent. The silence between us had taken form and slowly pushed me toward dread.

Betty asked a question, the question.

"*Do you believe in resurrection?*"

My hesitancy already constituted part of my answer. And, of course, she knew it.

"*Betty, you know I struggled with the question of resurrection through all my seminary studies. That's the reason we went to Germany in 1968 to enable me to study with Pannenberg. He had reopened the question of the resurrection of Jesus and made it central to Christology and his theology.*"

She said nothing for a long time. I felt trapped. When she did speak, she did so deliberately, precisely, dispassionately—with a voice quite unlike herself. But she did not intend to engage in conversation.

"*I did not ask you, 'What does Wolfhart Pannenberg believe about resurrection?'*"

"*I did not ask you, 'What did you believe about resurrection in 1968 while you worked on your dissertation?'*"

"*I asked you, 'Do you believe in resurrection?' Today. Now.*"

I said, "*Yes.*"

I was trapped. She knew me so well that she not only heard my answer but she also heard the level of conviction out of which my affirmation came. She had heard my uncertainty, because I had answered her question too slowly and reluctantly.

Silence descended between us, and dread settled around us. We both were trapped, the two of us, not entirely together.

June 1983. Betty had almost always been a realist, candid and straightforward. She lived within herself with considerable honesty and mostly without illusions, except those illusions necessary to live with the realities of family and with me. Now, quite frankly, she was afraid: afraid to die, without having lived enough; afraid to die, leaving her children; afraid to die, with so much left undone. She was afraid, afraid of death, afraid of the dying.

Earlier the gift of music had unexpectedly showered her with hope and joy. Now the music had died, drowned out in the constant clamor of the Storm. As the Storm raged unending between hospital and home, only one sound ranged above its roaring—the cackling laughter of Chaos echoing through the night.

Late one June evening Betty spoke to me softly, cautiously, and hesitatingly. She said, "*I want to tell you something that happened to me this morning.*"

A long pause. "*But I'm not sure you will believe me.*"

She had always been skeptical of escapist religious experience. Yet she had faithfully asked God for months to take away her fear of death and dying.

That morning—sitting at her desk adjacent to the small partition that separated her from the family room—she had continued that prayer. To her utter surprise she experienced the enveloping and uplifting Presence of God. And in the bliss of that majestic Presence she said: "*I heard children laughing, children laughing 'on the other side.*' "

She told me: "*I knew, if I die today, or if I stay with you a little while longer, I will enjoy the laughter of children on the Other Side.*"

As Betty described what had happened to her, she realized that she had misread me. I did not question her story or doubt the integrity of her experience. Thereafter we talked often and openly about resurrection, the hope for eternal life in God. We encountered conceptual and linguistic difficulties, and sometimes conversations ended in the silence of inaccessible mystery. Metaphors finally proved most meaningful for the journey: a brilliant Light, an open Door, a warming Presence—resurrection, eternal life, God.

Although she continued to experience a Mother's disappointment of leaving her own little children, she *never* feared death or dying again—never. So no matter how loud the wind howled in that relentless Storm or how difficult the discomfort of the night, she affirmed life and enjoyed living according to the measure of life available to her each portion of the day.

Sometime later a close friend asked her: "*Betty, are you afraid to die?*"

She answered with characteristic candor: "*No, if my faith is true, the Other Side is better than this one. And if my faith is not true, I'll never know it.*"

And she looked at me and smiled, because I knew that she had heard the laughter of little children on the Other Side.

So genuinely disappointed, sometimes unbearably so, but never afraid again—never—in that terrible Storm she died.

Conclusion

The Biblical Story concludes with a vision: the coming Home-Coming of God in the future of Jesus Christ. The Story of Jesus is the definitive Story of God, but the story ends outrageously with a Godforsaken death on a cross and a resurrected Nazarene from an empty tomb. The claim that God has endured the assault of death offends modern sensibilities as much as the claim that God has opened the door to eternal life. The death of Godforsakenness and the resurrection of the dead scandalized the gospel in antiquity and scandalize the gospel in the world today. The crucified Jesus who lives, the living Jesus once crucified, this Jesus invites us to trust our hope in the God of love. Does he ask us to do too much? Some prefer the cross without the problem of resurrection, while others prefer the resurrection without the path of suffering. Sometimes the pain of life runs so deep that the cry from the cross seems all that can be heard—almost. At other times the joy of life chimes such music that the song of resurrection sounds all that should be heard—almost. The song of resurrection cannot silence they cry from the cross, and the cry from the cross cannot silence the song of resurrection. The one cannot be heard without the other—at least not yet. Thus the providence of God disclosed in the story of Jesus remains a scandalous providence, for God is the God of a vulnerable compassion. God is vulnerable to the powerlessness of the cross and the ridicule of the empty tomb. The crucified God is as scandalous as the resurrected Jesus.

First and foremost the Biblical Story is the Story of God, the Gospel Story its hermeneutical key. We make the Biblical Story our story, the Story that incorporates and transforms all our stories. Yet the Biblical Story remains essentially the Story of God: The cry from the cross is the death cry of Jesus of Nazareth, the Beloved Child of God, a lament of Godforsakenness, and the echo that reverberates in the depths of Darkness is not the cry of humanity at death but the mystery of God in dereliction. Jesus was one with God in the whole of his life, and God was one with Jesus in the moment of death. Jesus trusted his hope to God, and God established our hope in Jesus. God reached through death and beyond it with the gift of eternal life: God raised the crucified Jesus from the dead. He is risen. And what God has done in Jesus, God intends to do for all of us. The song of resurrection concludes the Biblical Story with "Alleluia," an ending already transcended in a new beginning. We live into that new beginning that lies beyond this side of the ending. In the hope of Jesus we trust the God of love. Ridiculous? Incredulous? Absurd? The resurrection of a crucified Nazarene! Scandal. Scandal, all of it, from beginning to end. Scandal . . . scandal indeed.

Appendix

Gilkey on Providence: A Tillichian Revision of Process Thought

IN ONE OF THE MOST CAREFUL AND CREATIVE STATEMENTS of the providence of God in contemporary theology, Langdon Gilkey correlates providence, Christology, and eschatology in a significant revision of process theology, a revision that identifies him less with process theology and more with the theological perspective of Paul Tillich. "Historical passage" that informs and defines "modern consciousness" is the context for his interpretation of the providence of God, which is from the outset a historical and political-theological exercise.[1] A brief and modest analysis of crucial aspects of his proposal is appropriate, because Gilkey intends for his interpretation of providence to address sociopolitical processes.

Aspects of a Reinterpretation of Providence

As an essential starting point Gilkey understands modern historical consciousness to exclude the classical vision of God as the all-determining sovereign of past, present, and future. Rather, modern historical consciousness—a consciousness of historical contingency, relativity, transience, autonomy, and radical evil—requires a different perspective on historical causality within the givens and decision-making of a specific human community. Gilkey is quite precise: Historical causality is "*a dialectical interrelation between destiny from the past,*" which includes

---

[1]Langdon Gilkey, *Reaping the Whirlwind: A Christian Interpretation of History* (New York: Seabury Press, 1976). Peter C. Hodgson, *God in History: Shapes of Freedom* (Nashville: Abingdon Press, 1989) 260, n.72, says: "Although Gilkey employs Whiteheadian conceptualities, his basic theological outlook is closer to Tillich's."

the continuation of the structures of common life and the goals of a society, *"combined with new possibilities"* that are related to *"that given actuality"* in the present, *"possibilities* that are *projected into the coming future* and that are *embodied* into action through *decision and intention,"* which is our responsibility, "all aimed at a *new and better situation."*[2]

How does God work in this understanding of historical causality? Gilkey appropriates the Old Testament theology of Gerhard von Rad to construct a "model" of God's activity with Israel. God calls, delivers, and establishes Israel in its covenantal life on the one side; God judges, recalls, and offers new possibilities to Israel out of the nemesis of its past on the other. This is the dialectic of the hidden work of God in history. The initial task is to understand how God unites the polarity of destiny and freedom, establishes the unity of past and present, and correlates historical actuality with new possibilities without recourse to a "super-naturalistic" explanation of God's action in history. Rather, Gilkey proposes a "naturalistic" model that maintains historical causation wherein God acts through the secondary causes of destiny and freedom, but God has nonetheless a critical constitutive and renewing role in the history of the people of Israel. The divine ultimacy in history, the shaping of providence, is not an ultimacy that determined Israel's historic response to its covenant with God, but an ultimacy that then and now establishes, undergirds, limits, judges, and rescues the present. The providence of God occurs *through* the contingency, relativity, temporality, and freedom of finite being, and not contrariwise.[3]

On the basis of the dialectic of the hidden work of God in history, Gilkey refuses to equate the providence of God with the events that actually occur in the world of contingent history. "In the sense of ground, limit, and resource of our being and its powers—*and in that alone*—God is ultimate." God as the creative and providential sovereign is not only essentially active, dynamic, and present to us in all the changing of time, sustaining and driving forward all that is as well as the creative possi-bilities for the new. "He is also, as creative ground of our being, essentially *self-limiting*, producing a free, contingent being that is not God or a part of God and whose actions are not God's actions, for finite

---

[2]Gilkey, *Reaping the Whirlwind*, 246 (italics added).
[3]Ibid., 246-48.

actuality comes to be through its own actualization of its destiny." We who are creaturely, however, cannot participate in time nor experience meaning and hope without a continuing relationship to "God's present being, intentions, meaning and love—which together form his providence."[4] Though creation and providence may be conceptually distinguished for the sake of analysis, God creates, preserves, and guides through time. Contrary to most forms of process thought, therefore, creativity belongs in the being of God: God is the source of our total existence, the creativity and flux of the origin of life as well as the creativity and risk of creaturely freedom. The providence of God means that God preserves us in time and provides the ground of possibility for our finite autonomy and creative possibility—which are not predetermined or otherwise determined by God but, as modernity affirms, by us.[5]

Finally, God's providence relates unrealized possibility to achieved and achieving actuality, moving the historical process into the future. The not yet of possibility impinges on the present, creative possibility that can effect more relevant and meaningful changes in history. Destiny can be reshaped through freedom only by a creative appropriation of these new possibilities. Thus the logos of God in creation is God's envisioning and ordering of the infinite range of possibility *as possible*. A distinct creative role of God is "that he gives to each occasion, and so to each person and community, an ordered vision of possibility, a leap beyond the present actuality yet one in relation to it."[6] Though providence does not determine historical creativity, it makes such creativity possible and relevant and thereby limits and guides indeterminate human history. New possibilities, therefore, do not appear in history as "neutral" but as "demands," a moral claim on our conscience and sense of responsibility, the kairos of a demanding possibility that evokes decision and commitment with specific reference to more humane political possibilities. These moments can be interpreted as the "call" of providence within the ambiguity of historical life.

Precisely because human freedom in the ambiguity of history contains alienation and estrangement, i.e., "fallenness," sin threatens every destiny with fate. Sin has warped the past that comes to us in our present and

---

[4]Ibid., 248.
[5]Ibid., 248-50.
[6]Ibid., 252.

corrupts the future that we create for our children. Problems of warped social, economic, and political structures require the continuing liberation of the gospel, but the new structures always retain elements of the old, which cause and contribute to the inevitable warping of the new, and therefore necessitates the ongoing judgment and transformation of grace. Gilkey says: "The political action that undertakes *legitimately* to liberate itself and others from fate must *itself* stand under a more final judgment for its own continuing ambiguity, and hope for a grace wherewith it can itself be cleansed."[7] The corruption encompasses aspects of all that is human, and the destructive power of demonic evil can live through the past into the future, warped power that enables the mighty to impose fate on multitudes of the weak. The demonic aspects of our own creativity produces in the objective social world—institutions, systems, and symbols; structures of roles, rights, opportunity and reward—demonic power full of evil consequences housed in warped institutional form that breeds more evil through survival in time.

New Elements in the Conception of God

The relation of the concrete experience of historical passage and its interpretation through the symbols of the Christian faith provide the framework for Gilkey's understanding of God. The conception of God moves through ontological intuitions, Christian existence in the polarities of finitude and freedom, sin and grace, and "in major part through the shaping power of the biblical witness." Three new elements are essential to his conception of God. Unsurprisingly Gilkey begins candidly and consistently with the basic principle of the self-limitation of God in relation to finite being in the movement of human history. Each event that comes to be and its freedom of self-actualization arise concretely in the present through the power of the being of God. "It is through God's power of continuing, conquering the non-being of temporal passage, that moment follows moment, that cause impinges upon effect, that objects become object for subjects, that subjects remain in some sense identical over time —in sum, that the accumulated actuality of the past, now objectified and

---

[7]Ibid., 258.

so gone, becomes the ground for the new present." As the principle of creation of every aspect of finite being who sustains all actuality in the power of being in time, God is the creator and preserver of finite creation in all its dimensions. Since God *alone* does not create the present, God is not the sole shaper of the historical process who determinatively directs our freedom or ordains us to will God's will. "The divine creativity out of which the present arises from its past establishes a *self-creative* process: God creates by giving each occasion the power of self-creation out of its destiny."[8] We actualize our being in each present out of the destiny given us from the past combined with new possibilities and their demands offered to us from the providential future. God is inescapably an aspect of the ontological structure of the process as its ground and its possibility. Thus God is the alpha and omega of each moment of the process, and process is "a union of past actuality and future possibility in the present event of freedom made intelligible." Precisely as self-limited God is ontologically and necessarily present, but through our freedom we effect and complete self-actualization in the shaping of events. Gilkey says: "But if this divine self-limitation be constitutive of history, as essential an ontological structure as the polarity of destiny and freedom, then God will have to act in the future as he has in the past, namely *through* our freedom and *limited by* our freedom."[9] History will remain open, therefore, to creative possibility and freedom as well as destructive conflict and oppression. Divine grace acting on our freedom but not determining it is the only redemptive activity of God in our histories and therefore in history itself. Though our freedom is the gift of God to us, we are self-determinative through the power of self-determination given to us. We shape what is given to us into what we are, and thereby help to shape the historical process into what it is. Gilkey carefully distinguishes the relationship of God and humanity in history:

> [A]s the power alike of being, of freedom and of possibility, [God] is the ground of the process. The limitation on God's sovereignty is understood as the self-limitation of God in creating and preserving a finitude characterized by freedom and so by self-actualization. The concrete character of actuality, then, is not wholly of God, though every

---

[8]Ibid., 307.
[9]Ibid., 279.

aspect of its being arises from God and is preserved by God's power. For actuality is self-creative of the destiny given it by the divine power. As destiny and freedom unite to form event, divine creation and providence, as the possibilities or conditions of that union, unite with finite self-creation in the becoming of each creature. Thus again, the *character* of that destiny, which may be fate, arose from the work of finite freedom on its destiny.[10]

Of major importance he concludes: "In past, in present, and in future God's sovereignty is a self-limited sovereignty because it is the creative intention of God to *create* and *re-create finite freedom.*"[11] Self-limitation is central, perhaps the key to Gilkey's reformulation of the providence of God.

Beyond the self-limitation of God, the second new element in Gilkey's conception of God is the participation of God in historical passage, which entails the *temporality* of God. He writes: "The moving process in all its structural aspects is his creation; it arises out of his own power of being; his continuing being, therefore, is received from himself not from elsewhere." God is the ground of being of all process, the creative and temporal ground of temporality itself. Gilkey insists nonetheless on the modal distinction between actuality and possibility for finite being and for God as the absolute ground of finite being. Before actualization, "actuality *is* only as possibility."[12] Even for God the future is possibility and not actuality, which God does not foreknow as "already actuality" but only as the envisionment of infinite possibility. Thus for Gilkey: "God thus experiences temporal passage as constitutive and so essential to his own being: the past as achieved actuality, the present as self-achieving actuality, and the future as possibility"—but noncontingently.[13]

As the third and final new element in his conception of God, Gilkey understands that God, though transcendent to mere becoming—as non-contingent—nonetheless "*himself 'becomes,*' " that is, subject to change. "Consequently," he says, "as possibility *becomes* actuality, as change and process occur, God's creative and providential relations to process

[10]Ibid., 307-308.
[11]Ibid., 308 (italics added).
[12]Ibid.
[13]Ibid., 309.

themselves change, and God's 'experience' and 'knowledge' of his world change."[14] Gilkey posits "a crucial difference between possibility and actuality, *a difference contributed by the creature and not by God.*" History, which is the arena of finite being, is self-creative under God but not determined by God. Therefore, Gilkey concludes, as history changes, God changes, because "God is in an essential relation to a world he does not in its final and determinative form ordain or make—although each aspect of its being comes to be through the power of his creative being and through the possibilities of his providential envisionment."[15]

God as Being, Logos, and Love

Gilkey concludes his reinterpretation of God's providence in history with a positive reformulation of the Christian symbol of God, three historic aspects of God characteristic of the Christian tradition: God as Being, God as Logos, and God as Love. *God as being* underscores the continuous creativity of God, the necessary, eternal, yet moving ultimate ground of the evolutionary process and the process of history. God transcends time as the source of all that is, but God is in time illuminating in the creative life of God the modal distinction between possibility and actuality.

God as logos shares in the process of guiding, directing, and fulfilling the process as it moves toward its impinging future. The divine life nurtures movement toward an as yet unrealized range of possibilities, new possibilities that will find fulfillment in the eschatological end. Since becoming is the self-actualization of novel events, the rational structure of experience includes the *ingression* of possibilities from the *future* into self-creative actualities. Indeed, what God does in history, i.e., providence, is not determined through the orders of creation but according to God's eschatological promises toward a liberated future.

God as love means that God acts in new and varied ways to reconcile, reunite, and heal a world already disrupted and broken from creative providence through human sin and demonic power. The aspects of God's

---

[14]Ibid.
[15]Ibid., 310 (italics added).

reconciling love are communicated to us in Jesus Christ: incarnation, atonement, and resurrection. Through these three symbolic interpretations of Jesus the Christ, we experience the new presence of the spirit within whom in faith and hope we live toward the future in a new way.[16]

Strengths

Several aspects of Gilkey's proposal are of major significance for a constructive interpretation of the providence of God. (1) Providence must address the social and political processes within historical passage and not be reduced to the provident will of God for pious individuals. People live in systems—family, social, economic, racial, political, and religious systems; structures that enhance or deprive persons in the actualization of their freedom in the fulfillment of their destinies. The providence of God requires a political theology to address the network of systems grounded in institutions and symbols within which people live, usually the powerful on top of the weak. At the descriptive level Gilkey's analysis of the dialectic of the hidden work of God in historical causation through human agency to accomplish structural and political change is viable, if not entirely convincing.

(2) The radical self-limitation of God and a corresponding human responsibility for actualization of the most equitable possibilities open to us in situations of blind violence, obvious injustice, and intransient oppression constitutes a providential "call" to moral responsibility for the sake of reconciliation, justice, and peace. We who are the benefactors, however indirectly, of the oppressed and dispossessed are not at all likely to initiate change, but we have the greater responsibility through the compassion of Christ to encourage personally, support publicly, and demand politically that the possibilities for the needy be actualized—not whether it will cost us, but regardless of what it will cost us.

(3) The continuing problem that haunts human history is the destructive power of the demonic, which cannot be abstracted from but occurs within the distortion of the union of freedom and destiny of a person or a people into fate and estrangement. The problem of sin and

---

[16]Ibid., 310-18.

evil makes all history ambiguous, because the judgement against as well as the reformation of systems of violence and injustice contain elements of corruption that warps the best achievements of historical creativity and change, a corrupt warping of all liberation movements and reactionary reforms in continuing need of judgment and grace.

(4) The unique, active creativity of God and the intentional, envisioning love of God nurtures hope for each and all that the promise of God for fulfillment *in* human history, a fulfillment that refers to real possibilities that can be actualized. The integration of providence, Christology, and eschatology moves the vision of providence beyond the traditional categories of preservation, concurrence, and governance into a creative proposal that contains theological possibilities that are otherwise unavailable. Whether Gilkey's program adequately accomplishes this new configuration of providence is another question entirely, but the insight of the necessity to integrate providence, christology and eschatology for a Christian interpretation of providence endures.

Problems

The problems inherent in Gilkey's proposal are not obvious but significant, yet difficult to evaluate because these problems are blurred in the comprehensiveness and depth of Gilkey's work. The deficiencies are nevertheless identifiable.

(1) *Historical Causation.* Through a critical appropriation of von Rad's Old Testament theology, Gilkey distinguishes a supernaturalistic model of God's work from a naturalistic model. In the patriarchical, exodus and conquest narratives God unilaterally intervened to accomplish God's purpose; however, from the monarchy through the prophets God ceased to act as one independent cause among other causes but acted "in and through the ordinary creative and destructive actions of men in history," which Gilkey describes as a naturalistic model of God's activity. These models constitute the options for interpreting providence today: a model of supernaturalistic activity with periodic miraculous intervention to accomplish God's purpose, or a model of naturalistic explanation on the basis of the dialectic of the hidden work of God in history through human agency. The traditional supernaturalistic model and all its variations ultimately locate history entirely under God's control, whereas

alternative naturalistic process models locate the ground, meaning, and possibilities in God, but the ongoing actualization of possibilities in the freedom of humanity (the possibility of any moment nonetheless dependent upon God in all its aspects).[17] The question in part is the fundamental reality of human freedom, but another central aspect of the question is the characterization of God's relationship to history.

That God is the source and ground of our becoming, *that* God envisions the possibilities and limits of our future, *that* God enables providence to occur through the human actualization of possibility within the polarity of destiny and freedom, *that* God intends history to be *self-creative* under God but not under the control of God—these affirmations magnify the relationship of God to history. This relation of God to the dynamic realities of human history, however, is very abstract conceptually and descriptively. Is the sense of abstraction simply the style of Gilkey's presentation, or is it a characterization of the model of providence described? Does God actively engage persons and communities in the dynamic movement of history, a reciprocity of mutual contribution to the historical process? Gilkey's naturalistic model does not portray God as an engaging participant with humanity in the process. The character of personal relationship does not stamp, much less define, Gilkey's naturalistic model of the dialectic of the hidden work of God in history. If God *only* acts as one independent cause among other causes in history, engaging and engaged in the actualization of possibility, Gilkey thinks that God's ultimacy is reduced and human freedom is destroyed. However, strike "only"—affirm God's creativity in the entirety of the process *and* God's participation as one engaging agent among others contributing to possibility becoming actuality in the process, and not necessarily the most powerful agent in a given context—and another model emerges. This model is a personal model, wherein God's engaging Presence occasions the radical possibility of the transformation of actuality in the process. This model is *supernatural* without an interventionist mode of God's activity, and it is *natural* through God's engaging Presence and guidance, hidden though it is: This personal model of engaging transformation disavows God's control of history, but it affirms the interaction of God with humanity in the cooperative shaping of history. The symbol

---

[17]Ibid., 246-48.

of the Incarnation authorizes this model, and the activity of the Holy Spirit is its ongoing reality in the church and the world.

(2) *Christology.* While recognizing the importance of Christology for formulating a wholistic interpretation of providence, Gilkey affirms Incarnation in terms of a dramatic description of the powerlessness of God. Within the themes of Jesus' person and destiny, Incarnation and atonement, the difference between divine power and human power is incongruent, because "powerlessness and not power, suffering and not dominion, were the central characteristics of [Jesus'] life and destiny." The Incarnation does not mean that "the divine power is weak and suffers *now* but will rule in God's history *in the future.*" Rather, what Jesus did and what was done to him represent the essential and permanent realities of human history. "Jesus Christ is the center of history not only by what he promises for the future—though that is crucial—but even more by what he discloses of God's relation to history in the continuing present."[18]

Though all power to be is of God, we humans misuse power in history to escape suffering and death. Gilkey sees God's alienation from and judgment of the corrupted powers in all human history in the powerlessness, suffering, and death of Jesus. Gilkey is eloquent but even more radical: "The final manifestation of this strange or 'alien' relation of God to human power, universal in historical life, is therefore in terms of *total* self-limitation, *almost total non-being* [!] and so total alienation: in terms of powerlessness." God cannot reveal Godself unequivocally in historical power, i.e., eschatologically, because all history participates in the demonic. Yet God is revealed "hiddenly" as creative ground, as judgment, as new possibility on the one side, and "as nothingness or powerlessness in Jesus' weakness, suffering, and death, i.e., in Jesus' total participation in the weak *and* vulnerable conditions, *the non-being*, of existence" on the other. God in Christ not only reveals how the suffering of others results from our grasping for power, but the Christ also reveals his willingness to suffer that fate of the powerless and to die with all who die. "The resolution of sin, participation in God again, is manifested in the new reality of Jesus' life. And the consequences of that problem, fate, suffering and death, are now shared and conquered by God."[19]

---

[18]Ibid., 280-81.
[19]Ibid., 282 (italics added).

What is the problem? Gilkey has concentrated his presentation of the Christ event almost entirely in the weakness of Jesus in his passion and ignores the power of Jesus in his ministry: He forgave sins; he healed the sick; he exorcised demons; he confronted his adversaries confidently; he reinterpreted the law authoritatively; he hosted the anticipation of the messianic banquet of the Kingdom of God with outcasts and sinners; he had to resist the temptation to become a conqueror and king, because of his great compassion and charismatic impact among the people. Jesus exercised power, but he redefined power through his relationship to others: not dominating power but donative power; not lording it over others but serving in behalf of others; not with an overwhelming threat but with a vulnerable compassion. One could characterize Jesus' ministry as the unique expression of the power of love. Yet a notable transition to powerlessness occurs in Jesus' passion and execution, events preceded with the cleansing of the Temple, teaching daily in the Temple, and predicting the destruction of the Temple, a dangerous prophecy. The point of transition beyond confrontation to powerlessness occurs in Gethsemane.

(3) *Eschatology*. Despite occasional references beyond history, Gilkey focuses his understanding of eschatology in the providential and Christological work of God in history. Redemption and meaning in history is possible only if the unrighteous are not judged and punished but forgiven and healed. "For this reason," says Gilkey, "the meaning of history both within and beyond it comes more from the principles of justification and grace than from the promise of eschatological fulfillment; or better, eschatology must be interpreted in the light of justifying and sanctifying grace."[20] He understands the principle of meaning in history to have different but related levels: the level of creative providence, another level of redemptive grace, and a final level of eschatological fulfillment. These "multi-leveled" redemptive powers in history are always present in history but most fully revealed in Jesus. Our certainty about them and our inward participation in them is fullest in the Christ event.

The Kingdom of God is "not yet," but it continually comes in the new possibilities for a fated existence in history and points to a more

---

[20]Ibid., 282-83.

ultimate resolution beyond history. So the lure of the new possibilities for more humane structures of social existence, essential to creative politics for justice and peace, is defined eschatologically within history. The eschatological symbol of the Kingdom of God as the goal of providence has a double reference: "First and foremost," the *immediate* and *immanent* possibilities for sociopolitical progress toward the utopian ideal; and, second, the transcendent hope beyond history in the ultimate future of God. Here, however, theology is "vastly tentative and hypothetical in form." Does history have an eschatological destiny for humanity gathered into the life of God? Gilkey simply says: "Perhaps one day we shall know."[21] The immanent sociopolitical possibilities on the way to the Kingdom of God is the focus and concentration of the eschatological hope of providence in Christ.

(4) *The Self-limitation of God*. First, Gilkey's brilliant integration of providence, Christology, and eschatology stumbles on the *normative* principle of the self-limitation of God. Some kind of divine limitation is necessary for the openness of history, the relative autonomy of the natural world, and the authenticity of human freedom. For Gilkey, God's preservation of past actuality becomes the ground for the new present, and the present entails possibilities, some so new to be novel possibilities that a person or community actualizes in a *self-creative* process through the union of destiny and freedom. God does not participate in the process as one agent among others, nor does God determine the shape of the human history. Gilkey puts such emphasis on the self-limitation of God that we humans have almost all, if not exclusive, responsibility for what happens in the possibilities actualized as well as those that are not, because God does not work in the immediacy of personal engagement with an individual or community. Does such a sharply defined self-limitation of God put too much responsibility on wayward humanity for radical evil in the inevitable corruption of power and the warping of history, always ambiguous and sometimes demonic, despite all the possibilities God gives to it? Does such a sharply defined self-limitation of God inevitability minimize the personal character of God's engaging participation with humanity in the dynamics of history? Second, whether or not the Kingdom of God ever arrives in its transcendent fulfillment of

---

[21]Ibid., 292, 295, 298-99.

the goal of history is a question Gilkey minimizes, leaving it unnecessary and unlikely. The Kingdom of God as the transcendent goal of history has conceptual value, but little more. Gilkey simply leaves the possibility open. Third, because God's relationship to the process remains limited to its ground and envisioning of historical possibilities that confronts us with an "ought," a moral claim toward the betterment of social and political existence, God does not act as one agent among other agents working toward specific goals in a given trajectory of a particular process. Gilkey lacks, therefore, a theological rationale for the Incarnation and a "place" for the activity of the Holy Spirit. Coming full circle, the identification of "the *normative* principle of the self-limitation of God" makes it exceeding difficult to imagine if, when, and how God could ever transcend the principle of self-limitation. In fact, Gilkey suggests that God does not: As in the past, in the present and in the future God intends to create and to re-create finite freedom.

Indexes

Persons

Subjects

mystery of the death of 345,
348, 375, 382, 384, 395
name of 8, 49, 59-62, 118, 136-
38, 183, 224, 246, 247
pathos of 325
as personal 45, 73
and physical illness 74-75
and power 66, 76, 131-35, 151-
54, 221, 295, 330-31
Presence of 16, 17, 40, 41, 43,
44, 45, 47, 48, 62, 69, 79, 129,
138, 155, 159, 162, 179, 181,
182, 190, 192, 194, 196-200, 202,
215, 221-25, 226, 273, 279, 287,
308, 314, 315, 349, 350, 361,
362, 364, 370, 372, 374, 379,
382, 384
provision of 341
responsibility of 342-43, 381-85
self-abandonment of 375-77
self-consistency of 62, 85, 109,
111, 135, 138, 336
self-expenditure of 68, 133-35,
136, 137, 172, 179
self-limitation of 32, 33, 35, 37,
38, 58, 61, 63, 64, 68, 70, 71,
110-11, 113, 115, 118-19, 130-
31, 136, 191, 209-10, 219, 220,
329, 332-36, 338, 386, 442, 445-
48, 451, 453-54, 455, 457, 459
silence of 17, 29, 118, 121, 133,
193-94, 197, 199, 316-17, 318,
323-26, 343-45, 361-64, 366
and suffering 72, 75, 79, 111,
193
temporality 448
testing of 122
trust in 123, 127, 135-36
as Victim 384-85, 387, 388
weakness of 224, 343, 369-61,
362-64, 429-30
godforsakenness 17, 199, 318, 322-24

goodness of creation 12, 17, 79, 125-
28, 137, 145, 146, 157
Gospels as dramatic history 22-27, 29
Gospel genre 22, 24-26, 29
governance 13, 35-38, 39, 452
grace 17, 18, 22, 43, 56, 61, 66, 71,
90, 117, 118, 121, 128, 129, 146,
158, 159, 177, 190, 193, 196,
211, 216, 223, 224, 226, 227,
260, 271, 273, 274, 275, 276,
282, 284-87, 289, 290, 298-303,
305-308, 311-15, 319, 321, 331,
445, 446, 452, 457
as healing grace 280-85, 301
as sustaining grace 285-305
as promissory grace 305-12
and providence 42
Head Start 235-37, 239, 242, 243
healing grace 273, 276, 282, 285-87,
289, 305, 307, 308, 311, 312
hermeneutics 27-29
Hiroshima 148, 149, 153-55, 215
historical context 47, 71, 107, 109,
207, 211, 275, 279, 280
holocaust 83, 84
hope 22, 27, 40, 47, 48, 65, 71, 73,
79, 81, 82, 90, 159, 174, 190,
196, 197, 206, 220-22, 225, 228,
242, 244, 250, 254, 257, 259,
260, 262, 265, 271, 275, 280,
299, 311, 312-15, 323, 324, 336,
339, 340, 344, 443, 445, 451,
452, 459
human finitude 125, 144, 339
human agency 34, 68, 71, 112, 451,
452
human contingency 30, 32, 35, 38,
60, 62, 69, 71, 106, 110, 126,
211-12, 241-42, 328, 441
human freedom 131, 180, 335, 446
human history 8, 216

Scripture References

believe in God / Jesus p 19